The publisher and the University of California Press
Foundation gratefully acknowledge the generous support of
the Robert and Meryl Selig Endowment Fund in Film Studies,
established in memory of Robert W. Selig.

Transatlantic Cinephilia

CINEMA CULTURES IN CONTACT

Richard Abel, Giorgio Bertellini, and Matthew Solomon, Series Editors

1. *The Divo and the Duce: Promoting Film Stardom and Political Leadership in 1920s America,* by Giorgio Bertellini
2. *Relaying Cinema in Midcentury Iran: Material Cultures in Transit,* by Kaveh Askari
3. *Sirens of Modernity: World Cinema via Bombay,* by Samhita Sunya
4. *World Socialist Cinema: Alliances, Affinities, and Solidarities in the Global Cold War,* by Masha Salazkina
5. *Transnational Trailblazers of Early Cinema: Sarah Bernhardt, Gabrielle Réjane, Mistinguett,* by Victoria Duckett
6. *Transatlantic Cinephilia: Film Culture between Latin America and France, 1945–1965,* by Rielle Navitski

Transatlantic Cinephilia

Film Culture between Latin America and France, 1945–1965

Rielle Navitski

UNIVERSITY OF CALIFORNIA PRESS

University of California Press
Oakland, California

© 2023 by Rielle Navitski

Library of Congress Cataloging-in-Publication Data

Names: Navitski, Rielle, author.
Title: Transatlantic cinephilia : film culture between Latin America and France, 1945-1965 / Rielle Navitski.
Other titles: Cinema cultures in contact ; 6.
Description: Oakland, California : University of California Press, [2023] | Series: Cinema cultures in contact ; 6 | Includes bibliographical references and index.
Identifiers: LCCN 2023013083 (print) | LCCN 2023013084 (ebook) | ISBN 9780520391413 (cloth) | ISBN 9780520391437 (paperback) | ISBN 9780520391444 (epub)
Subjects: LCSH: Motion pictures—Social aspects—Latin America—20th century. | Motion pictures—Political aspects—Latin America—20th century. | Motion pictures—France—Influence.
Classification: LCC PN1993.5.L3 N38 2023 (print) | LCC PN1993.5.L3 (ebook) | DDC 791.43098/09045—dc23/eng/20230712
LC record available at https://lccn.loc.gov/2023013083
LC ebook record available at https://lccn.loc.gov/2023013084

32 31 30 29 28 27 26 25 24 23
10 9 8 7 6 5 4 3 2 1

For Amalia, with hopes for a better world

Contents

Acknowledgments   *xi*
List of Abbreviations   *xv*

Introduction   *1*

1. The Cineclub Movement in Latin America: Transatlantic Cooperation, Local Frictions   37

2. Toward a Global Film Preservation Practice? FIAF and the Emergence of Latin American Archives   85

3. Brokering Art Cinema: Latin America and the Festival Circuit   125

4. Film Pedagogy between Latin America and France: Training Professionals, Fostering Film Culture   174

Conclusion   227

Notes   233
Bibliography   283
Index   309

Acknowledgments

As a study of how individual mobility and cultural institutions together forged a transatlantic film culture, this book would be incomplete without reflection on how both factors made it possible.

I am deeply indebted to the George A. and Eliza Gardner Howard Foundation housed at Brown University and the Willson Center for Humanities and Arts at the University of Georgia. Each awarded me a providentially timed fellowship that let me dedicate a semester to writing and research, allowing me to finally bring a project I started researching in 2014 to completion.

As we emerge from a time of lockdowns and travel restrictions, even those of us lucky enough to have monetary reserves and passport privilege can no longer take for granted the ability to hop on an international flight. The kind of research travel necessary to write a book of this nature is an immense boon that nevertheless comes at a significant financial, environmental, and personal cost. Howard Foundation funds supported trips to Chile and France; two Travel Ambassador grants from UGA's Latin American and Caribbean Studies Institute, funded by the Title VI National Resources Center program, helped cover visits to archives in Argentina, Brazil, Colombia, and Uruguay. I am truly grateful to my family for making it work when my travels cut into precious time together. Sincere thanks to Marta León and Jairo Ospina, who hosted me in Bogotá and generously made sure I saw something of the city outside the archives' walls; to Luciana Corrêa de Araújo, who put me up in São

Paulo even when a university strike upended her plans; and to Misha Maclaird, who generously offered me a place to stay in Mexico City.

A study of this kind would be quite literally unthinkable without the labor and expertise of archivists and librarians. My gratitude to Jorge Moreno and Mónica Andrea Melo Cely at Fundación Patrimonio Fílmico Colombiano; Matías Clarens at the Cinemateca Uruguaya; Andrés Levinson and Celeste Castillo at the Museo del Cine Pablo C. Ducrós Hicken; Adrián Muoyo and the Biblioteca ENERC staff; Christophe Dupin at the FIAF archives; Antonia Rojas and the staff of the Filmoteca UNAM; Cuitláhuac Oropeza Alcántara and the personnel of the Archivo Histórico UNAM; Adolfo Marinello at the Archivo Histórico de la Pontificia Universidad Católica de Chile; Renato Noviello, Elisa Ximenes, and the rest of the Cinemateca Brasileira staff; Bertrand Kerael and the personnel of the Cinémathèque française; and the staff of the Servicio Oficial de Difusión Radio Eléctrica's Archivo de la Imagen y la Palabra, John Hay Library at Brown University, and France's Archives diplomatiques (La Courneuve), Archives nationales (Pierrefitte-sur-Seine), and Bibliothèque nationale. Special thanks to Rafael de Luna Freire for arranging a visit to the Cinemateca do MAM-Rio at a time when its collections were not readily accessible to researchers.

For their generosity and speed in the process of securing images and permissions, I thank these archive and library workers as well as the staff of the Boston Public Library; Hélène Foisil at the Muséum national d'Histoire naturelle (France); Christine Laurière, Jean-Pierre Castelneau, and Sophie Castelneau; Sophie Cazes, deputy director of La Fémis; Adán Griego and Dinah Handel at Stanford University Libraries; Nicolás Erramuspe Tejera of Cine Universitario; and Lúcia Telles.

Much like the figures whose trajectories I trace in this book, in bringing it to completion I have found myself enmeshed in a transnational web of cooperation and intellectual kinship. Sarah Ann Wells, a treasured friend and steadfast fellow-traveler on a parallel journey in book-writing, generously read and offered feedback on the entire manuscript. I am grateful, as well, to Kelley Conway, Tamara Falicov, Brian Jacobson, and Gabriel Rodríguez Álvarez for reading work in progress and offering insightful comments. I have had the good fortune to collaborate in various capacities with Mariana Amieva Collado and Irene Rozsa, exchanging work-in-progress, research materials, and ideas. My gratitude to Gabrielle Chomentowski for helping to unlock the secrets of IDHEC's files; to Sergio Becerra Venegas for the endless stream of contacts and recommendations in Bogotá; and to Charles Tepperman for digital humanities advice. My deep gratitude to Marta Rodríguez, Carlos Álvarez, and Manuel Vargas, giants of radical cinema and architects of film culture, for sharing their stories with me. Ramiro Arbeláez, Ana Broitman, Ainamar Clariana Rodagut, Olivia Cosentino, Alejandro Kelly-Hopfenblatt, Julio Lamaña, Rafael Morato Zanatto, Fabián Núñez, María Paz Peirano, Isabel Restrepo, Israel Rodríguez Rodríguez, Juana Suárez, Paulina Suárez Hesketh, Isabel Wschebor Pellegrino, and the steering committee of the Seminario de Cineclubismos Latinoamericanos offered suggestions, encouragement, and research materials, and more broadly, make the growing research area of Latin American film culture a stimulating and welcoming one to work in. Thanks to Juan Ospina León, Nicolas Poppe, and (once again) Rafael de Luna Freire for always staying in touch. The mentorship of Colin Gunckel, Laura Isabel Serna, and Ana M. López has been invaluable to my professional endeavors over the past decade. I am also indebted to colleagues and friends at the University of Georgia who have supported me professionally and personally during my work on this project.

I cannot thank this book's peer reviewers, Alice Lovejoy, Masha Salazkina, and Cristina Venegas, enough. They offered enthusiastic encouragement and constructive comments on countless aspects of the manuscript, saving me from innumerable missteps. Any failure to implement their excellent suggestions, like those of my colleagues mentioned above, is entirely due to my own deficiencies. Masha went far beyond her original role, plowing through the entire manuscript a second time, and also played a decisive role in this book's fate by giving me a push in the right direction at just the right moment.

My deep gratitude to Raina Polivka and to the Cinema Cultures in Contact series editors Richard Abel, Giorgio Bertellini, and Matthew Solomon, for their faith in this project. I am beyond delighted that the book found a home at University of California Press. Special thanks to Giorgio for his detailed comments and suggestions. My gratitude to Sam Warren, Stephanie Summerhays, Jon Dertien, and Sharon Langworthy for shepherding the project through the publication process.

I was fortunate to have the opportunity to present work in progress from this book, virtually and in person, at the Universidad de Buenos Aires; Northwestern University; the University of California, Santa Barbara; Concordia University; Tulane University; the École nationale des chartes; the Universitat Oberta de Catalunya; the Seminario de Cineclubismos Latinoamericanos; the Grupo de Estudios Visuales symposium at Uruguay's Universidad de la República; the Society for Cinema and Media Studies conference; the Latin American Studies Association congress; the Modernist Studies Association conference; and the Association of Moving Image Archivists' annual meeting. My gratitude to the organizers of these events for their interest and to audiences for their feedback.

Portions of chapter 1 appeared in an earlier form as "The Cine Club de Colombia and Postwar Cinephilia in Latin America: Forging Transnational Networks, Schooling Local Audiences," *Historical Journal of Film, Radio and Television* 38, no. 4 (2018): 808–827. Sections of chapter 2 were originally published as "Toward a Global Film Preservation Movement? Institutional Histories of Film Archiving in Latin America," *Journal of Cinema and Media Studies* 60, no. 4 (2021): 187–193. I thank the publishers for permission to reprint this material.

Eternal thanks to my parents, Regina Edmonds and Al Navitski, who, on top of everything else, let our family of two adults, a toddler, and a dog move into their house for an entire summer to allow for a major push on this project. As the only other caretaker for our daughter during the pandemic, my mother has continually moved heaven and earth to help keep us sane and, to boot, read and gave me feedback on the entire manuscript, twice. Love to my sister Alanna Navitski and to Aster and James. Deepest love and gratitude to my husband José Guadalupe Vázquez Zavala, who, in trying times, does his utmost to keep my phone battery, our car battery, and my reserves of inner strength from draining down completely; and to Amalia, who makes it all worthwhile.

Abbreviations

ACCA	Asociación de Cronistas Cinematográficos Argentinos
AF	Alliance française
AGN	Archivo Gráfico de la Nación
ANL	Aliança Nacional Libertadora
APDPM	Asociación de Productores y Distribuidores de Películas Mexicanas
BFI	British Film Institute
CCC	Cine Club de Colombia
CILECT	Centre international de liaison des écoles de cinéma et télévision
CNC	Centre national de la cinématographie
COFRAM	Consortium franco-américain
CSC	Centro Sperimentale di Cinematografia
CUEC	Centro Universitario de Estudios Cinematográficos
DGCN	Direction générale de la cinématographie nationale
DGRC	Direction générale des relations culturelles
FCCB	Foto Cine Clube Bandeirante
FIAF	Fédération internationale des archives du film
FIAPF	Fédération internationale des associations de producteurs de films
FICC	Fédération internationale des ciné-clubs

FIFA	Fédération internationale du film d'art
FIPRESCI	Fédération Internationale de la PRESse CInématographique
FTIP	Film and Television Institute of Pune
ICAIC	Instituto Cubano de Arte e Industria Cinematográficos
ICUR	Instituto de Cinematografía de la Universidad de la República
IDHEC	Institut des hautes études cinématographiques
IFAL	Institut français d'Amérique latine
IICI	Institut international de coopération intellectuelle
INC	Instituto Nacional de Cinematografía (Argentina)
MAE	Ministère des affaires étrangères
MAM-Rio	Museu de Arte Moderna do Rio de Janeiro
MAM-SP	Museu de Arte Moderna de São Paulo
MASP	Museu de Arte de São Paulo
MoMA	Museum of Modern Art (New York)
MPAA	Motion Picture Association of America
NAM	Non-Aligned Movement
NATO	North Atlantic Treaty Organization
NLAC	New Latin American Cinema
OCIC	Office catholique international du cinéma
PCB	Partido Comunista Brasileiro
PCF	Parti communiste français
RPF	Rassemblement du peuple français
SICA	Sindicato de la Industria Cinematográfica Argentina
SIPE	Subsecretaría de Informaciones y Prensa del Estado
SODRE	Servicio Oficial de Difusión Radio Eléctrica
SOFE	Service des œuvres françaises à l'étranger
UCAL	Unión de Cinematecas de América Latina
UFOCEL	Union française des offices du cinéma éducateur laïque
UNAM	Universidad Nacional Autónoma de México
UNESCO	United Nations Educational, Scientific and Cultural Organization
VGIK	Vsesoiuznyi Gosudarstvennyi Institut Kinematografii

Introduction

This book tells a story of cinema and mobility. It explores the transatlantic circulation of both films and film culture—the institutions, ideas, and social practices surrounding the medium—and the kinds of movement cinema affords, the international horizons it can open up. More precisely, it traces how, following World War II, film became intertwined in novel ways with individual desires for geographic and class mobility and the global ambitions of nations. My focus is an especially fruitful set of exchanges between France—a pioneer in cultural diplomacy and the global export of films—and Latin America.[1] In the postwar period, the region possessed large and profitable film markets, notably in Mexico, Cuba, and much of the Southern Cone, with the number of movie theater seats per capita rivaling that of France in several countries.[2] It was also home to growing urban middle classes who sought to build their cultural capital through the consumption of cinema, increasingly viewed in this period as a legitimate art with unprecedented mass appeal and influence.[3] This period witnessed the mass expansion of what we now call *cinephilia*—though the terms *culture cinématographique* and *cultura cinematográfica* were far more widely used among film enthusiasts in the period—after its initial emergence alongside the interwar avant-gardes in France. Recent scholarship has rightly sought to expand our conventional understanding of cinephilia, drawn from aesthetic preferences and cultural practices developed in 1920s and 1940s–1960s France, by highlighting affective investments and sociabilities inspired by cinema

TABLE 1 TOTAL MOVIE THEATERS AND MOVIE THEATER SEATS PER CAPITA IN LATIN AMERICA, FRANCE, AND THE UNITED STATES, 1950*

Country	Total Movie Theaters (Commercial)	Inhabitants per Movie Theater Seat (Commercial)
United States	19,311	12.4
France (excluding colonial territories)	5,163	20.9[a]
Argentina	1,547	19.7[a]
Brazil	1,490	56.2
Mexico	1,369	21.0
Cuba	485	19.0[a]
Colombia	445	45.0[a]
Venezuela	338	22.2
Chile	312	21.4[a]
Peru	252	42.0[a]
Uruguay	178	22.1[b]
Ecuador	84	36.2
Costa Rica	73	19.8
Panama	60	16.4
Bolivia	48	94.3
Dominican Republic	47	105.6
Nicaragua	44	25.7
Guatemala	39	168.9
Honduras	30	73.0
El Salvador	28	56.8
Paraguay	26	100.4

SOURCES: *The 1950 Film Daily Year Book of Motion Pictures* (New York: Wid's Film and Film Folk, 1950); and *United Nations Demographic Yearbook 1951* (New York: United Nations, 1951).
*Arranged in descending order by total number of theaters.
[a] Indicates a 1950 population estimate was used for calculations in the absence of 1950 census data.
[b] Indicates a 1949 population estimate was used for calculations in the absence of census data or estimated population for 1950.

that predate and exceed these cultural formations.[4] This book takes an alternate path by tracing the reverberations of this normative concept of cinephilia on the other side of the Atlantic.

By expanding the distribution of French film and disseminating French institutional models of film culture—embodied in cineclubs, cinémathèques, festivals, and film schools—diplomats, policymakers, and film enthusiasts worked to bolster France's soft power in the face of military defeat and occupation.[5] Like other European cinemas of the period, France's industry faced profound postwar challenges, in particular an onslaught of Hollywood imports—a condition of the Blum-Byrnes

TABLE 2 TOTAL MOVIE THEATERS AND MOVIE THEATER SEATS PER CAPITA IN LATIN AMERICA, FRANCE, AND THE UNITED STATES, 1960*

Country	Total Movie Theaters (Commercial)	Inhabitants per Movie Theater Seat (Commercial)
United States	16,103	17.9
France (excluding colonial territories)	5,793	16.3[a]
Mexico	2,185	17.4
Brazil	1,998	51.2
Argentina	1,900	20.0[a]
Colombia	560	56.5[a]
Cuba	525	14.4[a]
Venezuela	496	21.8[b]
Chile	399	23.4
Peru	334	36.2[a]
Uruguay	211	24.0
Ecuador	150	66.4[a]
Costa Rica	113	23.3[a]
Nicaragua	84	28.3[a]
Bolivia	82	77.3[a]
Dominican Republic	68	94.2
Panama	57	21.2
Guatemala	41	80.1
El Salvador	39	60.9[a]
Honduras	32	70.0[a]
Paraguay	24	104.0

SOURCES: *The Film Daily Yearbook of Motion Pictures 1960* (New York: Wid's Film and Film Folk, 1960); and *United Nations Demographic Yearbook 1961* (New York: United Nations, 1961).

*Arranged in descending order by total number of theaters.

[a] Indicates a 1960 population estimate was used for calculations in the absence of 1960 census data.

[b] Census data from 1961 used for calculations in the absence of 1960 census data, given a large discrepancy between the 1960 population estimate and the 1961 census figures.

accords that forgave France's debt to the United States—and it sought to (re)conquer foreign markets by capitalizing on emerging notions of film as art. Cultural diplomacy through cinema promised to yield both box office profits and intangible benefits by raising the international profile of French cultural products. These efforts found especially fertile ground in Latin America, where French influence had historically been strong, ranging from the impact of the ideals of the French Revolution on newly independent Latin American republics in the nineteenth century to the prevalence of French language instruction and the popularity of French consumer goods.[6] Even the notion of *Latin America* itself is a nineteenth-century French invention, used by Napoleon III to justify the French intervention in Mexico (1861–1867) by evoking *latinité*, a supposed cultural kinship based on a common linguistic heritage.[7] This book retains the concept of Latin America as a frame, despite its limitations and despite the fact that I focus on Mexico, the Andean countries, and the Southern Cone and devote limited attention to Central America and the Caribbean (with the exception of Cuba). This is because the term accurately evokes the regional imaginary that shaped the work of the region's film enthusiasts (who collaborated extensively across national borders) and of French cultural architects seeking to challenge the rising postwar hegemony of the United States.

Connections and collaborations between Latin American and French cinephiles helped foster an extraordinary blossoming of institutions of film culture in postwar Latin America. Over 250 cineclubs, a dozen film archives (some ephemeral), six film schools, and two major film festivals were established in the region in the two decades after World War II. The activities of these Latin American organizations frequently intersected with the work of supranational bodies like the Fédération internationale des ciné-clubs (International Federation of Film Societies; FICC); the Fédération internationale des archives du film (International Federation of Film Archives; FIAF); the Fédération internationale des associations de producteurs de films (International Federation of Film Producers' Associations; FIAPF); the Centre international de liaison des écoles de cinéma et télévision (International Liaison Center for Film and Television Schools; CILECT); and the United Nations Educational, Scientific, and Cultural Organization (UNESCO), which were all based in Paris and influenced by French priorities. I argue that the emergence of a transatlantic film culture between Latin America and France in the postwar period led to a mutually beneficial exchange of cultural capital that served both the geopolitical aims of the French state and the social ambitions of Latin America's middle classes, participating in broader efforts to regulate and instrumentalize cinema in the service of postwar aspirations and Cold War politics.

Even as upwardly mobile Latin Americans sought distinction—in Pierre Bourdieu's dual sense of aesthetic discernment and elevated social status—by watching films deemed artistically important by erudite film critics, film appreciation was cultivated as a moderating and modernizing force.[8] While often spearheaded by left-leaning film enthusiasts, Latin American institutions of film culture rarely engaged in political activism before the early 1960s. Despite major differences in economic and political development between Latin American nations, as a whole the region's expanding middle classes were accorded outsized geopolitical significance in the polarized Cold War climate. According to interested observers from capitalist nations, particularly the United States, emerging middle classes would be pivotal for promoting peace and democracy, especially in developing regions like Latin America that were viewed as vulnerable to the spread of communism. The expansion of the middle classes, which somewhat narrowed the profound and enduring split between a small elite and an economically disenfranchised majority in Latin America, was imagined as a bulwark against the region's supposed tendencies toward the extremes of socialism and right-wing authoritarianism.[9]

Ironically given their avowedly apolitical nature, postwar Latin American institutions of film culture helped create the preconditions for the politically radical, formally experimental New Latin American Cinema (NLAC) of the 1960s and 1970s by disseminating socially engaged filmmaking movements, including Soviet montage and Italian neorealism, as film historians often note in passing. NLAC has been incorporated into Anglo-American canons of film history as a radical Other to Hollywood, a role that so-called non-Western cinemas are often drafted to fulfill in film histories that seek to be global in scope but nevertheless continue to center Europe and the United States. Yet the vibrancy and complexity of postwar Latin American film culture cannot be reduced to a mere prehistory of this celebrated movement. Rather, it simultaneously participates in and exceeds a binary Cold War logic that, in most historical accounts, pits capitalist Hollywood against a leftist, anti-colonial Third Cinema.[10] Over the past decade, and especially in the past five years, Latin America's postwar film culture has inspired a new crop of insightful book-length studies.[11] Yet these works have invariably focused on a single country (while nonetheless attending to transnational connections). My interest, by contrast, is to plot the dense institutional networks that arose across national borders in this period.

The cultural and political circumstances that nurtured Latin America's postwar film culture were distinct from the turbulent social context of NLAC, characterized by powerful currents of leftist and anti-colonial politics stirred by the 1959 victory of the Cuban Revolution, which would be brutally repressed by US-backed regimes in the 1960s, 1970s, and 1980s. After a brief political opening across much of Latin America in 1945–1946, inspired by pro-democratic propaganda and antifascist mobilization, national governments moved to sharply limit leftist agitation and labor activism, particularly as Cold War conflict intensified in 1947 and 1948.[12] This move was partly rooted in a bid to attract international investment as countries across the region pursued economic development through import-substitution industrialization, a policy of building up domestic manufacturing and internal markets to replace the export of raw materials and agricultural products as a country's main economic activity.[13] (Ironically, this bid for economic independence often required foreign capital.) In a political climate where any hint of ideological extremism could alienate overseas investors, Latin American film enthusiasts tended to position their interest in cinema as purely aesthetic, operating in a space outside partisan politics.

This is not to say that postwar institutions of film culture in Latin America had no politics, but rather that they espoused a supposedly apolitical dedication to transcendent values like global peace and human progress that resonated deeply after the war. In the wake of a world conflict waged in part through media propaganda, policymakers and film enthusiasts on both sides of the Atlantic championed the creation of institutions of film culture as a means of honing viewers' critical sensibilities, thus inoculating them to morally or politically threatening content or simply against what some intellectuals saw as the crass commercialism of mainstream film. These institutions cultivated specific modes of interpretation—such as attention to film style over star appeal—that demanded detachment from the emotional and sensual responses roused by cinema. In theory, these practices would prepare audiences to navigate problematic film texts and ultimately to curate their viewing habits in a manner that would promote social well-being. Within this framework, films by avowed communists (such as works from the Soviet montage movement or Italian neorealist films scripted by Cesare Zavattini) could be embraced in bourgeois Latin American cineclubs not only for their celebrated aesthetic achievements but also for their humanism. Furthermore, cinephiles hailed film as a mass art that could facilitate intercultural understanding, a goal advanced most directly by the emerging festival circuit's role as a showcase for national industries. Cineclubs, archives, festivals, and film schools were all deeply shaped by an internationalist spirit that transcended efforts to build cultural capital for patriotic purposes or individual benefit, aligned with a humanism that fully embraced neither socialist nor capitalist ideologies as adequate for ensuring human happiness.

Postwar institutions of film culture in Latin America and France collaborated to advance a liberal-democratic internationalism, albeit on unequal terms. While somewhat tainted by the legacy of the Vichy regime, France was well positioned among major European film producers to embody this liberal spirit in the postwar period. Italy and Germany could hardly carry this torch as defeated Fascist aggressors, at least not immediately. Furthermore, French cinema had prospered during the war thanks to a captive audience for domestically produced films (Hollywood imports were banned under the occupation) and new levels of industry regulation under Vichy, though it would face new challenges in the postwar era.[14] Latin America was imagined as an especially promising terrain for the implementation of French and France-based institutions' global designs. Organizations like FICC and FIAF supported the propagation of nontheatrical venues, including film societies and the archives that nurtured them, in the region. The growth of cineclubs, cinémathèques, and film festivals had the collateral effect of boosting the commercial distribution of French films, which could reap promotional benefits from their presence in these non-commercial circuits. Representation from Latin America, especially its major film industries (Argentina, Brazil, Mexico), was key for asserting the internationalism of events like Cannes. Like its counterparts elsewhere in Europe, France's national film school, the Institut des hautes études cinématographiques (IDHEC), strategically recruited aspiring filmmakers as de facto cultural ambassadors. IDHEC's international students, it was hoped, would bolster the French film industry's reputation in their home countries through their newly acquired expertise. For their part, Latin American film enthusiasts leveraged their links to French organizations to gain access to material resources and skills—prints of film "classics" hard to source locally, professional training in filmmaking—and to enhance their local prestige.

Despite these gestures toward reciprocity, profound imbalances remained between France and Latin American nations when it came to access to the means of film production, imbalances that French officials and film enthusiasts naturally had little interest in redressing. Under the circumstances, French and Latin American institutions of film culture alike encouraged the region's cinephiles to valorize themselves primarily, though not exclusively, as sophisticated *consumers* rather than cultural producers. Cineclubs across the region screened mostly US and European features, dedicating limited time to Argentine, Mexican, and Brazilian cinema and homegrown amateur and nontheatrical film. Film society leaders, encouraged by Henri Langlois of the Cinémathèque française to establish archives in order to receive prints from FIAF members, amassed French, German, Italian, and US titles to furnish a growing network of clubs with programming and gave only belated attention to collecting and safeguarding a national film heritage. Local boosters in Punta del Este, Uruguay, organized a film festival in the absence of a commercial film industry to showcase the elevated film tastes of local viewers while promoting tourism and real estate development. The more ambitious Mar del Plata festival tried to compensate for its geographic remoteness from the United States and Europe and the less-than-stellar international reputation of Argentine film by styling itself as a center for the serious discussion of the cinematic medium, organizing an annual summit of film scholars and critics. Even Mexico's Centro Universitario de Estudios Cinematográficos (University Center for Cinematic Study; CUEC), the oldest continuously operating film school in the region, initially emphasized the training of filmmakers as critically inclined viewers more than as creators. Yet for French cultural architects and Latin American film enthusiasts of the postwar period, consumption was the pivotal terrain on which battles not only for national and class prestige, but also for the fulfillment of cinema's aesthetic and social potential, would be waged.

RETHINKING CINEMA AND THE "CULTURAL COLD WAR"

In a history of Unifrance, the government agency dedicated to promoting French film abroad, its longtime director Robert Cravenne reflected, "If the Second World War revealed to military men the absolute weapon, the bomb, it showed civilians that there existed a less deadly weapon that was nonetheless an effective auxiliary in winning the war: the media [*l'information*] and public relations."[15] In suggesting an equivalency between the power of modern communication technologies and that of nuclear arms, Cravenne signals how the rationale for Unifrance's creation in 1949 was shaped by wartime experiences with film propaganda. At the same time, his phrasing suggests how media might be mobilized in the service of the French state when its military might had proved inadequate. Notably, France lacked nuclear weapons capacity in the decade and a half after the war and performed its first nuclear test only in 1960.[16] Seen in this light, Cravenne's comment prompts us to consider how France instrumentalized culture in the face of perceived military weakness and postwar economic crisis, and more broadly, how media can serve strategic geopolitical ends.

Cultural diplomacy and cultural relations—a broader term encompassing forms of cultural exchange that are not directly sponsored by the state but nevertheless serve national interests—enter more or less tangentially into myriad works of film history.[17] The powerful influence of Hollywood's trade organization, the Motion Picture Association of America (MPAA), and the role of the US Department of State in eliminating international trade barriers to Hollywood films, informed by the belief that these works promote American ideologies and products, is widely known.[18] Accordingly, much of the literature on cinema's implications for international relations focuses on the diplomatic maneuverings of the United States. Ruth Vasey's *The World According to Hollywood, 1918–1939* and Hye Seung Chung's recent *Hollywood Diplomacy: Film Regulation, Foreign Relations, and East Asian Representations* examine the impact of diplomatic pressures on the narrative content of US films, while in *Hollywood's Cold War*, Tony Shaw explores explicit efforts by the state to utilize commercial film for anticommunist messaging.[19] Other recent books like Ross Melnick's *Hollywood's Embassies* and Sangjoon Lee's *Cinema and the Cultural Cold War: US Diplomacy and the Origins of the Asian Cinema Network* explore how diplomatic aims shaped the material and administrative infrastructures underpinning film circulation, an interest this study shares.[20] Melnick considers overseas movie theaters owned by Hollywood studios as de facto US outposts that promoted American-style consumption of both films and other commodities and became focal points for both pro- and anti-American sentiments. Lee explores how US policies designed to preserve a bloc of capitalist nations in East Asia reverberated in the region's film industries, fostering the creation of an anticommunist network that fostered co-productions and region-wide distribution, with assistance from the CIA-backed Asia Foundation.

Attending to postwar Latin American film culture not only promises to expand our knowledge of the forms of cultural diplomacy exercised through cinema outside the US context but also prompts us to reconsider our understanding of the medium's relationship to Cold War politics. As the widespread influence of French cultural organizations in postwar Latin America attests, the dynamics shaping the region's film culture cannot be reduced to an opposition between nationalism and cultural colonization by Hollywood. Latin America's institutions of film culture prompt us to reevaluate the politics of postwar art cinema, understood—following scholars like Steve Neale, Janet Staiger, and Barbara Wilinsky—not solely or even primarily as a corpus of films defined by particular aesthetic criteria, but as a set of social spaces (such as festivals and arthouses) and interpretive practices.[21] Idealized for its textual complexity and credited with fostering more sophisticated forms of spectatorship, art cinema's ideological dimensions—such as the way that cineclubs' efforts to mold spectators functioned as a form of social discipline, and the diplomatic maneuvering that shaped the global festival circuit—have yet to be fully explored.[22]

At the same time, the circulation of art cinema in the context of Cold War–era culture wars requires us to rethink conventional understandings of postwar modernism's political charge and to revisit core assumptions of scholarship on the "cultural Cold War" by considering cinema's medium specificity.[23] The characteristics of acclaimed postwar films do not map meaningfully onto the opposition between Stalinist socialist realism and American abstraction that informed a major strand of US cultural propaganda of the period, most notoriously in the 1946 exhibition Advancing American Art mounted by the US State Department. Slated to tour Eastern Europe and Latin America, the show was recalled in 1947 amid a furor over the use of taxpayer dollars to buy and display abstract works, many created by left-leaning artists.[24] As a result, the international promotion of modernist painting was outsourced to private institutions, notably New York's Museum of Modern Art (MoMA), which continued to champion abstraction as a marker of the aesthetic freedom lacking in socialist countries.[25] While often hailed as modernist, postwar art cinema occupies "a space of aesthetic and commercial distinction that is neither mainstream nor avant-garde."[26] If one accepts David Bordwell's definition of the notoriously slippery concept of art cinema, it is representational rather than abstract, narrative in nature (though its narratives tend to be meandering, marked by randomness and ambiguity), and invites interpretations rooted in directorial subjectivity, contrasting sharply with the nonfigurative works of postwar abstract expressionist painting or the cinematic vanguards of the interwar period.[27]

If, as Neale has argued, European film industries leveraged the concept of art cinema to differentiate their products from Hollywood's, postwar art film from capitalist and socialist nations alike tended to circulate internationally in proportion to the degree that it embodied not only an easily consumable version of a distinctly national ethos, but also the qualities of a "universal" humanism.[28] At the same time, celebrated works of art cinema typically embodied a consciousness of social issues and problems that exceeded liberal capitalist notions of the free market as the guarantor of human prosperity and happiness. This ambivalence resonates both with the ambiguities of French foreign policy—which, as I explore later, advocated a moderate path between US capitalism and Soviet socialism with an eye to maintaining France's independence within the US-led Western Alliance of capitalist nations—and those of Latin American populisms, whose rhetoric championed social justice and improved living standards through a planned economy while insisting that class conflict should be mediated by the state.

Examining French cultural diplomacy in Latin America allows us to nuance prevailing narratives of the "cultural Cold War"—a phrase popularized by Frances Stonor Saunders's influential book of the same title—as a binary confrontation between the First and Second Worlds. Saunders offers sensational revelations of the Central Intelligence Agency's covert support of a broad range of cultural activities—including cinema—with the hopes of influencing public opinion, a line of inquiry that Patrick Iber expands to Latin America in his 2015 book *Neither Peace nor Freedom: The Cultural Cold War in Latin America*.[29] Yet the literature on the cultural Cold War largely remains focused on the dueling cultural projects of the United States and the Soviet Union. Recent works like Masha Salazkina's *World Socialist Cinema*, Rossen Djagalov's *From Internationalism to Postcolonialism*, and the anthology *The Cultural Cold War and the Global South* are beginning to offer a more complex picture of cinema's place in Cold War–era cultural politics by considering the networks and alliances facilitated by the Non-Aligned Movement (NAM), a group of new postcolonial states that sought to preserve their autonomy amid the ideological polarization of the Cold War.[30] While it deals specifically with European–Latin American exchanges, *Transatlantic Cinephilia* builds on recent scholarly interest in the "global Cold War," as historian Odd Arne Westad terms his attempt to recenter the conflict's reverberations in the Global South.[31] Revisionist histories treat the Cold War less as an "all-encompassing bipolar struggle, and more a multisided conflict in which power flowed in multiple directions, even if some powers wielded far more control than others," increasingly considering the "plurality of multidirectional Third World experiences" that marked the Cold War in the Global South.[32] These accounts offer localized, bottom-up histories rather than grand narratives of the clash of superpowers and are marked by the growing incorporation of cultural and social history alongside methods from diplomatic history and international relations, which traditionally dominated studies of the Cold War.[33]

In the pursuit of a more nuanced Cold War history, it is vital to consider—though not overstate—the complexities of France's position within the post–World War II order, which cannot be reduced to its status as a member of the Western Alliance. Historian Georges-Henri Soutou contends that "for the French the Cold War was not so much an outside event as an internal problem: the question of whether France itself would not become a kind of popular democracy was often more urgent than the overall East-West balance."[34] Trading on the moral authority attached to its participation in the Resistance, the Parti communiste français (French Communist Party; PCF) was also a powerful political force, garnering the most votes in France's 1946 parliamentary elections and fielding five ministers to one of the Fourth Republic's early cabinets.[35] Though these ministers were ousted in May 1947 as Cold War battle lines began to be drawn, the party remained influential in France into the early 1980s. Furthermore, as Tony Judt observes, "The issue of communism—its practice, its meaning, its claims upon the future—dominated political and philosophical conversation in postwar France."[36] Although the possibility of a French alliance with the Soviet Union in the immediate postwar period was remote given Stalin's reticence and the pivotal importance of US economic aid to France, a considerable contingent of intellectuals, primarily from the non-Stalinist left, called for France to remain neutral in the standoff between the two superpowers.[37] Neutralism largely ceased to be a tenable foreign policy position for France in 1948 after the Communist Party's assumption of power in Czechoslovakia—which had also expressed a desire for neutrality in the immediate postwar period—led to the creation of a socialist state. Yet throughout the 1950s, polls indicated that a significant sector of French society favored neutrality over alliance with the capitalist or communist blocs, ranging from 43 percent in 1952 to 57 percent in 1958.[38]

Neutrality, the pursuit of an independent foreign policy, and the possibility of pursuing a "third way" between capitalism and communism—a concept that was flexible enough to encompass a range of distinct and even opposing ideological positions—deeply shaped French politics in the two decades after World War II. The most consequential of these alternate paths emerged from the worldwide tide of anti-colonial resistance that led to France's surrender of most of its colonial possessions through the Indochina War/War of Anti-French Resistance (1946–1954) in present-day Vietnam; the Algerian War (1954–1962); and the "year of Africa" (1960), during which fifteen nations on the continent opted for independence under the terms of a 1959 declaration by de Gaulle, who had returned to power after a 1958 political crisis triggered by the Algerian War. With the 1955 Bandung Conference, a watershed summit of Asian and African nations, and the development of NAM, formerly colonized countries asserted themselves on the world stage as a force to be reckoned with that claimed autonomy from both the First and Second Worlds. Yet the alliances that emerged from these geopolitical projects could be counterintuitive. While *tricontinentalism*—solidarity between African, Asian, and Latin American nations on the basis of a shared colonial or neo-colonial condition—proved influential in Latin America in the late 1960s, official Latin American participation in NAM was sharply limited by intense US pressure. Only Cuba fielded a delegate to the 1961 conference where the movement was formally constituted (Bolivia, Brazil, and Ecuador sent observers).[39] Despite belonging to the capitalist bloc, in 1968 France was invited to future conferences of non-aligned nations by Yugoslav head of state Josip Broz Tito—who himself embodied a socialism aligned with neither East (after his 1948 split with Stalin) nor West—given France's status as a "peace-loving" member of the Western Alliance.[40]

Such rapprochements ultimately would not alter France's position as a capitalist economy aligned with the United States, but the relationship between the two nations was far from harmonious. As Frank Costigliola puts it, "More than any Western ally, France has challenged American foreign policy by maintaining a coherent, often distinctly French global view and policy," although it "often lacked the necessary national power and international backing to carry out its ambitions."[41] Most dramatically, in 1954 this stance led France to scuttle the European Defense Community Treaty, which would have created a unified European army as a means of containing West Germany after its re-armament. The United States considered re-armament indispensable for containing the Soviet Union while France opposed it. Surprisingly, four months later France's legislature voted in favor of the German Federal Republic's re-armament and its admission to the North Atlantic Treaty Organization (NATO).[42]

Yet clashes between France and the United States over Cold War strategy continued. In May 1964 French president Charles de Gaulle presented France (however incongruously) as a curb to the ascendant neo-colonial ambitions of the United States. He affirmed: "France is violently opposed to the blatant American imperialism now rampant in the world. France will continue to attack and to oppose the United States in Latin America, in Asia, and in Africa."[43] These bold declarations appear to have been rooted in de Gaulle's failure to secure greater influence for France within the Western Alliance. Yet they also signal French efforts to exercise soft power in the developing world, including Latin America, at a moment when France's hard power was curtailed by the realities of Cold War politics. In 1966, with US-French relations at a low ebb, de Gaulle announced

France's withdrawal from NATO's military command (though not from NATO itself), necessitating the removal of US troops and bases from national territory and threatening US foreign policy aims in Europe.

Beyond these confrontations with the United States, the championing of a "third way" (*troisième voie*) between communism and capitalism, to be achieved through an "'association' between employers and workers, capital and labour," was a recurring (if vaguely defined) strain of de Gaulle's political thought.[44] A towering figure of wartime and postwar politics, de Gaulle had headed the forces of the Free French, who continued to fight against the Axis and the Vichy regime after the German occupation and French surrender in 1940, and served as the French head of state from 1944 to 1946 and again from 1958 to 1969. In his youth, de Gaulle was a follower of the Ordre Nouveau. This "nonconformist" political movement was closely aligned with German National Socialism, sharing its rejection of both communism and free-market capitalism, its penchant for charismatic leaders, and its ultranationalism.[45] According to John Hellmann, Ordre Nouveau's ideology was retooled in the postwar period in the "new discourse of the European federalists promoting a united Europe—a white, Christian, federated Europe, uniting Germany and France against the Stalinist East, Third World immigration, Islamic fundamentalism, and American influence."[46] Elements of this ethos informed the Rassemblement du peuple français (Rally of the French People; RPF), the political party founded by de Gaulle after he resigned as leader of France's interim government in 1946, dissatisfied with the limits on executive power taking shape in France's new constitution. The RPF ostensibly sought a *troisième voie* between established left- and right-wing parties but had a largely conservative following. De Gaulle tried to use the RPF's impressive success in the 1947 municipal elections to call for the legislature to be dissolved, paving the way for new elections and a new constitution, but his gambit failed.[47]

Frustrated, de Gaulle cut his ties with RPF legislators in 1953.[48] Yet the notion of the *troisième voie* resurfaced during de Gaulle's month-long tour of Latin America in late 1964, which he saw as "central to his strategic calculus to chisel away at US-Soviet bipolarity in order to foment a multipolar landscape" of geopolitical power.[49] Delivering a series of speeches that emphasized *latinité*, or the ostensible ties of linguistic and cultural kinship between France and Latin America, de Gaulle championed the principle of national independence against competing efforts to exercise global hegemony, alluding to the United States and the USSR without naming them explicitly.[50] His rhetoric echoed Argentine president Juan Domingo Perón's championing of a *tercera posición* (third position) between capitalism and communism. Perón's populist politics combined a pro-labor stance with anti-democratic policies and the conviction that class conflict must be neutralized by the state to advance the collective good.[51] However, the indirect allusion to Perón's third position in de Gaulle's speeches met with a cool reception in Argentina (where Peronism was still proscribed by the military government that had ousted President Arturo Frondizi in 1962 after important Peronist victories in midterm elections) and Brazil, where a US-backed military dictatorship assumed power six months before de Gaulle's visit.[52] Furthermore, de Gaulle's championing of political self-determination rang hollow given Latin America's economic dependence on the United States. France lacked the means to offer the kind of direct economic aid to Latin America provided by the United States through the Alliance for Progress, which sought to promote economic development as a means of forestalling socialist revolution. Instead, France proposed to boost its "intellectual cooperation and technical assistance" in the region, and the repercussions of de Gaulle's visit can largely be found in the cultural sphere.[53]

Like the efforts of the French state to bolster its geopolitical standing by presenting its political model as an alternative to both Soviet-style socialism and American-style capitalism, France's cultural diplomacy in this period was a bid for influence made from a weakened position. The battered yet resilient ideal of "French universalism," which posited French culture and intellectual life as embodying the highest ideals of Western civilization, served as a powerful reserve of international prestige. This self-aggrandizing notion of French universalism as a vehicle for the betterment of humanity nevertheless resonated with the humanism embodied by much of postwar art cinema and the institutions that nurtured it.

If examining French–Latin American cultural relations offers us a more complex picture of the cultural Cold War that cannot be reduced to East-West binaries, this exploration also prompts us to reconsider commonplace assumptions about Latin American film history (especially in the eyes of non-specialists), rooted in notions of cultural colonialization and dependency that have decisively shaped the field since the late 1960s. Accounts of the "Golden Ages" of the Argentine, Brazilian, and Mexican film industries (1930s–1950s) offer satisfying affirmations of cultural nationalism—though the transnational aspects of these industries are now being more fully explored—while NLAC represents a form of continent-wide (and tricontinental) solidarity that fits into global understandings of the 1960s as a decade of political upheaval.[54] Latin America's postwar film culture, by contrast, is suffused with a Europe-oriented cosmopolitanism that clashes with prevailing perceptions of Latin America as a hotbed of leftist resistance. In accounts of NLAC's development, film societies, archives, festivals, and film schools—particularly Italy's Centro Sperimentale di Cinematografia—(Center for Experimental Cinema; CSC)—are credited with exposing leaders of the movement, most notably filmmaker-theorists Fernando Birri and Julio García Espinosa, to socially engaged filmmaking movements that decisively shaped NLAC's strategies and aesthetics. Yet the undeniably bourgeois and often conservative character of the cultural institutions that helped introduce these movements in Latin America has gone largely unacknowledged. NLAC filmmakers and critics—many of them middle class or upper middle class—tend to rewrite their personal histories in light of the radical political projects of the 1960s and 1970s, recasting cinephilic practices that valorized European and US film, including their own, as manifestations of cultural colonization.

Scholarly accounts of Latin American film history have largely followed suit, mostly glossing over the reception and production of art cinema in the region in the 1940s, 1950s, and early 1960s. Few scholars have followed Paulo Antonio Paranaguá's call to attend to the 1950s as a pivotal decade of transition for Latin American film culture.[55] Although Paranaguá and Paul A. Schroeder Rodríguez highlight how the region's cinema has historically been marked by a process of "triangulation," or strategic navigation between US and European reference points, it continues to be interpreted largely through the lens of nationalist and anti-imperialist politics.[56] To be sure, this model of triangulation, like the scope of this book, does not encompass transpacific or South Atlantic exchanges, which have long been obscured by Eurocentrism but have garnered fresh attention in recent years. Nonetheless, in the case of postwar Latin American film culture, transatlantic connections were among the most influential transnational links in the period; sidestepping them would reproduce enduring perceptions of Latin American cultural formations as radically Other from and resistant to their North Atlantic counterparts, rather than deeply intertwined with them. Complicating this perception is pivotal for developing more nuanced accounts of Latin American cultural politics.

MIDDLE-CLASS POLITICS AND FILM CULTURE IN POSTWAR LATIN AMERICA

Grasping the distinctiveness of Latin America's postwar institutions of film culture requires insight into the ideologies and practices of the region's middle classes, who have alternately been championed, denigrated, and overlooked as a historical force. As leftist intellectuals embraced working-class political power in the wake of the Cuban Revolution, they increasingly dismissed the middle class as an irrelevant or even a destructive force in national politics.[57] Notably, the 1964 military coup that ousted Brazilian president João Goulart after he proposed to strengthen government control over the economy and redistribute uncultivated land had broad middle-class support. For their part, US observers and policymakers who had placed their faith in the power of the region's middle classes to guarantee democracy and moderate politics saw these developments as a sign of the region's failure to develop "true" middle classes and thus its deficient modernization.[58] Only in the past two decades have Latin America's middle classes again inspired sustained academic study.[59]

Latin America historically has been, and continues to be, marked by a high degree of economic inequality based in extractivist economies and rigid social and racial hierarchies rooted in its colonial past. Yet middle classes began to emerge in the region as a distinct social sector during the first three decades of the twentieth century. In Peru and Brazil, export-driven economic booms fueled the growth of white-collar employment in banks, customs houses, and retail stores; the emergence of the *social question* (a term encompassing class relations, wages, and living standards) as a matter of public debate; and a push for collective organizing by these emerging social sectors.[60] In Mexico, white-collar employment swelled under the dictatorship of Porfirio Díaz (1876–1911), a moment of accelerated industrialization underwritten by foreign capital. During and after the Mexican Revolution of 1910–1920, often imagined as an uprising of *campesinos* (rural agricultural workers), the state nonetheless made important concessions to middle-class interests.[61]

After World War II—a moment of economic turmoil in Latin America given the loss of access to European markets for the agricultural products and raw materials that sustained many of the region's economies—the middle classes expanded apace with the rapid urbanization of the region and the accelerating shift from an agrarian to an industrial economy. The difficulties of the war years, which drastically increased dependence on the United States as an export market, made the prospect of developing the manufacturing sector for domestic consumption an appealing one.[62] Import-substitution industrialization promised to increase national autonomy by minimizing the impact of global fluctuations in commodity prices, which could devastate national economies.[63] As the percentage of employment in agriculture shrank significantly between 1940 and 1960 (declining approximately 12 percent in Peru, 13 percent in Brazil, 14.5 percent in Colombia, and 16 percent in Chile and Mexico), the share of urban, non-manual employment in fields like retail, banking, and business administration increased, though less rapidly than other types of manual labor.[64] In Chile and Mexico, for instance, white-collar employment grew approximately 4 percent in this period. Nations like Argentina and Uruguay, which were already significantly urbanized and industrialized and had substantial middle classes before World War II, saw lower levels of middle-class growth.[65] As noted previously, the immediate postwar period was a moment of democratic opening in Latin America but had uneven effects on the middle classes' political engagement. With the exception of historically stable democracies like Chile and Uruguay, this interlude of increased participation was quickly overshadowed by military dictatorships and populist regimes that gave little quarter, rhetorically or politically, to moderate middle-class citizens.[66]

As A. Ricardo López-Pedreros and others have noted, the middle class was nonetheless envisaged—most influentially in John J. Johnson's 1958 book *Political Change in Latin America*—as having a pivotal role in postwar designs for global progress and peace conceived by wealthy North Atlantic countries, including the Alliance for Progress, launched by President John F. Kennedy in 1961.[67] The initiative drew on the precepts of modernization theory—the belief that developing nations in what we now call the Global South could thrive by adopting the cultural values and economic strategies of industrialized countries—that took hold during the 1950s. The hope was that improved living standards would further fuel the growth of the middle classes, mitigating social pressure for the redistribution of wealth by radical means. Perceived as having an inherent affinity for (capitalist) democracy, Latin America's expanding middle classes were hailed as a bulwark against communism and right-wing authoritarianism alike. As such, they were a prime target of the ideologically motivated cultural diplomacy implemented by North Atlantic countries across the Global South. As late as 1986, J. M. Mitchell of the British Council cautioned, "The extension of Marxist theory to development economics is an argument in favor of revolution in Third World countries to which some intellectuals are prone." He stressed "the need to reach the semi-westernized intellectuals (e.g. schoolteachers, middle-rank officials and media personnel), who should constitute one of the most important target groups, standing as they do between the westernized elite and the diffused mass of the population."[68]

As the limits of import-substitution industrialization became clear by the mid-1960s and economic growth slowed in Latin America, modernization theory was increasingly superseded by dependency theory. This school of thought posits that the economic underdevelopment of nations on the global periphery is not a historical accident nor a result of cultural backwardness, but rather is perpetuated for the benefit of wealthy countries, allowing them to obtain natural resources and agricultural products cheaply. Within the framework of dependency theory, the middle classes were felt to be all but irrelevant in the struggle of exploited and impoverished workers against a haute bourgeoisie in league with foreign capital. As political polarization intensified across Latin America, fueled in part by the Cuban Revolution, the middle classes' former champions in the United States and elsewhere concluded that they had failed to fulfill their desired social and historical role. Furthermore, as inflation and other economic woes eroded gains in living standards, domestic and international observers judged Latin America's middle classes to have fallen short of the (idealized) historical experiences of the United States and United Kingdom, and some questioned if they had ever existed.[69] If these normative understandings of the middle class kept scholars from grasping the specificity of Latin American cases, they were also internalized by middle-income Latin Americans themselves. For instance, Brian Owensby stresses that middle-class identity in Brazil was always marked by implicit comparisons to North Atlantic countries and thus by cosmopolitan aspirations.[70]

In the postwar period, this often unstable middle-class identity was articulated in part through cultural consumption. At a moment of increased upward mobility and urbanization—but also, often, of runaway inflation—consuming cultural goods imbued with aesthetic sophistication might reflect an individual's newfound buying power, or alternatively, might be used to distinguish oneself from arrivistes, as Barbara Wilinsky observes in her study of arthouse cinemas in the postwar United States.[71] The social meanings attached to cinema in Latin American contexts made it especially suited to fulfill such ambivalent and even contradictory functions. If literary culture had long been the near-exclusive province of elites, international art cinema was ripe for appropriation as a marker of cultural distinction by an emerging (upper) middle-class intelligentsia, as is suggested by the dominance of professionals, businessmen, white-collar workers, and university students in the region's film societies.[72] In broad strokes, in mid-century Latin America the working classes tended to gravitate toward Argentine, Brazilian, and Mexican popular melodrama and comedy, while well-off spectators typically preferred Hollywood films or other imported fare. Cineclubs, archives, festivals, and film schools promised to bridge this gap by creating favorable conditions for "elevating" the aesthetic quality of domestic film industries or fostering commercial film production where none existed. Film enthusiasts argued this could be accomplished by training spectators to embrace more aesthetically sophisticated and narratively complex films. To accomplish this goal, they adopted practices that were especially widespread in the postwar French cineclub movement, such as post-screening discussions and the distribution of audience questionnaires.

More broadly, Latin American institutions of film culture were galvanized by the threat and promise of cinema as a mass art, particularly its perceived capacity to shape the habits, fashions, and morality of society at large. In the view of film enthusiasts, it was imperative to cultivate desired modes of spectatorship—namely an active and critical engagement with cinema, as opposed to the passive consumption of visual and narrative pleasure. As I explore in more detail in chapter 1, these cinephiles insisted on erudition and often narrow canons of film art and film history as guiding principles for the consumption of films. This approach contributed to a split—though not always an insurmountable one—between the preferences and practices of an organization's leadership and its members, which allowed organizers to claim aesthetic and social superiority over the rank and file even as they sought to shape their tastes. At the same time, within this self-consciously sophisticated film culture, the object of aesthetic contemplation was unequivocally a mass medium that, in comparison with alternate entertainments such as classical music, was relatively affordable and spatially accessible to most social classes.

Ironically, in many cases the often paternalistic architects of postwar Latin American film cultures were both privileged members of the middle or upper-middle classes and avowed leftists. Danilo Trelles, who ran Uruguay's state film archive for nearly two decades, was a card-carrying member of the Communist Party.[73] Manuel González Casanova, a key player in postwar Mexican film culture, got his start running a cineclub with a group of Venezuelan communists in exile.[74] The trajectory of Paulo Emílio Salles Gomes, one of Brazilian film culture's major institution-builders in the postwar period, is especially revealing of how the social mobility and capital afforded by an upper-middle-class background shaped Latin American film enthusiasts' work as cultural mediators.[75] As his biographer José Inácio de Melo Souza shows, Salles Gomes's politics were left-leaning from his teenage years but did not translate directly into a militant or revolutionary approach to film culture until well into the 1960s. Salles Gomes was a sympathizer (but not a member) of both the Partido Comunista Brasileiro (PCB) and the Aliança Nacional Libertadora (ANL), a broad-based anti-imperialist and pro-worker party with significant middle-class membership founded under the regime of Getúlio Vargas, who came to power in the Revolution of 1930. Salles Gomes was arrested by Vargas's political police after an attempted coup organized in November 1935 by members of the ANL, which became increasingly dominated by communist activists after PCB leader Luís Carlos Prestes joined the movement. Though he was not involved in the uprising, Salles Gomes spent fourteen months in prison before escaping. Police located the young fugitive but opted not to rearrest him. Salles Gomes chose self-exile in Paris, where he frequented the screenings of Henri Langlois and Georges Franju's Cercle du cinéma and became enthralled with film. At the same time, the Stalinist purges and the German-Soviet Pact of 1939 fueled Salles Gomes's disillusionment with the Communist Party and his turn toward democratic socialism.

After spending the war years in Brazil, where he helped to found the Clube de Cinema de São Paulo and agitated against Vargas's dictatorial Estado Novo, Salles Gomes returned to Paris, enrolling in IDHEC, though he never completed his studies. His geographic location allowed him to broker contacts with France-based organizations on behalf of the club, including FICC and the Cinémathèque française founded by Langlois and Franju in 1936. After the Clube de Cinema's reorganization as a film archive—a bureaucratic fiction that allowed it to participate in exchanges of prints with FIAF members—under the umbrella of the Museu de Arte Moderna de São Paulo (MAM-SP), Salles Gomes organized its earliest acquisitions from the Cinémathèque française. Langlois was later feted as a guest of honor at the 1954 Festival Internacional de Cinema organized in São Paulo, which brought Salles Gomes back to Brazil to organize its retrospective programming. Assuming the leadership of the Filmoteca do MAM-SP, which became independent of the museum and was renamed the Cinemateca Brasileira in 1956, Salles Gomes remained deeply involved in FIAF, serving as its vice president and helping to coordinate the organization's regional section in Latin America.

Salles Gomes's involvement in a myriad of film-related cultural projects spanning the Atlantic was by no means unique. As I explore in more detail in chapter 2, the majority of Latin American cineclub organizers became de facto film archivists. Many, like Salles Gomes, were also journalists who covered festivals and served on juries, and also became film educators at the university level. For instance, Argentine film critic Andrés José Rolando Fustiñana, known by the pen name Roland, spearheaded the creation of the Gente de Cine film society in 1942, edited the magazine of the same name, and founded the Federación Argentina de Cineclubes and the Cinemateca Argentina, which provided film programs to the federation's network of film societies. Fustiñana attended Cannes, served on the jury of the Punta del Este film festival, and participated in a parallel conference of film critics and scholars at Mar del Plata. He taught in the Departamento de Cine at the Universidad Nacional de La Plata—which he briefly headed in 1962—and later at Argentina's Escuela Nacional de Cinematografía. González Casanova became the coordinator of film-related activities at the Universidad Nacional Autónoma de México (UNAM), fostering campus film societies, creating the Cineteca Universitaria (now the Filmoteca UNAM), and leading CUEC, founded in 1963. Eugenio Hintz and Walther Dassori Barthet (who was also a Communist Party member), respectively leaders of the Montevideo film societies Cine Club del Uruguay and Cine Universitario, created two film archives under the auspices of their respective clubs that later merged to become the Cinemateca Uruguaya.[76] Hintz became the secretary of FIAF's Latin American section, whose history is discussed in chapter 2, and later assumed the leadership of the state film archive, Cine Arte del Servicio Oficial de Difusión Radio Eléctrica (SODRE). Furthermore, Dassori Barthet and Hintz both worked at the Instituto de Cinematográfía de la Universidad de la República (Film Institute of the University of the Republic; ICUR), an institute dedicated to the production of scientific films, but also an important hub for practical training in filmmaking. Nobel Prize–winning novelist Gabriel García Márquez, whose involvement with cinema is less widely known (though it has become the object of sustained study over the past decade), was a member of Bogotá's Cine Club de Colombia, served as a delegate to FIAF for its associated film archive, and taught screenwriting at CUEC.[77]

These individuals' trajectories suggest how institution-building efforts centered on cinema not only nurtured their cosmopolitan and artistic aspirations but also opened up a novel—if often precarious and underfunded—sphere of professional activity for well-to-do and upwardly mobile Latin Americans, one that spanned private, philanthropic, and governmental initiatives. At the same time, this dense web of cultural organizations emerged in symbiosis with the geopolitical and cultural ambitions of the French state, the subject to which I now turn.

TRANSNATIONAL CULTURAL INFRASTRUCTURES: FRENCH CULTURAL DIPLOMACY AND SUPRANATIONAL ORGANIZATIONS

In 1958 a representative of France's Ministère des affaires étrangères (Ministry of Foreign Affairs; MAE) observed, "More than any other means of communication, cinema assures a French presence in all milieux."[78] This statement signals a belief that film was uniquely equipped to attract a mass audience through its international circulation, making it an eminently useful diplomatic tool. Yet given over three decades of Hollywood domination of global screens, French authorities were disinclined to rely on market forces alone to ensure the dissemination of French cinema. Instead, in the postwar period the state leveraged existing cultural networks—most notably the Alliance française (AF), an independent organization heavily subsidized by the French state—for the distribution of nonfiction films and the occasional feature. At the same time, the foreign ministry worked to build a non-commercial distribution and exhibition infrastructure that operated through its embassies. In parallel, the recently created Centre national de la cinématographie (CNC) financially supported both commercial ventures like the state-backed distributor Consortium franco-américain (COFRAM) and "para-commercial" initiatives like Unifrance, a state agency designed to promote the distribution and exhibition of French film abroad, which played an especially active role in coordinating French participation at international festivals.[79] These multifaceted efforts to facilitate the circulation of French film cultivated non-commercial circuits as alternatives to the theatrical exhibition spaces dominated by Hollywood film. In the process, they nurtured Latin American institutions of film culture and helped to fulfill film societies' need for alternative programming (for example, repertory titles and educational films) while ensuring the presence of French films, stars, and critics at festivals in the region. Broadly speaking, cinema promised to expand French cultural influence in Latin America beyond social elites, who had cultivated Francophilia for over a century.

Official manifestations of French cultural diplomacy date back to the early modern period and intensified after France's 1871 defeat in the

Franco-Prussian War.[80] France's deep cultural influence in nineteenth-century Latin America can be traced to the impact of the French Revolution's ideals on newly independent Latin American states, which sought a set of cultural models outside the former colonial metropolis, Spain. With the exception of Cuba and Puerto Rico, all of Spanish America became independent in the decade and a half between 1810 and 1826. (Brazil followed a distinct trajectory of historical development, becoming the seat of the Portuguese monarchy in 1808 when the royal family fled the advancing armies of Napoleon I. The country adopted a republican form of government only in 1889.) French immigration, while accounting for only a small percentage of massive migratory flows to South America in the nineteenth century, at times had an outsized cultural impact.[81] In Mexico, immigrants from the French town of Barcelonnette established an enduring commercial empire, rendering French goods all but synonymous with department store–style retail during the regime of Porfirio Díaz.[82] Yet according to Denis Rolland, France's prestige in Latin America was already in decline during World War I given (among other factors) the weakening of French capital investment in the region, sparking new forms of cultural diplomacy in response.[83] During the interwar period, the Service des œuvres françaises à l'étranger (Service of French Works Abroad; SOFE) founded in 1920 instituted a series of intellectual exchanges between Latin America and France via institutions of higher education.[84] Yet blows to French prestige accumulated after 1940 with the German occupation and the installation of the Vichy regime—though solidarity with the Free French was strong in Latin America, home to three-quarters of the world's Free French committees—and the rapid rise of the United States to economic dominance.[85]

Before the war, France's film-related cultural diplomacy was limited to scattered efforts to promote the commercial distribution of feature films.[86] After the conflict, France's diplomatic corps took new advantage of the existing network of the AF to boost the *rayonnement* (literally, radiance or radiation, implying a process of diffusion; figuratively, influence or standing) of French film and culture. The most enduring and best-known institutional network dedicated to promoting French culture abroad, the AF was founded in 1883. It was initially conceived as a means of bolstering French soft power in response to a profound blow to the nation's hard power, namely its defeat by Prussia in the 1870 Battle of Sedan. In addition, the AF was designed to help shore up French control of its colonial possessions through French-language education.[87] Later, language instruction would become the AF's main focus. The AF's efforts found especially fertile ground in Latin America, the world region with the largest number of branches (four hundred) and students (107,000) in the two decades after World War II.[88]

The French state made limited use of cinema as a pedagogical and propaganda tool in the 1930s, including via AF branches abroad, but greatly expanded its film-related activities after the war.[89] Many AF branches operated their own film societies. Others disseminated French film through partnerships with independent cineclubs and other organizations, offering auditorium space and furnishing prints from their collections of nonfiction film. For instance, the Cine Club de Colombia in Bogotá, Gente de Cine in Buenos Aires, and Cine Club Mendoza in western Argentina all sourced films from the local AF. This last organization also held its 16mm screenings in the AF's facility. The Cine Club de Lima in Peru and the Casa de la Cultura Ecuatoriana in Quito also collaborated with the AF.[90] These film-related activities appear to have been largely complementary to the AF's main mandate of language instruction. Nevertheless, the links between the AF and the growing postwar film society movement suggest how Latin American organizations strategically used a cultural infrastructure designed to build French soft power to accomplish their own institutional goals. Naturally, the AF faced competition from the cultural institutes of other nations, including the British Council, Germany's Goethe-Institut, Italy's Istituto Dante Alighieri, and the United States Information Agency's cultural centers, which developed their own film programming.[91] Yet even when it lacked the financial backing of some of its rivals, the AF proved made savvy use of cinema to promote language instruction and, more broadly, boost French soft power.

In addition to supporting the AF's film-related activity, the French foreign ministry's newly created Direction générale des relations culturelles (Office of Cultural Relations; DGRC) instituted a non-commercial exhibition infrastructure, purchasing and shipping 16mm projectors of French manufacture to embassies, legations, and AF branches.[92] By the late 1940s, most of Latin America's French embassies and legations held modest collections of nonfiction shorts to which the French state held non-commercial exhibition rights. A much smaller number of feature films were occasionally loaned to embassies for special screenings.[93] Diplomatic collections included promotional tourist films; *films sur l'art* (nonfiction films on art and artists); profiles of prominent public figures; and a few industrial, scientific, and medical films. As France's ambassador to Peru noted in 1953, the titles sent to embassies were primarily concerned with "literary or artistic culture" and served to "maintain admiration for our culture in intellectual groups." He requested more films on topics like aviation and electrical infrastructure to counteract prevailing local perceptions, writing, "It is acknowledged here that France is the land of the arts, good wines, fashion, and perfumes, but that she is incapable of any interesting accomplishments in the industrial realm."[94] Beyond objections to the tenor of the diplomatic service's films, ambassadors and cultural attachés complained about the lack of Spanish- or Portuguese-language voiceovers or subtitles on many prints, which limited their dissemination.

Yet by their own account, the reach of French embassies' film-related activities was impressive. In the last four months of 1949, the Brazilian embassy reported screening 113 titles for 18,633 viewers, including members of newly founded film societies at AF branches in Rio de Janeiro, Belo Horizonte, Porto Alegre, and Recife.[95] The Chilean embassy recorded comparable numbers four years later.[96] Also in 1953, the Colombian embassy reached 75,980 spectators with its screenings in the first three months of the year alone, though its audience numbers dropped by half in the following quarter due to a dearth of new films in its collection.[97] In 1951 the French embassy in Argentina possessed 159 titles, which it loaned out over fourteen hundred times (often for multiple screenings) to cineclubs (which accounted for just under 10 percent of the total), AF branches, educational institutions (France-affiliated and otherwise), governmental and religious groups, and cultural centers.[98] Despite these numbers, which far surpassed the reach of most private film societies, the DGRC often devoted a much greater portion of its budget to producing radio broadcasts than to coordinating film screenings. For instance, film accounted for just 6 to 7 percent of the combined radio/cinema budget in Brazil and Chile in the early 1950s.[99] (These figures do not include the cost of the films already provided to embassies by the DGRC.) Of course, French embassies' film-related cultural activities faced competition from other foreign diplomatic missions. Surviving programs from Latin American film societies indicate that they also sourced prints from the Austrian, British, Canadian, Czechoslovak, Dutch, Italian, Swedish, and US embassies.[100]

Latin American film societies also benefited from the activities of COFRAM, a joint-public private distributor founded by producer Jean Séfert in 1948 to boost the dissemination of French films in Latin America.[101] Their circulation in the region remained minimal in the interwar period despite isolated successes and had ceased almost completely between the German invasion in 1940 and the liberation in 1944 and

1945.[102] At its peak, COFRAM had local branches in Latin America's six largest film markets—Argentina, Brazil, Colombia, Cuba, Mexico, and Venezuela—and a network of local agents in other countries. Its business strategy included signing contracts with individual movie theaters to provide all or part of their programming, thus creating established destinations for viewing French films; distributing French newsreels; and working closely with film societies. COFRAM managed to increase its profits nearly ten-fold between 1948 and 1955, reaching a peak of more than a billion francs per year in 1960.[103] Yet the company collapsed in 1963 after suffering serious losses stemming from the erosion of Latin American currencies' value due to high inflation; declining numbers of film viewers due to television's expansion in the region; and, in Cuba, the nationalization of foreign-owned distributors and movie theaters and the freezing of COFRAM profits. COFRAM's fate signals the limits of a commercial distribution model for the ends of cultural diplomacy. The efforts of Unifrance, which is still active today, would prove to be a more enduring model for fostering cultural relations through cinema.

Unifrance was established in 1949 under the auspices of the CNC to promote the dissemination of French films. Upon its founding, Unifrance was defined by its executive director Robert Cravenne as a "para-commercial, para-diplomatic organization" designed to "promote the penetration of French films in foreign markets."[104] This phrase captures how economic aims became entwined with geopolitical ones in Unifrance's program of action. The agency's activities included lobbying against protectionist measures like tariffs and quotas, helping to negotiate commercial treaties and co-production agreements, handling relationships with state distribution monopolies in occupied nations like Germany and Japan and in socialist countries, and generating market reports that allowed distributors to more effectively sell French films overseas. Better known, however, is Unifrance's labor in promoting French cinema by disseminating publicity materials for new releases and films in production; coordinating the presentation of French films at international festivals; and organizing the Semaine du cinéma français (French Cinema Week), an oft-imitated strategy of cultural promotion.[105] Unifrance's efforts complemented diplomatic achievements with bilateral trade agreements; for instance, the 1953 Semaine du cinéma français in Buenos Aires was intended to "highlight with flair the re-entry of French films to the Argentine market following the recent film trade agreement. It will contribute, furthermore, to creating a favorable atmosphere for negotiations surrounding the renewal of this accord."[106]

Unifrance's program of cultural action was carried out by a network of agents, many of whom worked as cultural attachés or journalists, roles that positioned them effectively to organize events and place news stories. Argentina, Brazil, and Mexico—the Latin American nations with the largest film industries and markets—were deemed countries of secondary importance in Unifrance's original plan of action, which privileged European nations like Germany, Switzerland, Italy, the United Kingdom, Belgium, and the Netherlands for "geographic as well as commercial reasons."[107] Yet three years after its founding Unifrance had as many delegates in Latin America (just two, in Mexico and the Río de la Plata region) as it did in Europe, although the balance later shifted to favor Europe once more.[108] As discussed in more detail in chapter 3, the work of Unifrance agents encompassed information-gathering and negotiations surrounding the selection of films for the Cannes festival, along with the coordination of French representation at newly created Latin American festivals like Punta del Este and Mar del Plata. When salaries for local agents were cut from Unifrance's budget in the 1980s, the agency shifted its functions to AF personnel, suggesting that official and semi-official mechanisms of French cultural relations were closely intertwined.[109]

Beyond these direct forms of cultural diplomacy, the French government and individual cultural architects sought to shape to the ends of the state the supranational cultural organizations that emerged in the postwar period. Dudley Andrew describes the post–World War II period as a "federated phase" of film culture, when international organizations emerged to temper unbridled nationalism with a spirit of "international humanism."[110] In the period under study, the major international organizations dedicated to promoting cineclubs, archives, festivals, and film schools—FICC, FIAF, FIAPF, and CILECT—were all headquartered in Paris with the temporary exception of FIAPF, which was housed in Rome from 1950 to 1956.[111] Despite their multilateral character, these organizations remained intertwined with the French diplomatic infrastructure, in some cases receiving financial support from France's MAE, and were well-positioned to advance French cultural ambitions.

The case of UNESCO suggests both the ambitions and the limits of French efforts to advance a patriotic agenda through international organizations amid the political pressures of the Cold War. UNESCO was established on the principle that "co-operation in education and furtherance of cultural interchange in the arts, the humanities, and the sciences will promote the freedom, the dignity, and the well-being of all and therefore assist in the attainment of understanding, confidence, security, and peace among the peoples of the world," a sweeping mandate that purported to be politically neutral.[112] Yet the fulfillment of these ideals was necessarily conditioned by growing Cold War polarization and accelerating decolonization (which would shift the organization's approach decisively in the late 1960s and early 1970s), as well as by the strategic interests and decisions of individual member states. Notably, the Soviet Union declined to join UNESCO until 1954 following Stalin's death the previous year, allowing the United States to dominate the organization's policy agenda and prioritize liberal, democratic, and capitalist values in its programs.

Yet US strategic interests were far from the sole guiding principle of UNESCO's activities during its first decade. As William R. Pendergast has shown, French delegates endeavored to "ensure UNESCO's functional preoccupation with intellectual and cultural affairs" in the face of US, British, and Third World interest in educational and scientific activities as a vehicle for economic development.[113] Hopeful that UNESCO might help build French cultural capital abroad, the country's delegates sought to model the organization on the Institut international de coopération intellectuelle (International Institute of Intellectual Cooperation; IICI) founded in 1922 and headquartered in Paris.[114] Ultimately, UNESCO would also be housed in Paris thanks to the efforts of French delegates. French policy proposals to UNESCO emphasized intellectual and artistic production over direct education and development efforts. Yet efforts to ensure UNESCO's investment in culture outside the areas of fundamental education (a term referring to literacy programs and the mastery of basic skills to promote economic activity and public health) and technical assistance (the transfer of skills and expertise) met with only limited success. UNESCO participation in UN programs like the Expanded Program of Technical Assistance and Special Fund—earmarked for projects in developing nations—guided the agency's priorities, and French lobbying resulted only in a modest increase in the portion of the budget dedicated to cultural activities, from 6.7 percent in 1949 to 11.1 percent a decade later.[115]

French efforts to exercise hegemony over UNESCO ultimately had limited impact on its film-related activities, which de-emphasized erudite forms of film culture despite early assertions of their importance. At UNESCO's 1946 General Conference, the concept of art cinema and the need for institutions to promote it were championed by Salles Gomes, who represented Brazil on the conference's Sub-Commission on Mass Communication. Salles Gomes successfully introduced a resolution establishing that "cinema be considered an art." His remarks "stressed the artistic side of the cinema," affirming that it "should contribute to the democratization of culture, provided that care was taken to secure artistic quality. For this purpose, he urged the development of cinema clubs and libraries."[116] The conference's final resolutions also referenced the need to cultivate non-commercial infrastructures of film culture, namely the establishment of "*National Visual Councils or Institutes*, to facilitate the provision of films and film information services to educational and community organizations.... Complementary to this, Unesco should encourage the promotion of National Film Societies and Scientific Film Societies for the provision of specialized programmes in the fields of Unesco interests" (emphasis in original).[117]

Ultimately, UNESCO's main lines of film-related activity were distributing educational and "useful" cinema; producing educational cinema (after 1951); publishing a book series dedicated to media's uses as an pedagogical tool, including titles on film appreciation and education; and compiling surveys assessing the state of national media industries.[118] Alternately considered a noncontroversial initiative designed to satisfy opposing factions within UNESCO (as they simply collated information without making policy recommendations) or intelligence-gathering efforts that facilitated Cold War–era psychological warfare, these surveys were among the earliest fruits of UNESCO's Mass Communications Program.[119] Initiated in 1947 with data on twelve "war-devastated" nations—all in Europe, except for China and the Philippines—the survey was expanded in 1948 to seventeen countries with media industries that were "not yet sufficiently developed."[120] Over half of them were located in Latin America and the Caribbean (namely Cuba, the Dominican Republic, Ecuador, Haiti, Honduras, Mexico, Peru, Uruguay, and Venezuela), giving some credence to the idea that the reports prioritized territories of strategic importance to the United States.[121] Other film-related UNESCO endeavors included a 1959 catalog entitled *Orient: A Survey of Films Produced in Countries of Arab and Asian Culture*, a collaboration with the British Film Institute (BFI) designed to enhance understanding of the "East" in the "West" by facilitating awareness and distribution of films.[122]

Initially, due to the channeling of limited funds toward the United Nations Film Board established in 1947, UNESCO was not involved in making films, but rather facilitated the circulation of educational cinema that aligned closely with the organization's goals.[123] Building on an accord established by the IICI in 1933, UNESCO brokered the multilateral

Beirut Agreement (adopted in 1948 but enacted only in 1954) and Florence Agreement (enacted in 1950) to facilitate the circulation of educational, scientific, and cultural materials.[124] To the chagrin of cineclubs and archives, UNESCO's definition of "educational, scientific, and cultural" media excluded commercial features, staples of their programming. UNESCO also found an ingenious solution to combat issues caused by international currency exchange rates—a significant issue for FIAF, as explored in chapter 2—which led to an imbalance in buying power for educational materials.[125] Film coupons could be purchased on a sliding scale by organizations depending on their location and exchanged for prints and raw 16mm stock. UNESCO also created its own archive of educational films to be disseminated through local branch offices, including both internally and externally produced materials. Efforts to create a transnational distribution infrastructure for educational film extended to the creation of the Instituto Latinoamericano de Cine Educativo (Latin American Educational Film Institute), established in Mexico in 1956 with UNESCO funding, although international demand for the institute's services proved to be essentially nonexistent through the end of the 1960s.[126]

A notable intersection between UNESCO endeavors and erudite institutions of film culture did, however, emerge in the immediate postwar period in the form of UNESCO support for the Fédération internationale du film d'art (International Federation of Art Film; FIFA), founded with the support of Henri Langlois; his partner Mary Meerson; and art aficionado Gaston Diehl, who later became a cultural attaché and one of the leaders of the Cine Club Venezuela founded in postwar Caracas. Despite its name, the federation did not promote art cinema in general, but rather the specific subgenre of documentary films on art (*films sur l'art*), many with experimental qualities.[127] FIFA worked closely not only with UNESCO, which published several catalogs of films sur l'art, but also with FIAF member archives who worked to organize festivals dedicated to the genre.[128]

As its ranks swelled with newly independent postcolonial states in the late 1960s and early 1970s, UNESCO was increasingly concerned with the contradictions of the guiding principle of the "free flow of information," since reducing barriers to the circulation of media (including film, radio, television, books, and periodicals) simply perpetuated the domination of a few wealthy, industrialized nations over global communications. These misgivings were crystallized in the concept of a New International Information and Communication Order, a parallel to the New

International Economic Order adopted by the UN in 1974 that aimed to combat neo-colonial dynamics (such as the exploitative extraction of natural resources and the vulnerability of developing nations that export agricultural commodities to fluctuations in their prices on the global market) under the influence of NAM and the Group of 77, a consortium of developing nations organized in 1964. Yet as Sarah Brouillette notes, UNESCO's radical turn was undermined by pressures from the United States and other leading capitalist economies and has now been fully superseded by a neoliberal notion of culture as an engine of tourism and economic growth.[129]

As suggested by the disconnect between UNESCO's activities and the aims of France's film-related cultural diplomacy, the aims of this study are akin to, but do not always overlap with, the growing research area of "useful cinema," which refers to the instrumentalization of film for openly educational and promotional ends outside the space of the commercial movie theater.[130] This area is just beginning to be explored with regard to Global South film cultures. The instrumentalization of cinema by colonial empires and the afterlives of colonial films have received the bulk of the scholarly attention, meaning that Latin America, which was largely though not entirely decolonized during the nineteenth century, is not typically included in the conversation.[131] Postwar Latin American cineclubs, archives, festivals, and film schools were principally, but by no means exclusively, oriented toward the fiction feature. Nevertheless, the harnessing of commercial entertainment film in service of official and unofficial cultural diplomacy makes this context a productive one to explore through the lens of useful cinema. Given limited industrial film production outside Argentina, Brazil, and Mexico, the activities of postwar Latin American institutions of film culture often blurred the boundaries between professional and amateur cinema—an area of activity often pursued by cineclubs, even if their screenings focused on narrative features—and between commercial and non-commercial film, suggesting the need to avoid a rigid separation between these categories in developing a more nuanced understanding of global film cultures.

OVERVIEW OF THE BOOK

Transatlantic Cinephilia maps postwar networks of film culture by examining distinct types of institutions—cineclubs, archives, festivals, and film schools—in turn, offering an overview of their development and delving more deeply into one or more case studies in each section. I trace personal and institutional connections and reconstruct the ideals, aims, and tensions that informed these organizations through internal records like correspondence, meeting notes, bylaws, reports, and conference proceedings; public-facing documents such as cineclub and festival programs and entry guidelines for film schools; and accounts of organizations' activities in the press and secondary sources.

The first chapter explores the most expansive network of film-related cultural institutions that emerged in postwar Latin America: namely, the more than 250 cineclubs established between 1940 and 1965. The film society movement intersected with the cultural projects of a wide range of local and international organizations, from private clubs and universities to state-supported French cultural organizations like local AF branches and the Institut français d'Amérique latine (French Institute of Latin America; IFAL) in Mexico City, as well as the Brussels-based Office catholique international du cinéma (OCIC), which sought to regulate film's moral effects on a global scale. As social organizations that offered a sense of prestige to their members, film societies leveraged their international connections both for practical purposes like securing prints and to highlight their cosmopolitanism, which served as a source of cultural capital for members. I offer a case study of the Cine Club de Colombia founded in Bogotá in 1949, whose programs and meeting notes register the influence of an implicitly French model of the cineclub characterized by retrospective programming and spirited audience discussions. Yet friction resulted when the club's organizers attempted to impose these ideals on a reluctant local audience. The Cine Club de Colombia's history highlights how hierarchies of class and nation were reproduced through networks of film culture, even as cineclubs aspired to transform the mass audience by forging active spectators.

Chapter 2 examines the wave of cinémathèques founded in the region between the late 1940s and the mid-1960s, most often with the encouragement of Henri Langlois. These institution-building efforts advanced Langlois's ambitions for the broad global dissemination of film materials—especially French cinema—while also supplying him with ready-made allies to back his agenda for FIAF. Offering an overview of Latin American film archives' development from the late 1940s through the mid-1960s, I focus on the Latin American Pool (known as the Sección Latinoamericana in Spanish and the Seção Latino-americana in Portuguese), a subsection of FIAF created in the mid-1950s to facilitate regional cooperation. Although FIAF saw collaboration with Latin American archives as a promising means of propagating the film preservation movement worldwide, a profound disconnect emerged between FIAF's institutional procedures and the priorities and circumstances of newly created cinémathèques. Rooted in the film society movement, these archives (unlike their Euro-American counterparts) privileged the collection not of national moving-image heritage, but rather of European "classics" whose established prestige meant they could be screened for audiences and rented to affiliated cineclubs for a fee. Borrowed cultural capital thus literally bankrolled the activities of the precarious Latin American film preservation movement. Even as they leveraged their connections to FIAF to obtain programming, early Latin American cinémathèques were often marginalized within the organization due to difficult financial and political circumstances, compounded by FIAF practices and policies like holding conferences exclusively in Europe for over two decades and requiring that dues be paid in European currencies at a moment of runaway inflation in many Latin American nations. The troubled histories of the Latin American Pool and its independent successor, the Unión de Cinematecas de América Latina (UCAL), which both failed to effectively foster joint archival initiatives in the region, exemplify both the global aspirations and the structural inequalities that marked film preservation's international expansion in the postwar period.

A third chapter turns to the French/European model of the film festival and its adoption in Latin America. The circulation of Latin American cinema at Cannes reveals how its function as a showcase for world cinema with a diplomatic mission came into conflict with its role as an arbiter of cinema's status as art, ultimately leading the festival to privilege aesthetic qualities over nationality. As documents from Cannes's archives reveal, films from Latin America helped fulfill the imperative that as many nations as possible be represented. Yet internal communications show that the festival's organizers sought to exclude works selected by government officials or industry representatives that failed to conform to their notions of art cinema, while soliciting films from a handful of celebrated directors like Luis Buñuel and Leopoldo Torre Nilsson. At the same time, newly founded Latin American festivals in coastal resort towns like Punta del Este in Uruguay and Mar del Plata in Argentina modeled themselves on European events in the pursuit of both prestige and financial gain. In countries where domestic film industries were nonexistent or seen as troubled, festivals served not so much to advance the cause of national cinema as to promote tourism and to demonstrate the sophistication of local audiences to the world, a goal embodied by Mar del Plata's move to organize a parallel gathering of film critics and intellectuals during the first half of the 1960s. By acting as meeting places for film enthusiasts, critics, and educators, festivals strengthened connections between institutions of film culture on both sides of the Atlantic.

The study's final chapter looks at how French and European models of film pedagogy, which combined practical training with extensive coursework in the humanities, shaped a postwar generation of Latin American directors as well as the beginnings of professional film education in Latin America. While Latin Americans' presence at Italy's CSC is better known, France's IDHEC trained a larger number of Latin American students and actively promoted the enrollment of foreigners, albeit on unequal terms with native-born students. IDHEC's leadership recruited international students as de facto cultural ambassadors, whose training in France served as a testament to the national film industry's technical and creative superiority and thus amplified its international prestige. Early Latin American film schools—some of which employed IDHEC graduates—built on the notion of critical spectatorship championed both by their European counterparts and broader transatlantic efforts to foster film culture, approaching the absence or crisis of domestic production as a problem of film culture that could be addressed by the cultivation not only of erudite filmmakers, but also of cinephilic audiences. By the late 1960s, these top-down models of film education increasingly entered into crisis in the face of growing political polarization. As cinema was increasingly enlisted as an agent of social change, authoritarian regimes moved to shutter many of the region's film schools. At Mexico's CUEC students appropriated its equipment and facilities to document the 1968 student uprising. This chapter reconstructs ideals and practices of Latin American film pedagogy as they emerged in dialogue with European institutions and local politics.

The chapters are organized chronologically in terms of each type of institution's emergence in Latin America, but they cover overlapping periods and intertwined developments. Broadly, each traces a shift from historical moments characterized by an uneasy postwar consensus to those marked by more open polarization and political conflict. Overall, the case studies move from organizations primarily concerned with fostering the circulation of cinema and shaping its reception to those more intimately concerned with film production. Yet their complexity frustrates any neat narrative of a shift from a passive, colonized film culture based on consumption to a radical anti-colonial mode of film production. Instead, it charts a far more politically ambiguous and knotty set of transatlantic relations.

CHAPTER 1

The Cineclub Movement in Latin America

Transatlantic Cooperation, Local Frictions

In a program commemorating the thirtieth anniversary of the Cine Club de Colombia in Bogotá, its leadership claimed credit for a sweeping transformation of the movie-going public: "When the cineclub movement began in Colombia in 1949 [with the club's founding], one still remembered with horror that only seven years earlier, in 1942, an infuriated audience almost destroyed the Teatro Colombia (now the Jorge Eliécer Gaitán) in Bogotá due to the projection of Orson Welles' *Citizen Kane*, a masterpiece of cinema that nearly cleaves its history in two. Thanks to cineclubs, now familiar points of reference for the majority of spectators, they no longer generate the destructive furor caused by *Citizen Kane*."[1] Consistent with reports of disturbances and vandalism among Colombian audiences during the first half of the twentieth century, the program's reference to a "destructive furor" also evokes an event more deeply seared into popular memory: the Bogotazo, a popular uprising in Colombia's capital triggered by the assassination of Liberal presidential candidate Jorge Eliécer Gaitán on April 9, 1948.[2] The politician's death foreclosed hopes for social change awakened by his fiery speeches condemning Colombia's oligarchy and entrenched two-party system, which won him broad working-class support.[3] In particular, the program's phrasing echoed the tendency of "elites of both parties [Liberal and Conservative] to speak in the most extravagant and racist terms about the impossibility of civilizing the Colombian masses" after the Bogotazo.[4] On its anniversary, the Cine Club de Colombia (CCC) affirmed

37

its success in "imposing good cinema" and restraining the exuberant and even violent behavior of film audiences.[5] These comments highlight the film society's efforts to discipline film publics in a period of political upheaval, mass migration from the countryside, and the consequent transformation of urban spaces and class hierarchies.[6]

The early years of the CCC's operation coincided with La Violencia (1946–1966), a wave of conflict rooted in the stark divide between Liberals and Conservatives that intensified after the Bogotazo, encompassing guerrilla and paramilitary activity along with killings without apparent links to politics. La Violencia's most devastating impacts were felt in rural areas. Yet it is nonetheless striking that references to the conflict are almost entirely absent from the CCC's programs, though the club did screen a short documentary on the topic, Gonzalo Canal Ramírez's *Esta fue mi vereda* (This was my path, 1959).[7] This silence is consistent with broader tendencies among Colombian intellectuals of the period, who privileged internationalism over nationalism and cultivated a formalist mode of criticism that divorced aesthetics from politics.

Referring to the Colombian artworld of the mid-1960s, Ana María Reyes ponders how intellectuals could "so conspicuously evade issues of violence as the country was emerging out of La Violencia, one of its darkest historical moments, and embarking on another phase involving Cuban-inspired guerrillas and counterinsurgency initiatives" and instead "aspir[e] to an ideal of artistic autonomy" unhampered by political commitment.[8] According to Reyes, this tendency was cultivated by economic and political elites aligned with the United States in order to "redirect the attention of artists toward participating in a cosmopolitan culture, coded as universal, and away from political involvement and ongoing armed struggles taking place in the Global South."[9] Though many of Reyes's critiques apply to the CCC's cultural project, it cannot be reduced to a US-aligned cosmopolitanism. Rather, the CCC's activities were shaped by multiple cultural reference points—particularly French ones—that exceed the binary logic of the cultural Cold War, and it engaged in an often contradictory class politics.

The CCC's self-proclaimed goal of "improving the taste of the moviegoing public" embodied the local bourgeoisie's striving for distinction (in Pierre Bourdieu's sense) at a moment of rapid growth for Colombia's urban middle classes.[10] The postwar development of art cinema as a concept and phenomenon imbued the medium with significant prestige. Yet film culture remained distinct from the "lettered" culture that had traditionally yoked literary production to political power in Latin

America.¹¹ Viewing films that had been celebrated by erudite critics and on the international festival circuit became a mark of sophistication that distinguished members of the middle-class intelligentsia from other upwardly mobile Colombians. Yet cinema offered a mass appeal that established artforms like literature and painting could not match, and thus an opportunity to influence the tastes of supposedly unenlightened social sectors—the very groups cineclub organizers were presumably seeking to differentiate themselves from.

As surviving documents of the CCC's operations make clear, the club sought to democratize access to art cinema by offering alternatives to commercial programming and to empower viewers by prompting critical reflection through post-screening discussions and audience questionnaires, participatory protocols that were embraced by (though not exclusive to) the French film society movement of the period, as Léo Souillés-Debats and Kelley Conway have pointed out.¹² Yet these ideals of access and empowerment were curtailed by the CCC's efforts to exercise social discipline. The CCC's leadership relied on the club's rank and file to help elevate local film taste; yet it alternately criticized them as unruly and as passive, rather than actively engaged, in the face of the moving image. For instance, a 1957 program chided members who, faced with last-minute programming changes or projection problems, "manifest their displeasure with shouts and protests, which, if they are undesirable in any film screening, are worse in the case of a meeting of the Cine Club, where the spirit of camaraderie and tolerance among friends should be the norm."¹³ Four years later, a program described "melancholy results in the discussion following the screening of the film. With inexplicable anxiety, the members leave the theater as if fleeing from a disaster, without considering the necessity of expanding on the thoughts inspired by the film screened through the commentary of the attendees themselves."¹⁴ These criticisms signal the club's efforts to enforce an ideal of the film society defined by lively yet carefully regulated audience engagement, an ideal closely associated with French cineclubs. The club's ideals for member participation reinforced a distinction—in Bourdieu's dual sense of taste and social status—*within* the film society membership (some members embodied the ideal while others fell short) as well as *between* the membership and the broader movie-going public.¹⁵

The CCC's history also attests to the difficulties in reconciling imported institutional and aesthetic norms with local tastes and social practices. In 1961, Brazilian film enthusiast and archivist Rudá de Andrade wrote in a report prepared for a UNESCO-sponsored roundtable at the second Rassegna del Cinema Latino-americano in Santa Margherita Ligure, Italy:[16] "The influence of European culture determines the structure of [Latin American] cineclubs, which follow the example of the old continent, up to and including the details of programming, courses, and screenings, their methods of presentation, their intellectual orientation and even the practical organization of these bodies. This cultural imitation occurs without the leaders seeing the cultural differences that separate the two continents. To put it this way, one never finds a conscious quest to adapt European experiences to local problems."[17] Writing at a moment marked by leftist intellectuals' efforts to forge an "authentically" Brazilian national culture and challenge the neo-colonial cultural influence of Europe and the United States, Andrade describes an incomplete process of cultural translation. Yet this transaction generated cultural capital for both Latin American intellectuals and French institutions. I argue that the efforts of postwar Latin American film societies—which sought to transform film spectatorship by cultivating participatory modes of viewing and to develop alternative film programming, prompting them to tap into transatlantic institutional networks to secure films—proved mutually beneficial for Latin American film enthusiasts seeking personal prestige and France-based organizations eager to expand their global influence.

The social distinction conferred by film societies was reliant on the successful differentiation of their programming from mainstream theatrical fare. In locales where alternative distribution channels (such as firms specializing in educational titles or 16mm prints) were limited or nonexistent, Latin American film enthusiasts took advantage of diplomatic infrastructure and supranational cultural organizations to secure vintage prints and works of contemporary art film. Cineclubs in the region often sourced films from French embassies, local branches of the Alliance française, and the commercial distributor COFRAM, which had the financial backing of the French state. For their part, France-based entities like FICC and FIAF promoted non-commercial film culture while tacitly advancing French cultural interests. FICC and FIAF offered not only material resources but also institutional models, promoting the creation of national cineclub federations and archives as a means of advancing their own programs of global expansion.

In tracing the web of transatlantic connections in which the postwar Latin American cineclub movement was enmeshed, I shed light on an often overlooked period in the region's film culture and a Cold War–era cultural politics that precedes and exceeds the antimony between capitalist Hollywood and the radical NLAC that solidified in the mid-1960s. Although film societies are often credited with having a formative impact on NLAC directors, until recently they have garnered little attention as objects of study in their own right, perhaps because they forged circuits of cultural exchange that fall outside both Hollywood's global market domination and the shared "continental project" of political and economic liberation championed by radical 1960s filmmakers.[18] Touching on film society activity in Argentina, Brazil, Chile, Colombia, Cuba, Mexico, Peru, Uruguay, and Venezuela, I focus most closely on the case of the Cine Club de México, an influential Mexico City film society created within the cultural infrastructure of the French state, and the CCC, whose comparatively rich institutional archive allows for a sustained discussion of its inner workings and tensions.

Situating Latin American cineclubs within a broader historical arc of film society activity, I first chart their emergence in elite literary and artistic circles during the interwar period. I then outline the varied institutional underpinnings of mid-century film societies, ranging from private clubs, universities, and national governments to diplomatic endeavors and religious initiatives, examining how film society pedagogy reinforced broader organizational goals. Finally, I highlight how the development of transnational film society networks generated both mutually beneficial cooperation, resulting in the expansion of institutional networks and the transnational circulation of film prints, and local frictions. As the case of the CCC suggests, dominant film society protocols modeled on their European (especially French) counterparts clashed with the tastes and habits of the rank and file. The expectation that members would participate in desired forms of discourse on cinema were continually met with frustration, signaling the constitutive contradictions of postwar Latin American cineclubs' cultural project.

PRECURSORS: TRANSATLANTIC CINECLUB ACTIVITY IN THE INTERWAR PERIOD

Six months before the famous first meeting of the Ciné-Club de France in June 1920—often pinpointed as the origin of the global film society movement—the inaugural issue of *Le journal du ciné-club*, edited by critic and filmmaker Louis Delluc, outlined the goals of the future organization. An editorial lists the club's proposed activities: lectures on cinema's history, aesthetics, and educational potential "accompanied by moving projections"; "referendums" on the year's best films that would communicate public tastes to studios and exhibitors; and experiments with amateur filmmaking. Most centrally, the cineclub would dedicate itself to "gathering around the [intellectual] elite and [industry] professionals, as intermediaries, an entire army constituted by the broad public impassioned by Cinema, in an age where the masses play such a large role and exercise such great influence on all things."[19]

The editorial's program of action presages the protocols—and the class dynamics—of postwar Latin American film societies. Through these organizations, middle-class and upper-middle-class members of the intelligentsia sought both to enlighten and to harness the power of a mass audience enthralled by cinema, training them to demand aesthetically superior films from production companies and theater owners. These parallels are not surprising given Latin American film enthusiasts' direct and indirect contact with the French cineclub movement before and after World War II. Yet the Ciné-Club de France's investment in art for art's sake was certainly not the sole aspiration cherished by film societies in the interwar period. Organizations like Les Amis de Spartacus in France, the Workers' Film Society in the United Kingdom, and the Volksfilmverband in Germany sought to use cinema to stir the working classes' revolutionary energies in order to transform not only the film industry but society as a whole. Tracing politicized and depoliticized models of the film society on both sides of the Atlantic makes clear that the apolitical or even conservative stance adopted by most Latin American cineclubs prior to the 1960s—with the notable exception of communist-front organizations like Mexico's Cine Club Progreso—was not inherent to the film society itself.[20] Rather, it reflected the limited political engagement of many middle-class Latin Americans in the late 1940s and 1950s after a brief period of democratic opening given, on the one hand, a swing of the pendulum back to the right in many nations, and on the other, the ascendancy of populist currents like Peronism in Argentina, which was strongly opposed by erudite film enthusiasts.[21]

Founded in 1928 by the communist writer Léon Moussinac, Les Amis de Spartacus was an outlier among erudite organizations like the Ciné-Club de France and the Club des Amis du Septième Art founded by Paris-based Italian filmmaker Ricciotto Canudo in 1921.[22] After a trip to the Soviet Union, where he forged ties with Vsevolod Pudovkin and Sergei Eisenstein, Moussinac created the club in order to screen Soviet films prohibited by the French censors.[23] The club attained a cross-class membership of eighty thousand, counting satellite cineclubs outside Paris, in the eight-month period before it was shuttered by Parisian authorities.[24]

A similar pattern can be observed in Britain. In 1925 Iris Barry, future director of the Film Library of New York's MoMA, co-founded the unapologetically upper-crust London Film Society.[25] Four years later, the Workers' Film Society was founded in London amid a boom in British cineclubs, quickly organizing a national network of local chapters.[26] In Germany the Volksfilmverband, founded in 1928, rallied members of the communist and non-communist left to lobby against low-quality and reactionary film entertainment.[27]

Latin America's earliest film societies emerged in the late 1920s and early 1930s, with documented groups operating in Argentina, Brazil, Cuba, Mexico, Uruguay, and Venezuela.[28] These clubs typically took shape under the umbrella of existing cultural institutions and literary groups, whose politics ranged from moderate liberalism to communism. In Argentina, the Cine Club de Buenos Aires began hosting screenings and film-related lectures in 1929 under the auspices of the Asociación Amigos del Arte (Society of Friends of Art), an initiative spearheaded by future filmmaker León Klimovsky. Invested in exploring modern trends in visual art and music, the society hosted illustrious guests like philosopher José Ortega y Gasset, playwright and poet Federico García Lorca, and architect Le Corbusier.[29] In Cuba, critic and future film educator José Manuel Valdés-Rodríguez organized informal cineclub sessions in his home between 1927 and 1929. Dubbed the Cine Club de la Habana, the organization attracted a group of leftist writers and intellectuals clustered around the *Revista de Avance*.[30] In Mexico City, European cineclubs garnered significant interest from the press beginning in the mid-1920s.[31] Yet it was not until 1931 that Bernardo Ortiz de Montellano, editor of the influential literary magazine *Contemporáneos*, and Agustín Aragón Leiva, a close associate of Eisenstein's during the shooting of his never-completed project *Que Viva México* (1931), helped organize a film society alternately known as the Cineclub Mexicano and Cine Club de México.[32] Photographer Lola Álvarez Bravo extended the club's activities under the auspices of the Liga de Escritores y Artistas Revolucionarios (League of Revolutionary Writers and Artists; LEAR) between 1934 and 1938.[33]

Less commonly, interwar cineclubs in Latin America emerged outside existing cultural institutions. The founders of Rio de Janeiro's Chaplin Club, Octávio de Faria, Plínio Süssekind Rocha, Almir Castro, and Claudio Mello, found themselves galvanized by the transition to sound, which they stridently rejected as a corruption of film art.[34] In June 1928 the young intellectuals created a monthly forum at which they read and discussed their critical writing on cinema, some of which later appeared in the club's magazine *O Fan*. Due to logistical challenges, the organization did not screen its first film, G. W. Pabst's *Die Büchse der Pandora* (*Pandora's Box*, 1929) until January 1930.[35] Finally, in Caracas, poet Ángel Miguel Queremel created the short-lived Cineclub Venezolano, which held its first screenings in 1933.[36]

While most were rooted in existing cultural infrastructures, Latin America's interwar cineclubs were decisively shaped by the transatlantic traffic of individuals and publications. Prominent visitors like Eisenstein and Spanish poet Guillermo de Torre, who traveled frequently to Argentina, gave impetus to the creation of cineclubs, while periodicals like Madrid's *La Gaceta Literaria* took a keen interest in European and Latin American film societies alike.[37] Accordingly, the self-fashioning of the region's early cineclubs—through the publication of announcements, manifestoes, and statutes that outlined ambitious goals, lending discursive weight to organizations that were often small and precarious—involved performative declarations of both nationalism and internationalism.

For instance, in a program of action published in *Contemporáneos*, the Cineclub Mexicano outlined plans to screen works from European, American, and Asian avant-gardes along with its commitment "to create a favorable atmosphere out of which a Mexican cinema art may emerge."[38] The text was reprinted in *La Gaceta Literaria* and published in English translation in the leftist US film magazine *Experimental Cinema*.[39] The document stressed the Cineclub Mexicano's links with its European counterparts, describing it as "an affiliate of the Film Society of London and the Parisian League of Cine-Clubs" with "a program of action identical to that of cineclubs around the world, with special affinities to the Cineclub Español," whose screenings were often covered in *La Gaceta Literaria*.[40] The statutes of the Chaplin Club, published in the group's magazine *O Fan* in January 1929, similarly framed cinema in both cosmopolitan and nationalist terms. The document declares: "Any preoccupation with being hostile towards or systematically favoring national cinema or foreign cinema of any nationality, is alien to the Club, given that there is only one cinema, universal and international." Yet the authors stress "it is with maximum sympathy that the Club views Brazil's cinematic movement and intends to be nothing if not a part of it."[41]

Despite their far-reaching ambitions, Latin America's interwar film societies were very modest in size compared with their European counterparts; the Chaplin Club had approximately fifty members in June 1930,

> Translated for "Experimental Cinema" by
> Abel Plenn
>
> # BULLETIN NO. 1
> ## OF THE MEXICAN CINE CLUB
>
> The Cine Club of Mexico has been organized and affiliated with the Film Society of London and with the League of Cine Clubs of Paris. Its program is the same as that of the cine clubs throughout the world, but it is especially akin to the Spanish Cine Club which has achieved great success in the two years of its existence.
>
> The essential points of its program are: (1) to procure the showing of good European, American and Asiatic vanguard films; (b) to establish the educational cinema, with special attention to the systematic showing of scientific films; (c) to study the History of the Cinema by means of film-exhibits dealing with the cinema in retrospect; (d) to hold lectures on the esthetic, scientific and social importance of cinematography; (e) to create a favorable atmosphere out of which a Mexican cinema art may emerge.
>
> The Mexican Cine Club will follow the plan of the successful foreign cine clubs in linking its activities with a conscientious study of our necessities. Its purpose is highly social and not lucrative.
>
> The Executive Committee of the Cine Club is comprised of the following:
> Art Director: Bernardo Ortiz de Montellano.
> Technical Director: Emilio Amero.
> Secretaries of Finance: Manuel Alvarez Bravo Maria Izquierdo.
> Sec'y of Propaganda: Carlos Merida.
> Directors: Maria M. de Alvarez Bravo and Roberto Montenegro.
> General Secretary: Agustin Aragon Leiva.
>
> The organizers of the Cine Club are among the most serious-minded writers, artists, journalists and critics in Mexico, who have been able to see that our environment is a sufficiently cultured and mature to make possible the existence of a Cine Club whose prime mission is to give the cinema the place which it deserves as a powerful vehicle of culture.
>
> In order to make known the circumstances which have determined the creation of the Cine Club and to point out the details of its program, these organizers will shortly circulate a manifesto calling for general active cooperation in the establishment and functioning of the Mexican Cine Club.
>
> *By-laws of the Mexican Cine Club*
> Article 1. The Cine Club's social residence will be in Mexico City.
> Article 2. The object of the Cine Club is:
> (a) to show films, provided the Film Society of London, the International League of Cine Clubs, the Film Amateurs' League and similar organizations, as well as films which in the opinion of the Cine Club directors merit consideration at the Club's sessions. To cooperate in the establishment of a Mexican cinematography.
> (b) to show factory-films of high artistic quality, either at the expense of the Cine Club itself or in combination with some promoting management.
>
> (c) to organize lectures and publish articles and critical reviews on cinematography.
> (d) to work for the establishment of the educational cinema by means of scientific films; to see that the social function which cinematography can fulfill be made effective in Mexico.
> Article 3. The Mexican Cine Club proposes to work together with the foreign cine clubs, but at the same time to investigate the problems of its own surroundings.
> Article 4. The Cine Club will be comprised of an unlimited number of members. These will be divided into active members and subscribing members. Active members and subscribers will pay the same amount of dues and will enjoy equal rights, but active members will be given various duties to fulfill.
> Article 5. Active members are obliged to cooperate by means of work and commissions toward the development of the Cine Club. Their number will be unlimited, but every candidate for membership must be proposed by two active members in good standing and be passed upon by the respective committee.
> Article 6. Any person, without distinction of nationality or social category, may become a subscribing member of the Cine Club.
> Article 7. Active and subscribing members of the Cine Club have the following social rights: (a) to attend all the cinematographic sessions of the Cine Club; (b) to enjoy any privilege which the Cine Club may obtain for its members.
> Article 8. The sessions of the Cine Club will be of two kinds: business and cinematographic. Only active members will be entitled to attend the former. The cinematographic sessions will be held at stated intervals, preferably every month as soon as this is possible. They will consist of the showing of films, of short lectures, reading of reports, suggestions, etc.
> Article 9. The cinematographic sessions will be public, and non-members will pay an admission charge. The difference between the total dues and that of the admission charges, together with the right to receive mal lat the club's post-office box, constitute the member's privilege.
> Article 10. Those joining the Cine Club will pay a membership fee of one peso, Mexican silver currency, and monthly dues of one peso fifty centavos, Mexican silver currency. Payments will be made in advance.
> Article 11. Each member of the Cine Club will receive two tickets for every cinematographic session and a 25 percent discount on tickets obtained from non-members.
> Article 12. The administration of the Cine Club will be carried on through a Directorial Council consisting of an Art Director, a Technical Director, a General Secretary, two Secretaries of Finance, a Secretary of Propaganda and two Directors. This Council will be elected by the active members for a period of two years.
> Article 13. When the Cine Club attains a membership of one thousand, it will form itself into a Cooperative Society, Ltd.
> Article 14. The financial reserves which the Cine Club may possibly own at some future date will be spent on artistic films to be produced by the Cine Club itself.
> Mexico City, June 4, 1931.
> General Sec'y, Agustin Aragon Leiva.
>
> 34

FIGURE 1. The language of the Cine Club de México's bylaws and their appearance in international journals like *Experimental Cinema* signal the film society's cosmopolitan aspirations. Source: *Experimental Cinema*, no. 4 (1932): 34.

and the Cineclub Venezolano forty in early 1933.[42] Yet they nonetheless could count an impressive number of literary and artistic luminaries within their ranks. Members of the Cine Club de Buenos Aires included Victoria Ocampo, a wealthy patron of the arts and founder of the influential literary magazine *Sur*; writer Jorge Luis Borges; and aspiring photographer and filmmaker Horacio Coppola.⁴³ The Cine Club de la Habana drew in intellectuals like Raúl Roa García, César García Pons, and Fernando Ortiz, while the Cineclub Mexicano's organizers and allies included modernist photographer Manuel Álvarez Bravo and writer and future diplomat Jaime Torres Bodet.⁴⁴ As these partial lists suggest, the interwar cineclubs, like their postwar counterparts, tended to be male-dominated. Ocampo and Lola Álvarez Bravo nonetheless played decisive roles in obtaining avant-garde films for club screenings.⁴⁵

The programming of Latin America's interwar film societies coalesced around two main tendencies. First, cineclubs offered a retrospective look at cinema's past, which took on new interest and cultural value in light of the transition to sound. Slapstick comedy, especially the films of Chaplin—who was valorized as a uniquely modernist and socially critical figure in Latin America—tended to stand in metonymically for silent cinema as a whole, as is suggested by the choice of the name "Chaplin Club" for a group that passionately lobbied against synchronized sound.⁴⁶ Second, film societies showcased filmmaking movements that bucked Hollywood norms, particularly French avant-garde cinema, German Expressionism, and Soviet montage.

As Sarah Ann Wells has shown, Soviet cinema in particular commanded attention from Latin American film enthusiasts because of its aesthetic radicalism, its rapid growth as an industry despite challenging conditions (rendering it a possible model for incipient Latin American cinemas), and the politically motivated censorship measures that often rendered the films difficult or impossible to see.⁴⁷ Cineclub organizers were divided in their response to Soviet cinema. Some, like Faria, insisted on bracketing its politics in favor of artistic questions. Others, such as Valdés-Rodríguez, were deeply invested in its revolutionary potential; his private cineclub screened Soviet and German films almost exclusively.⁴⁸ The Cineclub Mexicano also prioritized Soviet montage and works associated with the movement, however tangentially.⁴⁹ Reportedly, the club projected Eisenstein's *Oktiabr': Desiat' dnei kotorye potriasli mir* (*October: Ten Days That Shook the World*, 1928, USSR) for a thousand workers, signaling a politicized programming practice that continued under the auspices of LEAR.⁵⁰ Other clubs offered more balanced programming slates. For instance, the Cine Club de Buenos Aires presented a notable number of Soviet films alongside a cycle devoted to lesser-known slapstick comedians and a series of French avant-garde titles like Man Ray's *L'étoile de mer* (1928) and Luis Buñuel's *Un chien andalou* (1929).⁵¹ The Chaplin Club screened features starring its namesake, *The*

Pilgrim (1923, United States) and *The Gold Rush* (1925, United States), along with Abel Gance's *La roue* (*The Wheel*, 1923, France), Vsevolod Pudovkin's *Potomok Chingis-Khana* (*Storm over Asia*, 1928, USSR), and Mário Peixoto's legendary work of Brazilian modernism, *Limite* (1931).

The international film society movement experienced immense disruption with the outbreak of World War II in 1939. In occupied France, cineclub activity officially ceased, and non-commercial screenings could be held only in secret.[52] While it was largely spared military conflict, Latin America suffered significant economic turmoil during the war due to the loss of European and Asian markets for its agricultural products and raw materials. To my knowledge, film society activity continued only in Brazil, with the founding of the Clube de Cinema de São Paulo in 1940, and Argentina, where the Gente de Cine film society was established in 1942. Between 1940 and 1945, Klimovsky organized commercial screenings in the Cine Arte repertory theater (see cover image), comprising largely animation and silents, including works of early cinema billed as *cine de museo* (museum cinema).[53]

European and Latin American film societies experienced a resurgence in the postwar period, swelling far beyond their interwar proportions, and cineclubs began to emerge in locales like the Belgian Congo, India, Indonesia, South Africa, Tunisia, and New Zealand.[54] Building on renewed interest in popular education at a moment of national reconstruction, the number of film societies in France expanded rapidly from 12 in June 1945 to 83 in 1946 and 185 in 1948.[55] According to data gathered by the Centre national de la cinématographie, 10,735 cineclubs—organized in multiple federations associated with the popular education movement, the PCF, and the Catholic and Protestant churches—were active in the country in 1957, attracting a total audience of over five million.[56]

The Fédération française des ciné-clubs (FFCC) traces its origins to the erudite cineclubs of the interwar period. Yet much of the federation's leadership, including its secretary-general Georges Sadoul, came from the ranks of the leftist Resistance, and the PCF directly encouraged its members to join FFCC-affiliated film societies.[57] Both the FFCC and its Catholic rivals sought to educate filmgoers as a bulwark against cinema's seductions, though religious reformers were most concerned with sexual morality and communist film enthusiasts with the passivity encouraged by entertainment film.[58] Despite their influence, the scope of the FFCC and the religious film federations was limited in comparison to the Union française des offices du cinéma éducateur laïque (French Union

MAP 1. Locations of known cineclubs in Latin America through 1950. *Source*: Cartography by Jeff King/Mapping Specialists, based on data compiled by the author.

of Secular Educational Film Offices; UFOCEL). Roughly 70 percent of French film society members belonged to UFOCEL-affiliated clubs from the mid-1950s to the early 1960s. Affiliates of FFCC and the three religious film federations combined respectively accounted for 8 and 10 percent of total members in this period.[59]

While Latin American film society activity was far more limited in numerical terms, the movement gained considerable momentum at the end of the 1940s. Close to 30 cineclubs were founded in the region between

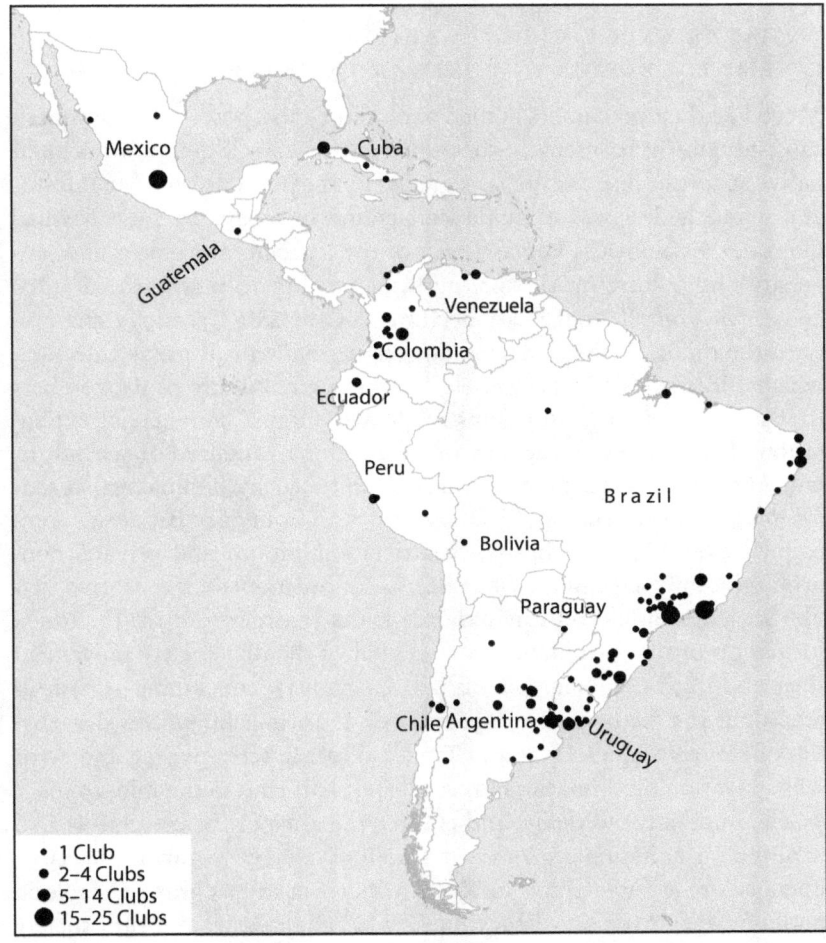

MAP 2. Locations of known cineclubs in Latin America through 1965. *Source*: Cartography by Jeff King/Mapping Specialists, based on data compiled by the author.

1948 and 1950. Over the next decade and a half, more than 230 new clubs emerged. As in France, the cineclub movement in the region was nurtured by a range of institutions, from private clubs that advanced intellectuals' quest for distinction through cultural consumption to the expanding university system, to Catholic lay organizations that sought to neutralize cinema's perceived threat to public morality. In the process, new spaces of film consumption and novel modes of viewing began to take shape in Latin America.

"WHAT IS A CINE-CLUB?": BUILDING CULTURA CINEMATOGRÁFICA IN POSTWAR LATIN AMERICA

Much like their precursors in the 1920s and 1930s, postwar Latin American cineclubs were intensely concerned with their self-definition as alternative spaces of film culture, as signaled by the publication of manifestos and manuals designed to guide leaders and members. In 1962 Manuel González Casanova, a key architect of the cineclub movement and university film culture in Mexico, published a slim volume entitled ¿Qué es un cine-club? (What is a cineclub?).[60] González Casanova championed the model of the "cineclub de vanguardia" (avant-garde cineclub), which "does not limit itself to elevating the film culture of its members [by] showing them quality films while avoiding all commercial exploitation . . . but takes on the task of organizing a vanguard of spectators, with the aim of sustaining the struggle initiated by filmmakers so that cinema may be a true art."[61] Drawing a firm boundary between "commercial exploitation" (that is, theatrical exhibition) and private, non-profit cineclub screenings, González Casanova nonetheless affirms that film societies should reform audience tastes in order to drive the transformation of film production, a core goal of the film society movement since its origins. Tellingly, González Casanova's concluding statement regarding the "vanguard of spectators" is an unacknowledged verbatim quote from Louis Daquin, a French director, screenwriter, and actor whose writing the Mexican film enthusiast had read in the mid-1950s.[62]

The imperative to define and enforce the aims of the cineclub is also manifest in communiqués directed at film society members. In 1959 Buenos Aires's Cine Club Núcleo distributed a mimeographed bulletin outlining the "Mission of the Cine Club," adapted from a film society operating in Zaragoza, Spain: "One goes to the cineclub to study, to learn, to strip the cinema of the usual frivolity of its plots, its industrialization, to convert it into a pure art that deserves and demands as much study as any other."[63] In this definition of the cineclub, the act of informed viewing promised to transmute the film itself, elevating it from a base entertainment commodity to a privileged aesthetic object.

In the same bulletin, Cine Club Núcleo offered guidelines for proper member behavior, again borrowing from one of its counterparts—this time, Cine Universitario in Montevideo, Uruguay, which had previously reprinted the Zaragoza club's manifesto.[64] The *buen cineclubista* (good film society member) described in the document "should be, according to internationally known experience, an ideal being" who "cultivates human relations outside the auditorium" rather than during the screening, and refrains from kicking, whistling, and shouting when problems arise with the projection (a not-uncommon occurrence, it seems, given the precarious condition of many prints screened in film societies).[65] The values outlined in this leaflet signal how cineclubs aimed to transform spectators' relationship to the moving image, but always within strict parameters. Protocols developed in the French film society movement and elsewhere to encourage audience participation, such as post-screening discussions and questionnaires, promised to remake a spectator imagined as passive and unquestioning into an active and critical viewer. Yet cineclub organizers explicitly discouraged more boisterous forms of spectator engagement in the name of decorum. This tension suggests class hierarchies embedded in the simultaneously elitist and democratizing project of the cineclub, which sought to disseminate erudite forms of film appreciation to the masses, even as their leadership and membership remained largely middle- and upper-class.

In an effort to reeducate their members and the broader public, cineclubs not only held screenings but also published magazines, amassed collections of books and periodicals for member use, organized classes in film appreciation and production, sponsored amateur film competitions, and surveyed members to select the best film screened locally in a given year.[66] Film societies championed dissemination (expanding the circulation of films whose exhibition was limited by censorship or lack of commercial appeal), propagation (encouraging the creation of cineclubs where none existed), and affiliation (forging cooperative links with other institutions of film culture, mediated by national and international federations). As suggested by the foreign provenance of the texts reprinted by Cine Club Núcleo, the resulting networks were highly international in character, involving the cross-border circulation not only of film prints but also institutional models and ideals.

The exchanges brokered by cineclub networks were deeply entangled with the broader "global designs" at work in the postwar period. I use this term in Walter Mignolo's sense to refer to a "cosmopolitanism [conceived as] a set of projects toward planetary conviviality" that is nonetheless inseparable from colonial logics.[67] Alluding to the devastating events of World War II and the ongoing Cold War conflict, González Casanova declared in ¿Qué es un cine-club?, "It is also the mission of avant-garde cineclubs to highlight the importance of cinema in acquainting [the world's] peoples with each other and for making their relations firmer and more cordial, while fighting against the spurious use of the cinematic art for ends that are contrary to the progress and well-being of mankind."⁶⁸ Such internationalist sentiments—which highlighted the dangers of film propaganda while hailing the medium's potential to promote international understanding—were central to cineclubs' efforts to retrain audiences. Intellectuals and religious reformers alike sought to inoculate viewers from the influence of ideological extremes or morally questionable film content by cultivating their critical sensibilities. In 1955, Chilean Catholic film educator Rafael Sánchez affirmed that cineclubs should provide an intellectual framework for film viewing that would "create a critical and reflexive position. Orient [the viewer] in relation to the values of the film. Immunize [them] against moral dangers."⁶⁹ Such objectives overlapped with secular film societies' efforts to instill exacting aesthetic standards in their members as a safeguard against the potentially debasing effects of mass-cultural products. According to González Casanova, cineclubs sought to "teach the spectator to appreciate [cinema's] artistic and human values and reject all distortions of reality. That is to say, train the spectator so that he ceases to be a simple receiver of cinematic images and becomes an active element, capable of judging and understanding everything that passes by onscreen."⁷⁰

As the convergence between Catholic and secular cineclub ideals suggests, a broad range of institutions nurtured non-commercial film programming in postwar Latin America, including private clubs, universities, and museums, as well as national and supranational initiatives that were governmental, diplomatic, and religious in character. Cineclub organizers invoked the malleable notion of *cultura cinematográfica* for a variety of institutional ends. Cultura cinematográfica was discussed as a property of social milieux, referring to the general level of film taste and the state of film-related institutions in a particular locale. It was also understood as a property of individuals, entailing connoisseurship, awareness of the medium's unique aesthetic resources, possession of a keen critical sense that could temper its powerful psychological and ideological effects, morally upright viewing habits, or a combination thereof. Championing the development of cultura cinematográfica could yield cultural capital for growing urban middle classes, moral influence for the Catholic Church, and soft power for foreign nations like France.⁷¹

In mid-century Latin America, the most familiar institutional model for the film society—that of a private club whose screenings were open only to dues-paying members, thus guaranteeing their non-commercial character—emerged through the initiative of intellectuals, most often film critics. Founded in 1942 with the backing of Cine Club de Buenos

Aires veteran León Klimovsky, the Buenos Aires club Gente de Cine (Film People) grew out of a radio program co-hosted by journalist Andrés José Rolando Fustiñana, known by the pen name Roland.[72] One of Gente de Cine's members, critic Salvador Sammaritano, founded the Cine Club Núcleo—which is still active as of this writing—in 1952, with the society holding its first screenings in 1954.[73] In 1950 the French Bulgarian journalist and future Unifrance delegate Amy Bakaloff Courvoisier founded the Cine-Club Venezuela, based in Caracas, in partnership with French cultural attaché Gaston Diehl.[74] Other cineclubs again coalesced around influential cultural magazines and their associated circles of intellectuals. In 1948 students Germán Puig and Ricardo Vigón organized the Cine Club de la Habana. The club later operated, albeit temporarily, in partnership with the Sociedad Cultural Nuestro Tiempo (Our Times Cultural Society), a coterie of left-leaning intellectuals who published a magazine of the same name.[75] In 1949 a group of film enthusiasts including bookseller Luis Vicens, artist Enrique Grau Araújo, and journalist Jorge Valdivieso Guerrero created the CCC in Bogotá. Its membership overlapped closely with the group of intellectuals linked to the cosmopolitan literary magazine *Mito* (1955–1962).[76]

While many private cineclubs were dedicated to film appreciation first and foremost, others emerged due to organizers' interest in amateur filmmaking.[77] Some clubs encouraged amateur production on occasion—for instance, the CCC sponsored a contest for "cine-aficionados" in 1952—while others made it their principal focus, such as the Cine Club Argentino.[78] Founded in 1932 and active through the early 1950s, the Cine Club Argentino hosted nearly 230 screenings of work by members and other amateur filmmakers.[79] In the postwar period, several Latin American photography clubs branched out into cinema. For example, São Paulo's preeminent amateur photo club created a film section in 1945, renaming itself the Foto Cine Clube Bandeirante (FCCB).[80] Operating in close contact with the Amateur Cinema League, FCCB also exchanged amateur films with its counterparts in Argentina and Uruguay.[81] Photo clubs were also active in the Argentine municipalities of Rosario, Santa Fe, La Plata, Mendoza, and Tucumán during the late 1940s. A film society existed in each of these locations by the mid-1950s, though these organizations were not necessarily connected.[82] Amateur filmmakers founded Peru's Cine Club Cusco in 1955—which became a nucleus for documentary film production and fostered the making of the first Quechua-language feature film, *Kukuli* (Luis Figueroa, Eulogio Nishiyama, and César Villanueva, 1961)—and Chile's Cine Club Viña del Mar in 1962. In addition to offering screenings and courses in film technique, Cine Club Viña del Mar organized international festivals of amateur cinema that gave rise to the famous 1967 Festival del Cine Nuevo Latinoamericano, which is credited with galvanizing a regional movement.[83] In Montevideo, a group of film enthusiasts created the Cine Club del Uruguay in 1948 as a means of financing their filmmaking endeavors.[84] Also sparked by an interest in amateur production, its rival Cine Universitario emerged from the activities of the Teatro Universitario (the university theater company) at the country's leading institution of higher education, the Universidad de la República.[85] The two clubs sponsored several amateur cinema competitions between 1949 and 1958.[86]

As the case of Cine Universitario suggests, academic settings were fertile ground for the creation of cineclubs at a time when higher education, which had traditionally been the privilege of a tiny elite, was expanding rapidly. Campus cineclubs catered to an upwardly mobile, intellectually curious student body and took advantage of existing gathering spaces. In 1940 students at São Paulo's Faculdade de Filosofia (School of Philosophy) founded the Clube de Cinema de São Paulo. The initiative was spearheaded by Décio de Almeida Prado and Paulo Emílio Salles Gomes, who had encountered cineclubs while living in Paris in voluntary political exile between 1937 and 1940. Perhaps due to Salles Gomes's participation, the club was quickly shut down by the regime of dictator Getúlio Vargas under suspicion of leftist agitation. Revived in 1946, the Clube de Cinema later reorganized as a film archive under the umbrella of MAM-SP, as I explore in more depth in chapter 2.[87] In 1953 students at the Universidad de Chile founded the Cine Club Universitario, which encouraged the creation of several campus film societies by the early 1960s.[88] In the late 1950s and early 1960s university cineclubs proliferated in Colombia—including in Bogotá, Medellín, Manziales, and Bucaramanga—and Venezuela, where student cineclubs operated at Caracas's Universidad Central and in the cities of Mérida and Valencia.[89]

As I detail in chapter 4, the construction of a modern campus for UNAM in Mexico City ushered in an ambitious program of cultural activity, including several campus cineclubs and a screening series open to the public.[90] University leadership hailed the development of film culture as pivotal to the university's pedagogical mission. For instance, in 1955 the *Gaceta de la Universidad* (university bulletin) applauded the efforts of the Cine Club de la Universidad and the independent Cine Club Progreso, which had a significant student contingent, to actively engage audiences and shape film tastes, "promoting in the public curiosity and discussions that will help orient them and lay the foundations for their preferences within this artistic genre."[91] As the book's final chapter explores, cineclubs helped foster new forms of film pedagogy at the university level and participated in a growing politicization of culture by the late 1960s.

If private and university film societies treated cinema as an object of formal or informal study or experimentation, supranational organizations and national governments mobilized film societies for their own pedagogical and political ends. State-sponsored film societies or screening series were rare but impactful in postwar Latin America. In Uruguay, SODRE first offered a cycle of "art cinema" to the public in 1944 as part of a broader project of cultural uplift, exemplified by its broadcasting of classical music.[92] SODRE's Cine Arte series attracted a broad audience totaling, by its own account, 2,638,693 viewers between 1950 and 1961 in a country whose population was 2.5 million in the early 1960s. SODRE also hosted screenings for elementary, high school, and university students, accounting for 905,008 spectators during this period.[93]

Whereas SODRE supported private cineclubs by furnishing them with film programs from its archive (see chapter 2), the Instituto Cubano de Arte e Industria Cinematográficos (ICAIC), created shortly after the triumph of the Revolution in 1959, instead seized control of both commercial and non-commercial distribution and exhibition infrastructure to further the aims of the Cuban state. As Irene Rozsa has shown, ICAIC and the Consejo Nacional de Cultura (National Cultural Council) effectively suppressed independent film society activity, instead holding public screenings referred to as *cine-debates populares* to help align spectators' ideological orientation with the Revolution's. Even as existing Catholic and secular cineclubs were marginalized, access to film programming beyond standard commercial fare—namely Hollywood genre films and Mexican cinema—was expanded to broader sectors of the population, while the post-screening discussion was transformed into a vehicle of political education.[94]

If Cuban and Uruguayan states leveraged film societies for cultural uplift and political reeducation, respectively, transnational initiatives that spanned religious activism and cultural diplomacy also proved pivotal in the formation of postwar cineclubs. The most far-reaching of these was the extensive network of Catholic film societies coordinated by the OCIC, which sought to inoculate viewers against the medium's powerful social and emotional effects by strengthening their critical capacities. Nora Watson, a leader of Argentina's Catholic film society movement, affirmed in 1956 that film education would prepare the viewer "not only to take maximum advantage of all of a film's values in terms of form and content, but at the same time will induce him to reason and use his intelligence during the film, so that it will not represent for him—as it does for the vast majority of the public—a mental opiate that makes thought impossible and weakens his intellectual and moral faculties."[95] While they were most immediately concerned with spiritual matters, Catholic film activists also expressed strong anticommunist positions, most prominently Andrzej Ruszkowski, a Polish lawyer who resided for several years in France and later became the OCIC's chief emissary in Latin America.[96] In a 1960 interview, Ruszkowski spoke of morality and politics as intimately intertwined. Admitting that Soviet cinema rarely involved displays of "immorality," he criticized the permissiveness of capitalist film industries, declaring, "Motion picture makers should feel an extra responsibility at this time when the West is struggling with the bitter ideological propaganda of communism. They must understand that if they present a decadent picture of the West, they'll open the doors to communist propaganda. Many people begin to believe that if moral regeneration is not possible they must turn East."[97]

Catholic film activists channeled their efforts to tame cinema's ethical and ideological menace through lay organizations known as Catholic action groups, whose film-related activities were coordinated by the OCIC. The OCIC had taken shape in 1928 at a conference convened at the Hague by the International Union of Women's Catholic Leagues.[98] During the 1930s, Catholic activism surrounding cinema focused on influencing film content and discouraging consumption of questionable films. Famously, in 1934 the Catholic Legion of Decency helped usher in stronger enforcement mechanisms for the 1930 Production Code, an effort explicitly praised by Pope Pius XI in in his 1936 encyclical *Vigilanti Cura*. Catholic action groups also rated films' suitability in an effort to shape the viewing choices of the faithful, a practice adopted in Argentina, Brazil, Cuba, and Colombia by the 1930s.[99] Catholic exhibition circuits also took shape in this period; Argentine parishes hosted Sunday screenings, while Catholic action groups in Colombia controlled 130 theaters by 1938.[100]

The wartime and postwar activities of the OCIC signal the pivotal importance of Latin America as a refuge for transnational cultural organizations based in Europe. After the Nazis shuttered OCIC's offices in Brussels and pursued its personnel, the organization's leaders turned to the Americas in hopes of guaranteeing its long-term survival.[101] In 1941

OCIC board member Father Félix Morlion embarked on a tour of film-related Catholic organizations that included stops in the United States, Brazil, Argentina, Chile, Ecuador, Peru, Mexico, and Canada.[102] After the war, OCIC sought not only to strengthen its international presence but also to reorient Catholic film activism away from a repressive policy that sought to eliminate problematic film content and restrict Catholics from viewing questionable films toward a model that stressed the capacity of film education to neutralize cinema's seductive effects.[103] At a 1947 OCIC conference, J. Van Liempt, the director of the Documentation cinématographique de la presse (an office that served as a liaison between the OCIC and Belgian newspapers) observed, "The majority of people who consume film entertainment go *only for distraction* and show little or no interest in the moral, human and artistic value of films" (emphasis in original). Cineclubs, he argued, had the potential to create "select groups within the mass of film spectators," leading them to "choose their entertainments and prefer good films to bad or merely superficial ones," to "effectively stimulate the production of good films," and to disseminate these ideals and practices within their social circles—all goals shared with the secular cineclub movement.[104]

During the 1947 conference, Ruszkowski assumed the position of general secretary of foreign affairs; the following year, he made his own tour of the Americas, visiting the United States, Cuba, Venezuela, Colombia, Ecuador, Peru, Bolivia, Chile, Argentina, Uruguay, and Brazil.[105] OCIC's presence in Latin America was strengthened when Cuban Catholic activist América Penichet became vice president of OCIC in 1954; after the Revolution, she settled in Lima and established the OCIC's Latin American office.[106] By 1962 OCIC's branches in Latin America and the Caribbean—typically known as Centros de Orientación/Orientação Cinematográfica Católica—were nearly as numerous as its European ones and frequently offered film appreciation courses.[107] Catholic film society activity proved especially robust in Brazil, where religiously affiliated film societies numbered close to a hundred, and in Cuba, where forty such clubs operated in 1959.[108]

Rather than seeking to enforce religious orthodoxy by suppressing problematic works, postwar Catholic cineclubs openly confronted films' challenges to conventional morality and religious doctrine.[109] Buenos Aires's Cine Club Enfoques, founded in 1956 by the Acción Católica Argentina, screened *Fröken Julie* (*Miss Julie*, Alf Sjöberg, Sweden, 1951), which was classified as "prohibited" in the ratings generated by the Acción Católica itself. Based on a play by August Strindberg, this sexually frank tale of cross-class romance and suicide had won the Grand Prix at the 1951 Cannes film festival. The Cine Club de Lima, founded by Ruszkowski in 1953 after he settled in Peru, also screened *Fröken Julie* along with *Los olvidados* (Luis Buñuel, 1950, Mexico), a searing portrait of Mexico City's underclass that had been banned by Peru's censor board, and *Jeux interdits* (*Forbidden Games*, René Clément, 1952, France), which contained potentially blasphemous elements.[110] (In the film, two children living in the French countryside try to make sense of their wartime experiences with death by stealing crosses from a nearby cemetery and creating their own burial ground for animals.) Like its secular counterparts, the Cine Club de Lima reinforced an upwardly mobile middle-class identity while bolstering France's soft power through its programming. Jean Binoche, the French ambassador to Peru, commented approvingly in 1954, "The elite appreciates [French cinema] as much as the masses; during the eight months of operation of the recently founded Cine Club de Lima, to date French films have been programmed most frequently."[111]

However ironic, Catholic cineclubs' screenings of controversial films demonstrates the faith placed in the power of cinematic education to effectively neutralize morally harmful effects on the viewer.[112] A revealing 1957 editorial in the *Revista de Cultura Cinematográfica* (1957–1963), a publication of the União de Propagandistas Católicos (Union of Catholic Publicists) based in Belo Horizonte, Brazil declared it would "treat the defense of MORALITY IN CINEMA as a closed matter. Everything but this [topic] can be found in our pages. For when the [cinematic] work is directed towards the elevated purpose of ennobling art, harmful and pornographic tendencies will disappear. Here, in these pages freedom of expression only reaches its limits when it confronts the obstacle of immorality" (emphasis in original).[113] Such statements suggest a convergence between religious orthodoxy and the valorization of cinema as art, rooted in a liberal postwar humanism that championed individual self-expression. This ethos extended to the prizes awarded by OCIC at international festivals, including controversial films on religious themes like Pier Paolo Pasolini's *Il vangelo secondo Matteo (The Gospel According to St. Matthew*, 1964, Italy).[114]

Whereas OCIC initiatives crossed national borders to advance spiritual aims, national governments mobilized cinema for more worldly reasons: namely, to advance their geopolitical agendas by building their soft power. As noted in the introduction, embassies and consulates—particularly those of France, the United States, Canada, Sweden, and the Netherlands—often furnished promotional documentaries and shorts to Latin American film societies.[115] Signaling these sources' importance for film society programming, the Federación Argentina de Cineclubes offered to send its affiliates catalogs of prints available from each embassy.[116] Film societies organized special events in partnership with national cultural institutes like the AF (which also ran its own cineclubs) and Germany's Goethe-Institut, as well as government agencies dedicated to promoting national film industries abroad, including Unifrance and Unitalia. Suggesting the significance of the diplomatic film service in general and French sources in particular, the Cine Club Mendoza in western Argentina reported that its films were sourced from the "Cinemateca Argentina [the archive that emerged from Gente de Cine, discussed in chapter 2], the Alliance française, the French embassy, and from the commercial field." French cultural diplomacy also aided Latin American cineclubs in solving infrastructure problems; the Cine Club Mendoza held some sessions in the AF's headquarters, while COFRAM's director Jean Séfert helped Gente de Cine secure the use of the Cine Biarritz for late-night screenings.[117] The French diplomatic apparatus also served as a point of entry into transatlantic cultural networks. For instance, during the CCC's first months of existence, its leaders contacted the French embassy and AF seeking film prints and contacts.[118] As suggested by the case of the film society founded in Mexico City's IFAL, French cultural diplomacy was pivotal in fostering the transnational connections that nurtured Latin America's film society and film preservation movements.

Circulating French Cinema in Latin America: The Cine Club de México

Established under the auspices of IFAL in 1950, the Cine Club de México exemplifies the intersection between French cultural diplomacy and the postwar Latin American film society movement and became a de facto node for the non-commercial distribution of French cinema in the region. IFAL was founded in 1943 on the initiative of French anthropologist and Resistance fighter Paul Rivet in an effort to burnish French prestige, which had been tarnished by military defeat and the installation of the Vichy regime. Rivet enlisted the aid of Mexican writer and diplomat Alfonso Reyes, who had spearheaded (unsuccessful) efforts to transfer the Paris-based IICI, the cultural wing of the League of Nations, to Latin America after the IICI was shuttered in 1941 following France's military defeat.[119] Established, by its own account, "in

FIGURE 2. Exterior of the Institut français d'Amérique latine, late 1940s or early 1950s. *Source:* Fonds Paul Rivet, Muséum national d'Histoire naturelle (France).

the certitude of France's coming deliverance which would permit it to again illuminate the world with the flame of its genius," IFAL operated under the auspices of the DGRC, a branch of the MAE of Charles de Gaulle's Free France government-in-exile.[120] Like the worldwide network of the AF, IFAL became a "global cultural front" in the struggle between Vichy and Free France, boosting the latter's cultural influence to build international solidarity and support for its military campaigns.[121] Mexico had broken off diplomatic relations with Vichy in November 1942 while maintaining ties with de Gaulle and welcomed a small but influential group of French exiles during the war.[122] Initially focused on the social and hard sciences, IFAL later sought to propagate a French intellectual tradition in Mexico through language instruction and lecture series.

On the initiative of French envoy Jean-François Revel, IFAL added non-commercial film screenings to its cultural programming. In a letter to Henri Langlois of the Cinémathèque française requesting the loan of archival prints, Revel described his venture as "a cineclub designed to familiarize a cultured Mexican public, along with the numerous non-Mexican residents of Mexico's capital, with the great masterworks of French cinema. We are convinced that the success of this endeavor will not only be very important from a cultural point of view, but will also aid French cinema in general, making our production better known in Latin American countries."[123] Revel's comments signal how aspirations regarding intellectual exchange, international influence, and the commercial potential of French film became intertwined in the cineclub's cultural project. Notably, the revenue generated by the club's membership fees came to sustain IFAL financially; rentals of its auditorium for screenings accounted for three-quarters of the institute's budget by mid-1951.[124]

In its first year, the Cine Club de México attracted an estimated one thousand viewers, 80 to 90 percent of them Mexican. The composition of its audience left it well positioned to influence the local milieu.[125] The French ambassador in Mexico noted approvingly, "As the majority of our lectures attract to the Institute only a public of amateurs, often elderly and without occupation, French almost in their entirety, it is encouraging to see that, through the channel of the Cine-Club, the Institute is regularly frequented by six to seven hundred intellectual Mexican students, artists, painters, critics, who are generally young and enjoy, on the whole, considerable influence on public opinion."[126] The club's members included industry luminaries like actor Dolores del Río, director Emilio Fernández, and cinematographer Gabriel Figueroa.[127] Its organizers cultivated such links in hopes that contact with European film would mitigate the "inexperience and even ignorance" of local creatives, raising the artistic and technical quality of Mexico's commercially successful cinema and leading to "interesting artistic and commercial collaborations."[128] The Cine Club de México's screenings also proved formative for future architects of Mexican institutions of film culture like González Casanova. The club's audience and organizers included several future members of the Grupo Nuevo Cine, who lobbied for the aesthetic and economic revitalization of Mexico's film industry in the 1960s (see chapter 4). Film historian Emilio García Riera and cultural critic Carlos Monsiváis attended its screenings, poet and future filmmaker José Miguel "Jomí" García Ascot introduced films and offered simultaneous translation for those that lacked Spanish subtitles, and writers Salvador Elizondo and José de la Colina offered courses in film theory and history at IFAL in the early 1960s.[129]

By 1951, the Cine Club de México also became the origin point for the non-commercial circulation of French films sourced from the

Cinémathèque française in Latin America, conceived as a means of amortizing the high cost of transporting prints to the region.[130] This practice was contrary to FIAF regulations, which specified that archives were permitted only to exchange films with fellow FIAF members. While Langlois encouraged his Latin American contacts to create their own cinémathèques, these institutions did not yet exist. From his earliest letters to Revel, Langlois recommended that he create a Mexican film archive—which would have helped mitigate the high cost of sending prints across the Atlantic—but this never came to fruition.[131] Nevertheless, Langlois directed the IFAL staff to dispatch programs to Caracas for screening at the Cine-Club Venezuela run by Amy Courvoisier and Gaston Diehl.[132] This Latin American distribution circuit also took shape via an agreement between Langlois and Luis Vicens of the CCC, reached during Vicens's trip to Paris in the winter of 1950–1951. After meeting with Langlois, Vicens contacted Diehl to arrange the transfer of 16mm prints of early French films—made at the expense of the France's MAE—via the embassies in Caracas and Bogotá.[133] However, the use of diplomatic channels failed to prevent confusion and delays. Dispatched in May 1952, the films appear not to have been exhibited in Bogotá until mid-1953, when the CCC screened three programs featuring works by the Lumière Brothers, Georges Méliès, Émile Cohl, Louis Feuillade, and Jean Epstein, which were likely drawn from the lot of prints in question.[134] In the meantime, Langlois berated Revel for not returning his films, although he was the one who had asked for them to be sent on to Venezuela.[135] On other occasions, programs sent to Havana with instructions to forward them to Mexico City never arrived.[136]

As these anecdotes suggest, the diplomatic distribution circuit linking Paris with Mexico City, Havana, Caracas, and Bogotá—which Langlois had hoped to extend to the Southern Cone as well—proved fragile and prone to disruption.[137] Programs of films from the Cinémathèque française continually arrived in Mexico City late or incomplete, to the point that IFAL sent an extensive list of "disappointments caused by the cinémathèque" to the MAE.[138] Revel was forced to rely on New York's MoMA for three-quarters of the films screened by the club.[139] The circuit's precarious functioning nonetheless signals how diplomatic endeavors forged both transatlantic and intraregional connections in the film society movement. The circulation of French film "classics" brokered by Revel and Langlois formed part of an overall strategy of cultural diplomacy that advanced France's wartime and postwar ambitions. Yet it also resulted in contact and cooperation between film enthusiasts across the region. These connections proved formative as Latin American film enthusiasts built networks of film culture in hopes of distinguishing their programming from commercial fare, while also grappling with the preferences of cineclubs' rank and file.

COOPERATION: FILM SOCIETY PROGRAMMING AND TRANSATLANTIC INSTITUTIONAL NETWORKS

In the programming of Latin America's postwar film societies, the notions of art cinema cherished by organizers ran up against constraints on access to prints and the demonstrated preferences of the membership. The tensions are illuminated by quantitative data on cineclub screenings, by the explanations leaders offered for their curatorial choices, and by reflections on whether the slate of films offered (and members' attendance patterns) lived up to dominant cineclub ideals forged abroad. Reconstructing the full breadth of Latin American film society programming of this period is impossible given gaps in the archival record. Yet surviving programs and bulletins reveal how both commercial and aesthetic hegemonies—in particular, the economic dominance of Hollywood and the widespread critical acclaim accorded French cinema—shaped cineclubs' offerings. Not surprisingly, film society leaders were guided by emerging canons of film taste derived largely from European criticism, as references in program notes and cineclub magazines attest.[140] This orientation led them to try, often without success, to avoid mainstream distribution outlets (local branches of the Hollywood majors in particular) while embracing alternative ones (such as diplomatic and archival channels), strengthening transatlantic institutional links in the process.

In a data set I compiled from programs available in public archives, comprising over twenty-five hundred unique screenings at cineclubs in four Latin American capital cities (Buenos Aires, Bogotá, Mexico City, and Montevideo) between 1942 and 1965, the preponderance of French and US films quickly becomes clear.[141] Across all available programming, French titles account for 30 percent of the total and US films 25 percent. A similar proportion, plus or minus 2 percent, is found in Gente de Cine's programs, which are complete from 1942 through 1955 with the exception of nine months in 1954. In the case of the CCC, for which the full slate of programming is available for the years 1949–1965, the ranking is reversed; 35 percent of all titles screened were Hollywood films, and 23 percent were French releases. These figures reflect the club's heavy reliance on gratis loans from the Hollywood majors. Nevertheless, the state-backed French distributor COFRAM may have been the CCC's single leading supplier of films. Its local branch Francia Films furnished at least fifty-three prints to the CCC between its founding in 1949 and the mid-1960s, corresponding to 10 percent of all titles screened during this period in cases where print provenance is known.[142] The abundance of French films, despite Hollywood's dominance of commercial screens, suggests the success of French promotional efforts through Unifrance and COFRAM and the impact of France-based organizations like FIAF and FICC in securing a privileged place for French cinema in film society canons.

In comparison, major producers like the United Kingdom, Germany, and Italy—despite the significance of neorealism for NLAC in the 1960s—account for only between 6 and 7 percent of known screenings, though some titles from these countries became film society staples. *Umberto D.* (Vittorio De Sica, 1952, Italy), for example, was shown four times by the CCC in the period under study, and neorealism received ample attention in film society magazines like *Gente de Cine*, *Film*, and *Cine Club*.[143] Suggesting the postwar cineclub movement's almost total lack of a pan-Latin American consciousness, just over 5 percent of unique screenings in the data set were Argentine films and under 2 percent Mexican ones, in spite (or because) of Mexican cinema's important presence in commercial exhibition circuits in Latin America, where it often accounted for up to 40 percent of local releases.[144] Mexican melodramas by Emilio Fernández and Roberto Gavaldón that were viewed (including by French critics who saw them at Cannes) as transcending popular cinema and entering the realm of art were most frequently screened.[145] Titles from other Latin American countries, such as the Cannes prize winner *O cangaceiro* (The bandit, Lima Barreto, 1953, Brazil), appear only sporadically.

Whether chosen for aesthetic, political, or practical reasons, cinema from socialist nations had a small but persistent—and sometimes controversial—presence in available cineclub programming. Films from the Soviet Union and Czechoslovakia each account for approximately 2 percent of known cineclub programming. Along with Soviet silents, works of animation by directors like Jiří Trnka, Hermína Týrlová, and Karel Zeman (some provided by the Czechoslovak embassy) and tendentious dramas like those of Karel Steklý were most frequently programmed. (The 1933 erotic drama *Extase* [Ecstasy, Gustav Machatý], infamous for featuring a nude Hedy Lamarr, was another perennial cineclub favorite from Czechoslovakia, but naturally it predated the country's socialist government).[146] Mexico City's Cine Club Progreso, founded by a group of Venezuelan political exiles affiliated with the Communist Party, screened an unusually high number of Soviet and Eastern bloc films, almost a quarter of the total in the second half of 1954.[147] Despite the apparent ideological neutrality of most other cineclubs, showing works from socialist countries raised scrutiny from local authorities. In the 1950s and 1960s, the political police of the province of Buenos Aires investigated film societies for showing Soviet, Czech, and Hungarian films.[148] By the mid-1960s, some Latin American clubs had begun to organize screenings for the residents of impoverished informal communities that included Soviet cinema, including the CCC and a film society operated by the Universidad de Buenos Aires's extension school, but I have found no trace of such activities in earlier periods.[149]

Overall, movements hailed as milestones in film history through the present—slapstick comedy, German Expressionism, Soviet montage, Italian neorealism, and the French New Wave—figure prominently in Latin American cineclub programming through the mid-1960s. The solidification of canons of (silent) film history is suggested by the titles most often repeated in available programs. In descending order, these were *Un chapeau de paille d'Italie* (*The Italian Straw Hat*, René Clair, 1928, France), *Das Cabinet des Dr. Caligari* (*The Cabinet of Dr. Caligari*, Robert Wiene, 1920, Germany), *Bronenosets Potiomkin* (*Battleship Potemkin*, Sergei Eisenstein, 1925, USSR), and *Mat'* (*Mother*, Vsevolod Pudovkin, 1926, USSR). Cineclubs' efforts to build film collections led to a self-reinforcing process of canon formation: clubs sought out consecrated "classics," repeated them in their programs, and loaned them to their counterparts. For instance, Gente de Cine owned a copy of *Un chapeau de paille d'Italie*, which the club showed on a near-annual basis for almost a decade.[150] After it became the property of the associated Cinemateca Argentina, the print screened at clubs in Ciudad Eva Perón (present-day La Plata) and Santa Fe.[151] Institutional links with archives abroad also shaped cineclub programs. In 1958 the CCC screened a copy of *Potemkin* from the BFI to commemorate the club's ninth anniversary.[152] When Czechoslovakia's Národní filmový archiv (National Film Archive) sent the Cinemateca Colombiana (the club's associated archive) a 35mm print of the film two years later, a CCC program hailed it as an "immortal film" that "should be re-shown at least once a year."[153] In the 1960s the USSR's state film archive Gosfilmofond furnished the Cinemateca Colombiana with prints of Eisenstein's *Stachka* (*Strike*, 1925) and Pudovkin's *Storm over Asia* and *Mother*.[154] As the initial screening of *Potemkin* shows, the CCC's organizers already considered Soviet montage historically significant, but gifts from Eastern bloc archives helped to ensure its long-term presence in the club's programming.

Although the canon of film history promoted by postwar Latin American film societies shows clear similarities to that of today, genres that historically have been overlooked abounded in their programs: animation; *films sur l'art* (films on art and artists); and educational, promotional, and travel films (often provided by local embassies). After René Clair, the director whose work most often appears in available programs is Scottish Canadian animator Norman McLaren (though as his films were shorts, the total screentime dedicated to his films was considerably less). The presence of McLaren's films—many of which were sponsored by the National Film Board of Canada and UNESCO—suggests cineclub programming was also deeply shaped by the geopolitical and ideological agendas advanced by "useful cinema."[155]

The heterogeneity of film society fare reflects a wide range of print sources, including commercial 35mm and 16mm distributors, private collections, archives, and foreign cultural institutes and embassies. Tapping into these alternative circuits often entailed considerable logistical difficulties. Prints might arrive late or not at all from overseas. Some films lacked subtitles or were so damaged they caused projectors to break down, halting screenings. Film society leaders tried to smooth over these less-than-ideal viewing conditions by emphasizing the rarity and significance of films sourced through unconventional channels. Cine Club Núcleo stressed in a 1957 program, "We should . . . remind members that many of the films screened in the club are unique copies, taken out of commercial circulation or non-commercial [in nature], that can only be seen in entities like ours, compensating for the fact that the projection is sometimes less perfect than desirable." The program went on to note, "The leadership of this cine club considers that, in the case of important films where there is a copy in the country but no Spanish-language version, it is preferable to see them in this manner than not at all, given that documentary, experimental and art films rarely screen in commercial movie theaters."[156]

In some cases, members' resistance to film society programming—whether due to language barriers, technical problems, or matters of taste—led cineclubs to adjust their offerings. The leadership of the Cine Club Mendoza reflected, "In the year 1952, the projection of avant-garde films dominated in our sessions; notably, given that the level of film culture of the members is mediocre for obvious reasons, these could not be widely evaluated and appreciated, and for this reason it was decided that this year's programming would be more accessible, with the goal of preparing the membership to enjoy [avant-garde] films." In consequence, the club managed to boost average attendance from 60 percent of the membership to 75–87 percent.[157] Other clubs apparently achieved a more harmonious fit between their organizers' ideals and the preferences of the rank and file. A 1955 survey of Gente de Cine's membership suggests members were largely sympathetic to the leadership's programming practices; for instance, 90 percent appreciated screenings of "archival films."[158] (Of course, the respondents were no doubt a self-selecting group; fewer than 150 members completed it out of the approximately 500 who belonged to Gente de Cine at the time).[159]

Despite their investment in sourcing rare prints, many cineclubs relied heavily on local infrastructures of commercial film distribution for practical and financial reasons. This dependence limited their attempts to implement dominant cineclub standards, which privileged repertory programming over the commercial logic of novelty. In the case of the CCC, commercial distributors furnished most prints screened without cost or for a nominal fee during the first decade of the cineclub's existence.[160] Although the club's financial records are incomplete, it appears distributors' policy shifted in the late 1950s and early 1960s; film rentals grew from 1.5 percent of the organization's budget in 1955 to 13 percent in 1963.[161]

In return for distributors' cost-free loans, "the Cine Club [took] on a certain labor of promotion and dissemination," hosting sneak previews of new releases that could boost their box-office potential.[162] The circulation of films through the CCC thus functioned as a "value-adding process," as Marijke de Valck has argued with regard to film festivals, imbuing them with added prestige.[163] In a 1958 interview, Hernando Salcedo Silva, a critic who assumed the leadership of the CCC after Vicens left Bogotá for Mexico City in 1960, was quick to align distributors' interests with the club's declared objective of elevating local film taste. According to Salcedo Silva, the CCC actively helped distributors launch films seen as challenging in the local exhibition market: "With commentary and articles in the press, and personal promotion by the members, we efficiently aid in the commercial release of a film that, in the final analysis, contributes to the establishment of good cinema among us."[164] As Álvaro Concha Henao observes, in 1950 praise for *Sciuscià* (*Shoeshine*, Vittorio De Sica, 1946, Italy) from CCC members was used in print advertisements, contributing to the film's successful run.[165] Similarly, the Cine Club del Uruguay entered into an agreement with a local distributor, the Compañía Central Cinematográfica, to use sneak previews to promote films like *Sommarlek* (*Illicit Interlude*, Ingmar Bergman, 1951, Sweden) and *Rashomon* (Akira Kurosawa, 1950, Japan).[166]

On occasion, the CCC's members were even asked to offer insight on films' commercial potential, acting as a sort of test audience or focus group. Their input seems to have been especially valued in the case of controversial titles. A 1954 program asked spectators to provide their opinion on *Fröken Julie*, inquiring "Do you consider it to be appropriate to be presented to the Bogotá audience, and how will it be received?"[167] Requests for audience feedback, which the CCC championed as a core part of viewers' critical reflection on the films screened, also seem to have been motivated by the club's eagerness "to return the favor to the distributors who so kindly lend their films."[168]

Yet the CCC's programs and internal documents also signal a tension between the accessibility of recent and upcoming commercial releases and the cineclub's self-proclaimed goal of showcasing films its organizers judged artistically and historically significant. Meeting notes attest to the popularity of sneak previews and risqué films prohibited by the censors with members.[169] Even as the CCC's leadership recognized the need to attract viewers to remain financially solvent, programs lamented the rank and file's taste for novelty over "classics." One chided the membership for the poor attendance at an Orson Welles retrospective—along with "a very interesting program of Colombian cinema," a rarity for the organization—in comparison with sneak previews. For the film society's leadership, such selective viewing undercut the organization's non-commercial status and its pedagogical aims: "Showing only sneak previews places the Cine Club on the level of any commercial movie theater and furthermore, no Cine Club in the world gives sneak previews except on very special occasions. Good—or at least interesting—films should be rescreened for the purpose of evaluating their merits or defects through time. For this reason the Cine Club insists—and will continue insisting—on the rediscovery of good cinema."[170] As these admonishments suggest, the CCC's reliance on commercial distributors and its members' preference for new releases threatened the organization's claims to the status of elevated cultural institution that lived up to international (that is, French/European) standards.

In their efforts to embody these international cineclub norms, Latin American cineclubs actively worked to insert themselves within expanding global circuits of film culture, as we have seen in the case of IFAL's Cine Club de México. As film societies sought to broaden and

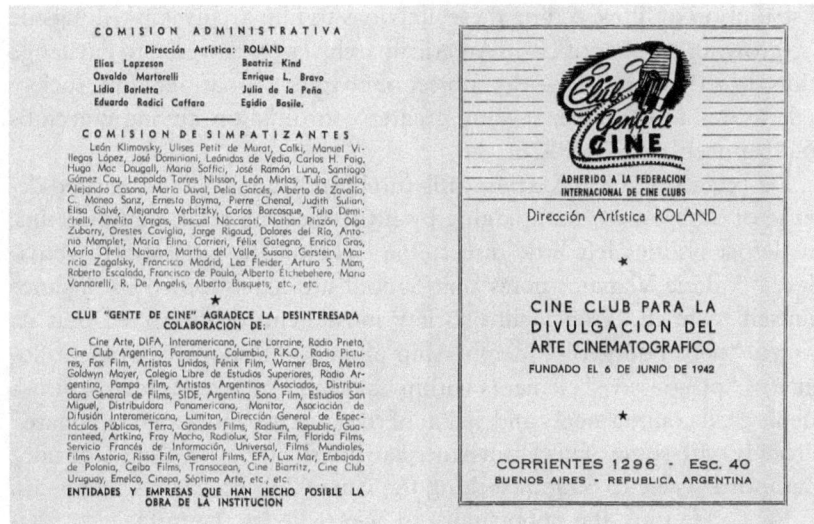

FIGURE 3. Program from Gente de Cine (circa 1948) highlighting the club's affiliation with FICC. Note the long list of commercial distributors, together with a few noncommercial entities, thanked by the film society for supporting its work. *Source:* Cinémathèque française.

differentiate their offerings, they tapped into regional, national, and international networks to access prints and seek organizational guidance from their foreign counterparts and supranational bodies. Archival exchanges accounted for only a small percentage of cineclub screenings.[171] Yet the transnational connections that made them possible were touted in programs and press accounts, suggesting how such links helped boost the prestige of film societies and, by extension, that of their organizers and members.

A promising, but ultimately ineffectual, node of transatlantic film culture was the FICC, established in 1947. FICC's creation was spearheaded by Georges Sadoul, a prominent communist activist, former surrealist, and film historian and educator, who also served as secretary-general of FFCC from 1945 to 1949.[172] Through FICC, Sadoul sought to rally an international group of film societies to negotiate with FIAF, whose member cinémathèques held the prints coveted by cineclub organizers for their programs. In 1949 FICC and FIAF made a joint commitment to regulate the flow of film materials and guarantee the non-commercial nature of cineclub exhibition in order to avoid industry backlash. FICC agreed that its members would renounce the collection and international distribution of films, ceding these activities to film archives.[173] Alongside the growing number of Latin American archives empowered to exchange films directly with FIAF—the subject of chapter 2—national film society federations took shape, seeking greater coordination among cineclubs and connections with FICC.

Despite the FFCC's Marxist affiliations and Sadoul's own spirited defense of Stalinist cinema, judging by FICC meeting notes and bulletins, his leftist politics left little discernible trace on the federation's activities.[174] Valérie Vignaux notes that Sadoul ultimately opted to distance himself from the French film society movement, disillusioned that its largely "petit bourgeois" membership proved unresponsive to the influence of "progressive" elements within its ranks.[175] Nevertheless, Sadoul's ideological commitments and vision of the cineclub movement resonated strongly with some of his Latin American interlocutors. In 1954 González Casanova wrote to Sadoul seeking the Cine Club Progreso's admission to FICC. He took the opportunity to acknowledge the influence of Sadoul's writing (together with that of Louis Daquin) on Progreso's efforts to embody the "avant-garde cineclub." In the same missive, González Casanova uses the language of Marxist orthodoxy to attack the cultural bona fides of a personal rival, Álvaro Custodio, a Spanish exile writer who had taken over the administration of the Cine Club de México. He denounces Custodio as "a Trotskyite with a checkered past. . . . With the support of the French embassy, he organizes a pseudo-cine club of the snobbish elite that allows him to speculate commercially [via theatrical releases of the films]. It's true that he shows some Soviet films, but only to profit from the interest that the public now shows in this type of cinema."[176] Playing to Sadoul's political sympathies, González Casanova's jabs at Custodio impugn his ideological correctness in order to undermine his social prestige. Yet despite Progreso's leftist orientation, González Casanova's own politics are all but imperceptible in *¿Qué es un cine-club?*, which instead advances liberal-humanist ideals of aesthetic progress and international understanding.

Although González Casanova first connected with Sadoul and FICC through correspondence, individual geographic mobility—whether facilitated by family wealth or scholarships that allowed film enthusiasts to study abroad, awarded by the French government or their home countries—often facilitated the initial contacts between Latin American film enthusiasts and French institutions of film culture. Throughout the 1950s cinephiles from Argentina, Uruguay, and Colombia attended the annual seminars organized by FFCC at Marly-le-Roi, where they watched films and rubbed shoulders with prominent creatives and critics.[177] Encounters with Henri Langlois had an even more formative impact on the Latin American cineclub movement. Salles Gomes first met Langlois through the Cercle du cinéma film society he co-organized with Georges Franju, during the young Brazilian's political exile in the 1930s.[178] Salles Gomes's future role as a Paris-based agent for Brazilian institutions of film culture is prefigured in a 1939 letter from his friend Décio de Almeida Prado, who requested his help furnishing film prints to "a kind of Cercle du Cinéma."[179] Almeida Prado predicts that mimicking aspects of the Cercle du cinéma, screening "(mostly French films, art films, meetings in a small group), may contribute to the success of [the São Paulo version of] the 'Cercle,' which could become something very chic, very 'snob,' which would translate into revenues indispensable for the continuation of the plan," thus linking French cultural capital to the promise of financial resources.[180]

This initiative bore fruit the following year with the creation of the Clube de Cinema de São Paulo; however, Salles Gomes only took on the role of intermediary between Brazilian cinephiles and Parisian institutions during his second sojourn in Paris, where he traveled in 1946 to study at IDHEC.[181] At the behest of his compatriots in São Paulo, Salles Gomes successfully requested the Clube de Cinema's admission to FICC, although he was unable to attend the 1947 meeting at the Cannes film festival where the federation was officially constituted.[182] Salles Gomes attended his first FICC conference two years later alongside Roland of Gente de Cine.[183] In talks with Langlois to acquire copies of French films and aware that FIAF members could technically provide such materials only to affiliated archives, Salles Gomes instructed his contact Francisco Luiz de Almeida Salles to create "a department called Filmoteca Brasileira, or Filmoteca de São Paulo, or something of the sort, in order to join FIAF," signaling how institutional connections with FIAF channeled the film society movements' energies toward the creation of archives, even if these initially existed only on paper (see chapter 2).[184]

Exemplifying what Dudley Andrew calls a "federated phase" of world film culture—in that it was marked by a postwar spirit of cooperation between national institutions mediated by supranational ones—FICC worked to coordinate national film society federations and to help foster their creation.[185] Early FICC documents register a desire to duplicate the massive growth of cineclubs in postwar France by facilitating the global circulation of film prints. Notes from a 1946 meeting state, "It is quite plausible that the rapid rise [of film societies] observed in France

FIGURE 4. Advertisement for a theatrical run of *Fröken Julie*—whose Latin American circulation suggests the synergy between cineclubs, festivals (it screened at Cannes and Punta del Este), and commercial exhibition—in a Montevideo film society magazine. *Source: Cine Club*, June 1952. Scan courtesy of Stanford University Libraries.

after October 1945 could be reproduced with the same rapidity in most European countries. But this rise is largely a function of [available film] programs. In numerous countries, as well, the future of cineclubs is linked to the existence of cinémathèques, to their development and their richness."[186] Latin America is not explicitly mentioned as promising terrain for the film society movement's expansion, but the meeting notes do reference cineclub activity in Argentina, Chile, and Uruguay, the only locales outside Europe and the United States referenced at the meeting.[187]

Within a decade, the Southern Cone would become home to Latin America's most robust film society federations. In Argentina and Uruguay, they developed in close connection with incipient film archives, helping to fund their activities through rental fees and ticket surcharges.[188] Elsewhere in Latin America, they proved more precarious. In Brazil, attempts in 1950 to create a national film society federation led by São Paulo's Centro de Estudos Cinematográficos (Center for Film Studies) failed, though the Centro dos Cine-Clubes do Estado de São Paulo (Center of Cineclubs for the State of São Paulo), founded five years later, joined FICC in 1957.[189] The Federación Mexicana de Cineclubes (Mexican Cineclub Federation), established in 1955, lasted only three months, bringing an inglorious end to an ambitious program of action that fused nationalism and internationalism.[190] Perhaps inspired by the visit of neorealist screenwriter Cesare Zavattini to Mexico that year, the federation championed "the development of national cinema [which] not only represents having the best means to educate the Mexican people on Mexican questions, to elevate the average level of national culture and to aid the collective search for solutions to the country's problems, but also the clearest path to fostering Mexico's relations with other nations . . . in pursuit of a better homeland, a [more] fraternal world."[191] After helping to foster film societies in Barranquilla, Cali, and Medellín during the 1950s, the CCC spearheaded the creation of the Federación Colombiana de Cineclubes (Colombian Cineclub Federation) in 1960 under the direction of poet Álvaro Cepeda Samudio.[192] Unfortunately, in a sign of the entity's general disorganization, he forgot its newly minted statutes in a taxi, and the federation began to function in earnest only after 1976.[193]

Linking existing clubs to facilitate the enforcement of institutional norms and streamline their functioning—creating efficiencies by circulating pre-constituted film programs or series, sharing program notes and information about print sources—Latin American film federations exemplified the self-propagating nature of the film society movement and promoted the transmission of imported institutional models and film canons.[194] At the same time, their failures highlighted local obstacles to effectively reproducing these models, including the resistance of cineclub members to their core ideals.

FRICTIONS: CINECLUB AUDIENCES AND THEIR DISCONTENTS

Assembling a slate of distinctive programming was only half the battle for film societies as they sought to reshape the tastes of the masses and ultimately improve the quality of film production. Instituting protocols of critical reflection that took their cue from European models was equally pivotal. These practices included contextualizing films with introductions and program notes; stimulating critical debate via post-screening discussions, questionnaires, and member reviews published in film society magazines; and suppressing audience behavior viewed as undesirable. Cineclub organizers were tasked with cultivating the membership, who—whatever their deficiencies—were assumed to possess tastes superior to those of the mass audience, the ultimate target of cineclubs' pedagogical mission.

Befitting the film society membership's desired role as a cultural mediator, its ranks were mostly comprised of middle-class individuals. Members of this social sector were well-positioned to benefit from the cultural capital attached to film society attendance at a moment when cinema was increasingly legitimated as an art but remained more accessible than consecrated cultural forms like literature and visual art. While cineclubs varied in size from the seventy-five members of the Cine Club Tucumán in northwest Argentina in 1952 to the two thousand affiliated with Uruguay's Cine Universitario in 1953 and the nearly three thousand who belonged to the Cine Club del Uruguay in the 1960s, they were remarkably homogeneous when it came to their members' class status.[195] Most groups gathered together middle-class professionals, creatives, academics, and students. These occupations were closely correlated with phenotypic whiteness, an unspoken prerequisite for middle-class status in Latin America.[196] In a 1950 survey, the Cine Club del Uruguay identified its members as "professors, students, painters, office workers [*empleados*], critics, photographers, engineers, illustrators, etc."[197] Similarly, Argentina's Cine Club Mendoza was "comprised in its majority by a professional and university element. After that are artists and businessmen." Unusually, the club's membership also included "a working-class element" [*elemento obrero*], whose representation among the ranks of film society members in the 1940s and 1950s appears to have been limited.[198] (For comparison, an analysis of twenty-seven French cineclubs conducted in the mid-1950s found that only 6 percent of their members were workers or artisans).[199] Catholic film activists even recommended convening an audience that was "homogeneous" in terms of social class and age in order to create "an atmosphere of greater balance, spontaneity, and comfort" for post-screening discussions, in Watson's words.[200] Irene Tavares de Sá, who organized film courses through a Catholic lay group in Rio de Janeiro, the Ação Social Arquidiocesana, similarly suggested that cineclub members should comprise "a homogeneous group with some specialized knowledge," although larger, less cultivated audiences could be accommodated in a more structured discussion she referred to as a cine-forum.[201]

Beyond this uniformity in class identity, leadership rolls and responses to polls suggest that postwar Latin American film societies were overwhelmingly male-dominated. In the aforementioned survey administered by the Cine Club del Uruguay in 1950, the respondents were 75 percent male and 25 percent female.[202] Yet by the 1960s its fellow Montevideo club Cine Universitario had a slight majority of female members, estimated at 50 to 60 percent by one of its organizers.[203] Only a handful of women seem to have spearheaded the creation of film societies. In Cali, Colombia, Maritza Uribe de Urdinola created the influential Centro Cultural La Tertulia in 1956, founding the Cine Club La Tertulia three years later. Beatriz Navia established a film society in nearby Palmira in the early 1960s.[204] In Rosario, Argentina, "Isabel Larguía de Pastor, married, 22 years of age, [directed] the activities of the Cine Club de Rosario as her only current activity," according to a 1953 club report.[205] The class and gender composition of postwar Latin American film societies suggest the forms of exclusion at work in the cineclub movement, despite its stated goals of transforming the mass audience.

Cineclubs' contradictions also become clear in materials designed to shape audiences' reactions to the films they viewed, thereby transforming them from passive consumers to active viewers. Audience responses were solicited in a variety of ways: post-screening discussions, questionnaires, and short reviews published in cineclub periodicals. Ironically, the publication that dedicated the most space to such reflections, *Gente de Cine* (printed by the club of the same name), moved in September 1952 to limit reader contributions. The magazine stated, "It has been decided we will not accept film reviews in this section, except when these—of an obviously polemical nature—render the inclusion of opinions other than those of the editorial board a matter of public interest. In this

FIGURE 5. Italian actor-director Vittorio De Sica interacts with members of Gente de Cine, who appear to be almost exclusively men, during an Italian film week in Buenos Aires. *Source: Gente de Cine*, November 1953, 1.

regard, we want to clarify that by no means are we restricting freedom of expression, but rather that we reserve for ourselves the review of new releases, a fundamental section for a film magazine."[206] Ultimately, *Gente de Cine* refused to cede certain forms of critical judgment—which the club's leader Roland exercised professionally as a film critic—to readers/ club members.

In a similar fashion, manuals offering advice on leading post-screening discussions instructed moderators in how to invite audience commentary while guiding conversation in a predetermined direction, operating on the premise that the critical sensibilities of discussion leaders were superior to those of members. Watson's *Elementos para un cine-debate* (1957) suggested that moderators should highlight aspects of the film neglected by viewers—particularly its formal qualities, often overlooked in favor of plot—without taking on an authoritative position in order to effectively stimulate dialogue. Watson proposes the following structure for a post-screening discussion: classify the film by genre, then discuss its plot and acting before turning to cinematography, mise-en-scène, sound, and editing.[207] This protocol allowed the moderator to move from familiar, mainstream interpretive frames for reading a film to more specialized ones. Watson stresses that, overall, "The moderator should speak little, always listen with real interest to the different points of view of the audience, and never impose his own, even when these are excellent and superior to those of the attendees."[208] In a similarly contradictory fashion, Colombian priest and film educator Jaime Serna celebrated the innate human capacity for analysis while stressing the need for informed guidance. He wrote in a 1959 cineclub manual, "Since passivity is so harmful in the case of cinema given that the most valuable thing about man is his ability to criticize, the Church recommends a well-directed and well-guided cineforum."[209] These comments crystallize the contradictory orientation of many Latin American film societies' leadership, which encouraged viewers to engage with cinema in an active and theoretically unfettered manner while nonetheless seeking to influence them from a position of presumed intellectual and cultural superiority.

For their part, audience questionnaires stimulated viewer reflection through open-ended questions but also offered more structured means of evaluation, asking members to make a positive or negative judgment or to quantify their opinions. For instance, an undated form from Cine Club Enfoques encouraged members to provide their overall opinion of the film while also listing the most notable aspects of its execution, its flaws, and the rating they would assign it.[210] Other questionnaires were more pointed in nature. For instance, on the filmmaker's request, Cine Club Núcleo solicited members' opinions about *Buenos Aires*, a 1958 short exploring urban poverty and alienation by David José Kohon.[211] Kohon's involvement with the club foregrounds film societies' role as an incubator for the *generación del 60* (generation of 1960), Argentina's own new wave or young cinema.[212] Questions like "Do you believe that 'Buenos Aires' accomplishes its goal of documenting and denouncing a social problem with legitimate cinematic means?" and "Are the composition of the frame and the rhythm marked by montage appropriate for the subject and the purpose of the film?" prompted viewers to reflect on the relationship between aesthetics and politics, suggesting that some of the critical frameworks they were offered would stimulate their analytical skills.[213]

Yet the active engagement sought from cineclub members often proved elusive. Some film society leaders considered soliciting spectator responses at all to be premature. In 1953 Argentina's Cine Club Santa Fe reported that organizers "commented on [the film's] value, on the director and their collaborators, on the school to which it belongs, [and] ma[de] known the opinion of some critics, etc." but "did not yet do discussions about the films, estimating that the members are not yet sufficiently equipped in terms of film culture [*cultura cinematográfica*]."[214] Other clubs considered post-screening discussions and questionnaires indispensable but had trouble generating the desired audience response. In 1952 film enthusiast José Sanz commented skeptically on Rio and São Paulo cineclubs, claiming that with few exceptions, they were "practically just commercial houses. There is not the least interest in discussing cinematic problems."[215] A bulletin from Colombia's Cine Club de Medellín that directly addressed (male) members using the future tense, attempting to create a sense of reciprocity that might stir them to action, is worth quoting at length:

> MR. MEMBER:
> you are a member of this cine-club.
>
> the cine-club looks out for you.
> you will look out for the cine-club.
>
> The cine-club will prepare bulletins for you.
> you will write for the bulletins.
>
> The C.C. seeks out the best programming for you.
> you will suggest films for cine club.
>
> The cine-club wants discussion for you.
> you will collaborate in the discussions.
>
> cine-club is yours . . . help it out!

The bulletin continued, "we've been in operation for eight years. we have the best programming in the country. but we don't have commentators—yes, plural. nor do we have a cine-forum. and without people with personality, people who aren't afraid to write in a bulletin or say what they think in a cine-forum, a cine-club is not a cine-club. it is simply . . . well, anything but a cine-club."[216] Such statements suggest how audience participation was often held to be inherent to a film society's identity, even when members balked at engaging in participatory rituals that were imposed in a top-down fashion. While it was by no means unique, Bogotá's CCC is an especially trenchant example of the tensions between localized forms of spectatorship and imported cineclub ideals, and between the elitist and democratizing impulses that defined mid-century film culture.

Resisting Imported Cineclub Norms: The Cine Club de Colombia

The founding of the CCC coincided closely with the postwar expansion of film society activity in Latin America and the growth of commercial film exhibition in Bogotá as its population increased rapidly through migration from rural areas. Nearly fifty movie theaters were constructed in the city during the 1940s, almost quintupling the number present in the late 1930s.[217] While the flourishing of commercial exhibition was likely a contributing factor, details on the immediate impetus for the CCC's creation are scarce. According to one account the idea emerged during the visit of German photographer Julius Meyer to Bogotá.[218] Founded by a small group of enthusiasts led by Luis Vicens, the CCC's membership included future Nobel Prize–winning novelist Gabriel García Márquez; visual artist Enrique Grau Araújo; and writers Jorge Gaitán Durán, Otto de Grieff (who served as the club's president), and León de Grieff.

Notes from the CCC's first meeting in September 1949 indicate that the organization defined itself as a non-commercial "cultural association dedicated to improving the taste of the movie-going public," one explicitly patterned on imported models. Vicens shared his knowledge of the "functioning of cineclubs in various European countries," while another attendee "referred to the magnificent work of French cineclubs [and] insisted on the enormous possibilities of an Association of this type in Colombia."[219] Yet Meyer also declared that the organization "could represent the first step in the creation of a film industry in Colombia."[220] Beyond "the presentation of special works of the Seventh art, of high artistic quality, both National and foreign, and to encourage debates on cinematic topics," the CCC pledged to support amateur cinema and photography.[221]

The CCC launched its public activities on September 6, 1949, with a screening of *Les enfants du paradis* (*Children of Paradise*, Marcel Carné, 1945, France), followed by commentary and discussion. Encapsulating the cineclub's often contradictory goals—to embody elevated taste while cultivating mass appeal—a newspaper account of the event noted that "the opinions of the *numerous and select public* were deeply divided relative to its value" (emphasis added).[222] One commentator, leftist writer Jorge Zalamea, questioned the labor of cultural recovery in which the CCC was engaged, declaring, "art, like old houses, has an attic where useless, unserviceable items collect; yet when the nouveaux riches enter the attic and exhume its contents, they believe they are working wonders."²²³ Highlighting the intertwining of social class and taste implicit in the CCC's activities, Zalamea's comments devalue the academic capital (in Bourdieu's terms) that emerging middle classes could acquire through study in a cineclub setting by contrasting it with the social capital conferred by aristocratic origins.²²⁴ These comments suggest the relative precariousness of the organizers' claims to refined taste (and by extension, elevated class status).

Perhaps as a result of these claims' precarity, the CCC made only a limited effort to offer mass access to non-mainstream film programming by opting to restrict its membership, creating a sense of exclusivity.²²⁵ Unlike its counterparts in Uruguay, whose membership numbered in the thousands, the CCC's size was deliberately limited to three hundred, with the argument that it "would otherwise lose the intimate character that these type of organizations should have."²²⁶ Salcedo Silva recalled in an interview conducted in the 1980s that "there was a moment when not being a member of the Cine-club was considered in bad taste," highlighting the film society's role as an arbiter of social status.²²⁷

Beyond its restricted membership, the CCC sought to discipline spectators in a dual sense, repressing boisterous forms of audience engagement while encouraging members to produce sanctioned forms of discourse on cinema. Both audience decorum and verbal and written performances of participation and discernment were seen as essential in order to legitimate the CCC and place it on a par with its international counterparts. Programs urged members to arrive punctually for screenings and implored them not to bring more than the single permitted guest or to smoke in the auditorium.²²⁸ Beyond such transgressions, post-screening discussions threatened to escape the control of their moderators in the club's early years. In a 1952 letter to Courvoisier penned in French, Vicens observed, "We are at the mercy of a mob [*foule*] that does not even know what a cine-club is and that very easily slips from praise to the most ferocious criticism."²²⁹ Members' failure to adhere to international film society norms is cast in class-based terms, suggesting how divides of status and taste operative within Colombian society were reproduced within the club's social space.²³⁰

Beginning in the mid-1950s, the CCC's organizers were more troubled by viewer indifference than by their unrestrained reactions to films. While the club's leadership made periodic attempts to facilitate post-screening discussions, these seem to have been poorly attended.²³¹ In 1963 a commentator for the left-leaning magazine *Guiones* noted that in the CCC's sessions, "The film is not discussed and if it is, it's by five members, answering the moderator. [The club's] interesting programming becomes useless."²³² Ironically, much of the CCC's leadership apparently failed to model the spectatorial norms that the organization was striving to enforce. One officer, Rosa Halaby, noted in a 1966 meeting that "with the exception of herself, [she] had never seen any members of the Board stay for the discussions, giving in this manner a bad example to the members," suggesting a gendered division of labor in the fulfillment of cineclub ideals.²³³

Given the disappointing results of post-screening discussions, the CCC's leadership shifted its focus to audience questionnaires, but these hardly proved more successful in provoking reflection from members. Yet the surveys do give a sense of the schemas offered to members for evaluating films, including the quality of the cinematography, direction, and acting, and whether the respondent considered the film worthy of the awards and accolades it had received from international festivals, signaling these events' pivotal role in canon formation in the period.²³⁴ Although a handful of viewer comments were published in the CCC's programs, more common were reminders that "it is an obligation of the members to respond to the questionnaires."²³⁵ One program lamented that only three out of three hundred members had submitted their questionnaires, urging members to help the CCC "achieve the principal objective of any cine-club in the world: that members critique and comment on the films that they see."²³⁶

During the 1960s, lack of member engagement with the CCC's programming seemed to deepen into greater and greater indifference to the programming itself. One board member blamed Salcedo Silva's "exclusive attention to the cultural side" of the CCC to the detriment of member recruitment and retention.²³⁷ Referring to Colombian film societies as a whole, the leftist film magazine *Cinemés* attributed cineclubs' indifference to member taste to a slavish imitation of foreign models: "They disregarded the preferences of the majority, the spiritual and economic soul that causes a cine-club to *be* and imposed upon it, quickly and by force, a bourgeois-ified taste brought from abroad. . . . They believed that a cineclub here, in the midst of a very different social reality, should function as in Paris, and not as it should here, in Latin America" (emphasis in original).²³⁸ At the same time, the CCC faced competition from a growing number of cineclubs, especially those in university settings. An account of this shift, published by filmmaker Abraham Zalzman in *Cine Cubano* in 1963, is worth citing at length for its caustic take on cineclubs as generators of cultural capital:

In 1959, Colombia had five cineclubs, distributed in five large cities.²³⁹ The life of these organizations had become routine. They existed through their own inertia and because of the number of members, for whom paying their dues was paying for the right to belong to a "chic" organization, where intellectual circles paraded by and where actual film enthusiasts could be counted on one hand. With the irruption of the university clubs in 1959 and 1960, the concept of the Cine-club was enriched by the word *action* and a real interest in cinema began to awaken in university milieux and adjoining ones.²⁴⁰

The CCC managed to survive in this shifting cultural landscape by scaling back on its screenings and rebuilt its membership in the early 1970s, though it struggled to reach the desired complement of three hundred.²⁴¹ The club's longevity signals its impressive, if partial, success in defining a distinct space within the local landscape of commercial and non-commercial exhibition, if not in enforcing the pedagogical model of the cineclub that underpinned its activities. The CCC's achievements in its first two decades were limited both by structural constraints and by its conflicting impulses toward elitism and the democratization of film culture. Lacking ready access to sources of repertory programming, the CCC was reliant on the very system of commercial film distribution from which it sought to distinguish itself. The limitations of this approach pushed the organization to connect with cultural institutions with an international scope, which envisioned Colombia and other Latin American nations as fertile ground for their global designs.

As the case of the CCC makes clear, organizations like FICC and FIAF worked to regulate film culture on an international scale—for example, by setting the terms for the non-commercial exchange of film prints—even as they fostered institution-building and regional cooperation in the Latin American cineclub and archiving movements. Ultimately, sourcing prints proved less problematic for the CCC than forging an idealized film public that embraced repertory programming and demonstrated discerning spectatorship through sanctioned forms of written and verbal reflection. The persistence of these elusive aims—used to shore up the CCC's cultural legitimacy and to draw internal divisions of class and taste within the membership—signal how the organization's labor of cultural uplift reinforced social and global hierarchies, even as it forged transnational connections. The history of the Cine Club de Colombia thus reveals how film society norms established abroad were instituted and challenged in the local context, to the point of being met with resistance—or simply indifference—from the public.

CONCLUSION

The challenges the CCC experienced in the mid- to late 1960s were far from unique to Colombia, where the growth of film societies more attuned to the political upheaval of the period diminished its potential audience. In Argentina, cineclubs came to face intense competition from the expansion of commercial arthouse programming, rendering them (like their French precursors in the 1920s) victims of their own success in cultivating public taste for art cinema.[242] Roland commented in 1969, "The cineclub sensitized the spectator, cultivated him, and revealed cinema as something more than a pastime or entertainment. Bergman, Antonioni, Resnais or Godard would not have been accepted before. An assimilated aesthetic taste now permits the successful exhibition of films that were previously [too] difficult. The audience sees them in arthouse theaters or even common cinemas."[243] More radically, by the late 1960s NLAC movements were calling for an even more sweeping transformation of the spectator, who was charged with becoming not only an active, critical viewer but also a political actor, a stance exemplified in Fernando Solanas and Octavio Getino's quotation of Frantz Fanon in their film *La hora de los hornos* (*The Hour of the Furnaces*, 1967, Argentina): "Every spectator is a coward or a traitor."[244]

This chapter has traced the transatlantic connections that linked Latin American film societies with France-based institutions, seeking to illuminate how Latin American intellectuals' desires for cultural cachet converged with the interests of the French state and France-based supranational bodies like FICC and FIAF. Latin America's intelligentsia gained prestige by implementing an imported institutional model of the cineclub, which promised to redeem the seductive mass medium of cinema through sanctioned practices of cultural consumption. For their part, Latin American interest allowed France-based organizations and individuals to advance a variety of goals. IFAL's collaboration with the Cinémathèque française promoted the consumption of French film, complementing other means of French cultural diplomacy like language instruction and scientific cooperation. As I explore in the next chapter, Langlois's dealings with Latin American cineclub organizers furthered his efforts to disseminate films while swelling the ranks of FIAF with his allies. For its part, FICC leveraged the admission of new national film society federations to improve its bargaining position in negotiations with FIAF. At the same time, the film society movement and its institutional allies abroad sought to nullify film's potentially negative ideological and moral effects by transforming spectatorship into a self-aware act of artistic contemplation. Whether they explored film aesthetics while asserting political and moral neutrality or turned film appreciation to explicitly ideological and religious ends, Latin American cineclubs strove to remake the mass audience, an inherently contradictory project that foregrounded the disconnect between institutions' cosmopolitan aspirations and the viewers they sought to transform.

CHAPTER 2

Toward a Global Film Preservation Practice?

FIAF and the Emergence of Latin American Archives

Upon its founding in 1938, the world's oldest organization dedicated to film preservation announced its global ambitions in its choice of name, the Fédération internationale des archives du film (FIAF). Yet only US and European institutions participated in FIAF's creation: the Film Library of New York's MoMA, the United Kingdom's National Film Library (now the BFI), Germany's Reichsfilmarchiv (which ceased to exist upon Germany's military defeat and the occupation of Berlin), and the Cinémathèque française, which housed FIAF's headquarters until 1960.[1] Archives located in other world regions would not join the organization's ranks until a decade later as its activities regained momentum in the post–World War II period. In 1948 the Filmoteca do MAM-SP, now the Cinemateca Brasileira, and Uruguay's state cinémathèque, housed in the film division of SODRE, became the first archives outside the North Atlantic countries to gain admission to FIAF as full members.[2]

In the two decades after World War II, over a dozen cinémathèques were founded in Latin America (some short-lived), marking the first widespread expansion of the film preservation movement beyond the United States and Europe. By the end of the 1950s, only three cinémathèques in Asia and Africa—Iran, Japan, and Morocco—had joined FIAF, compared with five in Latin America alone.[3] Suggesting profound obstacles to the creation of archives in recently decolonized nations, FIAF's first member in sub-Saharan Africa, the Republic of Congo's Cinémathèque nationale populaire, joined only in 1976, although the FIAF leadership

85

sought to encourage the creation of archives on the continent beginning in the mid-1960s.[4]

European and US members are still predominant in FIAF today, despite efforts to support Global South archives, such as the School on Wheels training program held in several locations across Africa and Latin America between 2002 and 2015 and the Film Preservation and Restoration School organized in Mumbai, Pune, Chennai, Buenos Aires, and Mexico City in recent years.[5] As of this writing, only a quarter of FIAF's members and just over a third of its associates are based in Africa, Asia, Latin America, or the Middle East.[6] Naturally, FIAF is not the sole organization that fosters international cooperation in moving-image preservation. Initiatives like the SouthEast Asia-Pacific AudioVisual Archive Association and the Audiovisual Preservation Exchange run by New York University's Moving Image Archiving and Preservation program promote regional coordination among and outreach to "non-Western" archives.[7] Yet given FIAF's longevity and institutional weight, its history demands special scrutiny. The organization's recent move to catalog its internal documents, many of which are digitized and freely available online, has opened up new opportunities in this regard.

Archives define the horizons of possibility for film culture and history by (selectively) safeguarding the material supports of moving images and making them available to researchers and broader audiences through public programming. It is thus imperative that we attend to the structural inequalities—and mutually beneficial exchanges—that define the history of the film preservation movement, which continue to condition the long-term survival of audiovisual materials outside wealthy North Atlantic countries. These long-standing disparities compound local factors responsible for regional gaps in film preservation, including climate—heat and humidity accelerate the decay of film and magnetic videotape—and institutional crises stemming from financial precarity and political neglect or interference.

For instance, in August 2020 the Cinemateca Brasileira was forced to close its doors after over seventy years in operation and its entire staff was fired. Eight months earlier, the federal government had abruptly terminated a contract awarded to the Associação de Comunicação Educativa Roquette Pinto, a nonprofit organization, to administer the Cinemateca. During the closure, in July 2021 a devastating fire destroyed not only an undisclosed number of films but also the records of Brazil's former film agencies, the Instituto Nacional de Cinema (1966–1976) and Embrafilme (Empresa Brasileira de Filmes, 1969–1990). The archive finally reopened in March 2022 after an existing nonprofit, the Sociedade Amigos da Cinemateca, won a temporary contract to administer it. The crisis was a clear instance of the right-wing administration of Jair Bolsonaro's onslaught on the cultural sector, which included the dissolution of the Ministry of Culture and the freezing of subsidies for Brazilian film production administered by the state film agency ANCINE (Agência Nacional do Cinema). Yet the Cinemateca has long suffered from inadequate financial support and precarious infrastructure, a contributing factor in fires that struck the archive in 1957, 1969, 1982, and 2016.

In order to fully grasp the contemporary challenges facing audiovisual archiving in Latin America, we must turn to the early history of the region's cinémathèques, which illuminates both the successes and limitations of the film preservation movement's internationalization. In the mid-1950s Latin American archives served as a laboratory for FIAF's expanding global ambitions, most notably with the creation of a regional subsection known as the Latin American Pool in English and the Sección/Seção Latino(-)americana in Spanish and Portuguese. Spearheaded by Henri Langlois of the Cinémathèque française, the creation of the Pool responded to structural barriers that hampered the full participation of "non-Western" institutions in FIAF.[8] These ranged from the locations chosen for its annual congresses—held exclusively in Europe from 1946 to 1968—to unfavorable currency exchange rates that made it difficult or impossible for Latin American archives to afford FIAF dues. At the height of its activity between 1955 and 1960, the Latin American Pool sought to address these obstacles through decentralization, most notably by convening regional meetings. Yet the initiative was faced with geographic, financial, and administrative hurdles that stymied exchanges between member archives, and it never successfully addressed their marginalization within FIAF. The history of the Pool—a largely failed experiment in both transatlantic and regional cooperation—illuminates early Latin American archives' distinctly cosmopolitan approach to film preservation, the profound challenges they faced in developing and circulating film collections, and the frictions that marked their relationship with FIAF.

The creation of cinémathèques in postwar Latin America exemplifies the widespread, if often fraught, export of a particular institutional model of the film archive in the postwar period and the disparate organizational, personal, and diplomatic agendas it served. With a handful of exceptions, postwar Latin American archives operated as private ventures without robust governmental support. Many of them emerged from personal connections between leaders of the film society movement and Langlois, whose institution-building efforts in the region have been acknowledged in passing but rarely examined in depth.[9] In the late 1940s and early 1950s, Langlois encouraged Latin American film enthusiasts he met in France—including the film students Paulo Emílio Salles Gomes from Brazil and Germán Puig from Cuba, the Argentine critic Andrés José Rolando Fustiñana (Roland), and the Catalan Colombian bookseller Luis Vicens—to establish archives, even if these existed only on paper. This legal fiction allowed newly created cinémathèques and their associated cineclubs to receive prints from the Cinémathèque française, in compliance with FIAF regulations that limited the circulation of archival materials to exchanges between its members.[10] Beginning in the late 1940s, FIAF increasingly sought to monopolize this form of non-commercial distribution, wresting it away from film societies to minimize competition with theatrical exhibition and thus avoid industry backlash.[11]

Given their strong ties to the cineclub movement, postwar Latin American archives primarily sought out copies of canonized "classics," whose established prestige helped legitimate the activities of their associated cineclubs. (Note that because of these close links, many early Latin American film archives did not offer an extensive slate of their own programming; in consequence, I focus here on collecting, preservation, and loans of film prints).[12] In some cases, cinémathèques circulated these prints via national cineclub federations for a fee. Borrowed cultural capital thus quite literally bankrolled the activities of the early Latin American film preservation movement, most notably in Argentina and Uruguay.[13] The region's archives did not initially seek to valorize "national cinemas"—whose existence was debatable outside the major film-producing nations of Argentina, Brazil, and Mexico, despite vibrant amateur film cultures in countries like Chile and Uruguay—in the face of perceived cultural colonization by the United States and Europe. In fact, until the mid-1950s or even the mid-1960s, Latin American cinémathèques showed little interest in either physically preserving or rhetorically constructing the notion of a national film heritage, which Caroline Frick identifies as the guiding principles of US and European archives through the 1990s.[14]

In serving the programming needs of Latin America's growing film society movement, Langlois's institution-building activities advanced FIAF's efforts to expand and regulate films' non-commercial circulation on an international scale. The organization's leadership sought to increase global access to film "classics" in order to foster film culture and promote film preservation by helping to inspire the creation of new archives. In 1948 Iris Barry, the director of MoMA's Film Library, proposed the creation of a shared repository of prints for this purpose, which members would both borrow from and contribute to.[15] Acting as a preservation safeguard by multiplying the number of existing copies, the circulation pool would help meet growing demand from archives and other organizations for prints, supplementing existing archive-to-archive exchanges. While, as Catherine Cormon has shown, this general circulation pool did not begin operating until 1961, it provided the conceptual framework for the Latin American Pool.[16]

Faced with their growing success in creating a nontheatrical market for "classic" films, postwar film archives had to balance their interest in circulating their holdings with commercial stakeholders' fears of competition and copyright infringement—as Fausto Douglas Corrêa Jr. argues—but also with the material fragility of the prints themselves.[17] In their quest to secure programming, Latin American archives aligned themselves with Langlois in his well-known dispute with Ernest Lindgren of the United Kingdom's National Film Library, a conflict that structures many histories of the film archiving movement, sometimes to the point of oversimplification. Whereas Lindgren prioritized the physical preservation of film materials to the point of curtailing access, Langlois privileged their broad accessibility, even at the risk of damage or loss.[18] This carelessness in the physical preservation of films fueled open conflict between Langlois and FIAF in 1959 in the wake of a devastating nitrate fire that struck the Cinémathèque française, destroying a huge swath of its collection along with prints belonging to other archives. Langlois proved unable to produce an inventory of the films that had been destroyed, heightening concerns about his methods. He lashed out by leveling unfounded accusations of misconduct at Jacques Ledoux of the Cinémathèque de Belgique and stormed out of the conference. Langlois summarily dismissed FIAF's executive secretary Marion Michelle—although only the organization's president Jerzy Toeplitz had the right to do so, and she was later reinstated—before officially withdrawing from FIAF in mid-1960.[19]

In his influential book *Les cinémathèques*, Raymond Borde argues that the FIAF crisis of 1959–1960 signaled a shift from a "subjective" mode of film preservation embodied by Langlois's approach to archiving to one grounded in technical expertise.[20] Langlois seems to have cultivated Latin American archives in part because of their investment in dissemination, as opposed to the more pragmatic, technocratic approaches to preservation ascendant in the wake of the FIAF crisis. The creation of Latin American archives whose leaders were philosophically aligned with (and personally loyal to) Langlois bolstered his influence in FIAF, furnishing him with ready-made allies who could be mobilized as a voting bloc.[21] As Rudá de Andrade of the Cinemateca Brasileira noted, "The expansion of cinémathèques throughout the world also meant an increase in his power as leader."[22] Latin American archives often named Langlois as a proxy when unable to send a representative to FIAF congresses, a common occurrence given the high expense of traveling to Europe. Langlois leaned heavily on these existing alliances after his falling-out with FIAF; Andrade recalled, "Everything Langlois did for Brazil [i.e., the Cinemateca Brasileira] was repaid in 1960, with the crisis that struck FIAF."[23] By the end of the 1960s, nearly all Latin American archives had left the organization. Yet archival records suggest that this was due to runaway inflation and other financial problems that rendered them unable to pay their dues despite repeated attempts and negotiations with FIAF that lasted well into the decade, not blind loyalty to Langlois.

The region's cinémathèques again proved central to Langlois's bid for institutional influence in 1965, when he helped launch a new confederation of Latin American archives, UCAL. Operating independently from FIAF, UCAL offered a model of regional cooperation that was not beholden to North Atlantic models or priorities. Yet the organization dissolved by 1984, falling victim to ideological polarization and political repression as right-wing dictatorships swept the region.

As recent research by Beatriz Tadeo Fuica shows, in the early 1950s Langlois cultivated close relationships with incipient archives in Argentina, Brazil, and Uruguay, whose vibrant film markets had escaped wartime devastation. He sought these cinémathèques' assistance in finding prints of prewar German films—many believed lost—in an effort to replace the Reichsfilmarchiv's holdings. Langlois also inquired after Soviet productions, circumventing the politically tricky maneuver of trying to source these materials in the USSR given Cold War tensions.[24] Although FIAF resolved to accept a Soviet state archive as a founding member at its first postwar conference in 1946, Gosfilmofond joined only in 1957, after the death of Stalin in 1953 fostered greater Soviet involvement in international cultural organizations.[25] The Cinemateca Argentina, in particular, dispatched several Soviet and German titles to Langlois.[26] In return, the Cinémathèque française sent not only French films—the only ones that technically fell within its purview—but also German and Soviet ones, to archives in Argentina and Brazil.[27]

Langlois's personal ambitions and FIAF's global designs also became entangled with the aims of French cultural diplomacy. After the

1946 FIAF conference, Langlois wrote to DGRC head Louis Joxe to ask the agency to pay the Cinémathèque française's membership dues. Langlois reminded Joxe that FIAF had been created with the support of the DGRC's precursor, SOFE, which had helped ensure the organization would be headquartered in Paris at the Cinémathèque française. Langlois wrote, "Given the importance of Paris remaining the center of international exchanges between cinémathèques, which, as you know, have been charged with the dissemination of films in the noncommercial cineclub circuit in nearly all countries, we hope you will continue to support French participation in this institution."[28] Langlois framed his own investment in the global circulation of films as being in the French national interest, stressing the Cinémathèque française's role as a cultural mediator and arbiter. Langlois's (seemingly successful) appeal to the French state, despite the archive's status as a private organization, contrasts sharply with the inability of most of its Latin American counterparts to secure official backing.[29]

While I highlight such disparities between North Atlantic and Latin American cinémathèques, archival records demonstrate that the latter were central to FIAF's designs for global expansion in the postwar period, even as they were marginalized within the organization in practice. Yet the emergence of Latin American cinémathèques, like the history of Global South archives more generally, has received minimal attention in the Euro-American literature on film preservation that began to take shape in the 1980s and 1990s.[30] Only a handful of book-length studies of moving-image archiving exist in Spanish and Portuguese.[31] Most focus on individual institutions, though important comparative work has been done by scholars like Corrêa Jr. and Tadeo Fuica. Inasmuch as English-language scholarship has addressed Latin American archives at all, they are typically framed in terms of radical alterity and radical politics. In an essay on UCAL, Janet Ceja Alcalá contends that preservation in the region was a highly politicized practice that drew its inspiration from the leftist, formally experimental NLAC. This interpretation may hold true for the period she examines—the late 1960s and 1970s—but not for the nearly two decades of archival efforts that preceded it, which she characterizes as the work of "amateurs."[32] Focusing on Guatemala's Cinemateca Universitaria Enrique Torres, Caroline Frick offers a more nuanced take, emphasizing Latin American archives' historical and contemporary commitment to access over physical preservation. Yet in insisting that the activities of cinémathèques in the region thus constitute an "alternative preservation practice," she presents their work as out of step with or actively resisting the international consensus in the field. In fairness, she acknowledges that this approach stems from archives' need to boost public awareness of their collections in order to secure scarce financial resources.[33]

Contra these readings, the practices of early Latin American cinémathèques fail to fit neatly into prevailing narratives about the region's film culture. For the most part, Latin America enters canonical film histories only under the sign of social commitment, political resistance, and opposition to Hollywood, hallmarks of NLAC. Yet early cinémathèques in the region were neither overtly leftist nor explicitly nationalist. Rather than engaging in an "alternative" or counter-hegemonic preservation practice, they advanced a self-consciously cosmopolitan cinephilia. In this sense, postwar Latin American archives were not radically "other" from their European and US counterparts, since they also approached questions of access and preservation through largely depoliticized notions of film as art. Nor were they simply instruments of cultural colonization, although they enlisted the aid of foreign institutions to secure both material resources and prestige. Rather, these cinémathèques participated in mutual exchanges of cultural capital and institutional influence with FIAF, benefiting (though less than they would have liked) from the material resources of wealthier, better-established members to arrange programming, organize festivals, and build their collections. These young archives also capitalized on their connections to a widely recognized, supranational cultural organization to gain institutional legitimacy, which they could leverage locally to secure support for their activities. Responding to concerns about the influx of Latin American members in FIAF—some without the necessary infrastructure to effectively safeguard films—Salles Gomes declared at the 1956 FIAF congress in Dubrovnik, "FIAF is a sufficiently effective organization, endowed with sufficient prestige, that it can incorporate Latin America's nascent cinémathèques without harm, without fearing that their weakness will damage it. And their entrance into FIAF is the sole path by which these Archives can benefit from FIAF's prestige and consolidate themselves."[34]

This disconnect between FIAF's established international profile and the precarity of Latin American archives pervades the organization's internal records. While the establishment of cinémathèques in the region helped fulfill FIAF's ideals of a global film preservation movement, heightened Langlois's clout within the organization, and helped him prospect for rare prints, their presence ultimately exposed a Eurocentric institutional structure that failed to fully account for geopolitical disparities. Premised on the unequal global distribution of cultural capital, FIAF's Latin American Pool nonetheless fostered intraregional connections that fostered the regional solidarity characteristic of NLAC, despite being rooted in a markedly different regime of cultural value.

Because I focus on relations between postwar Latin American archives and FIAF, I attend most closely to the cosmopolitan cinémathèques that emerged and expanded through close contact with the organization. Yet their model of film preservation was certainly not the only one pursued in the region. The following section offers an overview of these preservation initiatives—which approached cinema not solely as art but also as pedagogical tool and historical document—and their antecedents in public discourse on cinema, before examining the development of self-consciously cinephilic archives after World War II. Finally, I turn to the question of regional cooperation in the film preservation movement. The histories of FIAF's Latin American Pool and UCAL, I contend, not only chart an ideological shift in the region's preservation practice but also highlight both the potential and the contradictions of globalizing film preservation.

THE EMERGENCE OF LATIN AMERICAN FILM ARCHIVES

The conviction that cinema was not solely an ephemeral entertainment, but rather a repository of enduring cultural value, emerged in Latin America decades before the founding of its first cinémathèques. As David Wood notes, upon cinema's debut as a commercial entertainment in Mexico City in 1896, observers stressed its potential contributions to the historical record.[35] A number of silent-era critics called for the preservation of films with educational or aesthetic merits to facilitate their commercial re-release. In 1912 a journalist proposed in the Rio de Janeiro magazine *Fon-Fon*: "Why don't our movie theaters institute a kind of archive for films that instruct, exhibiting them once in a while in the name of ... a valuable service rendered to today's vertiginous temperament, which no longer allows us to burn the midnight oil studying?"[36] Making reference to travel films and screen adaptations of literary classics, the magazine hailed film preservation as a means of fully exploiting film's educational potential. In the late 1920s, an article in the Brazilian fan magazine *Cinearte* aligned film archiving with salvage ethnography. Suggesting how cinema could preserve local customs in the face of rapid modernization, the writer (likely editor-in-chief Adhemar Gonzaga) observed that "we still possess certain traditions, picturesque aspects of life, especially in our interior, which are slowly disappearing ... it is exactly these fleeting aspects of an age that Cinema can fix forever and museums conserve forever. In other countries this is attended to with loving care."[37] Here, film preservation is simultaneously presented as a means of documenting local particularities and as a foreign practice that Brazil would do well to emulate, prefiguring the cosmopolitan orientation of Latin America's postwar cinémathèques.

Focusing on cinema's aesthetic qualities rather than its use as a teaching tool or ethnographic document, in 1926 Mexican writer Jaime Torres Bodet—a future diplomat, minister of education, and director-general of UNESCO—proposed the creation of an archive to facilitate what we now call repertory programming. Arguing for the need to create "a museum for a living art," he wrote, "The cinema has evolved enormously. ... Why not, then, establish a venue dedicated exclusively to placing this history within reach of aficionados who doubt the reliability of their memories? Why not make this potential venue the indispensable library that cinema deserves and demands?"[38] Torres Bodet's comments cast cinema as an emerging art that already possessed a meaningful history, aligning closely with the ideals that fueled Europe's interwar film societies. His text built on contemporary writings by film enthusiasts like Carlos Noriega Hope and Marco Aurelio Galindo, who sought to emulate the cineclubs of Paris, London, and Berlin in Mexico City, though these desires did not come to fruition until the early 1930s.[39]

Uruguayan film preservationist and critic Manuel Martínez Carril identifies three main waves of development for Latin America's cinémathèques, with the first emerging from the cineclub movement, the second linked to universities, and the third taking shape under the auspices of the state.[40] While this observation is broadly useful, state and university archives with an explicitly educational mandate in fact predated those affiliated with cineclubs. The Instituto de Cinematografía Educativa established at the Universidad de Chile in 1929 possessed over a thousand titles, while Brazil's Instituto Nacional de Cinema Educativo, founded in 1936 to produce pedagogical films, held approximately four hundred titles by the end of the 1940s.[41] In Mexico, in 1942 a presidential decree established Mexico's Filmoteca Nacional as the successor to the Ministry of Public Education's Cinema Department. In addition to safeguarding films made by government agencies and a few commercial features, the Filmoteca made and screened educational films, reaching nearly 340,000 viewers between August 1943 and July 1944.[42] The driving force behind the Filmoteca was Elena Sánchez Valenzuela, who

FIGURE 6. Elena Sánchez Valenzuela poses with reels from the Filmoteca Nacional's collection. Source: *Cinema Repórter*, February 26, 1944.

is best known as the star of the popular 1918 feature *Santa* but later worked extensively within the cultural infrastructure of the Mexican state. As Patricia Torres San Martín observes, Sánchez Valenzuela advocated (without immediate effect) for the creation of national film archives during visits to Guatemala, Argentina, Uruguay, and Peru in 1947 and 1948. Despite rivals' attempts to thwart her efforts and even have her removed from her post, Sánchez Valenzuela continued working at the Filmoteca until shortly before her death in 1950. The archive appears to have ceased operation after her departure, though its collection may have been transferred to the archive created at UNAM in 1960.[43] A cinema law passed in 1949 provided for the creation of Mexico's Cineteca Nacional, but this project would not come to fruition until 1974.[44]

The history of state-sponsored film preservation in Argentina roughly parallels the Mexican case, with its long-deferred promises of a robust national film archive. In a recent book, Eugenia Izquierdo highlights the little-known history of Argentina's Archivo Gráfico de la Nación (AGN).[45] Founded in 1939, the archive was charged with safeguarding filmic and photographic images of important historical events. During the presidency of Juan Domingo Perón, the AGN's mandate shifted, and it came to serve largely as a footage library for state-sponsored films. After Perón's ouster in a 1955 coup, the archive fell victim to a sweeping process of de-Peronization that actively sought to suppress images of the exiled leader. A law promulgated in 1957 to revive Argentina's flagging film industry made provision for a national film archive, and the AGN was absorbed into the Archivo General de la Nación. Concretized in 1963, Argentina's Cinemateca Nacional amassed approximately 350 titles that it loaned to the Cinemateca Argentina and the country's growing network of film societies.[46] Yet the project of a national film archive in Argentina lacked continuity. Its latest iteration, the Cinemateca y Archivo de la Imagen Nacional, was established by decree in 1999 and launched in 2017 but as of this writing has yet to open to the public.

The most enduring and influential archive founded in Latin America prior to the end of World War II was housed in Uruguay's SODRE, a pioneering example of Latin American public broadcasting established in 1929. Despite its official character, under the leadership of founder Danilo Trelles Cine Arte del SODRE (Cine Arte) followed the line of private cinémathèques that valorized film's aesthetic dimensions over its strictly pedagogical ones.[47] Cine Arte's orientation also contrasts sharply with the politicized state cinémathèques that emerged in the late 1950s and 1960s, including the postrevolutionary Cinemateca de Cuba and the Cinemateca Nacional de Venezuela, to which I return at the end of this section. In a 1948 report to FIAF, Cine Arte described itself as "an organization similar to European cine-clubs," though unlike most private film societies, its sessions were not limited to members.[48] The screening series launched by Cine Arte in May 1944 was part of a varied slate of edifying cultural activities offered by SODRE.[49] Promoting cultural forms deemed "high" art, such as classical music and ballet, the broadcaster boasted a choral ensemble and orchestra that performed on air and a collection of musical recordings, a precursor of its film archive.[50] By its own account, Cine Arte's programming primarily reached a middle-class audience of "student youth, intellectuals, professors, [and] white-collar workers."[51]

Nevertheless, Cine Arte's activities targeted a wide range of locales and audiences. In 1948 the organization coordinated screenings in twelve regional branches outside Montevideo and in K–12 schools and universities.[52] According to internal reports tabulated by Mariana Amieva Collado, between 1950 and 1961 Cine Arte organized over ten thousand screenings that reached more than 2.6 million total viewers—roughly equivalent to Uruguay's entire population in this period, though the count naturally includes repeat viewers. Over 900,000 of these spectators watched the films in educational settings.[53] Cine Arte also organized special events like a 1951 retrospective of French cinema and the Festival Internacional de Cine Documental y Experimental (Festival of Documentary and Experimental Cinema), first held in 1954, discussed in the following chapter.[54] To support its programming activities, Cine Arte began to amass prints sourced from European archives, material discarded by distributors, and private collections, including, by Trelles's account, five thousand films acquired in Argentina, Chile, and Peru in 1948.[55] Although the cinémathèque sought out and preserved a small number of Uruguay's earliest films, Soviet, German, and French cinema dominated both its early collection and its programming.[56]

Though Cine Arte was among the first Latin American archives to join FIAF, its director Danilo Trelles soon found himself at odds with Langlois, whose differences with Lindgren seem to have fueled hostility toward the state-sponsored model of preservation embodied by the UK's National Film Library. In March 1954 Langlois wrote to José María Podestá, a critic with links to the Cinemateca Uruguaya and Cine Universitario film society, to outline his plans for the creation of a "Latin American Bureau" within FIAF. Langlois observed: "Currently, two tendencies converge to favor [the development of] cinémathèques: one aristocratic and New York-influenced [i.e., museum-based archives like MoMA's Film Library], the other democratic and rooted in cineclubs."[57] Not surprisingly, given the Cinémathèque française's origins in the Cercle du cinéma film society he ran with Georges Franju, Langlois affirmed that "the future of non-millionaire cinémathèques in Latin America is with the cineclubs," including the Cinemateca Uruguaya, created through a merger between the archives of Cine Universitario and the Cine Club del Uruguay.[58] These comments casting doubt on the value of museum-based cineclubs may have been rooted in Langlois's recent dispute with Paulo Emílio Salles Gomes of the Filmoteca do MAM-SP over payment for prints furnished by the Cinémathèque française for the I Festival Internacional de Cinema in São Paulo, an incident I return to later. Yet the French curator reserved his harshest criticism for Cine Arte, claiming that it "takes advantage of and blocks the support of the state" from private archives like the Cinemateca Uruguaya, functioning as a "parasitic organism that must prove it exists and can only do so by impeding others' existence."[59] Langlois apparently hoped that the Cinemateca Uruguaya would someday come to occupy the Cinémathèque française's privileged position as an autonomous private entity with robust government support and viewed

Cine Arte as an obstacle. Research by Tadeo Fuica suggests that Langlois's antipathy for Cine Arte may have been due less to divergent institutional models than to Trelles's reluctance or failure to provide titles of interest to the Cinémathèque française in the early 1950s.⁶⁰ Regardless of the root cause, Langlois endeavored (often successfully) to marginalize Trelles from efforts at regional cooperation through the 1960s.

As Langlois's letter suggests, Cine Arte was something of an anomaly among postwar Latin American cinémathèques, while museums and private film societies proved more influential. As noted previously, MAM-SP, founded in 1948, nurtured the Cinemateca Brasileira, initially known as the Filmoteca do MAM-SP. Its comparatively well-documented history exemplifies how Langlois's institution-building efforts and FIAF's ambitions shaped Latin America's film preservation movement.⁶¹ While living in Paris to study at IDHEC, Salles Gomes frequented the Cinémathèque française and developed a friendship with Langlois. As noted in the previous chapter, in 1947 Salles Gomes took on the role of European correspondent for São Paulo's Clube de Cinema, which he had helped found in 1940. On Langlois's advice, Salles Gomes encouraged his contacts to establish a film archive under the auspices of MAM-SP. With the backing of the Cinémathèque française, FIAF's executive committee accepted the Filmoteca do MAM-SP as a member in April 1948. Beginning with the 1948 FIAF congress, Salles Gomes often served on the organization's executive committee through the mid-1960s, when the Cinemateca Brasileira was expelled for non-payment of dues.⁶²

Part of a crop of cultural organizations established by the city's industrial bourgeoisie in the late 1940s and 1950s in a bid for cultural hegemony, MAM-SP was established by industrial magnate Francisco Matarazzo Sobrinho in close contact with oil baron and philanthropist Nelson Rockefeller, who served as a trustee of New York's MoMA and head of the Office of the Coordinator of Inter-American Affairs during World War II.⁶³ As Salles Gomes commented a decade after the Filmoteca's founding, MAM-SP's institutional prestige lent legitimacy to film exhibition and preservation by associating it with already-sanctioned cultural forms.⁶⁴ Once incorporated into the museum, the Clube de Cinema benefited from Matarazzo Sobrinho's financial patronage and the institution's physical infrastructure. Its newly constructed facilities included a 180-seat auditorium equipped with 35mm and 16mm projectors, the latter on loan from the US consulate.⁶⁵

Beyond brokering the creation of the Filmoteca, Salles Gomes handled its earliest acquisitions from the Cinémathèque française during his stay in Paris, which lasted until he returned to Brazil in 1954 to handle the retrospective programming for the I Festival Internacional de Cinema. Salles Gomes's correspondence with Matarazzo Sobrinho registers competing notions of film as modern art, while also signaling how his relationship with the Cinémathèque française ensured a privileged place for French cinema in the Filmoteca's collection, reinforcing its place in the canon. The museum's investment in abstraction meant that films by the French avant-garde of the 1920s ranked high in its collection priorities. Yet Salles Gomes's recommendations, based on the titles Langlois offered him, promoted a broader conception of film art. In a 1949 letter to Matarazzo Sobrinho, Salles Gomes suggests that the Filmoteca postpone the purchase of experimental works like Germaine Dulac's *La souriante Madame Beudet* (*The Smiling Madame Beudet*, 1923, France) and Dimitri Kirsanoff's *Ménilmontant* (1926, France). Instead, he suggests assembling a collection that could help attune audiences to continuities within national cinemas and the work of individual directors. Making explicit the Filmoteca's pedagogical aims, he writes, "We should attempt to spark in the audience for whose cinematic culture we will be responsible, a consciousness of cinematic style. To arrive at this point I think the best way is to first give them the concrete elements for developing consciousness of *one* cinematic style, of an auteur. For this reason I propose René Clair, not only because he is one of the auteurs with the most personal style, but also due to the great unity of his work, in a particularly French style" (emphasis in original).[66] Weighing the merits of acquisitions in Soviet cinema (ultimately rejected for political reasons), the films of Jean Renoir, and those of German director G.W. Pabst, Salles Gomes convinced Matarazzo Sobrinho to acquire Clair's *Un chapeau de paille d'Italie* (*The Italian Straw Hat*, 1928), *Les deux timides* (*Two Timid Souls*, 1928), and *Le million* (1931). Spanning silent and sound cinema and experimental and narrative film, Clair's oeuvre offered a middle ground between competing visions of film art.

Despite the success of these early negotiations, the Filmoteca's relationship with the Cinémathèque française quickly became strained due to Langlois's questionable handling of film materials, justified in the name of broad access. One of Salles Gomes's contacts in the Clube de Cinema, Lourival Gomes Machado, reported, "The two René Clair films that were bought used have arrived in awful condition—after four screenings, we dare not show them again."[67] Sourced from a private collector, the films had apparently been loaned out for a screening after Salles Gomes inspected them (in fact, one print had to be hastily retrieved from the airport when he came to pick them up).[68]

Due in part to Langlois's unreliability, the Filmoteca soon sought out materials from MoMA's Film Library, leveraging existing connections between the two museums rooted in official and unofficial forms of US cultural diplomacy.[69] Referring to a program of D. W. Griffith films to be provided by MoMA, Salles Gomes asked, "Might it not be possible to play all our cards (the Good Neighbor Policy, Pan-American Union, Rockefeller) to obtain the films not only as loans, but also for our Archives?"[70] He directly enlisted the aid of Iris Barry to position the Filmoteca favorably within an emerging network of institutions of film culture.[71] In response to Salles Gomes's attempt "to try to get Mr. Rockefeller to approve of the Cinematheque Bresillienne [sic] acting as the central point of contact and distribution for South America" (a suggestion from Langlois), Barry wrote, "Naturally we shall do what we can to help the Museu especially as Mr. Rockefeller has promised them our best cooperation."[72] As this exchange makes clear, the Cold War–era cultural diplomacy promoted by the Rockefellers, including the equation of abstract painting with freedom of expression (in opposition to socialist realism), served as an alternative to the indirect forms of French cultural diplomacy exercised by Langlois through the Cinémathèque française.

The importance of the French archive to the Cinemateca Brasileira also waned as relations between Langlois and Salles Gomes deteriorated after 1954. While organizing a series of major retrospectives for the I Festival Internacional de Cinema in São Paulo, Salles Gomes negotiated the permanent loan of prints struck from the Cinémathèque française's holdings. Yet a year later, Langlois complained to FIAF's executive committee that the funds promised by the Cinemateca Brasileira to cover the cost of the copies had yet to be paid.[73] Langlois also chastised Salles Gomes for his failure to return films loaned in advance of the festival in 1953, which had instead been sent on to Uruguay.[74] Although the collaboration between the two archivists survived these tensions, their relationship continued to deteriorate. Apparently unsatisfied with Salles Gomes's response to the 1959 FIAF crisis, Langlois used his influence to damage him professionally. Learning that the Brazilian curator would be asked to serve as a juror at the 1962 Locarno film festival, Langlois threatened to withhold the prints he had promised for retrospectives of the work of King Vidor and Jean Vigo unless Salles Gomes was disinvited.[75]

As his early communications with both the Cinémathèque française and MoMA suggest, Salles Gomes's initial focus was on securing copies of foreign film "classics" that could be used in MAM-SP's programming and loaned to cineclubs. Although the Filmoteca organized a retrospective of Brazilian cinema in 1952, only in 1955 did its staff begin a systematic search for domestically produced films.[76] Ultimately, this campaign contributed to the Filmoteca's split with MAM-SP in 1956. While the Filmoteca's screenings had attracted members to the museum, its leadership balked at underwriting the growing costs of film preservation activities.[77] After this largely amicable split—which left Salles Gomes free to pursue (elusive) government support—the Filmoteca was renamed the Cinemateca Brasileira. Shortly thereafter, in January 1957, the archive suffered a nitrate fire, sparking a period of intense crisis.

That same year, film enthusiast and aspiring diplomat Ruy Pereira da Silva attended FIAF's annual conference in his capacity as head of the Departamento de Cinema do Museu de Arte Moderna do Rio de Janeiro (MAM-Rio). Like its counterpart in São Paulo, the museum was established with the support of the Rockefeller Foundation in 1948, and it played a key role in nurturing film preservation in Brazil, despite the tensions that emerged between the two archives over access to prints and institutional influence.[78] Under the leadership of Pereira da Silva, who (like Salles Gomes) had encountered Langlois and the Cinémathèque française while studying in Paris, MAM-Rio began offering screenings to museum members in 1955. That same year, MAM-Rio hosted the festival 10 Anos de Filmes sobre Arte (A Decade of Films on Art) originally organized by the Filmoteca do MAM-SP for the São Paulo Biennial.[79] After the 1957 FIAF conference in Antibes, where Pereira da Silva represented MAM-Rio in the capacity of an observer, he embarked on a tour of European and North American archives. Pereira da Silva chronicled his travels in the museum's programming bulletin, suggesting the importance of transatlantic institutional connections for legitimating MAM-Rio's film department.[80] In 1959 the museum organized major retrospectives of French and Italian cinema with the aid of the national film promotion agencies Unifrance and Unitalia; the Cinémathèque française provided three-quarters of the prints screened in the former event.[81] Also in 1959, MAM-Rio was admitted to FIAF as a provisional member and began collecting films, including prints discarded by França Filmes, a branch of the state-backed distributor COFRAM.[82]

The Cinemateca Brasileira and Cinemateca do MAM-Rio's grounding in the comparatively well-funded art world lent them an institutional stability and legitimacy that contrasts sharply with the more precarious archives that emerged from film societies. However, the character of these private archives ranged from comparatively isolated and underresourced institutions like the Cinemateca Colombiana to entities like the Cinemateca Argentina and Cinemateca Uruguaya, which profited from their links to robust local and national networks of film societies.

Perhaps the most embattled archive to emerge from the cineclub movement is the little-known prerevolutionary Cinemateca de Cuba. As Emmanuel Vincenot observes, Cuban film histories tend to gloss over the archive's existence and reduce its precursor, the Cine Club de la Habana, to a mere offshoot of the Sociedad Cultural Nuestro Tiempo (Our Times Cultural Society). Because of Nuestro Tiempo's close links to the Partido Social Popular, Cuba's communist party, this rhetorical move allows the Cinemateca de Cuba and the Cine Club de la Habana to be neatly reinscribed into a socialist history of Cuban film culture that culminated in the creation of ICAIC shortly after the Revolution. In fact, the Cine Club and Cinemateca were associated with Nuestro Tiempo only briefly, during 1951 and early 1952, when co-founder Germán Puig cut ties with the group upon his return to Cuba from France, displeased with its politicization of the club's activities.[83]

As Vincenot and Irene Rozsa have shown, the histories of the Cine Club de la Habana and its associated archive exemplify struggles for control over Cuba's cultural field marked by generational conflict and growing politicization. In hopes of creating a film society, Puig approached film educator and leftist critic José Manuel Valdés-Rodríguez after taking his pioneering film studies course at the Universidad de la Habana's extension school. Yet Puig was brusquely rebuffed, perhaps because Valdés-Rodríguez was concerned about competition with the Cine Arte screening series attached to his course. Puig's efforts regained momentum when he met Langlois in 1951 after traveling to Paris in an unsuccessful bid to enroll in IDHEC. After consulting with the French curator, Puig enlisted Tomás Gutiérrez Alea to establish an archive so that the film society could receive prints from the Cinémathèque française. Langlois privately debated whether to choose a "semi-official but very disagreeable figure" (Valdés-Rodríguez) or "young lovers of cinema who seem to be the future" (Puig and his associates) as his point of contact in Havana, ultimately opting for the latter.[84] Yet Valdés-Rodríguez diverted the first batch of films at customs, appropriating them for use in his own screenings.[85]

After Puig's return to the island, Valdés-Rodríguez continued to sabotage the Cinemateca's efforts. When the archive resumed its screenings at the Instituto Nacional de la Cultura (National Institute of Culture) in 1955 with programs furnished by MoMA, Valdés-Rodríguez used his influence in the Agrupación de Repórteres Teatrales y Cinematográficos (Association of Theater and Film Critics) to block press coverage of the sessions.⁸⁶ Aggravating matters, a faction within the Cinemateca's leadership—including writer Guillermo Cabrera Infante—interrupted its screenings in early 1956 in protest against the dictatorship of Fulgencio Batista, leading the Cinemateca to lose the support of the institute and thus its auditorium and library space.⁸⁷ Although screenings continued at the Lyceum Lawn Tennis Club, thanks to Valdés-Rodríguez and Cabrera Infante's efforts to sabotage them, the Cinemateca's activities ceased shortly thereafter.⁸⁸

While it did not suffer the direct attacks experienced by the prerevolutionary Cinemateca de Cuba, the history of the Cinemateca Colombiana similarly demonstrates the profound challenges faced by Latin American archives that failed to find strong institutional or financial backing. Once again, the archive was founded "at the behest of the director of the Cinemathèque française Henri Langlois."⁸⁹ Around the time of Puig's sojourn in Paris, Luis Vicens of the Cine Club de Colombia met with Langlois in hopes of obtaining programming, as noted in the previous chapter. However, no mention is made of the Cinemateca Colombiana (or Filmoteca Colombiana, as it was originally called) in the cineclub's programs until 1955, when it screened the archive's first acquisition, Dimitri Kirsanoff's early sound film *Rapt* (*The Kidnapping*, 1934, France/Switzerland).⁹⁰ The same year, future Nobel Prize–winning novelist Gabriel García Márquez, who was working in Europe as a journalist, represented the Cinemateca Colombiana at the FIAF conference in Warsaw. He secured the archive's admission as a provisional FIAF member, although it possessed only three films at the time.⁹¹ In 1957 the Cinemateca Colombiana reported acquiring another four titles but still fell far short of the twenty to twenty-five prints it estimated to be necessary for its plans to "stimulate the formation of Cine-Clubs (especially in universities) and constitute a lending circuit" for these film societies.⁹² Furthermore, its efforts to recover early Colombian productions, launched the same year, did not immediately bear fruit, and the minimal levels of film production in Colombia hampered exchanges with European archives.⁹³ In 1966, over a decade after its founding, the Cinemateca Colombiana listed only fifteen titles, including just two Colombian films, among its holdings.⁹⁴ Over a third of its holdings were Soviet silents, some of which originated at the USSR's Gosfilmofond and Czechoslovakia's Národní filmový archiv (National Film Archive).⁹⁵ The Cinemateca Colombiana is perhaps the clearest example of an institution that was essentially an archive in name only but nevertheless sought to participate in transnational exchanges.

Elsewhere in the Andean region, ephemeral archives emerged from both cineclubs and universities. In 1953 Gaston Diehl, a French cultural attaché and co-organizer of the Cine-Club Venezuela, founded the Cinemateca Venezolana. The archive screened films, including documentaries on visual art—a keen interest of Diehl's—in the Universidad Central's Instituto de Arte.[96] Five years later, Diehl joined forces with Amy Courvoisier (the other co-founder of the Cine-Club Venezuela) and distributor Georges Korda in a fresh attempt to establish an archive.[97] Yet no stable archive existed in the country until the establishment of the Cinemateca Nacional de Venezuela in 1966. In Peru, the founders of the Cine Club de Lima, including the Office catholique international du cinéma's international secretary Andrzej Ruszkowski, established the Cineteca del Perú in 1953 to support their activities.[98] The Cineteca received close to sixty documentary films from the French embassy and acquired early Peruvian sound features like *El gallo de mi galpón* (The rooster on my ranch, Sigifredo Salas, 1938) and *Las palomillas del Rímac* (The butterflies of Rímac, Sigifredo Salas, 1938) but lost momentum shortly thereafter.[99] Over a decade later, in his capacity as a law professor at the Pontificia Universidad Católica del Perú, Ruszkowski helped establish the Cinemateca Universitaria del Perú together with film society organizer Miguel Reynel. Hosted by a consortium of Lima-area universities, the Cinemateca furnished prints to university classrooms, cineclubs, and the Catholic Centro de Orientación Cinematográfica.[100] Suggesting Langlois's pervasive influence on the region's archives, the Cinemateca Universitaria launched its activities with a French cinema retrospective provided by the Cinémathèque française.[101] An inventory of the now-defunct archive lists only a handful of Peruvian titles—including the Quechua-language drama *Kukuli* (Luis Figueroa, Eulogio Nishiyama, and César Villanueva, 1961) and the Argentine-Peruvian co-production *Intimidad de los parques* (Intimacy of parks, Miguel Antín, 1965)—among its approximately 170 films, with Soviet, Scandinavian, and French titles predominating.[102]

By contrast with short-lived and precarious archives in Andean countries, where the commercial exhibition sector and non-commercial cultural infrastructure were comparatively less robust, in the Río de la Plata region private cinémathèques were relatively stable entities backed by national film society networks. Roland, the main organizer of the Gente de Cine film society, met Langlois during a 1949 trip to Europe to attend the Cannes Film Festival and the FICC conference in Venice. Langlois encouraged Roland to create the Cinemateca Argentina and provided him with prints, which together with the cache of films amassed by León Klimovsky while running the Cine Arte repertory theater, formed the core of its collection.[103] Beginning in 1954, an agreement between the Cinemateca Argentina and the recently created Federación Argentina de Cineclubes granted member film societies preferential access to five film programs annually in exchange for a flat fee.[104] The transnational networks that facilitated the Cinemateca Argentina's access to archival prints thus became an important source of financial support. Yet cooperation between the archive and the federation stalled in 1957. According to Roland, poor behavior by clubs (damage to films, late returns, failures to pay rental fees) soured the relationship, along with his refusal to loan out one-of-a-kind or damaged prints.[105] The conflict was not resolved until 1961 with the intervention of longtime FIAF president Jerzy Toeplitz.[106] This incident suggests that FIAF not only regulated the circulation of archival copies but also mediated conflicts between institutions of film culture in order to maintain international standards for the circulation and preservation of vintage prints.

A similar symbiosis—but also similar frictions—between the cineclub and archiving movements existed in Uruguay. The country's film enthusiasts first learned of the advantages of FIAF membership through a film society conference held in Argentina.[107] In 1952 Cine Universitario established the Cinemateca Uruguaya; not to be outdone, the rival Cine Club del Uruguay created the Cineteca del Cine Independiente soon after. Representatives of both archives attended the 1952 FIAF conference and gained admission as members, sparking a conflict that unfolded in the pages of the Cine Club del Uruguay's magazine *Cine Club*.[108] The tension was resolved only December 1953, when, as noted previously, the film societies decided to merge the two entities. The Cinemateca Uruguaya remained closely linked to both clubs, sourcing much of its budget from a surcharge on their membership fees.[109] The archive also collaborated closely with the national film society federation (also established in December 1953) comprising fourteen cineclubs and two educational institutions.[110] In 1954 the Cinemateca Uruguaya provided roughly 20 percent of federated clubs' programming.[111] Yet the following year the archive had few films on hand—70 percent of its prints were on loan abroad—leading to reduced income from rentals.[112] This move signals how the dilemma of access versus preservation was intensified for archives that had emerged from—and were largely funded by—the film society movement.

FIGURE 7. Participants in the 1956 meeting of FIAF's Latin American Section. Back row, left to right: Julio Arteaga, Antonio Grompone, Paulo Emílio Salles Gomes, Eugenio Hintz, Francisco Luiz de Almeida Salles, Roland. Front row: Lida Barletta de Fustiñana. *Source*: Fundo Paulo Emílio Salles Gomes, Cinemateca Brasileira. Courtesy of Lúcia Telles.

In the 1960s and beyond, Latin American cinémathèques increasingly took root within universities, as Martínez Carril points out. Emerging in tandem with the expansion of campus film societies and pedagogical uses of cinema, these archives took advantage of educational institutions' financial resources and infrastructure. University cinémathèques in Latin America invested in film as art (rather than pedagogical tool first and foremost) trace their roots at least to 1949, when Valdés-Rodríguez began collecting films for use in his course El cine: Arte e industria de nuestro tiempo and the associated Cine Arte screening series at the Universidad de la Habana. Thanks to acquisitions funded by these public screenings, the collection contained over 150 films by 1957 and nearly 250 in 1966.[113] Latin America's largest and most enduring university film archive, the Filmoteca UNAM, was founded just over a decade later in 1960 as an initiative of the Sección de Actividades Cinematográficas (Section of Cinematic Activities), a division of the university's Coordinación de Difusión Cultural (Cultural Dissemination Department).[114] Like Valdés-Rodríguez's Filmoteca Universitaria, the Filmoteca UNAM funded its acquisitions through public screenings.[115] Suggesting the Filmoteca's investment in an alternative Mexican cinema, its first two acquisitions were *Raíces* (*Roots*, Benito Alazraki, 1955) and the documentary *Torero* (*Bullfighter*, Carlos Velo, 1955).[116] The films were a gift from their producer Manuel Barbachano Ponce, whose work embodied a countercurrent to Mexico's commercial industry. *Raíces* is especially notable for its open criticism of the social marginalization of Mexico's Indigenous peoples, who were romanticized and played by light-skinned actors in popular films like Emilio Fernández's *María Candelaria* (1943).[117] After the creation of a film school at UNAM in 1963, the Centro Universitario de Estudios Cinematográficos (see chapter 4), the Filmoteca began collecting 16mm prints for classroom use.[118] Although the Filmoteca participated in UCAL and was in touch with the FIAF throughout the 1960s, it joined the organization only in the following decade.[119]

The year 1960 also saw the founding of the Universidad de Chile's Cineteca Universitaria, an initiative of the Cine Club Universitario. As early as 1956, the club's organizers had sought to recover Chilean films through a campaign announced in the pages of their magazine *Séptimo Arte*.[120] The university's Centro de Cine Experimental, a laboratory for documentary production (see chapter 4), later invited Langlois to Santiago to explore future collaborations.[121] The Cineteca Universitaria became a provisional member of FIAF in 1961 but lacked an operating budget until the following year.[122] Although the archive safeguarded works by members of the Centro de Cine Experimental, its limited budget—compounded by unfavorable foreign exchange rates—hampered the acquisition of the foreign titles often used in its weekly screenings.[123] As Chilean politics swung toward the left, culminating in the election of socialist president Salvador Allende, the Cineteca's activities grew increasingly politicized. In a 1972 report to UCAL, the archive's director Pedro Chaskel reflected, "The aspiration to disseminate a strictly cinematic culture, conventional to some degree and governed by foreign models, gives way to the conscious integration of cinema in the battle to reunite with our own cultural identity, for decolonization. . . . Thus, the Cineteca concentrates its human and economic resources in the dissemination of national and Latin American cinema oriented fundamentally towards a popular audience, workers, peasants, and students." In these screenings held in "union halls, [squatters'] encampments, towns, neighborhood associations, schools, rural villages," Latin American documentaries comprised 85 percent of the films viewed and discussed.[124] The Cineteca's activities in the early 1970s signal a fundamental shift away from a cosmopolitan canon of art cinema consumed largely by middle-class intellectuals to a national-popular view of cinema (promoted, in many cases, by these same intellectuals) as a means of generating political consciousness.

Not surprisingly, the standard-bearer for the growing politicization of film preservation was the postrevolutionary Cinemateca de Cuba founded in 1960. Operating under the umbrella of ICAIC, the archive pursued an active role in the political and aesthetic re-education of audiences, though without rejecting the values of European art cinema altogether. As Rozsa argues, ICAIC effectively brought prerevolutionary institutions of film culture under its control, appropriating non-commercial circuits for overtly ideological ends.[125] In May 1961 the institute became the island's sole film distributor by nationalizing commercial agencies and confiscating their prints, thus determining the films available to an increasingly centralized and tightly controlled group of cineclubs.[126] ICAIC's success in both monopolizing and expanding film culture is suggested by the rapid growth of the Cinemateca's membership, which swelled to 11,500 by 1963—although only about a sixth of members regularly attended screenings—to the extent of interfering with its preservation activities. A report to FIAF noted, "The Cinemateca, needing to focus on the growing number of new registrations—which often exceed a hundred a day—has seen itself obliged to dedicate all its energies to this, neglecting its other responsibilities. As a result, for some months, the work of cataloging and inspecting films, its condition and laboratory reports, etc. has been practically paralyzed."[127]

Although many of its Latin American counterparts also lacked the funds, staff, and infrastructure to effectively carry out these activities, the Cinemateca's choice to prioritize exhibition suggests how it sought to instrumentalize alternative film programming for political ends. In a 1961 article in ICAIC's magazine *Cine Cubano*, the archive's director Héctor García Mesa gave concerns about cinema's influence on the masses an anti-imperialist twist. García Mesa wrote, "Cinema is perhaps the most effective method of dissemination known to man. . . . On the film screen things happen that affect the spectator's sensibility, their emotions and intelligence, very directly. . . . If we undertake a rigorous examination of those films that have contributed to generalizing the idea that cinema should serve only 'to entertain,' upon observing the situations proposed in them we soon discover, in the first place, that all elements of sense have been deliberately eliminated from them, and later how the reality of the facts and situations presented has been distorted."[128] He attributed this distortion to capitalist propaganda. Decrying how "constant American influence corrupted the taste" of the Cuban public, the curator contended that repertory programming could direct viewers' attention toward the "pure historic, artistic or technical values of a film," qualities that were unappreciated in a commercial exhibition environment premised on the pursuit of "the new in cinema, the sensational."[129] García Mesa's tendentious statements evoke notions of audience susceptibility and aesthetic merit familiar from the discourse of the film society movement, inflecting them with anti-colonial politics.

Accordingly, the Cinemateca de Cuba's programming quickly shifted away from US cinema—with the imposition of the US embargo in 1961, new releases became unavailable and Hollywood films already in the country were usually deemed too politically suspect to be shown—and toward European productions. Films from the Eastern bloc flowed into Cuba in response to the resulting undersupply of prints, reaching 92 percent of releases in 1963.[130] The archive's programming, however, combined film "classics" with recent European art cinema and a much smaller number of titles from socialist countries. Its inaugural season included screenings of Sergei Eisenstein's *Battleship Potemkin*, Chaplin's *The Gold Rush* and *Modern Times* (1936, United States), Luis Buñuel's *Los olvidados*, Cannes Grand Prix winner *Fröken Julie*, and Alain Resnais's *Hiroshima mon amour* (1959, France/Japan).[131] The Cinemateca de Cuba took the rubrics of national cinema and the auteur as organizing principles, offering series on Soviet montage and German expressionism and dedicating retrospectives to Luis Buñuel, Alfred Hitchcock, Carl Theodor Dreyer, Julien Duvivier, Alberto Cavalcanti, Andrzej Wajda, Ingmar Bergman, and Michelangelo Antonioni.[132] Beyond supplying films for the Cinemateca de Cuba's fifteen-hundred-seat auditorium and a national network of cineclubs, ICAIC famously created a fleet of mobile cinema units (trucks equipped with 16mm projectors) deployed to rural areas.[133] Offering free screenings of "scientific, artistic and cultural films in general, and in particular those that refer to the history, transformation, and social development of Cuba," the mobile cinema units reportedly reached over 42,500,000 spectators (including repeat viewers) between 1962, their first year of operation, and 1970.[134]

Despite the cosmopolitan character of its programming, the Cinemateca de Cuba moved swiftly to preserve ICAIC productions and sought out films from earlier periods, though prerevolutionary commercial film was often devalued by critics and scholars. As revolutionary Cuban cinema made a splash on the international festival circuit, recent productions became valuable currency in exchanges with FIAF member archives. The Cinemateca furnished Cuban films to archives in the

USSR, East Germany, and Czechoslovakia, which García Mesa visited in person in 1961. In return the archive received prints of Soviet films from the 1920s, 1930s, and 1940s.[135] While this close collaboration with Soviet bloc archives is not surprising in the Cuban case, as we have seen, archives behind the Iron Curtain were quick to offer prints to other cinémathèques in the region, sending works of silent-era Soviet montage to the Cinemateca Colombiana and 1930s dramas to Chile's Cineteca Universitaria.[136] By 1963 the Cinemateca de Cuba had amassed approximately 780 titles—some of them seized from commercial distributors after the revolution—and restored and duplicated 117 films.[137]

Even in the absence of socialist regimes, state-sponsored film archives had begun to adopt distinctly radical positions by the mid-1960s. In 1966 Paris-trained filmmaker Margot Benacerraf founded the Cinemateca Nacional de Venezuela within the newly created Instituto Nacional de Cultura y Bellas Artes.[138] The Cinemateca's first retrospective was dedicated to Brazilian Cinema Novo, a filmmaking movement that was previously unknown in Venezuela. Benacerraf told *Cine Cubano* in 1968, "for me it was very important that we had contact with these authentically Latin American works, full of force and denunciation. My aim was not to create a classical, orthodox cinémathèque."[139] These comments suggest how the Cinemateca Nacional defined itself against an earlier wave of archives that had disseminated a Eurocentric canon of film culture.

The programming and preservation efforts of the Cinemateca de Cuba and the Cinemateca Nacional de Venezuela constitute early examples of the politicization of film archiving in Latin America. Yet the Cinemateca de Cuba's programming in the early 1960s was still deeply indebted to a Eurocentric canon of art cinema. While the archive became an influential model for socially engaged preservation practices across the region, the forms of regional cooperation it helped facilitate—namely UCAL—were rooted in earlier institutional networks mediated by FIAF. The shift from FIAF's Latin American Pool to UCAL registers both the deep split in the film archiving movement created by Langlois's rupture with FIAF and the profound contradictions entailed in expanding the film preservation movement on a global scale.

THE LIMITS OF TRANSATLANTIC COOPERATION: FROM FIAF'S LATIN AMERICAN POOL TO UCAL

Alongside Langlois's strategic efforts to cultivate film archives in Latin America and beyond, FIAF as a whole sought to expand its international sphere of influence in the late 1940s and early 1950s. During this period, the organization pursued global initiatives that exceeded the notion of archives as guardians of national film heritage. As noted previously, Corrêa Jr. has shown that FIAF's success in helping to forge a global, non-commercial market for "classic" films created new challenges. Cinémathèques felt pressure to supply prints to a growing number of cineclubs and fellow archives while maintaining tight control over this material to head off attacks from the theatrical exhibition sector and maintain their own position as cultural arbiters.[140]

To address these issues, FIAF explored global and regional initiatives with mixed success. In its 1952 congress in Amsterdam, the organization revived Iris Barry's proposal for a global circulation pool, resolving that "each cinémathèque commits itself to entrust to FIAF's Executive Bureau the most representative films of its National Cinema to be circulated independently of bilateral exchanges, through FIAF member countries and *those countries where FIAF's steering committee deems it desirable to encourage or create a national film archive with an eye to its eventual admission to FIAF*" (emphasis added).[141] The resolution makes explicit the aim of propagating the film preservation movement globally through the increased circulation of film materials—precisely the logic that drove Langlois's institution-building efforts in Latin America. In theory, the circulation pool would have lessened the power of archives in countries with commercially or aesthetically hegemonic film industries (including France) to furnish or withhold prints. However, the pool was slated to be housed in Paris, and would have thus reinforced the city's status as a center for non-commercial film exchanges.[142]

As a supplement to the international circulation pool and existing archive-to-archive exchanges, the attendees resolved to create four subdivisions of FIAF that mapped out the organization's geographic extent in the period—Eastern Europe, Western Europe, North America, and South America—which would each be charged with coordinating the duplication of film materials on a regional level.[143] When introducing the resolutions at the 1952 congress, Langlois stressed how they could mitigate the fundamentally disadvantaged position of young, poorly funded cinémathèques within a system based on bilateral exchanges between institutions, considering that newly created archives typically had few prints to offer their counterparts.[144] His comments at the 1957 FIAF congress in Antibes, France, further fleshed out his position on the role of film circulation in assuring the future of the archiving movement. Langlois stated, "The goal of the pool is to help emerging archives obtain programming. It is absolutely certain that if, for example, M. Vicens in Colombia, or M. Roland in Argentina, or tomorrow someone in Karachi in India can obtain programming, the archive movement will gain momentum."[145] Langlois would have benefited from a lesson in Asian geography and history; Karachi had been located in Pakistan since Partition in 1947, and his confusion suggests he was ill-equipped to understand the circumstances and needs of emerging Global South archives. Further signaling Latin America's imagined role as a proving ground for the film preservation's global expansion, minutes from FIAF's 1954 congress in Lausanne, where the Latin American Pool was formally created, affirm that "upon the gradual creation of cinémathèques in Asia and Africa, the founding members of FIAF should take the initiative to constitute local bureaus and regional meetings on the South American model."[146] This never came to pass during the Latin American Pool's existence, likely because it failed to deliver the desired results and existing archive-to-archive exchanges presumably satisfied the needs of most North Atlantic cinémathèques.

Langlois and FIAF also saw Latin America as pivotal in interinstitutional struggles to control the international circulation of archival prints, in part by limiting the activities of an expanding network of cineclubs that collected, circulated, and screened films in a largely unregulated manner, threatening the broader ecosystem of non-commercial film distribution by arousing the ire of distributors and rightsholders. As noted in chapter 1, Latin American film enthusiasts were involved from an early stage in FICC, which gave cineclubs leverage in their negotiations with FIAF surrounding access to film materials by uniting film society federations.[147] Salles Gomes played a pivotal role in negotiating the agreement between FICC and FIAF in 1949, though not without arousing Langlois's ire at miscommunications that arose in the process.[148] Despite the cordial tone of extant meeting notes and resolutions, Sadoul described the negotiations as "a fratricidal struggle between our two organizations for the domination of one over the other" in the control of film circulation.[149] Yet once the agreement was reached, FICC promised to be a useful tool for ensuring this control, although its influence ultimately proved limited through the late 1950s.[150] Again signaling the importance of Latin America to FIAF's plans, Langlois urged the region's film enthusiasts to affiliate themselves with FICC as well as FIAF to ensure the viability of the FICC-FIAF agreement.[151]

Becoming a cornerstone, along with the FICC-FIAF pact, of FIAF's incipient global policy, the Latin American Pool took shape during

Langlois's 1954 trip to Montevideo and São Paulo, where he attended the Festival Internacional de Cinema discussed in the next chapter. Officially launched in 1955 during the Punta del Este film festival, the Pool was housed at the Cinemateca Uruguaya. Its members developed plans to inventory and compare their holdings, allowing for an efficient division of labor in the preservation of specific titles, and to pool funds to strike new prints that could be furnished to growing national networks of film societies. At the 1955 meeting, the Cinemateca Brasileira agreed to provide twenty-five programs to the Cinemateca Uruguaya and Cinemateca Argentina.[152] However, the devastating 1957 nitrate fire at the Cinemateca Brasileira put a halt to these plans, and they were never meaningfully revived before the Pool's activities ground to a halt in the early 1960s after the irruption of the FIAF crisis. Eugenio Hintz of the Cinemateca Uruguaya, who served as the Pool's secretary, lamented in 1962 that the initiative had failed to circulate a single program of films.[153]

The Pool also sought to facilitate exchanges of prints between members by lobbying for customs duties to be waived on prints destined for non-commercial exhibition.[154] Yet its members had little success establishing multilateral agreements that would allow the free flow of prints throughout the region. For instance, the Cinemateca Uruguaya negotiated free transport of outgoing films on the government-owned airline Pluna but was unable to convince Brazilian customs to waive import duties. Sending prints via the diplomatic pouch—a common means for obtaining duty-free entry through the suspension of standard import protocols, censorship regulations, and indeed national sovereignty itself—was problematic because they would arrive in Rio de Janeiro (Brazil's capital at the time), leaving the question of transport to the Cinemateca Brasileira in São Paulo unresolved.[155] Such obstacles suggest the juridical and logistical constraints on non-commercial film circulation in the period. Nonetheless, pre-existing exchanges of materials between film archives in the Southern Cone continued, while sending prints to more geographically distant members like the Cinemateca Colombiana remained challenging. Although Latin American archivists were eager to collaborate, the region's spatial vastness hampered any unified action. In a 1963 letter to Marion Michelle, Salles Gomes pessimistically reflected, "This idea of Latin America or of 'South-American Archives' [in English in original] . . . is a European abstraction or an act of wishful thinking on the part of Brazilians, Uruguayans, Argentines when random encounters create optimistic desires to act as a single community when the only reality is geography."[156]

In attempting against all odds to build a regional preservation movement, the Latin American Pool debated whether FIAF protocols could be effectively transferred to local contexts, given the precariousness of the region's archives and the institutional links connecting them. Roland of the Cinemateca Argentina noted at the Pool's 1955 meeting, "The Europeans . . . can give themselves the luxury of creating commissions, regulations, and structures, but we may not meet again for a long time."[157] The representatives of other archives insisted on developing structured guidelines modeled on FIAF's statutes. Yet Roland's comments suggest the frictions generated by transplanting North Atlantic institutional models, which often failed to account for the profound financial and administrative challenges faced by the region's archives.

In FIAF's global vision, the Latin American Pool would address structural issues that marginalized Latin American cinémathèques within the organization. Linguistic, geographic, and economic obstacles reinforced geopolitical disparities within the organization's structure. Reflecting the success of long-standing efforts to promote French-language instruction in Latin America and the Francophilia of many film archivists from the region, most communicated with FIAF in French, however imperfect their command of the language. For instance, Michelle, who was fluent in both of FIAF's official languages, English and French, congratulated Hernando Salcedo Silva on his progress in learning the latter in a 1963 letter.[158] Yet if she made any attempt to reciprocate by writing in Spanish—a language used by eight of FIAF's thirty-two members at the time—no trace seems to have survived in FIAF's files. By the turn of the twenty-first century, Spanish had become one of FIAF's three major working languages, but it was made an official language of the organization only in 2014.[159]

A more formidable barrier proved to be the travel expenses associated with attending the yearly FIAF conference, which were sizable for cash-strapped archives located at great distances from the conference sites (even if these cinémathèques' curators sometimes funded their own trips to Europe for festivals or vacations). The locations chosen for FIAF's annual meetings strategically navigated the East-West divide. Beginning with the conference held in Warsaw in 1955—at a moment when de-Stalinization was well underway in the USSR, but roughly a year before the Polish thaw—through the late 1960s, congress sites were evenly divided between communist and capitalist nations. Yet no postwar FIAF conference took place in the Americas until the 1969 meeting in New York; the first to be held in Latin America was the 1976 Mexico City congress. Langlois's initial plan for the Latin American Pool proposed that a meeting might be held in Brazil "every twenty years."[160] Hintz summed up the situation in 1962: "We all feel we have to keep more direct ties with FIAF, but for economical reasons we can't attend FIAF's congresses, with few exceptions. The only way out of this situation is to send a delegate for the whole of the Latin American Section (and again we have the famous economical difficulties) or else ask a member of FIAF to come here (which seems to be a little easier)."[161] But although FIAF leaders like Toeplitz and Langlois visited Latin America, often to attend film festivals, real reciprocity was never achieved.

As Hintz's comments suggest, efforts to minimize Latin American archives' travel costs by holding regional meetings of the Pool—these ultimately took place in 1955, 1956, 1959, and 1960—and then selecting a single representative to travel to the FIAF conference had limited success. Travel costs were reduced by planning the 1955 and 1959 meetings to coincide with film festivals held in Punta del Este and Mar del Plata, since attendees would have some of their expenses covered if participating as jury members or journalists. However, sending a Latin American delegate to the FIAF congress proved challenging, even when creative solutions were pursued, such as recruiting diplomats and intellectuals living in Europe. Tellingly, the delivery of the Latin American Pool's first report to FIAF, slated for the 1955 Warsaw congress, never happened. Salles Gomes volunteered to attend, but neither FIAF nor the Cinemateca Brasileira could cover his airfare, nor did the airlines or embassies he approached assist. Paris-based film enthusiast Martín Luis Lasala—who later played the starring role in Robert Bresson's *Pickpocket* (1959, France) under the name Martin LaSalle—was recruited by the Cinemateca Uruguaya to attend. While the archive covered his ticket, Lasala never arrived at the conference due to issues obtaining a last-minute flight to Poland—he reported that "the Polish embassy had blocked all flights for a week"—and miscommunications with the FIAF leadership.[162] The incident suggests how logistical challenges compounded financial ones.

Unfavorable currency exchange rates and banking difficulties also placed a disproportionate burden on Latin American cinémathèques, who were obliged to pay their FIAF dues in French and later Swiss francs. In some cases archivists' friends and associates living in Europe managed to pay on their behalf, but the impact of inflation on Latin American cinémathèques' meager budgets, especially during the early 1960s, compounded the issue.[163] In 1963 Salles Gomes observed, "Inflation is diminishing the value of the *cruzeiro* [Brazil's currency at the time] at an incredible rate, and thus the contribution to FIAF in foreign currency is more and more costly for us, since we receive a fixed payment in cruzeiros, [amounting to] a small fortune."[164] In Uruguay and Chile, devaluations caused the exchange rate of local to foreign currency to jump by a factor of two and one-half to three, greatly increasing the financial burden represented by FIAF dues.[165] FIAF again attempted to mitigate these problems via the Latin American Pool; beginning in 1957, members were permitted to pay half the sum directly to the Pool to fund regional activities, thereby avoiding the conversion to European currency.[166] In practice, these fees were rarely paid, and the Pool's office could operate only by siphoning off funds from the budget of the Cinemateca Uruguaya. Furthermore, the system generated significant confusion and even tensions. Cine Arte del SODRE, which enjoyed robust state support, insisted on paying the full amount of its dues directly to FIAF and rejected the Cinemateca Uruguaya's proposal that this payment cover the Cinemateca's share as well.[167] Overall, these accommodations failed to create parity between North Atlantic archives and their Latin American counterparts.

By 1960 persistent obstacles to intraregional cooperation—most notably a lack of funds for duplicating and transporting prints—had prevented the Pool's activities from gaining momentum.[168] The conflict that erupted between Langlois and FIAF in 1959 appears to have sealed the fate of the regional subsection, though its dissolution happened slowly. Latin American archives' close links with Langlois became a liability; they were often mistrusted despite expressing a neutral position in the conflict. As noted previously, Langlois's dramatic departure from FIAF unfolded in the aftermath of the 1959 nitrate fire at the Cinémathèque française. The revelation that Langlois had never legally registered FIAF with the French authorities further escalated the situation. Langlois blocked access to the FIAF office and its contents and rushed to register a false FIAF with Cinémathèque française staff as its officers, a legal action that would not be reversed until 1965.[169] Langlois also created a rival to FIAF, the Union mondiale des musées de cinema (World Union of Film Museums), although it existed only on paper for the most part.[170]

Since no representatives of Latin American archives had attended the 1959 conference in person, the Pool's members had little insight into what had transpired. Hintz noted in a February 1960 letter to Rudá de Andrade of the Cinemateca Brasileira, "The conflict appears to be serious, and we're fearful that Langlois has dragged us into a difficult situation with the proxies that we gave him."[171] At the Pool's 1960 conference, its members drafted a letter declaring their neutrality, pledging to maintain their affiliation both to FIAF and to the rival organization that Langlois had created, or failing that, to withdraw from both.[172] Yet given their subordinate place within FIAF, Latin American archives could exert little influence as mediators. Salles Gomes, who was present during Langlois's dramatic confrontation with Michelle, attempted to defuse the conflict in letters to Langlois and Toeplitz but was met with suspicion and alternately suspected of siding with Langlois and his rival Lindgren.[173] In a letter to his colleagues at the Cinemateca do MAM-Rio, Salles Gomes observed, "I have the impression that Brazil is more of a power in the UN than in FIAF, *c'est tout dire* [that says it all]. The situation of our underdeveloped, beggar cinémathèque constitutes a tremendous *handicap* [in English in original]."[174] Upon the founding of UCAL in 1965, the members petitioned Toeplitz to reconsider FIAF's blanket ban on collaboration with the Cinémathèque française but otherwise seem to have stopped short of direct confrontation with FIAF.[175]

Despite Latin American cinémathèques' avowed neutrality in the FIAF crisis, existing accounts suggest most left the organization out of loyalty to Langlois.[176] Yet there is no clear evidence of this in their correspondence with FIAF, although Langlois certainly may have pressured their leadership to disengage from the organization. He had the opportunity to do so during a 1960 trip to Argentina, where he attended the Mar del Plata film festival, and Uruguay.[177] Referencing Langlois's meetings during this trip—from which Cine Arte was excluded—Trelles complained to Toeplitz about the French curator's "peculiar policy of creating spheres of influence and treating problems related to Latin American film archives as if they were colonial possessions that he manages according to his desires and whims."[178] In a more balanced tone, Hintz acknowledged both Langlois's impact and the self-interested nature of his efforts in a 1962 letter to Michelle, stating "Let us say the truth: the only film labary [*sic*] who has been helping us a little was the Cinémathèque française. And now we know why: just to get our votes." As a result, Hintz noted, "the Latin American Section is suspected among other members of FIAF, to be a sort of 'Langloi's [*sic*] daughter', and looked upon with undeserved little sympathy. The only truth is that when Langlois asked our support during the crisis, we decided to join the legal forces which resulted to be a great mayority [*sic*]. We keep the same spirit up to now."[179]

Langlois boasted in 1960 that he still had some unshakeable allies in Latin America, including the Cinemateca do MAM-Rio and the precarious Cinemateca Venezolana organized by Courvoisier and Korda.[180] Yet FIAF correspondence suggests that it was non-payment of dues rather than outright withdrawals that led to the disappearance of most Latin American archives from the FIAF rolls. Though this might have been a calculated choice, FIAF files document persistent efforts to pay that were eventually abandoned. At the 1965 FIAF congress, the membership resolved that the Cinemateca Argentina, Cinemateca Brasileira, Cine Arte del SODRE, and the Cinemateca Venezolana would be deleted from the membership rolls for non-payment of dues, although a number of the archives petitioned to remain within the organization.[181] By the end of the 1960s, nearly all archives in the region had been expelled from FIAF or downgraded to the status of corresponding members (meaning they paid no dues but also lacked voting power). Only the state-supported Cinemateca de Cuba—ironically, one of Latin America's most politicized archives—remained a full FIAF member in good standing.[182] One exchange between Lindgren and Hintz—who assumed the leadership of Cine Arte in 1965, following Trelles's ouster from the archive in 1962—is particularly revealing.[183] In one of a series of stern letters, Lindgren wrote:

> We have tried for many years to gain your co-operation. We fully appreciate your financial difficulties, and we have resorted to various devices to try and meet them. . . . We have now reached the point where we feel that the attitude of our South American members is not really due to financial difficulties at all (with good will these can be overcome), but is quite simply the result of a lack of seriousness and a lack of interest. . . . Many of us therefore feel that the time has now come to accept the reality of this situation and to regard the South American film archives as deleted from membership and to liquidate all our memberships on your Continent.[184]

In response to a later rebuke from Lindgren, Hintz wrote, "I would like to avoid excuses in these circumstances, except to say that with a 135% rise in the cost of living . . . and a 101% devaluation of Uruguayan currency (both world records very probably) I feel sometimes happy when I find paper to write on."[185] Though his exasperation is understandable, Lindgren's position at the head of a well-funded state archive seemingly left him unable to grasp the challenges faced by his Latin American counterparts. Most egregious, from Hintz's perspective, was Lindgren's claim that South American archives had failed to collaborate with FIAF initiatives, despite what Hintz saw as a lack of reciprocity.

As FIAF was losing its Latin American members, UCAL was taking shape as an alternative venue for regional cooperation. At the 1965 Mar del Plata film festival, representatives of the region's cinémathèques gathered to form a new alliance with the encouragement of Langlois, who attended the festival along with Toeplitz, now his sworn adversary.[186]

An initial proposal for the creation of UCAL led by the Cinemateca Argentina and Argentina's Cinemateca Nacional dates to February of that year.[187] In addition to former members of the Latin American Pool—namely the Cinemateca Argentina, Cinemateca Brasileira, and Cinemateca Uruguaya—newer state-sponsored and university archives joined UCAL, including Chile's Cineteca Universitaria, Perú's Cinemateca Universitaria, and the future Filmoteca UNAM.[188]

UCAL pursued "a policy of integration and development of the Cinémathèques of Latin America" that included "broadening and coordinating their labors of organizing museums, research, conservation and dissemination of films and deepening their relationships and exchanges of information and materials."[189] Its charter lacks the overtly politicized rhetoric that would characterize UCAL in later years. Yet it highlighted Latin American archives' common challenges—including pervasive problems with funding, staffing, facilities, and collection-building—and utilized terms such as "development" and "solidarity" that evoked the "continental project" of NLAC.[190] Operating on the premise that the entire region suffered the negative effects of neo-colonial economic and cultural influence, NLAC sought to unite national filmmaking movements in the pursuit of social justice and economic development region-wide. UCAL was further solidified later that year at the Festival Internacional do Filme (International Film Festival) in Rio de Janeiro, where Langlois had organized a series of roundtables under the auspices of the Union mondiale des musées de cinema. Venezuela and Colombia's archives joined UCAL at this meeting, and the organization petitioned the Brazilian government for the long-sought exemption from customs duties for archival prints.[191]

In 1967 UCAL members gathered at the famous Primer Festival del Cine Nuevo Latinoamericano in Viña del Mar, a milestone for NLAC's consolidation, to approve the organization's statutes. Instructions given by Walther Dassori Barthet of the Cinemateca Uruguaya to Miguel Reynel of Perú's Cinemateca Universitaria in advance of this meeting suggest UCAL's complex relationship to the earlier, FIAF-led attempt to foster regional collaboration, a relationship marked by both adaptation and rejection. Dassori Barthet wrote, "I think that FIAF's statutes (which may have been modified by now) will only serve UCAL as a guide. UCAL must be different . . . for exchanges, ownership of prints, etc., there is something outlined there. . . . From a historical point of view, perhaps they will amuse you."[192] UCAL was viewed as a homegrown alternative and even a rebuke to FIAF, despite their common roots in Langlois's machinations. In the heated letter to Lindgren cited previously, Hintz wrote, "Believe me, if the U.C.A.L. (Union of Latin American Film Archives), to whom Cine Arte is the only organization in the continent *not* to belong"—likely due to Langlois's long-standing dislike of the archive—"is flourishing, something is wrong with FIAF."[193]

Despite hopes that UCAL would offer a solution to the constraints of working within FIAF, familiar challenges persisted. The idea of creating a regional circulation pool of "classic" films reemerged at Mar del Plata but proved difficult to concretize.[194] Financial difficulties and geographic distances continued to pose problems, and UCAL's activity was again concentrated in the Southern Cone.[195] Furthermore, lapses in contact between the members, which regularly extended up to two years, hampered print exchanges and the organization of UCAL conferences.[196] In November 1965 Manuel González Casanova, the director of UNAM's film archive, was obliged to cancel a planned UCAL meeting due to the lack of response from other archives.[197] The following year, in a letter to González Casanova, Dassori Barthet expressed his frustration over the lack of communication from the Cinemateca Argentina, which possessed a negative of *The General* (Buster Keaton and Clyde Bruckman, 1926, United States) that he needed in order to strike a print promised to the Cinemateca Brasileira. A postal workers' strike had interrupted the flow of letters, and long-distance telephone calls entailed long delays. Dassori Barthet observed, "These are misfortunes caused by the 'still shaky links of the UCAL' to which you so accurately allude."[198]

Despite UCAL's roots in dissatisfaction with FIAF, throughout the late 1960s and early 1970s its members debated a collective or individual return to the federation. In 1969 Hintz told Ledoux, who had replaced Langlois as secretary-general of FIAF in 1961, "An agreement through which all these organizations could join—or rejoin—FIAF, would be highly desirable," although only the Cinemateca Argentina had explicitly expressed interest in this possibility.[199] Yet Hintz also observed how UCAL had highlighted the drawbacks of FIAF's approach to Latin American archives. He noted that the region's cinémathèques had "found a 'modus vivendi' outside the FIAF, which looks very confortable [sic]. They don't pay any fees, invest all the money exclusively in films and although cut away from the rest of the world manage to carry [on] an exchange program. It's a limited horizon perhaps, but those who have belonged to the Federation feel that it does'nt [sic] make much difference with the previous status, as the Federation has never done too much for Latin America."[200] Suggesting that UCAL might step into the role of the defunct Latin American Pool as a representative for the region, Hintz reiterated long-standing structural problems: "Latin American film libraries have always felt too isolated from the rest. Congresses always take place in Europe and the members can hardly attend for strictly economic reasons. So they read the reports, see how active the movement is in Europe, how films are sen[t] from one country to another, and cannot but feel frustrated for an isolation which seems to have no solution. The ocean inbetween [sic] is too wide."[201] Reviving the idea of a regional circuit for archival prints, Hintz proposed that twenty or thirty programs of "much needed film classics" could be purchased and circulated throughout Latin America, allaying the concerns of European archives that were reluctant to send prints because of the long transport times involved.[202] While some Latin American archives retained ties with FIAF as observers or corresponding members, Hintz was unable to negotiate their return to the federation en masse, although UCAL's activities remained a topic of discussion at FIAF conferences in the period.[203] In 1973 Cuba, FIAF's only full-fledged Latin American member at the time, reiterated the problems of unfavorable exchange rates and geographic distance, suggesting a five-year exemption from dues for Latin American archives joining the federation and urging a FIAF representative to attend UCAL meetings, but these propositions appear not to have been adopted.[204]

If the divide between FIAF and UCAL ultimately proved impossible to bridge, by the early 1970s UCAL itself was increasingly split between its more conservative members and those who championed preservation practices that responded to the urgency of a historical moment marked by intensifying political polarization and violent repression. The utopian hopes for social justice and national liberation from their neo-colonial condition cherished by the region's left were met with the grim reality of right-wing military dictatorships backed by the US's Cold War–era policy of containment in Uruguay (1973–1985), Chile (1973–1990), and Argentina (1976–1983).[205] Brazil had been under a military dictatorship for nearly a decade at this point, although left-wing intellectuals maintained considerable hegemony prior to the Ato Institutional 5 (Institutional Act Number Five) of 1968, a decree that shuttered Brazil's legislature and allowed dissidents to be stripped of their political rights.[206] Under such circumstances, cinémathèques' mandate to preserve the past for future generations was judged insufficient; instead, they needed to intervene in the present. At its Mexico City conference in 1972, UCAL adopted the manifesto "Cultura nacional y descolonización cultural," which denounced the devastating impact of "economic colonization" and the "cultural colonization" that reinforced it, declaring that

> in Latin America, the cultural act par excellence is the liberation of our peoples, and all the cinematic activities on the continent should place themselves at its service. The first task of Latin American cinémathèques should be to promote, preserve, disseminate, and develop to the maximum of its possibilities, the cinema of their own countries and the Latin American [cinema] that authentically expresses our reality and the problems and tendencies of its transformation. . . . This does not imply neglecting the functions specific to all cinémathèques, such as preserving and disseminating international cinematic works with historical and/or artistic value. But it does oblige [us] to surpass the limitations of a traditional organization.[207]

The manifesto argued that cinémathèques had to transform themselves into a "new and total cultural structure that encompasses all aspects of present-day cinematic work."[208]

Founded in 1969, Uruguay's Cinemateca del Tercer Mundo was perhaps the UCAL member that best exemplified these ideals. Beyond collecting works of political cinema and screening them to an audience comprising largely workers and students, the organization offered hands-on training in filmmaking and made films of its own.[209] Its directors, Walter Achugar and Eduardo Terra, were arrested in 1972 along with five others, and though they were eventually freed, the archive's collection disappeared.[210] When informed of the arrests via a telegram sent by Pedro Chaskel of Chile's Cineteca Universitaria to the 1972 FIAF congress on behalf of UCAL, Ledoux insisted on consulting the Cinemateca Uruguaya and Cine Arte before moving to condemn the repression, since "neither the Cinemateca del Tercer Mundo, nor Pedro Chaskell are members of FIAF." The FIAF membership later resolved to send a telegram expressing concern about Achugar and Terra's arrest without waiting for word from other Uruguayan archives, but Ledoux's adherence to bureaucratic procedures suggests a failure to grasp the situation's potentially life-or-death stakes.[211]

Yet not all of UCAL's members embraced an openly politicized preservation practice, whether for ideological or pragmatic reasons. Cine Arte, a latecomer to UCAL's ranks, had refused to sign the manifesto adopted at the 1972 conference; at this time, Uruguay's government was already embroiled in the military repression of leftist guerrillas. The archive opted to withdraw from UCAL altogether after a 1974 conference in Caracas, citing the approval of "reports with ideological-political content that thus diverged from their specific purpose, meddling in the internal affairs of brother Latin American republics."[212] This complaint likely refers to a resolution condemning the 1973 coup d'état in Chile that ousted the government of Salvador Allende. As a state institution, Cine Arte presumably found it impossible to sign given that Uruguay was also under a right-wing military regime by that point; the Cinemateca Uruguaya and Cinemateca Argentina also declined to sign given the delicate political situation in both countries.[213] The split widened at the 1976 FIAF congress in Mexico City, where the Cinemateca Argentina and Cinemateca Uruguaya—both operating under dictatorships at the time—announced the founding of their own organization, the Regional de Cinematecas del Cono Sur.[214]

By Martínez Carril's account, philosophical differences between UCAL members—with the Cinemateca de Cuba and its allies championing the filmmaker's power to impose political consciousness on the spectator, and archives like the Cinemateca Uruguaya defending the audience's freedom of interpretation—contributed to the split.[215] In describing this first category, Martínez Carril appears to be alluding to the Cinemateca del Tercer Mundo, whose magazine had openly attacked existing institutions of film culture, including the Cinemateca Uruguaya, for their lack of political engagement.[216] As Germán Silveira, Isabel Wschebor Pellegrino, and Fabián Núñez point out, without adopting an openly militant stance, archives like the Cinemateca Uruguaya and Cinemateca do MAM-Rio nonetheless engaged in cultural resistance by convening oppositional publics at a time when freedom of assembly was limited; screening films that likely would have suffered censorship in commercial circuits; and supporting the production and preservation of political films.[217] While conflicts between members sapped whatever momentum UCAL had gained, the organization continued operating until its reorganization in 1985 as the Coordinadora Latinoamericana de Archivos de Imágenes en Movimiento, which is still active today.

UCAL's fate at once reflects major shifts in the Latin American film preservation movement in the late 1960s and early 1970s, most notably its growing politicization, and long-standing challenges that date back to the Latin American Pool, namely the structural barriers that hampered its functioning. Boldly asserting Latin American autonomy, UCAL made clear the tangible benefits of working outside FIAF's structure, namely more investment in film duplication and less in membership dues. Yet UCAL, like the Latin American Pool, ultimately traced its origins to Langlois's efforts to control the film archiving movement. UCAL built its foundations on the erudite film culture of previous decades even as it leveraged film archiving and programming in service of political aspirations.

CONCLUSION

Rather than pioneering a socially engaged preservation practice or a valorization of national film heritage in the face of cultural colonization, early Latin American film archives were profoundly shaped by the cosmopolitan cinephilia of the region's burgeoning film societies. Their goals converged with those of the European-dominated film preservation movement, whose leaders were eager to expand and demonstrate its global reach, but whose policies nonetheless reproduced structural inequalities. Archives that grew out of cineclubs tapped into transatlantic archival networks to access prints, ultimately advancing FIAF's efforts to regulate non-commercial film culture on a global scale. University film archives pursued similar links as they served both on-campus cultural activities and educational mandates. State-sponsored film archives alternately championed the values of erudite film culture and leveraged cinema for overtly ideological ends, most notably in the case of the Cinemateca de Cuba. While shaped by Euro-American canons of art cinema, the Cinemateca de Cuba steered Latin American archival practice—though not without controversy—toward greater politicization in the turbulent 1960s and 1970s.

In uniting these diverse institutions around common aims, the Latin American Pool and UCAL exemplify how film preservation in the region was shaped by national, regional, and global ambitions, from FIAF's attempts to regulate the dissemination of film heritage to UCAL's efforts to affirm national and regional identities in the face of "cultural colonization." Both initiatives faced systemic obstacles, including the institutional precarity of Latin American archives and the obstacles that geographic distance and national boundaries posed to the circulation of films. The Latin American Pool tried and failed to redress inherent imbalances within FIAF, even as its members largely maintained a cosmopolitan and depoliticized approach to film heritage. For its part, UCAL ultimately dissolved in the face of conflict about the political role of film culture. Despite, or perhaps because of, their failures, these organizations exemplify how Euro-American ideals and practices of film preservation were contested and transformed in the course of their globalization.

CHAPTER 3

Brokering Art Cinema

Latin America and the Festival Circuit

In a travel diary published in *Cahiers du Cinéma* in 1956, film critic and theorist André Bazin chronicled his trip to the coastal resort town of Punta del Este, Uruguay—a thirty-hour flight from Paris in a prop plane at the time—to attend a film festival.[1] Though Punta del Este had hosted international festivals in 1951, 1952, and 1955—becoming one of the first locales outside Europe to do so—the 1956 festival was its second to focus exclusively on French cinema (the first took place in 1953).[2] For Bazin, these two events attested to and reinforced France's soft power, indicating "the prestige of French culture in South America and in Uruguay in particular.... The manner in which our films are chosen and disseminated in Latin America is perhaps the most decisive factor in the maintenance or decline of our intellectual and moral position in these countries."[3] The 1953 and 1956 showcases of French film furthered the agenda of Unifrance, the government agency charged with promoting the French industry abroad, by acting as a ready-made venue for the French film weeks it organized across the globe. At the same time, the two events furthered local boosters' ambitions (albeit in a scaled-back form) to promote Punta del Este as a destination for tourism and real estate development.

Though local power brokers had initially pursued these goals through an international festival, an event of this scope proved difficult to sustain for both financial and geopolitical reasons. As Bazin describes, a major controversy had rocked Punta del Este in 1955:

The jury composed [entirely] of South American journalists refused, in a sweeping move of critical severity, to award the Grand Prize due to the mediocrity of the selections sent by the participating countries, they declared. This draconian judgment did not suit the authorities, nor the rest of the national delegations; there was quite a scandal. Without wanting to contradict the substance of my Latin American colleagues' position—all the more so as I have come to esteem them still more—I nevertheless wonder if their severity wasn't excessive and also due to an inferiority complex with respect to the great European festivals, where juries are not, in fact, totally indifferent to diplomatic considerations.[4]

Bazin's assessment of the 1955 Punta del Este incident highlights the structuring tensions of the postwar festival circuit, as well as the uneasy place of newly created Latin American events within it. He notes how festivals' declared goal of promoting cinema as art—embodied by juries' supposedly impartial selection of the highest-quality films—was inevitably tempered by the commercial and geopolitical factors that informed festival selections and prizes.[5] These were shaped by the need to flatter nations with economic or strategic importance to the host country, or simply to ensure the broadest possible international representation. Festivals were especially fraught during the polarized Cold War period, when they functioned as spaces of both tentative rapprochement and intense friction between the capitalist and communist blocs.

Providing opportunities to strengthen diplomatic and trade ties, festivals also offered reputational and material gains to their host cities (often tourist destinations), most notably an influx of visitors and press coverage. While styled as international showcases, they were calculated to present the host country's industry to its best advantage, as Loredana Latil demonstrates in the case of Cannes.[6] Conversely, festivals could benefit the industries of invited countries by raising their public profiles and facilitating commercial distribution of festival films. As Faye Bartram notes, they often made "the best candidates for exchange because much of the import/export paperwork had already been processed and approved, the necessary visas dispensed, and viewer and critical reaction gauged."[7] Furthermore, starting in the 1950s, festival selections were guaranteed commercial distribution despite any import quotas.[8] The festival circuit thus promised—but never quite delivered—a reciprocal exchange of films that would temporarily suspend stark imbalances in the global circulation of cultural goods and the soft power wielded by the countries involved.

The question of who profited from film festivals, which involved hefty state and private investment, was especially delicate considering the state of film production in Latin America during the 1950s and 1960s. Commercial cinema was largely nonexistent in Uruguay and Colombia, where a long-running film festival was founded in the Caribbean port city of Cartagena in 1960. When Argentina's first international festival debuted in the coastal city of Mar del Plata in 1954, that nation's once-robust industry was struggling. Production had yet to recover from the US refusal to furnish Argentina with raw film stock during World War II in retaliation for Argentina's decision to remain neutral for most of the conflict, despite protectionist policies enacted by Juan Domingo Perón's populist government. Argentina's *generación del 60* (generation of 1960), a cinematic "new wave" that portrayed disaffected middle-class youth and urban anomie, garnered critical acclaim at Mar del Plata but often faced hostility from industry players and government officials, hampering its circulation on the international festival circuit.

By contrast, Mexican cinema was thriving during and immediately after the war thanks to abundant allowances of film negative and technical cooperation and investment from the United States, though it faced its own challenges in the 1950s after this support was withdrawn and the US State Department and MPAA collaborated to head off protectionist measures implemented by the Mexican government.[9] Perhaps due to its industry's relative prosperity, Mexico did not host a film festival until 1958. Held in the popular resort town of Acapulco except for the first year, it was a noncompetitive event dedicated to showcasing the highlights of other festivals.[10] Even at their most prosperous, the major industries of Argentina, Brazil, and Mexico found greater success with popular audiences than with critics; their films were accorded the status of art cinema by European tastemakers only selectively and intermittently.

Given this discouraging outlook, I argue that Latin American film festivals of the 1950s and 1960s styled themselves as testaments to the elevated film taste of national audiences—that is, their embrace of an emerging international art cinema—even as they promised to further refine this taste. This emphasis on erudition was built into the very structure of Mar del Plata, which organized a summit of critics at each of its festivals between 1960 and 1965 (except in 1964, when the event was held in Buenos Aires). This chapter delves into the inequalities and contradictions of the postwar festival circuit by examining the reception of Latin American cinema at Cannes, where it was often dismissed as poor quality—to the point that festival organizers lobbied for titles to be pulled in order to preserve the event's artistic caliber—and the functioning of early Latin American festivals as a compensatory display of the host country's cinephilia. If (critically acclaimed) commercial filmmaking was not attainable locally, Punta del Este and Mar del Plata could nonetheless aspire to enter the prestigious ranks of competitive film festivals, whose centerpiece was a highly public act of aesthetic judgment. In this light, the 1955 Punta del Este jury's unusual refusal to compromise the integrity of their aesthetic evaluation, diplomatic fallout be damned, becomes more comprehensible. It suggests the disproportionate weight placed on film taste in the absence of a self-sustaining national industry.

By attributing this move to an "inferiority complex" rooted in Punta del Este's less-than-distinguished status, Bazin acknowledged the deeply hierarchical nature of the postwar festival circuit, despite its internationalist ideals. Beyond their inherent disadvantage as newcomers competing with established events, Latin American festivals faced infrastructural and logistical obstacles. Chief among these was their geographic distance from self-declared centers of film culture like Paris and Hollywood at a moment when the jetliner was just beginning to reshape commercial aviation, a shift that gained momentum in 1958 with the introduction of the Boeing 707.[11] When Cuban film critic and educator José Manuel Valdés-Rodríguez traveled from Havana to Mar del Plata for the first film festival held in the city (an event dedicated solely to Argentina's industry) in 1948, the round trip involved "65 hours in flight and 16 by bus and train, passing through ten countries."[12] While European festivals suffered their own logistical snags, the smooth functioning of transportation, electrical, and communications networks nevertheless attested to the modernity—or lack thereof—of Latin American festival sites in the eyes of guests.

Beyond such practical considerations, the festival pecking order was enforced by FIAPF, which defended and mediated between the interests of individual national industries. Founded in the 1930s and revived in 1948 with representatives from European industries, along with Mexico and Argentina, FIAPF regulated the number and type of festivals in order to safeguard the latters' role as arbiters of cultural prestige.[13] Beginning in the early 1950s, FIAPF began to accredit festivals, classifying them according to their national or international scope and competitive or noncompetitive character.[14] FIAPF exercised control through its member associations, barring them from participation in non-accredited festivals and thus limiting the supply of films available to any event not in compliance. Punta del Este first received FIAPF approval to hold a competitive international festival in 1955, making the jury's decision especially puzzling to foreign observers. As a *Variety* headline put it, "Uruguay

Festival, After Fight for Right to Give Prizes, Doesn't."[15] FIAPF also sought to preserve top festivals' impact by mandating that they alternate years, as was temporarily the case with Cannes and Venice among capitalist countries and Moscow and Karlovy Vary in the Eastern bloc.

Although socialist nations were not permitted to join FIAPF during the 1950s on the grounds that "only representatives of private, not state, business should belong," the organization nonetheless sought to balance the interest of industries on both sides of the Iron Curtain.[16] In 1956 FIAPF granted "A" (competitive, international) status to both Karlovy Vary and the Berlin film festival, which had been established on the initiative of US officials as a "western cultural showcase in the east."[17] Festivals' claim to internationalism, based on breadth of participation, required the inclusion of films from the Global South, which also became a source of East-West competition. US journalist Gideon Bachmann observed dismissively in 1963, "Festivals like Karlovy Vary and Berlin, who vie for first place in the number of countries represented, often accept trash because it comes from an obscure country. The amount of time I have wasted sitting through public-education features from Vietnam, Liberia, Korea, Hong Kong, Mali, Turkey, etc[.], etc[.], defies addition."[18] In 1962 a leaked report from the United States Information Agency cautioned that the representation of recently decolonized nations at the Moscow festival and the USSR's participation in festivals springing up in sub-Saharan Africa and the Arab world were bolstering Soviet soft power. *Variety* concluded in an article on the report, "Uncle Sam is an amateur in contrast to the all-out promotion of the reds in milking the film fairs."[19] In her recent book *World Socialist Cinema*, Masha Salazkina exhaustively charts the links between the Second and Third Worlds forged by festivals like Karlovy Vary—where nearly half of the participating countries hailed from the Global South by 1960—and in Tashkent beginning in 1968 (though Latin American cinema was not officially included in the festival until 1976).[20]

Within this competitive and politically charged atmosphere, the Punta del Este jury's decision staked a claim to aesthetic refinement—defiantly asserted, one imagines, in the face of international expectations to the contrary. At the same time, it signaled the perceived deficiencies of the festival's selection, which stemmed from its inability to land the most desirable productions due to the lack of an established reputation. The incident signals the double bind in which early Latin American festivals found themselves as they strove to insert themselves into the circuit from a subordinate position. By asserting their exacting standards, the jury lent legitimacy to the Punta del Este festival's role as a cultural arbiter. Yet their decision undermined the event's broader economic and political aims: raising Uruguay's profile abroad, promoting tourism, and encouraging real estate development.

Even as it evokes key dynamics of the postwar festival circuit, Bazin's take on the 1955 "scandal" at Punta del Este lacks important context. The jury's polemical decision was not a spontaneous act of rebellion, but rather rooted in pressures exerted by FIAPF that had already generated considerable frustration in Uruguay. During talks to accredit Punta del Este as an international, competitive event, FIAPF demanded that its top prize, to be renamed the Gran Premio Sud América, go to the film that "best corresponded to the taste of the South American audience."[21] FIAPF sought to limit competitive festivals in Latin America to one per year, envisioning that Punta del Este would alternate with Mar del Plata (which, after its 1954 debut, was not held again until 1959), with each festival awarding the regional prize in alternate years.[22] The scope of the award ignored local and national preferences by assuming the existence of a monolithic "South American" taste, as film critics in the left-leaning Uruguayan weekly *Marcha* observed with irritation. At the same time, the nature of the prize highlighted the tension between festivals' supposed devotion to cinematic art and their commercial motivations.[23] *Marcha*'s columnists lamented that the jury's "work will be not one of critical evaluation, but sociological prediction. They won't be able to vote for the film they consider best, but the one predicted to draw in the masses."[24] The 1955 incident thus illuminates both tensions inherent to the festival circuit and the unique challenges faced by early Latin American festivals.

Despite its somewhat condescending tone, Bazin's discussion of Punta del Este resonates with much local reporting on early Latin American festivals. Puff pieces in mainstream newspapers reveled in the glamor of visiting celebrities and quoted guests' flattering comments about the events and their host countries. But specialized film periodicals and skeptical general-interest magazines were quick to criticize their flaws, from chaos in the distribution of tickets and chronically late start times to inconvenient distances between venues and problems with telegraph and telephone communications needed to file stories. Implicit in these critiques is frustration with the festivals' failures to meet international standards, particularly when hefty government investment was involved. As a journalist observed with regard to the 1952 edition of Punta del Este, "We spent as if we were in Venice, but things weren't like in Venice."[25]

SONRISAS PREVIAS   Elías Ciurich (Comité), Hugo A. Rocha (Jurado), Jorge Suárez (C.), José Mª Podestá (J.), Jaime F. Botet (Jurado suplente), Rolando Fustiñana (J.), Paulo Emilio Salles Gomes (J.), Alberto Ugalde (C.), Francisco Luiz Almeida Salles (J.), Alfonso Delboy (J.), Carlos Ferreira (J.).

FALLO DEL JURADO

Reunido en Punta del Este, a 31 de enero de 1955, el Jurado designado por el Comité Organizador del III Festival Cinematográfico Internacional, considerando:

1) que no han sido presentadas por los países participantes películas de elevada calidad creadora, capaces de justificar la atribución de una recompensa de la importancia y el significado del Gran Premio Sud América, previsto por el inciso a) del Artículo 8º del Reglamento;

Considerando:

2) que el antedicho inciso, al preceptuar la correspondencia del premio con el gusto sudamericano, no tuvo la intención de excluir la exigencia de una calidad sobresaliente para las películas, por tratarse de una competición internacional;

Considerando:

3) que la misma situación se presenta para el caso de las películas de corto metraje, pues las mejores entre las inscriptas no alcanzan un nivel de méritos que justifique la atribución de un Gran Premio de Sud América para esa categoría, de acuerdo con el inciso c) del citado artículo;

Considerando:

4) que fueron presentadas en algunas selecciones nacionales películas de alta jerarquía técnica y artística, resuelve:

1º) Declarar por unanimidad desierto el Gran Premio Sud América 1955 para películas de largo metraje.

2º) Declarar por mayoría desierto el Gran Premio Sud América 1955 para películas de corto metraje.

3º) Conceder, de acuerdo con el inciso b) del Artículo 8º del Reglamento, los siguientes premios especiales:

Estados Unidos: *The Living Desert;* Francia: *Le Rouge et le Noir;* Inglaterra: *Hobson's Choice;* Méjico: *Robinson Crusoe;* Suecia: *En Lektion i Kärlek.*

El Jurado desea dejar expresa constancia de su pesar por no haber tenido a su disposición premios para distinguir algunos importantes valores parciales en otras películas presentadas. Asimismo, deplora el no poder hacer referencia a las películas exhibidas fuera de concurso y en los ciclos culturales, que tanto contribuyeron, unas y otras, a elevar el nivel artístico del Festival.

José María Podestá, Rolando Fustiñana, Francisco Luiz de Almeida Salles, Alfonso Delboy, Paulo Emilio Salles Gomes, Hugo Rocha, Carlos Ferreira.

FIGURE 8. Photo of members of the organizing committee and (all-male) jury of the 1955 Punta del Este festival and a collective statement on its refusal to award the Gran Premio Sud América. The statement was published in cineclub magazines in Argentina, Chile, and Uruguay. *Source: Film*, March 1955, 8. Courtesy of Cine Universitario. Scan courtesy of Stanford University Libraries.

Festival postmortems often prompted pessimistic reflections on the national character: *Marcha*, one of the Punta del Este festival's fiercest critics, cautioned after the first week of the 1955 event that it "already shows serious signs of being improvised, of its always clumsy (whether well- or ill-intentioned) efforts, of the typical *criollo* neglect and crackpot and scatterbrained ideas."[26] Similarly, a Buenos Aires newspaper described the 1963 Mar del Plata film festival as "a faithful reflection of our country today. There was disorder, confusion, a lot of frivolity, many words, a profound desire to succeed by the easiest method, and finally noise, just noise."[27]

If the press expressed skepticism about the value of these early Latin American festivals, scholars have followed suit; only a handful of studies exist, most on Mar del Plata.[28] Unlike the Primer Festival de Cine Nuevo Latinoamericano (First Festival of New Latin American Cinema) held in Viña del Mar, Chile in 1967 and the Primera Muestra de Cine Documental Latinoamericano (First Showcase of Latin American Documentary Cinema) organized in Mérida, Venezuela, the following year, these earlier, self-consciously European-style festivals fail to align with the narratives of regional solidarity and political resistance that mark the history of NLAC. More broadly, though important studies exist, non-European festival histories remain under-researched even as film festival scholarship has exploded over the past decade and a half.[29] Festivals' high public profile—bolstered by celebrity appearances—and their economic impact command a level of critical interest unmatched by other institutions of film culture. Festival screenings and prizes can lead to distribution deals and increased critical attention that boosts box office performance. Furthermore, through their associated film markets, major festivals also broker production financing and even fund films themselves through programs like the Rotterdam Film Festival's Hubert Bals Fund.[30] These functions, along with the work of festivals to develop individual film projects and careers through initiatives like Sundance Labs and Berlinale Talents, can have a profound impact on the fortunes of creatives and productions and shape broader industry trends.

These multifaceted activities are a logical outgrowth of festivals' role in gathering filmmakers, critics, and businesspeople in the heightened atmosphere of a time-limited event, as Janet Harbord stresses.[31] Most pertinently for the purposes of this study, festivals offered essential scaffolding for the administrative infrastructures of film-related institutions. As noted previously, Dudley Andrew describes the postwar period as a "federated phase" of film culture, in which supranational organizations mediated national interests in order to achieve global cooperation on cinematic questions.[32] Embodying a spirit of internationalism nonetheless reliant on the notion of distinctive national cinemas, film festivals functioned as gathering places that facilitated cross-border endeavors. Two key France-based international organizations took shape at Cannes: FICC was officially created at the festival in 1947, and the Première Rencontre Internationale des Écoles de Cinéma (First International Meeting of Film Schools) took place there in 1954, leading to the constitution of CILECT the following year.[33]

Early Latin American film festivals came to fulfill a similar role. Film school leaders from France, Poland, and Mexico gathered at Mar del Plata in 1966 to commemorate the founding of Argentina's national film school, an event to which I return briefly in the next chapter. Festivals also proved pivotal for the Latin American film preservation movement examined in chapter 2. FIAF's Latin American Pool first met during the 1955 Punta del Este festival, capitalizing on the fact that prominent critics and preservationists—Andrés José Rolando Fustiñana (Roland) from Argentina and Paulo Emílio Salles Gomes and Francisco Luiz de Almeida Salles from Brazil—were serving on the jury. In 1959 the Pool's meeting took place in Mar del Plata, taking advantage of the presence of its secretary, Eugenio Hintz of the Cinemateca Uruguaya, as a jury member. After the Pool lost momentum in the wake of the dramatic split between Henri Langlois and FIAF, Langlois proposed a new consortium of Latin American archives—which became UCAL—on his second visit to the Mar del Plata festival in 1965. Institution-building efforts thus built on film festivals' status as privileged sites of cultural exchange.

Drawing on festival archives and press accounts, this chapter explores the vibrant if unequal cinematic exchanges brokered by these events at the height of the Cold War.[34] I expand on existing accounts focused on East-West tensions to consider the circulation of films from the prolific (but aesthetically suspect, in European eyes) industries of the Global South.[35] The presence of Latin American cinema at Cannes—often deemed the preeminent postwar festival—advanced French cultural diplomacy but often conflicted with the event's role as an arbiter of art cinema. Conversely, Latin American festivals sought to establish new countercurrents of cultural exchange while affirming a local cinephilia rooted in consumption rather than production. My analysis focuses on Punta del Este and Mar del Plata, which explicitly modeled themselves on Cannes and its European rivals. Held in resort towns on opposite banks of the Río de la Plata, these events were respectively the earliest and the most sustained efforts to organize a competitive, international festival in Latin America in the 1950s and 1960s. (Ironically, the noncompetitive festival held in Cartagena proved to be much more enduring, running largely uninterrupted up to the present.) I touch more briefly on alternative models of the film festival developed in the region, including the Festival de Cine Documental y Experimental first organized by Uruguay's state broadcaster SODRE in 1954, and the Festival Internacional de Cinema de São Paulo, a one-off, noncompetitive event held the same year that privileged a retrospective look at film history. Ultimately, these events shared with Punta del Este and Mar del Plata both a performative internationalism—one that politely overlooked global disparities and divides—and a conviction that festivals could be "a means of cultivating the masses [*vehículo culturalizador de las masas*]" even as they demonstrated the existence of sophisticated national film cultures.[36]

BETWEEN INTERNATIONALISM AND ART CINEMA: LATIN AMERICAN FILM AT CANNES

The Cannes international film festival was born not from a spirit of global harmony, but rather from a confrontation between the cultural projects of fascism and democracy.[37] The inaugural Cannes festival of 1939—canceled on the eve of its opening after Hitler invaded Poland—originated as a nationalistic response to the Mostra Internazionale d'Arte Cinematografica (International Showcase of Cinematic Art) held at the Venice Biennale beginning in 1932.[38] In the postwar period, Cannes would become the site of a lower-stakes confrontation with an uneasy ally: the United States. By cultivating a cosmopolitanism counterposed to Hollywood's market dominance, France contested the global hegemony of the United States on the terrain of cinema. As Vanessa Schwartz argues, "France established its centrality to international film culture by playing host to the world's most important Festival and market. If French national products did not dominate the box office in most parts of the globe, Cannes promoted internationalism and eventually auterism."[39] The tension between such diplomatic and aesthetic concerns would decisively shape Cannes's history.

Organized by the Association française d'action artistique (French Association of Artistic Action) and sponsored by the MAE, with additional funding from the Ministry of Information, tourist commission, and city of Cannes, the first postwar Cannes festival cultivated a more expansive internationalism than the never-realized 1939 event, showcasing national industries while touting cinema's capacity to build global understanding.[40] Whereas the 1939 festival line-up included only European countries (the United Kingdom, USSR, Belgium, the Netherlands, Sweden, Poland, Czechoslovakia, Romania, Luxembourg, and Denmark) plus the United States, the geographic scope of the 1946 festival was significantly broader, though it still had limits. With the exception of Italy, the former Axis powers were persona non grata in Cannes's early years; Germany would not be invited until 1949 and Japan and Spain not until 1951.[41] Invitees to the first postwar festival included nations in Latin America (Argentina, Brazil, Chile, and Mexico), Asia (Turkey, India, China), Africa (Egypt, South Africa), and the Pacific (Australia), though not all participated.[42] Among Latin American industries, only Mexico sent films to Cannes that year. The festival's diplomatic function was reflected in the composition of its jury, comprising international delegates (mostly diplomatic personnel and representatives of national film associations) rather than prominent creatives or critics.[43]

Cannes's investment in film as a vehicle of international harmony lessened over time as the festival took on a more active role as an arbiter of aesthetic merit, as suggested by its changing approach to prizes. In 1946, Cannes organizers initially resisted awarding a top honor due to the transparently political motives that had guided awards at the prewar Venice festival. Most notoriously, in 1938 Leni Riefenstahl's *Olympia* had been co-awarded the Mussolini Cup, despite the fact that as a nonfiction film, it was ineligible for the prize.[44] At the first festival, the top selection from each country received a Grand Prix (which thus served as a sort of participation trophy), though the jury singled out René Clément's Resistance-themed drama *La bataille du rail* (*The Battle of the Rails*, 1946, France) for a prize. It was not until 1949 that the Grand Prix became the festival's top distinction; it was renamed the Palme d'Or in 1955.[45] Up to this point, "the prizes were a hodge-podge designed to honor as many films as possible," as they were tailored to the strengths of each year's entries.[46]

Although they were selected by officials and industry representatives from each country, the Latin American films screened at Cannes nonetheless suggest the festival's evolving identity as a showcase for more self-conscious and formally innovative works as it tried to stay abreast of industry trends.[47] From the 1940s through the mid-1960s, Mexican selections shifted from the ultra-nationalistic, visually stunning melodramas of director Emilio Fernández and cinematographer Gabriel Figueroa (e.g., *María Candelaria*, 1943, which screened at Cannes in 1946) to Luis

Buñuel's absurdist fantasies and trenchant deconstructions of Mexican national myths (*Los olvidados*, 1950; *Él* [*That Strange Passion*], 1953; *El ángel exterminador* [*The Exterminating Angel*, 1962]). In the case of Brazil, a similar transition can be observed from the prestige productions of the Companhia Cinematográfica Vera Cruz (*Caiçara*, Adolfo Celi, Tom Payne, and John Waterhouse, 1950; *O cangaceiro* [The bandit], Lima Barreto, 1953), a Hollywood-style studio that proposed to elevate Brazilian cinema above the popular industry based in Rio de Janeiro, to the "aesthetics of hunger" pursued by early works of leftist Cinema Novo like *Vidas secas* (*Barren Lives*, Nelson Pereira dos Santos, 1963) and *Deus e o diabo na terra do sol* (*Black God, White Devil*, Glauber Rocha, 1964). Entries from Argentina moved from noirish thrillers and melodramas to the moody dramas of Leopoldo Torre Nilsson and members of Argentina's generación del 60.[48] Yet many Latin American titles screened at Cannes in this period exceed this tidy narrative of a transition from classical industries to innovative new waves. Much to the organizers' chagrin, the region's industries fielded run-of-the-mill melodramas and even exploitation fare like *Marihuana* (1950, Argentina), directed by former Cine Club de Buenos Aires organizer León Klimovsky, which failed to conform to the notions of art cinema promoted by the festival.

Cannes's history is marked by a keen tension between the festival's political and diplomatic function—which placed a premium on the representation of a wide array of countries—and its role as an arbiter of film taste. As one representative of Unifrance noted in a letter to longtime festival director Robert Favre Le Bret in 1953, films might be selected by officials or producers' associations "for reasons more political than cinematic."[49] At times, countries fielded works of propaganda like *Osvobozhdionnyi Kitai* (*Liberated China*, Sergei Gerasimov, 1951), a Soviet documentary on the People's Republic of China that was pulled from the festival line-up on the grounds that it might "wound the national feelings" of a sovereign state, per Article 7 of the Cannes regulations. This clause remained in force until 1957, leading to tense confrontations between invited countries.[50] Beyond the fallout from these diplomatic incidents, controversy arose regarding the Cannes policy tying the number of films allotted to each country in the festival program to the yearly output of its film industry, which obviously favored the United States (but also relatively prolific industries like Argentina's, Brazil's, and Mexico's). The USSR declined to send films to Cannes in 1947 and 1949 (no festival was held in 1948 or 1950); after the troubled 1951 festival, the Soviet Union would not participate until 1954, following the death of Stalin the previous year.[51]

While Cannes placed certain limits on participating nations, film selection remained firmly in the hands of their governments and industry representatives—a principle enshrined in FIAPF regulations in 1958—though festival organizers adopted the practice of inviting additional films to enhance the program.[52] As Favre Le Bret noted, the organizers constantly faced the dilemma of how "to permit the entry only of films of real quality to the festival without, nonetheless, altering the universal character of the event."[53] Cannes's celebration of artistic achievement coexisted with a sympathetic—albeit paternalistic—attitude toward less established industries. Favre Le Bret noted on another occasion, "One must never forget that the liberal policy that has always been ours, especially toward countries where the Film Industry is not exactly flourishing (the festival should also be a means of encouragement and emulation) has contributed enormously to the global renown and the success of our Festival."[54] Given concerns about the growing length of the festival and the artistic level of the films presented, in 1962 the Cannes organizers sought to find a new balance between these priorities. The committee altered regulations to specify that all nations could "propose one feature and one short film," additionally noting that the festival reserved the right to reject official selections.[55] Further signaling the shift away from diplomatic and toward aesthetic concerns, that same year Cannes stopped automatically inviting all countries with which France maintained diplomatic relations.[56] Yet the selection of films did not pass entirely into the hands of the organizers until the 1970s.[57]

Behind-the-scenes negotiations surrounding festival selections signal how Cannes's organizers prized characteristics understood to define art cinema—most notably, the distinctive, recognizable style of an acclaimed director, but also qualities like formal or stylistic novelty, compositional beauty, narrative complexity and ambiguity, socially weighty themes, and subtle characterization and performance.[58] Favre Le Bret stressed to government and industry representatives that an insufficiently strong entry could be damaging to the national image, thus aligning his interests with their desires to promote their domestic film industries. If unsuccessful, Favre Le Bret resorted to intermediaries, including Unifrance representatives, who in some cases doubled as cultural attachés employed by embassies and consulates. In 1957 Favre Le Bret wrote to Nicholas Mouneu, the Unifrance agent stationed in Buenos Aires, "I would like ARGENTINA to be represented by a truly noteworthy film, it is in our common interest and if it seems to you that the entry does not have all the required qualities corresponding to an international event, I will be obliged to ask you to intervene with those responsible so that they can avoid at all costs sending us a film that is not within the line of the festival."[59] As this letter signals, Cannes organizers relied on cultural mediators embedded in local contexts, mostly Unifrance representatives but also intellectuals they recruited to report on national industries and evaluate individual films.

In negotiations between Cannes organizers and national film institutes and producers' associations, the latter held a trump card: they could threaten to pull their films and delegations from the festival entirely, thereby compromising its imperative of international representation. For instance, in 1953 the Asociación de Productores y Distribuidores de Películas Mexicanas (Association of Mexican Film Producers and Distributors; APDPM) threatened to pull its entries if the festival declined to show all three of them, although the submissions arrived late in violation of festival regulations.[60] Furthermore, Cannes organizers felt pressure to maintain friendly relationships with industry representatives in order to protect the interests of the French cinema in these territories. In 1961 Mouneu encouraged Favre Le Bret to invite a second Argentine feature—Torre Nilsson's acclaimed *La mano en la trampa* (*The Hand in the Trap*, 1961)—to safeguard the preferential treatment accorded French cinema in the country. Mouneu suggested France had "great obligations with respect to Argentina. During 1960, for example, 54 French films were able to be screened commercially although our quota is only 35. For this reason, a gesture on your part would have the happiest of consequences for the future of French cinema in Argentina."[61] Yet conversely, the prestige and material benefits attached to participating in Cannes could be used to secure significant concessions from invited countries. In 1963 French officials leveraged Cuban interest in sending a film to Cannes to pressure Cuba's national film agency, ICAIC, to remit frozen revenues of the state-backed French distributor COFRAM, which had ceased after the nationalization of the island's exhibition and distribution infrastructure.[62]

The standard of "quality" that Cannes organizers sought to maintain came into conflict with not only the principle of national representation, which left film choices in the hands of the participating countries, but also the national representativeness of film content. Subjects and settings were often expected to speak to national particularities—especially in the case of Latin American and other Global South cinemas—by offering "characteristic," even "exotic" portrayals, often linked to the depiction of a seemingly pre-modern rural existence. Often embraced by European festival audiences, such fare ran the risk of portraying the nation as backward or unmodern. At times, national film institutes suppressed titles considered unflattering or works of young directors that deviated from established industry conventions and production values. Argentina's Instituto Nacional de Cinematografía (National Cinema Institute; INC) rejected an invitation from Cannes to send *Los inundados* (*Flooded Out*, Fernando Birri, 1962), a comic portrait of an impoverished family displaced by rising river waters, given its pessimistic take on social conditions.[63] In other cases, festival organizers and officials were aligned on what qualified as a desirable representation of the nation, even if aesthetic innovation might be lacking. This appears to have been the case with *O pagador de promessas* (*The Given Word*, Anselmo Duarte, 1962), which chronicles how a rural man's pilgrimage sparks conflict between orthodox Catholicism and African-derived popular religion in Salvador da Bahia. In a letter to Favre Le Bret, critic Amy Bakaloff Courvoisier (who at this point was Unifrance's agent in Brazil) deemed the film "interesting" and noted "it has excited Brazilian critics. I am less enthusiastic, because the film seems to me too 'classical' and without great originality. But, it has a very Brazilian theme, and without being 'exotic,' it shows a curious side of popular Brazil."[64] Reportedly thanks to the pressure exerted by director François Truffaut on his fellow jury members, *O pagador de promessas* won the Palme d'Or, becoming the first Latin American film to receive Cannes's top honor.[65]

While offering a consumable form of cultural difference, Cannes selections were expected to be fully intelligible and palatable to French and international spectators, sometimes leading to alterations to the films themselves. In advance of the festival, Favre Le Bret sent a telegram to the producer of *O pagador de promessas* urging a re-edit: "To assure film's success with an international audience appears indispensable to consider cuts to give the best results."[66] Favre Le Bret also demanded changes to Nelson Pereira dos Santos's *Vidas secas*, a bleak portrait of a family of migrant farmworkers in Brazil's arid Northeast based on a novel by Graciliano Ramos, which had been invited by Cannes's organizing committee. (Brazil's official 1964 selection was Rocha's *Deus e o diabo na terra do sol*.) In the offending scene, Fabiano (Átilo Iório) is preparing to shoot his family's ailing dog Baléia before they leave the barren backlands, where they have been eking out a living, for the city. Festival organizers requested that the animal's "long agony" be excised, leaving only images of Fabiano taking aim, followed by a shot of Baléia's corpse.[67] Yet Luiz Carlos Barreto, the film's cinematographer and co-producer, refused to approve the cuts.[68] Baléia's onscreen death caused a

FIGURE 9. Still from *Vidas secas* (1964) showing Baléia's "long agony." The scene sparked controversy at Cannes despite Favre Le Bret's attempts to head off the furor by requesting cuts to the film. Source: *Vidas secas*, directed by Nelson Pereira dos Santos (New York: New Yorker Films, 2005), DVD.

furor among audience members—more so, it seems, than the human suffering on display in the film. As a result, the producers flew the dog to the festival at Air France's expense to prove she was alive and well.[69] While Favre Le Bret failed to forestall the controversy, his demands signal how Cannes did not merely showcase films but actively reshaped them.

While "exotic" visions of the national might have played well at Cannes, on the other hand, organizers' efforts to include international co-productions in its line-up suggests a prioritization of aesthetic qualities over the logic of national representation. Some co-productions were presented at Cannes as national selections with great success and without controversy surrounding their origins. Luis Buñuel's *Viridiana* (1961), a joint venture between Mexico and Spain, won the Palme d'Or in 1961, while Torre Nilsson's *La mano en la trampa*, an Argentine-Spanish coproduction, won the Fédération Internationale de la PRESse CInématographique (International Federation of Film Critics; FIPRESCI) prize the same year.[70] Two English-language films shot in Argentina a decade apart proved to be more problematic.[71] In the run-up to the

1951 festival, Favre Le Bret was initially receptive to proposals from the major studio Argentina Sono Film—which he had visited in 1950—that the country be represented by *Sangre negra* (*Native Son*).⁷² Directed by French filmmaker Pierre Chenal, this adaptation of Richard Wright's novel was a US-Argentine co-production shot in Buenos Aires. Unfortunately for its producers, Mouneu reported that, likely because of its English-language source text and dialogue, "the Office of Public Entertainments does not consider the film Argentine. So, there is nothing to be done in that respect."⁷³ Thy Phu argues that Argentine producers and audiences understood *Sangre negra*—however counterintuitively—as the embodiment of the national industry's export ambitions and thus as a patriotic endeavor.⁷⁴ Yet Argentina instead opted to send *La danza del fuego* (The dance of fire, Daniel Tinayre, 1949), a convoluted crime drama that delves, in a series of nested flashbacks, into the mysterious death of a concert pianist (Amelia Bence) with a traumatic past.

A decade later, Favre Le Bret again asked Mouneu whether Argentina might send an English-language literary adaptation to Cannes—this time, *A puerta cerrada* (Pedro Escudero, 1962), an adaptation of Jean-Paul Sartre's *Huis clos* (*No Exit*) shot in Buenos Aires with a Hollywood cast—as its official entry. After consulting with the film's producers Fernando Ayala and Héctor Olivera, Mouneu responded, "It seemed quite difficult to us to ask the Argentine government to send 'HUIS-CLOS' in representation of the national cinema."⁷⁵ In response, Favre Le Bret argued that a selection's national flavor was less important than its artistic quality. He urged Mouneu to work with the Argentine delegation to "find a film capable of representing Argentina in a dignified manner, as our purpose, this year more than ever, is to avoid any work that would weigh down our Event, which is in the common interest of the Festival and the participants."⁷⁶ The fact that *Sangre negra* and *A puerta cerrada* were both adaptations of celebrated literary works and that each had French connections likely added to Favre Le Bret's perceptions of their aesthetic value, lending them a cosmopolitanism at odds with the priorities of Argentine officials.

Whether privileging national specificity or artistic inventiveness, Cannes organizers and audiences remained deeply invested in a notion of cinema as an auteur's individual vision, as shifting attitudes toward the Mexican films shown at Cannes attest. As Ernesto Acevedo-Muñoz and Patrick Keating note, French critics' fascination with the films of director Emilio Fernández and cinematographer Gabriel Figueroa—including the Cannes selections *María Candelaria* (1943) and *La red* (Rossana,

1953)—quickly gave way to disenchantment.[77] Initially accorded the status of art cinema for their compositional beauty, serious themes of economic exploitation, and construction of a mythic sense of Mexican-ness that early reviewers experienced as novel and picturesque, the duo's films were later dismissed in favor of those of Buñuel, who was hailed as a true auteur. In an oft-cited review of Buñuel's *Subida al cielo* (*Mexican Bus Ride*), screened at Cannes in 1952, Bazin wrote:

> The surprise and admiration engendered by Mexican films right after the war were, unfortunately, short-lived—the feelings stemmed in large part from illusion. It is perhaps no surprise that film festival juries on both sides of the iron curtain were conned for two years longer than they should have been—juries seem to mistake cinema for photography. There was admittedly something more than beautiful photography in *María Candelaria* and even *La perla* (both by Emilio Fernández, 1944 and 1945). But it is easy to see, year in and year out, that physical formalism and nationalist rhetoric have replaced realism and authentic poetry. With the exotic surprises gone and Figueroa's cinematographic feats ultimately reduced to fragments of technical bravura, Mexican cinema found itself crossed off the critics' map. . . . It is entirely thanks to Luis Buñuel that we are talking about Mexican films again.[78]

As Susan Martin-Márquez observes, Buñuel's participation in the French surrealist movement early in his career lent him aesthetic legitimacy in European eyes.[79] The future Nobel Prize–winning writer Octavio Paz, who attended Cannes in 1951 as a representative of the Mexican embassy in Paris—explicitly evoked this trajectory in a manifesto entitled "Buñuel the Poet," which he distributed before the screening of *Los olvidados* in hopes of assuring a favorable reception. Paz wrote:

> The subversive nature of Buñuel's early films resides in the fact that, hardly touched by the hand of poetry, the insubstantial conventions (social, moral, artistic) of which our reality is made fall away. And from those ruins rises a new truth, that of man and his desire. . . .
> After a silence of many years, Buñuel screens a new film: *Los olvidados*. . . . Its characters are our contemporaries and are of an age with our own children. But *Los olvidados* is something more than a realist film. Dream, desire, horror, delirium, chance, the nocturnal part of life, also play their part. And the gravity of the reality it shows us is atrocious in such a way that in the end it appears impossible to us, unbearable.[80]

"Buñuel the Poet" situates the film's unforgiving realism in relation to Buñuel's avant-garde experiments, working to universalize—and thereby temper—its critique of the dark side of the costs of Mexico's "economic miracle," marked by rapid urbanization and persistent social inequality.

Los olvidados was authorized by the APDPM to represent Mexico's industry at the festival, but its nihilistic depiction of suffering and cruelty among Mexico City's underclasses had generated controversy at home.[81] Combined with European interest in the neorealist strategies on display in *Los olvidados*, Paz's efforts to reframe the film proved successful: the Cannes jury awarded Buñuel the prize for best director. After being panned by critics when it premiered, *Los olvidados* was re-released in Mexico and later racked up nearly a dozen wins at the national film awards.[82]

Accordingly, Buñuel became a sought-after guest of the festival. In 1953 Favre Le Bret urged Jean Sirol, French cultural attaché and Unifrance representative in Mexico, to "demand that [producer] Oscar Dancigers make every effort to send [Buñuel's film] *Robinson Crusoe*.... Insist on Buñuel's presence at Cannes."[83] Once again, Cannes's priorities clashed with the logic of national representation; Sirol noted that "the Mexicans do not consider him, and justifiably, as a characteristic representative of their country's cinema as he is Spanish," though the director had become a naturalized Mexican citizen in 1949.[84] As *Robinson Crusoe* was not yet complete, Mexico was instead represented by Buñuel's *Él* along with two other titles, while Buñuel himself missed the festival due to professional obligations.

A similar dynamic was at play in the case of Alberto Cavalcanti, the Brazilian-born filmmaker who became a key figure of the French avant-garde in the 1920s and British documentary filmmaking of the 1930s before returning to Brazil to become head of production at Vera Cruz. Favre Le Bret wrote in 1951: "I am quite annoyed not to have a definitive response from Brazil, especially since the Companhia Cinematográfica Vera Cruz is sending me the film CAIÇARA, which interests us in any case as it carries the signature of Cavalcanti."[85] Though Cavalcanti was the producer, not the director, of the film, his involvement nonetheless lent prestige to Brazil's entry, helping to further Vera Cruz's international ambitions.

Other Latin American directors who lacked these European connections became fixtures at Cannes without enjoying the acclaim accorded Buñuel or Cavalcanti, most notably Leopoldo Torre Nilsson, who straddled Argentina's classical film industry and its emerging new wave. His films *La casa del ángel* (*The End of Innocence*, 1957), *La mano en la trampa*, *Setenta veces siete* (*The Female: Seventy Times Seven*, 1962), *El ojo que espía* (*The Eavesdropper*, 1966; out of competition), and *La chica del lunes* (*Monday's Girl*, 1967) all screened at Cannes in the

1950s and 1960s. As Martin-Márquez argues, Torre Nilsson lacked the European avant-garde credentials of Buñuel or Cavalcanti. As a result, his work was often dismissed as derivative, given tacit assumptions that Argentina's industry was inevitably backward compared to its European counterparts.[86] This claim holds true for Mouneu's private assessment of *La casa del ángel* in 1957. He wrote to Favre Le Bret: "I see a mixture of [popular novelist Georges] Ohnet revised by [proto-New Wave director Alexandre] Astruc, which will no doubt seem very dated."[87] Ironically, four years later Mouneu called Torre Nilsson's *La mano en la trampa* "really exceptional" despite its strikingly similar themes of adolescent female sexuality alternately repressed by patriarchal religious morality and exploited by unscrupulous men, and Elsa Daniel's presence as the protagonist of both films.[88]

Despite this ambivalence, Torre Nilsson enjoyed the favor of Cannes's selection committee throughout the 1950s and 1960s. In 1965 Torre Nilsson petitioned Favre Le Bret to invite *El ojo que espía*, a US/Argentine co-production distributed by Columbia Pictures in both English- and Spanish-language versions. He flattered the festival director by stressing Cannes's role as an arbiter of prestige and commercial success: "Every director and producer tries to take advantage of his economic, political, and even sentimental influences to get his film selected for Cannes.... You know how much I owe to the Cannes Festival."[89] Perhaps foreseeing that *El ojo que espía* was unlikely to be selected by INC due to its status as a co-production, Torre Nilsson sent a print to France to be reviewed by the organizing committee. The film had failed to charm Franco-Argentine writer Gloria Alcorta, who reported on the Buenos Aires film scene for Favre Le Bret; she found it "glacial, cerebral, without the essential: life."[90] Yet concerns about *El ojo que espía*'s suitability paled beside those raised by INC's 1965 selection, *El reñidero* (The arena, René Mujica), which brought the simmering tension between Cannes organizers and Argentine producers and officials to a boiling point.

Alcorta's 1965 report is worth examining at length as a document of the interpretive frames and points of reference that could help make Latin American films legible to Cannes organizers and audiences. She prefaces her comments by stating, "I have taken this 'job' [in English in original] to heart because I would like not to suffer so much for my country at Cannes as I have had to suffer [in the past], and there are good films [in Argentina]."[91] Alcorta offers measured praise for the generación del 60, whose works she reads through the lens of France's nouvelle vague. She calls Rodolfo Kuhn's *Pajarito Gómez* (1965), a comic chronicle of a fictional pop star, an "excellent satire of the New Wave." Alcorta found Leonardo Favio's *Crónica de un niño solo* (Chronicle of a boy alone, 1965), which recalls François Truffaut's *Les quatre cents coups* (*The 400 Blows*, 1959) in its depiction of a young boy who flees a reform school—to be "very touching. Badly constructed at the beginning, but admirable in its honesty, of a spontaneous and poetic flavor." Alcorta described the film, Favio's directorial debut, as "perfect for Critics' Week," a parallel competition for first and second feature films that screened the generación del 60 films *Tres veces Ana* (David José Kohon, 1961) and *Alias Gardelito* (Lautaro Murúa, 1961) in 1962.

By contrast, Alcorta judged *El reñidero* as a work "TO BE AVOIDED AT ALL COSTS.... Refuse it if it is sent. Program it in the morning" (emphasis in original). Her negative evaluation may have stemmed in part from the fact that the film largely ignored the narrative and stylistic cues of global new waves. Adapted from a popular play by Sergio de Cecco that transplanted the Greek myth of Electra to a turn-of-the-century Buenos Aires neighborhood plagued by political vendettas and violence, *El reñidero*'s stylized dialogue and frank emotional intensity contrast sharply with the affects of detachment, irony, and ambiguity prevalent in early 1960s art cinema. Cannes's organizing committee privately described its approach as "pretentious and pompous [*solennelle*]."[92]

In transferring a theatrical production to the screen, *El reñidero* ran contrary to the distaste for adaptation expressed by the French *nouvelle vague*, given the movement's emphasis on the director's creative agency. Yet cross-pollination between theater and film was not unusual for Argentina's generación del 60, giving rise, for instance, to Simón Feldman's *Los de la mesa 10* (The ones at table 10, 1960).[93] By comparison, *El reñidero* was a mainstream production; it was produced by Martín Rodríguez Mentasti, who had also acted as producer for *La casa del ángel*, and shot in Argentina Sono Film's studios. Whereas *Los de la mesa 10* was classified as a grade B film by INC (meaning its exhibition was not obligatory under Argentina's screen quota, severely curtailing its chances of box office success), *El reñidero* was awarded third prize in an INC competition before being selected for Cannes.[94]

In *El reñidero*, Elena (Fina Basser) takes on the role of Electra in the original narrative. Her father Pancho Morales (Francisco Petrone), an enforcer/assassin in the pay of local politicians, stands in for Agamemnon. In the original myth, Agamemnon's unfaithful wife Clytemnestra (named Nélida in the film and played by Miriam de Urquijo) and her lover Aegisthus (replaced by Morales's right-hand man Santiago Soriano

[Jorge Salcedo]) conspire to murder him. In the original narrative, Electra goads her brother Orestes into killing Clytemnestra and Aegisthus; in the film, Orestes (Alfredo Alcón) kills Soriano, while Nélida falls onto the same blade, seemingly by accident.

El reñidero begins with a heavy-handed sequence that literalizes the film's title metaphor—dialogue compares the violence-plagued neighborhood to a *reñidero*, or arena used for cockfighting—by intercutting a cockfight with the fatal knife duel between Morales and Soriano, though the latter's identity is not revealed at this point. The opening contributes to an earnest tone that makes the film feel out of step with its period. Nor does *El reñidero* pursue many stylistic innovations, beyond brief moments of frenetic handheld camera movement and the use of a snap zoom and, a moment later, a circular matte to emphasize Elena's reaction to the unwelcome sound of Soriano playing the guitar during a flashback.

Whether guided by Alcorta's evaluation, his viewing of the film, or the fact that Greek director Michael Cacoyannis's adaptation of *Electra* had screened at Cannes three years earlier, Favre Le Bret wrote to INC to dissuade it from sending *El reñidero* on the grounds that "the film does not seem to be one that would serve Argentine cinema in an international competition as important as Cannes where the audience is always very demanding, quite skeptical, and of a critical spirit that is rather acerbic. To be sure, the qualities of *El reñidero* did not escape us, but it is quite obvious that they must be more perceptible to a national audience."[95] Favre Le Bret thus suggested that the organizing committee was (paternalistically) protecting the interests of Argentina by shielding its cinema from ridicule. His comments were doubtless intended to soften the blow of his negative assessment. Yet his characterization of the film's appeal as too localized suggests, once again, how nationally specific representations were often subordinated to supposedly universal aesthetic criteria. (Tellingly, this language appears to have been boilerplate; it was used verbatim to explain the rejection of *Runaway* [John O'Shea, 1964, New Zealand] a few days later.)[96]

In response to Favre Le Bret's letter, INC protested that it had already invested the funds to subtitle a print in French and assembled publicity materials for the film—a reminder that invited countries took on the labor of translating and contextualizing their films for festival audiences—and threatened to withdraw from the event.[97] Ultimately, Cannes organizers relented and agreed to show *El reñidero*, perhaps in part because antagonizing Argentine officials and industry players threatened to derail the re-negotiation of a bilateral trade accord between the two countries.[98]

Director René Mujica sent a furious telegram, refusing to attend the festival and railing that his film should have been accepted automatically under the Cannes regulations but once rejected, should not have been reinstated.[99] Although Argentina's withdrawal from Cannes was averted, the conflict indicates how the ideals of art cinema promoted by the festival might clash with the local particularities of new waves like the generación del 60 and adjacent filmmaking trends.

Beyond Cannes's indirect and direct curation of Latin American cinema, the festival's global aspirations facilitated links with the growing number of similar events emerging in Latin America. The presence of Cannes staff at Latin American festivals boosted these events' prestige and fostered hopes for future collaborations, although Favre Le Bret was selective in accepting invitations. In 1958 he declined to attend the Punta del Este festival (which was dedicated exclusively to European cinema that year) after festival director Alberto Ugalde Portela left Paris without scheduling a promised in-person meeting.[100] In 1962 INC encouraged Favre Le Bret to return to the Mar del Plata film festival to help select a title for Cannes, as he had done the previous year.[101] He declined, but Unifrance head Robert Cravenne and novelist Christiane Rochefort, who worked for Cannes's press service, both attended, and Rochefort continued on to Mexico to scout for titles for Cannes.[102] By contrast, Favre Le Bret visited Moscow every year between 1955 and 1972, suggesting his desire to head off further diplomatic incidents at the festival and the importance that the French state placed on cultural ties with the USSR.[103]

Prior encounters with representatives of Cannes and Unifrance became a kind of currency that Latin American festival organizers could leverage to advance their personal interests. In 1963 Ernesto Salcedo Salazar, the public relations director for the Cartagena festival, reminded Favre Le Bret of their conversation at Acapulco the previous year and the invitation he had extended to both Favre Le Bret and Cravenne to attend Cartagena in 1962. Although Favre Le Bret had failed to respond, Salcedo Salazar nevertheless took advantage of the prior contact to request an invitation to Cannes, where he hoped to solidify a co-production deal. Salcedo Salazar wrote, "With Cannes being the most important center of world cinema where the most prestigious directors and producers meet, you can understand, my dear friend, my interest in attending for the ultimate purpose of achieving my desire to produce in Colombia a homegrown film with French technique."[104] While Favre Le Bret claimed not to have received the invitation, he nonetheless welcomed Salcedo Salazar at Cannes.[105] Salcedo Salazar's letter suggests how the festival became a springboard for Latin American film enthusiasts' ambitions, including the creation of festivals in the region to stimulate film production and garner international attention. It is to these events that I now turn.

EXPERIMENTING WITH THE EUROPEAN FESTIVAL MODEL: PUNTA DEL ESTE, 1951–1955

In 1955 Arnold Picker, United Artists's vice president for foreign distribution, gave a somewhat backhanded compliment to Punta del Este's showcase of international cinema: "This is one of the few film festivals which are honestly judged because no local politics interferes in the judging. That country hasn't a film production industry."[106] Uruguayan film critic Homero Alsina Thevenet echoed this sentiment in a report from the rival Mar del Plata festival four years later: "It is easier to organize festivals where there is no [film] production industry. They are a bit more artificial, but they are free of the internal problems that arise where [films] are made. The list of intrigues, opinions, interests, and even hatreds there can be in Argentine cinema is incommensurable."[107] Highlighting the nakedly self-interested maneuvering that arose when festivals promoted homegrown cinema, Alsina Thevenet's comment also begs the question of these events' purpose in the absence of self-sustaining commercial film production. Beyond promoting tourism—also a core goal of Cannes and other established festivals—Punta del Este worked to present Uruguayan audiences and critics on the international stage as sophisticated consumers.

Punta del Este is one of the earliest instances of the festival circuit's expansion beyond Europe, though it was soon followed by the International Film Festival of India in 1952 and the covertly CIA-backed Southeast Asian Film Festival in 1954.[108] Yet Punta del Este's history is almost entirely unknown, reflecting a divide in film festival scholarship between studies of traditionally dominant European festivals—which continue to play an outsized role in shaping contemporary Latin American film as brokers of production financing and as a major distribution circuit for the region's art cinema—and the growing number of alternatives to the dominant festival model, including the openly politicized showcases of Latin American cinema that emerged in the late 1960s. Latin American festivals of the 1950s and early 1960s that sought to adapt the conventional European model lacked both the prestige of established, top-tier events and the oppositional nature of gatherings linked to NLAC and thus have been largely overlooked by scholars. Yet I contend that the histories of Punta del Este, Mar del Plata, and other festivals of the period offer important insights regarding the global ambitions attached to cinema in the region.

Punta del Este arose from the overlapping interests of local real estate developers and Uruguay's government. Both hoped to promote tourism at a moment when the numbers of visitors from neighboring Argentina had plummeted due to a precipitous drop in the value of the Argentine peso relative to Uruguay's gold-backed currency.[109] The event's organization was spearheaded by Argentine entrepreneur Mauricio Litman, the developer of Punta del Este's Cantegril Country Club, the festival site. Beginning in 1946, Litman constructed hundreds of bungalows—which could be purchased and paid off over ten years and thus were accessible to upper-middle-class or even middle-class consumers—around a golf course located at a distance from the existing town center.[110] In late 1950 construction began on the six-hundred-seat movie theater that would host the festival screenings. "Made mostly with red brick, but with touches of Madison Square Garden and El Morocco," according to the *New York Times*, the structure was completed in less than three months, with mere hours to spare before the festival began.[111] Litman also built a nightclub to accommodate festival receptions, all with an eye to boosting the value of his property.

As *Marcha* observed, "The goal was to lend prestige, with this ample publicity [connected with the festival], to the coastal zone of Punta del Este, and bolster the economic interests (the sale of lots, primarily)" of the Cantegril Country Club.[112] The *New York Times* also noted that "real estate salesmen were available, although discreetly" during the event.[113] In this sense, the festival advanced Punta del Este's development and urbanization. Journalist Gualberto Fernández, who managed the festival's press service, evoked Cantegril's relative isolation in the early 1950s: "In this area making a phone call is torture, buses do not exist, there are no bars and one lacks, in a word, everything that constitutes the 'modus vivendi' of city dwellers."[114] Not surprisingly, the event was plagued with infrastructural problems, including issues with telephone service and a power outage that delayed a screening.[115] Such incidents were certainly not unknown at European festivals; memorably, a blackout during the screening of the Soviet documentary *Bitva za Berlin* (*The Fall of Berlin*, Yulii Raizman and Elizaveta Svilova, 1945) led to accusations of sabotage at Cannes in 1946.[116] Yet in the case of Punta del Este, such snags interfered with the festival's efforts to project a sense of technical modernity.

FIGURE 10. Advertisement displaying festival infrastructure—a newly constructed movie theater—and logistics—a fleet of vehicles belonging to a car service engaged to transport festival guests. *Source:* Gualberto Fernández, *Travelling en el festival de cine de Punta del Este* (Montevideo: Talleres Gráficos Prometeo, 1951).

Architect Alberto Ugalde Portela, who worked closely with Litman on the country club, became the "ambassador of the event" in Europe. Enrique Palacio and Jaime Prades—the producer of *Sangre negra*, another testament to his international ambitions—did the same in Mexico and the United States, respectively, while Brazil and Argentina were invited directly through diplomatic channels.[117] Ultimately, six nations representing major film industries in Western Europe and the Americas participated—France, Italy, the United Kingdom, the United States, Mexico, and Brazil—together sending nearly forty features to be screened. Punta del Este thus proposed a geographically circumscribed notion of art cinema, excluding Eastern bloc countries. Argentine authorities declined to field an entry to the festival; its regulations stipulated that the films screened be Uruguayan premieres, and industry representatives protested that no suitable new releases were ready.[118] Argentina did send a contingent of stars to mingle at the event. However, Buenos Aires newspapers largely declined to cover it, perhaps out of pique that Uruguay had succeeded in organizing an international festival, an initiative that had been proposed by Argentina's Peronist government for 1949 but never materialized.[119]

In the face of difficulties in managing the entry of films and delegates into the country, Litman joined forces with the Comisión Nacional de Turismo (National Tourism Commission). State involvement in the festival was hotly debated not only in the press but also in the Senate. Even during an export-driven economic bonanza occasioned by the Korean War, the use of public funds in excess of 600,000 pesos (more than double the 270,000 initially promised) to mount an event that served private interests sparked controversy. Notably, by contrast with major festivals like Cannes, which only covered invitees' hotels, Punta del Este typically paid the full travel and lodging costs of its delegations, a courtesy later extended by the São Paulo and Mar del Plata festivals as well.[120]

Confusion about the respective duties of the event's private and public backers contributed to disorganization, including incidents like the organizers being caught one statuette short during the final awards ceremony.[121] Some international guests viewed these logistical problems through stereotyped notions of Latin Americans' supposedly laid-back character. *Variety* commented, "When natives were asked for help in straightening out the confusion, there was a stock answer: 'I'll take care of it right away.' But it was more like 'ma[ñ]ana.'"[122] The distribution of tickets proved to be a point of contention. Journalists and festival workers (including members of the Cine Club del Uruguay) protested that they were slighted in favor of government officials, who reserved the lion's share of the tickets for themselves and their families.[123] The handling of the tickets contributed to a heavy state presence that underlined the festival's role as a vehicle of international relations. For instance, the projection of *José Artigas, protector de los pueblos libres* (José Artigas, defender of free peoples, 1950), a poetic documentary portrait of one of Uruguay's independence heroes commissioned by the Uruguayan government from Italian filmmaker Enrico Gras, was interrupted and screened from the beginning when Uruguay's president at the time, Luis Batlle Berres, entered the theater.[124]

Following the opening screening, attendees were shown an eclectic mix of now-classic and forgettable titles, including *Sunset Boulevard* (Billy Wilder, 1950, United States), *Valentino* (Lewis Allen, 1951, United States), *The Fallen Idol* (Carol Reed, 1948, United Kingdom), Michelangelo Antonioni's *Cronaca di un amore* (Story of a love affair, 1950, Italy), Jean Cocteau's *Orphée* (*Orpheus*, 1950, France), Max Ophuls's *La ronde* (1950, France), and Robert Bresson's *Journal d'un curé de campagne* (*Diary of a Country Priest*, 1951, France). Several attendees admitted to sleeping through this last title after a champagne-soaked reception offered by the French delegation.[125] Brazil screened two films from Vera Cruz, including *Caiçara*, and Cavalcanti attended the festival in person. Mexico offered a slate of melodramas—Emilio Fernández's *Un día de vida* (A day in the life, 1950) and Roberto Gavaldón's *Rosauro Castro* (1950) and *Deseada* (*Desired*, 1951)—alongside the psychological thriller *El hombre sin rostro* (The man without a face, Juan Bustillo Oro, 1950).

Punta del Este's improvised nature led to last-minute changes that often responded to diplomatic pressures. France, fearing competition from Italy—whose selection *Domani è troppo tarde* (Tomorrow is too late, Léonide Moguy, 1950) ultimately took the festival's top prize—added an eleventh-hour submission, René Clair's *La beauté du diable* (*Beauty and the Devil*, 1950).[126] A minor scandal erupted when the festival's organizers rescheduled a morning screening of *The Breaking Point* (Michael Curtiz, 1950). When the film was replaced with *Deseada*—originally slated for a more prestigious evening slot—Mexico's representatives threated to leave in protest and were appeased only when *Deseada* was shown a second time at night.[127] Overall, the US delegation received preferential treatment at Punta del Este, no doubt due to the economic dominance of Hollywood film on Uruguayan screens. A member of the planning committee reminded the jury that positive attention to Hollywood entries was in the festival's interest, since it would help ensure the participation of US studios—generally skeptical of international festivals—in future editions of the event.[128] Responding to "a suggestion of the U.S. State Department that such a move would aid hemispheric solidarity," according to *Variety*, fifty-six American representatives attended at the expense of the Uruguayan government, nearly totaling the number of invitees from the five other nations combined.[129]

Given the festival's lavish expenditures, many observers were skeptical about the results. In *Marcha*, Alsina Thevenet commented acerbically on the "fantastical spirit with which [the festival] was approached, whose elemental manifestation was believing that with ostentation, luxury, publicity and bright lights they could obtain, by force, the good opinion of visiting film personalities." In his view, the press was to blame for failing to impress its celebrity visitors with Uruguayan audiences' erudition: "We were lacking in journalists who know how to talk about cinema, understand what they see, convince their foreign colleagues that in this country cinema is, demonstrably, a serious passion."[130] In the absence of real prospects for a commercial film industry, Uruguay could nonetheless distinguish itself as a country of sophisticated consumers. As

Mariana Amieva Collado observes, this notion of Uruguay as a "country of critics" that "did not produce cinema, but had a great film culture" reinforced a belief in "Uruguayan exceptionalism" rooted in the country's long democratic tradition, its comparatively advanced level of industrialization, and the economic bonanza of the 1950s.[131]

Despite the Punta del Este festival's mixed results, *Marcha* noted that the Cantegril Country Club's investment was so substantial it could not be recuperated in the course of a single event, thus incentivizing the organization of future events.[132] Yet despite slightly broader international participation in 1952—Japan, Sweden, Switzerland, and West Germany joined the festival's line-up—Punta del Este struggled to rekindle the excitement surrounding the prior year's event. Speculation encouraged by the festival had, by some accounts, contributed to a real estate bubble that quickly burst in the face of new economic pressures, which punctured the optimistic mood that had characterized the presidency of Batlle Berres (1947–1951).

Batlle Berres had adopted policies of "stimulating industry; state intervention in the economic and social spheres; a statist, planned economy; an increase in services offered by the state; the expansion of social rights through social and labor legislation; and efforts to secure the support of diverse social classes that approximated him to the region's so-called populist reform movements," despite his "emphasis on democratic liberties" and resulting animosity toward Perón.[133] Yet by 1952 the limits of import-substitution industrialization were becoming clear. A drop in international demand for Uruguayan agricultural products as the Korean War wound down dealt a blow to the economy, although the crisis would not become critical until 1957, contributing to the losses of Batlle Berres's Colorado Party in the presidential elections.[134] As land values dropped in Punta del Este, hotel rooms sat empty and homes languished on the market, while informal settlements on the outskirts of cities expanded.[135] Through ironic reference to the Cantegril Country Club, these marginalized communities became known as *cantegriles*.[136] Underlining the grave financial problems facing the country, *Marcha* mused tendentiously, "Can we waste time in Cantegril?"[137] Although some commentators found the 1952 festival "better run" than the previous year's, issues with organization persisted.[138] The event began without even a final list of films to be shown; several prints arrived late, to the point that a full day of screenings was canceled.[139] The Japanese selections were shown without subtitles, and explanatory programs with plot summaries were not distributed to all audience members; some tipsy viewers even mocked the films openly.[140]

International pressures appear to have further compromised efforts to establish the Punta del Este's aesthetic authority and legitimacy. The 1952 festival had no official jury or prize, a condition imposed by FIAPF, which had resolved that Cannes and Venice would be the sole competitive international film festivals held in 1952.[141] In Uruguay, this move was interpreted as a concession to Hollywood and its distaste for festivals, given that awards usually favored other nations and due to their market dominance, US studios had less to gain from the publicity.[142] Regardless, the MPAA declined to participate officially, though RKO and United Artists sent films independently.[143] With no jury or competition, the festival further compromised its own prestige by accepting films that had already screened at prior festivals, contrary to its own regulations. *Umberto D.* (Vittorio De Sica, 1952, Italy) was the sole major premiere, although other acclaimed films screened at the event, including *Rashomon* (Akira Kurosawa, 1950, Japan) and *Fröken Julie* (*Miss Julie*, Alf Sjöberg, 1951, Sweden)—top prize winners at Venice and Cannes, respectively—and Ingmar Bergman's *Sommarlek* (*Illicit Interlude*, 1951, Sweden). As critic Antonio Grompone put it, by "suppressing any official evaluation of the films, Punta del Este only throws into relief the hidden face of festivals, where, behind the display in favor of film art and culture, one finds the traffic in films and other interests foreign to cinema, often unutterable ones."[144] Worsening matters, the festival failed to effectively encourage tourism: *Marcha* noted that funds earmarked by the government to subsidize hotel stays went largely unspent.[145]

Over the next two years, without additional government support forthcoming, Punta del Este scaled back its ambitions, offering smaller events dedicated to the cinema of a single country. As noted previously, in 1953 the festival's organizers opted to collaborate with Unifrance on a two-week showcase of French cinema. Incentivizing tourism again became a priority after Argentina's Peronist government levied restrictions on exit visas to Uruguay, reducing the flow of visitors from across the Río de la Plata.[146] A letter from Édouard-Félix Guyon, France's ambassador in Uruguay, to foreign minister Georges Bidault reveals how Unifrance's efforts to promote France's cinema abroad ran afoul of French celebrities' limited familiarity with Latin America, product of an obvious imbalance in soft power. Guyon noted, with some sexism, "Due to our compatriots' ignorance in matters of geography, certain members—and above all, certain female members [of the delegation]—imagined finding the enchanting setting of a tropical forest in Punta del Este. Great was their disappointment upon seeing a landscape of sand and pines similar to that of the Landes coast" in southwest France.[147] Presented with apparent sameness instead of exotic difference, several stars moved to make an early exit, and Unifrance representatives narrowly averted an exodus of celebrities that would have undercut the festival's promotional and diplomatic aims.

The year 1954 proved to be a bumper one for Latin American festivals. New events were held in Mar del Plata and São Paulo, though FIAPF categorized them both as "Class B" (noncompetitive international showcases), and neither became an annual event at the time. Punta del Este was granted only a "Class D" rating by FIAPF, meaning its scope would be national and noncompetitive.[148] The coastal city opted to host an Italian film week, whose line-up included nine Uruguayan premieres (two from the 1940s) alongside reprises of popular Italian films.[149] Amid this wave of new Latin American festivals, FIAPF, as noted previously, secured a promise that beginning in 1955 Punta del Este would be held biannually. In return, the festival would gain the right to award the controversial Gran Premio Sud América. Underwhelmed by the results of prior year's festivals and battered by polemics surrounding its investment, Uruguay's government devoted just $350,000 pesos to Punta del Este in 1955, compared with over $600,000 in 1951 and $500,000 in 1952.[150]

Although Argentina, Cuba, Spain, and Finland participated in the festival for the first time in 1955, deference to US interests and the continued exclusion of socialist countries again compromised the festival, observers opined. Hollywood again turned out in force, motivated, according to *Variety*, by "the realization that Uruguay is one of the most democratic nations in South America and that heavy American representation at the Uruguayan event has definite political implications."[151] The contrast with Perón's populist government across the Río de la Plata in Argentina is clear, if unspoken. By contrast, Punta del Este invited only two delegates from Japan and offered to cover their airfare only from the United States to Uruguay, and Japan declined to participate.[152] For Montevideo film critics, the lone bright spot of the festival was a retrospective on Méliès and French fantasy cinema organized by the Cinemateca Uruguaya with materials from the Cinémathèque française, the Cinemateca Argentina, and the Filmoteca do MAM-SP.[153]

The challenges of the 1955 festival came to a head with the controversial decision by the jury discussed in this chapter's opening. Despite the presence of well-regarded films like Buñuel's *Robinson Crusoe* (1954, Mexico/United States) and Claude Autant-Laura's *Le rouge et le noir* (*The Red and the Black*, 1954, France/Italy), the jury affirmed in a statement that was reprinted in cineclub magazines in Argentina, Chile, and Uruguay: "The participating countries have not presented films of high creative quality worthy of a distinction of the importance and significance of the Gran Premio Sud América."[154] The president of the festival's organizing committee then declared the jury's decision null and void, leading jurors to fire back with a letter protesting that "there are no precedents in similar competitions of the jury's authority being rejected," presenting the decision as a violation of international festival norms.[155]

As suggested previously, the jury's polemical action arose from the dilemma faced by new festivals comparatively lacking in prestige. Unable to effectively compete with their rivals for the most desirable films, their juries would inevitably undercut their own critical authority if they awarded top prizes to mediocre titles. *Marcha*'s film columnists reflected:

> What these incidents reveal is a diametrical opposition between what the executive committee and the jury (or the majority of it) understand a Film Festival to be. For the executive committee, the festival seems to be a matter of a big show of publicity, sought-after stars (albeit bad actors), unforgettable parties in the hottest clubs, and a prize for every delegation so they go home happy and bring more films to the next festival. For the jury (or the majority of it), a festival is a competition of cinematic creation that should be organized using the values of the creators and not an international association of producers [i.e., FIAPF].[156]

Despite the jury's pan-Latin American composition, Alsina Thevenet seized on the opportunity to further highlight Uruguayans' discriminating tastes. He wrote, "A point of speculation . . . is that the level of Uruguayan film criticism was one of factors that drove the severity of the Jury, which refused to award a prize to [films] that the press had rigorously objected to or applauded in a lukewarm manner."[157]

In the wake of the controversial 1955 festival, Punta del Este's organizers again scaled back their international ambitions. After the French cinema week attended by Bazin in 1956, Punta del Este held two noncompetitive showcases of European film in 1958 and 1961.[158] Punta del Este's early experiment with a festival modeled on Venice and Cannes ultimately disappointed Latin American film enthusiasts and foreign observers alike, since the event proved unable to successfully create a self-perpetuating cycle of prestige.

Even before 1955, Punta del Este's emulation of European festivals was already being contested by events dedicated to nonfiction (SODRE), retrospective programming (São Paulo), and arguably, political theater.

Following a national film festival at Mar del Plata in 1948, in 1954 the first international film showcase held in the city harnessed the logic of the European festival to a spectacular display of Juan Domingo Perón's political support and infrastructural achievements, laying the groundwork for the most prominent and enduring Latin American festival of the 1960s. The following section highlights the year 1954 as one of fleeting experimentation with alternative—though not oppositional—festival models.

REVISING THE EUROPEAN FESTIVAL MODEL: PEDAGOGY AND POLITICS AT THE SODRE, SÃO PAULO, AND MAR DEL PLATA FESTIVALS, 1954

Roughly 150 kilometers from Punta del Este in Uruguay's capital Montevideo, the public broadcaster and cultural agency SODRE proposed an alternative ideal of cinematic internationalism. Cine Arte's inaugural Festival de Cine Documental y Experimental (Festival of Documentary and Experimental Cinema) in 1954 championed filmmaking practices beyond the fiction feature—not only feature-length documentary, but also advertising; animation; and children's, ethnographic, avant-garde, and scientific films—explicitly differentiating itself from the commercially motivated Punta del Este event.[159] Pointedly, the program booklet for SODRE's second festival in 1956 affirmed its "exclusively cinematic nature, its spirit of *disinterested* service to the cause of cinema the world over, welcoming all the richness of its varied range of styles" (emphasis added).[160]

SODRE's definition of documentary and experimental film was expansive, encompassing fiction features of neorealist inspiration like Nelson Pereira dos Santos's *Rio, Zona Norte* (Rio, Northern Zone, 1957) and Fernando Birri's *Los inundados*. Yet the festival's organizers nonetheless affirmed that nonfiction film had a privileged role to play in promoting international understanding. The 1956 program declared, "Cinema is closer to a direct reproduction of reality than any other medium of expression; it permits a more exact perception of the mysterious world in which we live.... Through cinema, the peoples of the world can see each other's faces, hear each other's voices, dialogue in the closest thing to a universal language."[161] By contrast with Punta del Este, which invited only a small number of capitalist nations to participate, the SODRE festival was open to any country that maintained diplomatic relations with Uruguay. Amieva Collado notes that the cinema of socialist countries had a significant (though sometimes controversial) presence at the festival, perhaps due to the communist affiliation of Cine Arte's director Danilo Trelles. Films from the Eastern bloc accounted for between a quarter and a third of all films screened in the first four festivals, held biannually between 1954 and 1962.[162]

Serving as an important point of contact with the socialist bloc, the festival also fostered inter–Latin American connections with the Primer Congreso Latinoamericano de Cineístas Independientes (First Latin American Congress of Independent Cinéastes) held in 1958, an important precursor to NLAC, as Ana López has noted.[163] Filmmakers and critics from across the region attended, including Pereira dos Santos, who would become a pivotal figure of Brazil's Cinema Novo movement, and Birri, founder of the Instituto de Cinematografía de la Universidad Nacional del Litoral, discussed in chapter 4.[164] Identifying common problems and opportunities for the region's cinemas, the conference delegates affirmed: "The peoples of Latin America have the right and the duty to have a cinema of their own that freely expresses their physiognomy and their national aspirations. . . . [C]inema in Latin America should fulfill the obligatory work of safeguarding [the] education, culture, history, tradition, and spiritual enlightenment of its population."[165] The resolutions also called on independent filmmakers to "tend to the development of national film cultures and cooperate with those entities that, like cinémathèques, cineclubs and other similar organizations, favor greater knowledge of the essential values of cinema."[166] Despite the strong Eurocentric orientation of such institutions in this period, here they are linked with the promotion of cultural nationalism through film.

Without yoking cinema to the lofty goals of human or national progress to the same degree, the Festival Internacional de Cinema held in São Paulo in 1954 trumpeted its efforts to cultivate local film culture by breaking with conventional festivals' investment in competition and novelty. The event's daily bulletin declared, "The Brazilian public, for reasons that are well known, is not educated cinematically; its orientation in the seventh art is faulty and full of gaps. On the other hand, without a deep film culture among this public, an artistically dignified national industry cannot develop. Therefore, it is for this public, broad, curious, eager for new things, that the Festival of São Paulo was organized, not, as is the custom elsewhere, for a limited group of the so-called elite."[167] The event featured a noncompetitive international showcase alongside three major retrospectives: one Brazilian, a second international, and a third dedicated to the work of Erich von Stroheim. This emphasis on repertory programming was a necessity given

FIAPF's stipulation that the festival not hold a competition.[168] Festival organizers admitted the lack of prizes was a disincentive for studios, who preferred to save their releases for competitive events. Given these constraints, they framed their approach as a victory over the base commercialism of existing (largely European) events. As the festival bulletin put it, "The São Paulo event will not resemble the famous traditional festivals, as it is lacking in touristic and social aspects. By a conscious choice of its organizing committee, the festival that is about to begin will be, above all, a festival of cinema, a festival of art."[169]

Planned as part of the festivities marking São Paulo's four-hundredth anniversary, the festival joined several initiatives of the late 1940s and early 1950s—from the establishment of the Companhia Cinematográfica Vera Cruz to the creation of the Museu de Arte and Museu de Arte Moderna to the development of the São Paulo biennial—that sought to burnish the cultural credentials of the city's wealthy industrial bourgeoisie.[170] The organization of the festival gained momentum through the efforts of Alberto Cavalcanti and poet and diplomat Vinícius de Moraes, under the auspices of the Ministries of Foreign Relations and Education.[171] As the Uruguayan magazine *Film* put it, for São Paulo the festival served "as a simultaneous demonstration of its modernity, its interest in culture, and of an economic position that allows it to incur great expenses."[172] Yet the plummeting value of the Brazilian cruzeiro against the dollar led to a precipitous drop in the budget's real value by the time the festival opened.[173]

The festival's organizers included Francisco Matarazzo Sobrinho, the main patron of São Paulo's Museu de Arte Moderna, and Francisco Luiz de Almeida Salles, a close contact of Paulo Emílio Salles Gomes at the museum. Almeida Salles enlisted Salles Gomes to organize the festival's retrospectives, a task that eventually led to his permanent return to Brazil from France. Salles Gomes leveraged his connections to FIAF to secure prints from the Cinémathèque française and other archives.[174] A number of conservators also attended the festival, including Henri Langlois; Ernest Lindgren of the BFI; and José María Podestá, a critic with links to the newly created Cinemateca Uruguaya.[175] However, the festival led to a rift between Langlois and Salles Gomes over payment for prints struck for the event (see chapter 2).

Although the São Paulo festival had always been envisioned as a one-off event, controversy surrounding the event would likely have precluded any hopes of a reprise. To recoup expenses, admission to festival screenings was double the customary ticket price, leading to public outcry.[176]

As Rafael Morato Zanatto observes, Brazilian industry players also protested the duty-free entry of prints for the festival, the limited attention accorded to Brazilian films, and the investment of funds that might have been used to subsidize domestic production.[177] Not all observers were convinced by the organizers' claims that fostering of film culture and building the national industry went hand in hand.

On the heels of the São Paulo festival, Mar del Plata held its first international edition, which would not become an annual event until five years later. Both the 1954 event and the national showcase held there in 1948 have been largely erased from the Mar del Plata festival's history due to their role in promoting the achievements of the Peronist state.[178] The organization of both the 1948 and 1954 festivals was closely linked with the administration's subsidies for the film industry and its protectionist policies, part of a broader program of import-substitution industrialization that favored domestic manufacturing over imports. The 1948 event served to publicize a new scheme of government support for film production; it was financed through a tax on foreign film exhibition levied by the province of Buenos Aires.[179] Its organization dovetailed with the transformation of Mar del Plata from a high-society destination modeled on the French resort town Biarritz to a space of mass leisure for the working classes, a shift that predated Perón's administration but accelerated during his presidency. The festival coincided with a mass campaign to promote state-subsidized tourism for the working classes, which included the construction of an enormous resort for this purpose, the Colonia de Vacaciones de Chapadmalal, located approximately thirty kilometers from the center of Mar del Plata. Also in 1948, a law was passed permitting ownership of individual apartments in a building for the first time, sparking a real estate boom that would populate Mar del Plata's horizon with skyscrapers in the 1950s and 1960s.[180]

Although only Argentine films were screened at Mar del Plata in 1948, the festival's ambitions were more expansive than they might appear at first glance. The event was envisioned as a dry run for an international festival set to take place the following year. Furthermore, according to *Variety*, the festival was designed to improve the Argentine industry's international reputation and thus boost exports: "Prime purpose is to make the world in general more conscious of Argentine pix production, and to offset the poor showing made by Argentine pix at recent European festivals."[181] To this end, critics from seventeen Latin American countries (including José Valdés-Rodríguez and Elena Sánchez

Valenzuela), France, the United Kingdom, Italy, Spain, and Canada were invited to Mar del Plata.[182]

During the opening ceremonies, government officials championed the festival circuit as a vehicle of international unity while cautioning against cinema's mass influence and its use as a propaganda tool. The governor of the province of Buenos Aires, Domingo Mercante, noted that European festivals served to promote "international connection and solidarity," but cautioned that "the cinema is by definition an art of the masses, and thus in an age of such high political tension as ours is, the cinematograph—often betraying its artistic aims through the systematic propaganda of foreign economic and political regimes—has become the most efficient and poisonous instrument of foreign ideological penetration."[183] Without naming specific adversaries, the speech seems to evoke the United States and the Soviet Union, resonating with Perón's call for a "third way" between capitalism and communism. Mercante's discourse is contradictory: he leans on the prestige of the festival's European precursors while declaring that "by sponsoring this exposition, we are laying the foundation for . . . a great national art in the near future."[184] This apparent tension is resolved rhetorically by affirming Peronism's cosmopolitan character. Mercante declares that "we men of the [Peronist] Revolution, because of our mentality and our purely democratic origins, repudiate narrow nationalisms," even as he calls for a cinema that would be "popular in its content and at the service of the nation in its patriotic intentions."[185] Reflecting the ideological contradictions that Peronism attempted to mediate, Mercante's speech signals the 1948 festival's nationalistic sentiments and international aspirations.

Though plans for an international festival in Mar del Plata did not come to fruition for another six years, the 1954 festival event was no less intertwined with the Peronist political project. On his first visit to Mar del Plata in a decade, the president launched his campaign in support of Peronist candidates in the 1954 midterm elections.[186] As Clara Kriger observes, the festival gave Perón the opportunity to showcase his administration's economic and infrastructural accomplishments and the fervor of his supporters, who turned out in the thousands to rallies that coincided with the festival.[187] In keeping with Perón's foreign policy, both capitalist and communist nations were invited. According to *Variety*, "the Soviet and satellite delegates [were] left much to themselves, not only because of language barriers, but because neither local nor other screen personalities care to be seen in their company," but this observation must be viewed critically given *Variety*'s anticommunist bent.[188]

The 1954 festival took shape through the initiative of Raul Alejandro Apold, a journalist and newsreel producer who served as director of the Subsecretaría de Informaciones y Prensa del Estado (State Press and Information Agency; SIPE). Allotted a 2 million peso budget by Perón himself, the festival organizers covered an additional two million in costs by selling tickets to screenings and associated sporting events.[189] Beyond securing this government investment, Apold negotiated on behalf of the Argentine state with FIAPF, which granted the festival a classification of "B" as a noncompetitive international festival.[190] Apold also traveled to Hollywood to meet with the MPAA, whose cooperation was deemed essential to secure Hollywood representation at the festival. The Argentine government promised to remit $500,000 out of over $3 million owed to US studios, a move that *Variety* interpreted as "a mere token of goodwill, possibly to induce U.S. companies to participate in the Mar del Plata festival."[191] While this promise was reiterated by Perón to MPAA president Eric Johnston at the festival's opening ceremonies, the funds did not begin to flow until several months later.[192] Such negotiations would recur in later years, as in 1965 when the United States declined to participate officially in the Mar del Plata festival due to new import quotas instituted by the Argentine government.[193]

Yet while the presence of Hollywood stars was considered indispensable, US cinema did not dominate the festival line-up. In 1954, rather than programming only new films, Mar del Plata screened productions released as early as 1950, including well-received titles like *Fröken Julie* and *Sommarlek*, both of which had been shown at Punta del Este two years earlier, along with Federico Fellini's *I vitelloni* (*The Loafers*, 1953, Italy), Michelangelo Antonioni's *I vinti* (*Our Sons*, 1952, Italy), Michael Powell and Emeric Pressburger's *Tales of Hoffman* (1951, United Kingdom), and Luis Buñuel's *La ilusión viaja en tranvía* (*Illusion Travels by Streetcar*, 1954, Mexico).

Beyond the diplomatic and commercial maneuvering that informed its planning, the Mar del Plata festival staged spectacles of technological modernity that showcased both Hollywood innovations and Argentine infrastructure. The festival marked the debut of both 3D projection and the CinemaScope format in the country. The Ocean Rex movie theater invested $20,000 in renovations necessary to screen *The Robe* (Henry Koster, 1953, United States), the first CinemaScope release.[194] Later editions of the festival would also feature spectacular widescreen processes. In 1959 Abel Gance demonstrated the Polyvision process in which three synchronized projectors were used to create an expanded image, most famously used for his 1927 film *Napoléon*.[195] (The film and process had also been displayed at the São Paulo festival of 1954, albeit with technical problems.)[196] Nelly Kaplan, a Paris correspondent for the Argentine cineclub magazine *Gente de Cine* and future director of *La fiancée du pirate* (*A Very Curious Girl*, 1969, France), who was romantically linked to Gance (even though he was married), accompanied him to the festival.[197] At the 1961 festival, the largest screen in South America (according to *Variety*) was installed to showcase the ARC-120 format, a single-strip process that mimicked the proportions of Cinerama.[198]

In 1954, such displays did not solely serve to show off foreign technological achievements. In addition to Warner Brothers' *House of Wax* (Andre de Toth, 1953, United States), festival attendees—including Perón himself—watched *Buenos Aires en relieve* (Buenos Aires in relief, Don Napy, 1954), a production of Argentina's SIPE shot using a domestically developed 3D process. The film's voiceover misses no opportunities to highlight the Perón administration's infrastructural achievements, from the construction of housing and public parks to the nationalization of the railroad. Argentine infrastructure was also placed in a positive light through a subtler, somewhat deceptive strategy: the usual rationing of electricity was suspended for the duration of the festival, allowing for a fully illuminated skyline and sidestepping the power cuts that plagued other events.[199] Yet securing adequate electrical capacity to power projectors and air conditioners continued to be a concern for the festival into the 1960s.[200] In 1961 *Variety* griped about the inadequacy of telephone and telegraph connections at the festival. A journalist linked these limitations to the organizers' "lack of experience and/or global imagination," signaled by their tendency to favor correspondents from Buenos Aires and Montevideo newspapers over journalists based outside the Río de la Plata.[201] Such remarks suggest US journalists' difficulty in imagining a cultural sphere that did not revolve around Hollywood.

Criticized in retrospect as an expensive political stunt—one that, as Kriger shows, favorably impressed many foreign delegates with the accomplishments of Perón's "New Argentina"—the 1954 Mar del Plata festival also aroused skepticism internationally. *Variety* viewed the event as a counterintuitive means of combating industry crisis: "The methods used were peculiar, consisting mostly in staging a lavish International Festival, and demonstrating a spendthrift prodigality in entertaining foreign visitors."[202] Yet *Variety* also mentioned Apold's successful negotiation of co-production deals with the United Kingdom, Italy, and France. Regardless of the festival's mixed results, the 1955 military coup that ousted Perón scuttled any immediate plans for future festivals.

Whether they wholeheartedly embraced a European festival model centered on the fiction feature, like Punta del Este, or pursued alternative paths for promoting international understanding and developing film culture by focusing on nonfiction or retrospective programming, Latin American festival initiatives lost momentum in the mid-1950s in the face of public criticism, FIAPF pressures, and in the case of Mar del Plata, shifting political winds. Yet by the end of the 1950s, the consolidation of the Mar del Plata festival—currently the sole event in Latin America ranked "Category A" by FIAPF, a distinction conceded when the festival reopened in 1996 after a quarter-century hiatus—would come to embody a more lasting transplantation of the European festival model to Latin America and a significant battleground in the "cultural Cold War."

ESTABLISHING THE EUROPEAN FESTIVAL MODEL: MAR DEL PLATA, 1959–1970

In 1962, three years after Mar del Plata became an annual event, the magazine *Lyra* praised its efforts to cultivate a unique profile: "From its very birth, [the festival] has concerned itself with being a testament to contemporary film culture, a true point of confluence for these cultures, and [there] the most important names in the sphere of creation or film criticism have united as well with prominent figures of other intellectual orders."[203] As *Lyra*'s assessment suggests, Mar del Plata presented itself as a space for sophisticated discourse on cinema despite the nation's perceived dearth of high-quality film production. This tendency was especially strong in the first half of the 1960s, when a series of public discussions on cinema—referred to as Encuentros de Teóricos ("Encounters of Theoreticians")—became a staple of its programming. Similarly, in 1963 the magazine *Primera Plana* commented, "Since its birth, the Mar del Plata festival has insisted on having its own style, in distinguishing itself as a vast center of intellectual discussion."[204]

Yet foreign observers were not always impressed by these efforts, *Primera Plana* complained: "some disdainful French critic" (namely Pierre Billard, writing in the magazine *Cinéma 60*) compared them to "the impractical pretension of the ant." Furthermore, Billard is quoted as stating that "traveling to Mar del Plata is one way, and not the most pleasant, to bury oneself at the ends of the earth."[205] Yet if one returns to

Billard's original text, whose title indeed calls Mar del Plata "the festival at the end of the world," these dismissive comments are nowhere to be found.[206] A remark by Billard that is reproduced accurately—the description of Mar del Plata as "a jungle compared with public gardens"—reads as a compliment rather than the dig resentfully cited by *Primera Plana*. Unlike conventional festivals—"there is nothing more banal, more academic, more bureaucratic," Billard mused—Mar del Plata offered him a sense of adventure. The tone of Billard's festival diary, it seems, had been lost in translation, leading *Primera Plana* to stridently contest Mar del Plata's imagined place on the periphery of film culture. Despite being held in a country with a significant (if troubled) industry, Mar del Plata, like Punta del Este, sought to highlight the elevated tastes of local audiences as part of an international public relations strategy. Even as the festival advanced Argentine cinema's commercial interests through the brokering of distribution agreements and co-production deals, it actively combated its own subordinate position within the cultural economy of the festival circuit through the Encuentros de Teóricos. Although Mar del Plata was not the first festival to include such events—Karlovy Vary in Czechoslovakia held an Open Forum consisting of seminars and panel discussions beginning in 1958—it became a central aspect of its public profile.[207]

Mar del Plata's revival in 1959 took place amid a climate of optimism for Argentine cinema during the presidency of Arturo Frondizi (1958–1962), which ended the dictatorship of General Pedro Eugenio Aramburu that had followed the ouster of Perón. Frondizi came to power in the elections of 1958, during which the Peronist party was banned, receiving significant Peronist support based on a tacit understanding that he would work to lift the prohibition. Frondizi moved away from the import-substitution industrialization model pursued by Perón, increasingly seeking development through foreign investment. In 1962, on the heels of a Peronist resurgence, Frondizi was ousted in turn by a military junta headed by politician José María Guido. Despite robust state support for the film industry under Perón—support that often backfired, as producers pocketed subsidies rather than investing them in the productions themselves—many film critics and enthusiasts welcomed his fall, hailing the opportunity for the birth of a new cinema unconstrained by previous limits on freedom of expression. Though the sudden dismantling of state subsidies all but paralyzed the industry, a new cinema law promulgated in 1957 established INC and set aside funds for the production of shorts, viewed as a path for young directors to enter the industry.

In 1958 the Asociación de Cronistas Cinematográficos Argentinos (Argentine Film Critics' Association; ACCA) was approached by Mar del Plata's Chamber of Commerce to revive the festival.[208] ACCA's backing lent Mar del Plata its unique character; *Variety* described it as being "responsible for having made [the festivals] renowned as serious seminars of discussion on all screen problems."[209] ACCA's role in organizing the festival also granted it partial autonomy from both the state and the film industry. Surprisingly, the 1959 festival met with pushback from a newspaper owned by Frondizi himself and the Sindicato de la Industria Cinematográfica Argentina (SICA), the Argentine film industry union.[210] INC only grudgingly offered a last-minute infusion of funds to the festival, while the national air carrier, Aerolíneas Argentinas, reneged on its offer to cover the fares of foreign delegates.[211] Beginning in 1960, the festival enjoyed considerably broader support, including the backing of INC, Argentina's Ministry of Foreign Relations, the national tourism institute, the provincial government, Mar del Plata trade associations, and film industry unions, including SICA.[212]

An explosion on the rail line connecting Mar del Plata and Buenos Aires in the run-up to the 1959 event threw into relief ideological frictions both foreign and domestic. Historians speculate that Peronists were responsible for the blast, though one magazine brushed it off as a publicity stunt.[213] According to *Variety*, "The bombing of the Railway line caused a panic among the Mar del Plata police forces. This, combined with the attendance of so many Iron Curtain delegations, set up much cloak-and-dagger activity. Most waiters in the Provincial Hotel were cops, microphones were hidden in their lapels at diplomatic dinners, and more were probably hidden in hotel bedrooms, to discover whether any of the news folk were in league with the bomb-layers."[214] While this account reads as a colorful exaggeration, Carlos García-Rivas has shown that during the 1959 and 1960 festivals the province's secret police closely monitored contacts between foreign delegations and suspected communists, a practice that continued in later years.[215]

Like its counterparts abroad, the festival was also marked by East-West clashes. In 1963 the military government's Servicio de Inteligencia del Estado (State Intelligence Service) sought to pull the Hungarian social realist drama *Angyalok földje* (*Land of Angels*, György Révész, 1962) from the festival line-up due to its "tendentious" qualities, but proved unable to do so because it risked a complaint being filed with FIAPF.[216] The film went on to win the top prizes from the official and critics' juries. The same year, Tony Richardson, director of *The Loneliness of the*

FIGURE 11. Poster for the 1959 Mar del Plata film festival, positioning Argentina (whose flag is the last to appear on the reel) alongside major producers like the United States, Italy, the United Kingdom, and France and placing Mar del Plata on equal footing with established festivals in Cannes, Venice, and Berlin. Note the tiny size of the Mexican and Soviet flags (respectively fourth and seventh from the top) despite the geopolitical force of the USSR and the importance of Mexico's film industry. *Source:* Courtesy of the Museo del Cine Pablo Ducrós Hicken.

Long-Distance Runner (1962, United Kingdom), made a polemical public declaration of his support for the Cuban Revolution.[217] At the 1964 festival, held in Buenos Aires rather than Mar del Plata, the Soviet delegation declared a boycott on West German screenings after the projection of *Durchbruch Lok 234* (*The Breakthrough*, Frank Wisbar, 1963) which dramatized a railway engineer's efforts to escape East Germany by hijacking a train.[218]

Beginning in 1960, Mar del Plata's organizers sought to elevate the event above pragmatic concerns like subsidies, distribution deals, and co-production agreements through the Encuentros de Teóricos. The Encuentros' importance to Mar del Plata's cultural project becomes clear in a welcome speech by festival president Enzo Ardigó printed in Spanish, English, and French in the festival bulletin. Making the usual rhetorical gestures toward cinema as "the most formidable vehicle created by man for the promotion of knowledge and understanding among people," Ardigó's welcome was quick to yoke the quality of the films presented to Argentines' elevated taste and cosmopolitanism. He wrote: "We want you to know that we have not asked you here, prompted by simple cortesy [sic]. Argentina is a cultured and dynamic nation where in the last three years, perhaps the greatest number of foreign films presented in any country in the world have been screened. . . . We admire the creators of the different Motion Picture styles and our film clubs and public collections [*cinetecas*] devotedly review their classics."[219] Ardigó's speech strategically staked a claim to Argentine distinction not through the nation's film production—so often dismissed abroad as aesthetically uninteresting—but through its sophisticated consumers.

Following a 1960 session dedicated to hammering out an agreement to facilitate the international circulation of artistic film, the Encuentros de Teóricos tackled topics such as "freedom of expression" (1961), "the mission and ideology of criticism" (1962), and "cinema as expression of the modern city" (1963). French intellectuals figured prominently at the Encuentros, including historian and film society activist Georges Sadoul (1960), sociologist Edgar Morin (1961), and Henri Langlois (1960 and 1965). In the conference's final year, which saw the formation of UCAL, guests from across Latin America and Europe informed attendees about the state of film culture in their countries, including Roland and Salvador Sammaritano (Argentina), Rudá de Andrade (Brazil), Pedro Chaskel (Chile), Miguel Reynel (Peru), and Walther Dassori Barthet (Uruguay).[220]

Ironically, this component of the festival often failed to impress foreign observers. While largely complimentary about Mar del Plata, Billard criticized the inaugural Encuentro for involving "too many subjects to debate, too much time wasted in translations and procedure, too many improvisations [that] impede conclusions from being developed rationally."[221] For *Variety* reporter Hans Ehrmann, logistical problems hampered the Encuentro's success. He wrote in 1962, "Simultaneous translation was beamed at participants' earphones, but never a thought was given by the Argentinean hosts to the 200 spectators, whose understanding of the proceedings was hampered by the lack of audible translation, poor acoustics and—in some cases—by the so-called theoreticians' poor diction or low delivery. They sat with their backs to the public."[222] For Ehrmann, the conference was nothing more than "the usual stuff about objectivity and non-objectivity, whether criticism should be 'engag[é]' or not and finally an inoffensive little bout between Roman Catholics and Marxists." He reported that only half of the panelists and a third of the audience returned to the second session.[223] In 1963 local observers noted that only half the usual number of critics, approximately ten, had made the trip to Mar del Plata, further compromising the success of the parallel conference.[224]

While some critics insisted on film criticism's independence from ideological concerns, politics came to weigh heavily on the Mar del Plata festival, ultimately contributing to a hiatus of more than twenty-five years. In 1962 the event coincided with Frondizi's ouster. Yet although the abrupt dismissal of INC personnel derailed a co-production deal between Argentina and Brazil slated to be signed during the festival, foreign delegations and Argentines alike seem to have largely disregarded the president's overthrow.[225] Turmoil outside Argentina's borders—namely the overthrow of Brazilian president João Goulart by a US-backed military coup, which presaged the wave of military dictatorships that swept the Southern Cone in the 1970s—slowed the arrival of some foreign delegations traveling via Brazil to the 1964 festival in Buenos Aires.[226]

In the latter half of the 1960s, political repression weighed increasingly heavily on Mar del Plata. The 1967 edition was canceled altogether when the INC abruptly pulled its financial support, purportedly because the military government that came to power in 1966 with the overthrow of President Arturo Illia would not agree to the involvement of Eastern bloc countries.[227] In 1968 the festival was organized directly by the military dictatorship, yet these efforts to improve the regime's image

FIGURE 12. Images from the 1965 Encuentro de Teóricos, which focused on the problems of institutions of film culture, including archives and film schools, and saw the founding of the Unión de Cinematecas de América Latina. *Source: Gaceta del Festival*, March 27, 1965.

on the international stage failed spectacularly.[228] Industry professionals again threatened to boycott the festival if the government failed to pass a new cinema law, but they were forced to cede in the face of President Juan Carlos Onganía's intransigence.[229] Most damagingly, after INC's general administrator Adolfo Ridruejo agreed that films in the festival would not be subject to censorship, the Consejo Honorario de Contralor Cinematográfico (the governmental film review board) suddenly demanded cuts in four of the titles shown at the festival and even fined INC officials for screening films without review in an apparent turf war between government agencies.[230] The reverberations of this incident were still felt in 1970, when journalists threatened to boycott the festival if censors intervened, though ultimately this did not occur.[231] In light of these escalating tensions, the 1970 festival was the last until 1996. While Mar del Plata constituted a much more lasting transplantation of the European festival model to Latin America, both national factors and internal contradictions ultimately made it impossible to sustain.

CODA: FROM CINEMATIC INTERNATIONALISM TO CONTINENTAL SOLIDARITY

In a report on the inaugural 1960 Rassegna del Cinema Latinoamericano (Survey of Latin American Cinema) organized by the Fondazione Columbianum, a Genoa-based religious organization dedicated to strengthening ties between Europe and Latin America, French writer Simon Lantieri described it as a "first encounter with Latin American cinema." He continued, "we must consider as negligible what we knew up to this point of Argentina through *La casa del ángel* or of Mexico through *Raíces* [*Roots*, Benito Alazraki, 1955]," referencing titles that had screened at Cannes in 1957 and 1955, respectively.[232] Three years later, journalist Guy Gauthier similarly celebrated the Rassegna's capacity to expand French knowledge of Latin American films. Although he did not reference the famous festival on the French Riviera by name, his Latin American points of reference were drawn entirely from the directors (Emilio Fernández, Luis Buñuel, Leopoldo Torre Nilsson) and films (*Raíces*; *O cangaceiro*; *O canto do mar* [*Song of the Sea*, Alberto Cavalcanti, 1952]; *O pagador de promessas*) featured at Cannes.[233]

These two journalistic accounts suggest the Columbianum's role not only in broadening French familiarity with Latin American cinema beyond Cannes's programming (although it often overlapped with the Rassegna's), but also in disseminating of the idea of Latin American cinema itself. Designed to forge connections between the region's film industries and to identify solutions to common problems, the Rassegna challenged the internationalism of conventional film festivals, conceived as a set of relationships between nations that ignored disparities between them. In so doing, the festival helped lay the groundwork for the theorization of NLAC by practitioners and scholars as a "continental project" rooted in the region's shared struggles against neo-colonial economic and cultural domination.[234] Father Angelo Arpa, the leader of the Columbianum, explained the organization to the Argentine film magazine *Tiempo de Cine* in 1963: "The world is passing through a singular historical moment characterized by an intense movement of political, economic, and social liberation of the so-called Third World. Within it, Latin America has the function of a vanguard, due to its particular evolution and the degree of maturity reached. If Western civilization does not learn how to insert itself in this process, it runs the risk of being left behind entirely."[235] Arpa's remarks suggest the strategic nature of European cultural interest and investment in Latin America at a moment of sweeping cultural and political transformation.

Held at different locations in the Genoa region between 1960 and 1965, the Rassegna became a showcase for emerging Latin American new waves with varying degrees of politicization, including Argentina's generación del 60 (Leopoldo Torre Nilsson attended in 1960 and again in 1962, when he was accompanied by Rodolfo Kuhn and David José Kohon); Mexico's Grupo Nuevo Cine, most notably represented by José Miguel "Jomí" García Ascot's *En el balcón vacío* (On the empty balcony, 1962); and early works of Brazilian Cinema Novo, including Glauber Rocha's *Barravento* (*The Turning Wind*, 1962) and *Porto das Caixas* (Paulo César Saraceni, 1963).[236] Representatives of Cuba's emerging postrevolutionary cinema, including Julio García Espinosa and Alfredo Guevara, head of ICAIC, also attended, although Cuban films sent to the event were censored by local authorities on multiple occasions.[237]

Like Mar del Plata, the Rassegna included a series of public roundtables, including evaluations of the state of Latin American cinema and the role of film culture in fostering national industries, though some observers were unimpressed with European intellectuals' tendency to offer advice despite their limited familiarity with Latin American culture and cinema.[238] Most famously, Glauber Rocha's declarations at the 1965 festival became the basis for his famous manifesto "Estética da fome" (Aesthetics of hunger). Prefiguring contemporary debates about the marketability of "poverty porn" in the international festival circuit, Rocha wrote, "While Latin America laments its general misery, the foreign observer cultivates a taste for that misery, not as a tragic *symptom*, but merely as a formal element in his field of interest" (emphasis in original).[239] Insisting that Cinema Novo's aesthetic "violence" was "not primitive but revolutionary," Rocha hailed its ability to generate political consciousness and social change, though later manifestos like Fernando Solanas and Octavio Getino's "Towards a Third Cinema" would dismiss Cinema Novo as auteurist "second cinema," still beholden to bourgeois notions of art as individual self-expression.

Two years after the final Rassegna—the event and the Columbianum itself collapsed due to the high costs of the 1965 festival and resulting accusations of financial mismanagement—the Cine Club Viña del Mar organized the Primer Festival de Cine Nuevo Latinoamericano.[240] While historians have hailed this event as a watershed for the development of NLAC that fostered personal connections between filmmakers in the region as well as a shared political consciousness, few have remarked on its precedence in a national, and later international, festival of amateur cinema that the cineclub organized beginning in 1963.[241] This piece of historical context sheds light on how the festivals that helped inaugurate NLAC built on existing infrastructures of cinematic exchange that were shaped by distinct geopolitical configurations.

This chapter has traced Latin American involvement—in the role of both invited guests and hosts—in the competitive international film festivals that dominated the circuit in the first two decades after World War II. This participation proved problematic for two main reasons. The first was the frequent difficulty of reconciling the formal and narrative strategies of popular Latin American film industries with the conceptions of art cinema being codified internationally through festival prizes and film criticism. The second was the Europe-centered and inherently hierarchical nature of the postwar festival circuit, enforced by FIAPF to preserve events' prestige and their benefits for major film industries, which necessarily disadvantaged new festivals located at a great geographic distance from both Hollywood and Europe. Latin American festivals' efforts to showcase the refined taste and erudition of local cinephiles promised to address both challenges, glossing over perceived deficiencies in domestic film production (or its near-total absence) by placing the focus on consumption, valorizing national audiences as connoisseurs capable of appreciating complex works of cinematic art. From infrastructural challenges to dilemmas like that faced by the Punta del Este jury members in 1955, who found themselves obliged to assert the validity of their aesthetic judgments from a subordinate cultural position, the precarious career of early Latin American festivals exemplifies both the cosmopolitan promise and the structural inequalities of the postwar festival circuit.

CHAPTER 4

Film Pedagogy between Latin America and France

Training Professionals, Fostering Film Culture

At a ceremony held at the Mar del Plata film festival to mark the official founding of Argentina's Escuela Nacional de Cinematografía in 1966, Manuel González Casanova, the director of Mexico's CUEC, outlined a set of lofty goals for professional film training tied to broader hopes and anxieties surrounding the medium. Invoking the work of French sociologist Edgar Morin and echoing a constant theme of postwar discourse on cinema, his speech stresses the medium's social influence, declaring, "It is difficult to grasp the effect exercised on the average man's way of living and thinking by frequent attendance at theaters where empty, mediocre films that constantly falsify reality are screened."[1] González Casanova hails film societies and high school classes in film appreciation—initiatives he spearheaded at UNAM and its associated preparatory schools—as means of building the spectator's critical capacities. Yet he also notes the limitations of these methods in reaching the general public, especially given low levels of formal education in Mexico. "For this reason," González Casanova continues, "it's necessary to attack the evil at the root, that is to say, to awaken the conscience of the filmmaker with respect to his commitment to society, and give him the necessary technical and cultural training so that he can make cinema that does not shy away from its educational responsibilities, hiding behind its supposed goal of entertaining, because this entertainment is educating, education understood in its broadest sense."[2]

González Casanova's comments suggest the far-reaching hopes and anxieties attached to professional film training in the two decades after World War II. More broadly, they highlight film schools' often overlooked role in shaping aesthetic canons, production practices, and notions of filmmakers' ethical obligations.[3] Only in the past decade and a half have film schools emerged in force as an object of academic inquiry. Scholars have explored their roles both as vehicles of cultural nationalism—particularly through the "national conservatory" model pioneered by European film schools—and as nodes of transnational exchange, given that aspiring cineastes often sought out training abroad if it was unavailable locally.[4] The very existence of film schools suggests cultural ambitions beyond the capacity of commercial film industries to reproduce themselves through informal apprenticeships and other forms of on-the-job training. These educational institutions were charged with fostering domestic industries where none existed or actively fortifying existing ones against foreign competition by equipping film industry workers to develop a distinctive national style.[5] Furthermore, they could broaden access to industry careers for previously excluded sectors, including young people.

If the perceived need for film schools signals discontent with the capacity of existing industrial structures to fulfill cinema's desired social function, González Casanova's particular vision builds on the humanist ideals of postwar film culture while signaling a growing investment in the medium's power to reveal, critique, and transform social reality, core principles of the NLAC that was gaining momentum in the mid-1960s. For González Casanova, film schools were an especially promising means of advancing these ideals, since they could directly impact production via filmmakers' technical and cultural preparation. By contrast, cineclubs, archives, and festivals acted in a more roundabout manner by working to create a more educated and demanding spectator. Accordingly, film schools have been attributed with a much more direct role in shaping NLAC than other film-related institutions.

To wit, aspiring Latin American filmmakers' decision to pursue professional film training abroad is credited with helping to transplant Italian neorealism's critical, observational approach toward everyday life to the region. Like Italian neorealist works, many key films of NLAC critique social inequality, offer meandering narratives rather than tightly constructed plots, cast mostly non-professional actors rather than recognizable stars, and prefer location shooting over the polished production values made possible by the studio.[6] This transfer of neorealist principles is often attributed to the passage of key figures of NLAC, including Julio García Espinosa and Tomás Gutiérrez Alea from Cuba, Fernando Birri from Argentina, and Colombian novelist and screenwriter Gabriel García Márquez through Rome's CSC.[7] After returning from Italy, Birri founded the Instituto de Cinematografía at the Universidad Nacional del Litoral in 1956, whose pursuit of a socially engaged filmmaking practice became a major precursor to NLAC.

Yet as González Casanova's remarks aligning film schools with long-standing efforts to "improve" the film culture of the masses suggest, the legacy of postwar film pedagogy in Latin America cannot be reduced to the forms of social critique and political commitment fostered by contact with Italian neorealism. Rather, professional film training in the region was shaped both by the local needs of expanding and modernizing universities and by a broader tradition of European film pedagogy that combined technical instruction with humanistic study. France's national film school, IDHEC, in fact attracted a greater number of Latin American students than CSC, enlisting them in the French state's postwar cultural diplomacy. Building on the precedents of the Soviet Union's Vsesoiuznyi Gosudarstvennyi Institut Kinematografii (All-Union State Institute of Cinematography; VGIK) and Italy's CSC, IDHEC sought to bolster France's industry not only by training a new generation of practitioners, but also by developing the film culture of cineaste and audience alike. Furthermore, IDHEC actively promoted the enrollment of Latin Americans and other foreigners—albeit on unequal terms with native-born students—as a testament to the technical and creative superiority of French cinema and as a means of enhancing its international prestige. International students who returned to their home countries with French training were imagined as de facto cultural ambassadors.

Much like their counterparts in France, early Latin American film schools treated the mid-century crises that struck Argentina's and Mexico's film industries as problems of film culture that could be addressed by cultivating cinephilic audiences and erudite filmmakers. IDHEC's influence on Latin American film pedagogy was far less direct than France-based institutions' impact on the cineclub and film preservation movements. Yet the region's film schools nonetheless propagated ideals of the sophisticated spectator championed by these earlier initiatives and by European film pedagogy, even when their original purpose (such as the production of scientific and promotional films) was far removed from such goals. Latin America's oldest continuously operating film school, CUEC, founded by González Casanova in 1963, perpetuated models of film culture promoted by IDHEC and other film-related institutions as a necessary response to the challenges faced by Mexican cinema in the 1960s.

Responding to the perceived economic and aesthetic decline of the national film industry, CUEC took on the seemingly paradoxical task of institutionalizing innovation and freedom of expression, qualities that critics found lacking in commercial Mexican cinema of the period. Mirroring the contradictions of an institutionalized revolution, which increasingly came to the fore in the 1950s after more than two decades of one-party rule, CUEC's cultural project converged with a turn away from popular nationalism and toward the erudite and cosmopolitan in Mexican arts and letters. Amid the (limited) expansion and democratization of higher education in Mexico and across Latin America, CUEC instituted a largely top-down approach to reforming the industry and audiences alike, incorporating cineclub screenings and critical reflection on the state of Mexican cinema into its curriculum. These somewhat paternalistic methods would be challenged as students seized control of the school during an intense period of student activism in 1968, appropriating its equipment and facilities to document the movement.

In the late 1960s and early 1970s Latin American film schools experienced an intense politicization, characterized by the production of more overtly leftist films and, in turn, by repression by right-wing military governments as the Cold War turned hot in the Southern Cone. Across the range of institutional models that gave rise to Latin American film schools—from scientific and educational film institutes to hands-on workshops without formal curricula to more traditional professional training programs—film students began to pursue a socially committed cinema of direct action, whose efforts to transform the spectator into a political actor contrasted sharply with postwar efforts to "improve" audience taste. Yet these distinct tendencies were never diametrically opposed; the imperative to build film culture always carried with it a sense of social responsibility, albeit conceived in rather patronizing terms as a need to guide unenlightened spectators.

Tracing Latin Americans' experiences at European film schools and the emergence of professional film training in Latin America, this chapter highlights geopolitical investments and cultural trajectories that exceed NLAC's well-known appropriation of neorealist strategies. I examine how aspiring Latin American filmmakers in both Europe and Latin America were recruited into broader institutional and cultural projects as professional film training took shape through efforts to foster film culture and shore up national industries. I first delve into the roots of humanistic and technical training in European film schools before turning to IDHEC's use of film pedagogy as a form of cultural diplomacy. I then examine the emergence and development of Latin American film schools with varied institutional profiles, exploring the frequent tension between erudite film culture and (politicized) film practice, with a focus on CUEC and its transformation during the 1968 student movement.

THE ORIGINS OF EUROPEAN FILM PEDAGOGY

Arising from attempts to establish or strengthen national film industries through state intervention, early European film schools fused humanistic instruction and hands-on training, a model that would later shape film pedagogy in Latin America and beyond. In adopting the model of the "'national conservatoire,' a publicly funded institution providing high-level professional training in a specific field of cultural activity beneficial to the state," both CSC and IDHEC drew on the precedent of the earliest educational institution dedicated to training filmmakers, the USSR's VGIK.[8] Renamed and reorganized several times during its early years, VGIK's origins can be traced to Moscow's State College of Cinematography, founded in 1919 by filmmaker Vladimir Gardin at the behest of the Soviet state's Commissariat of Enlightenment.[9] Due to limited resources, the school initially focused on experimental approaches to the training of actors. This notion of the film school as laboratory attracted prominent figures of the emerging Soviet montage movement. Lev Kuleshov ran his famous workshop within the school, Vsevolod Pudovkin was enrolled as a student, and Sergei Eisenstein formally joined the faculty in 1932.

Throughout the late 1920s and early 1930s, Eisenstein lobbied the administration to incorporate classes in humanistic disciplines like art history and literature, stressing cinema's links with other arts.[10] By 1930 this shift culminated in the school's reclassification as an institute of higher education rather than a technical school. In parallel, its administration moved away from the mass enrollment of peasants and workers that had begun in the late 1920s, whose limited academic preparation had contributed to high drop-out rates.[11] Over the next two years VGIK began to develop infrastructure for the study of film history and aesthetics, assembling a collection of five hundred films and establishing a center for Russian and Soviet film history.[12] Yet unlike its successors CSC and IDHEC, VGIK did not enroll foreign students until 1953.[13] Through 1957, its students generally hailed from socialist republics, but

VGIK attracted a strong contingent of African, Middle Eastern, and some Latin American students in the 1960s and beyond.[14] Despite its historically more insular nature, VGIK's emphasis on humanistic inquiry alongside technical training proved highly influential.[15]

Despite the clashing political orientations of the Soviet Union and Fascist Italy, Italian film educators were nonetheless fascinated by VGIK's attempts to harness the Russian Revolution's radical energies in its pedagogy. The initial impetus for the creation of CSC, one of the Fascist state's many film-related initiatives, can be traced to a visit by Alessandro Sardi to VGIK in 1932.[16] At the time, Sardi headed L'Istituto LUCE (L'Unione Cinematografica Educativa; Educational Film Union), the Fascist government's educational and newsreel organization. As Masha Salazkina has shown, Futurist artist Anton Giulio Bragaglia, who first proposed the creation of a Scuola Nazionale di Cinematografia, referred directly to VGIK as a model.[17] Established in Rome in 1932, the school was reorganized as the CSC two years later. Suggesting the mix of affinity and antipathy that marked Fascist Italy's relationship to Soviet Russia, Umberto Barbaro, a left-leaning Futurist writer who developed the school's curriculum jointly with its staunchly Fascist director Luigi Chiarini, embraced Pudovkin's theories of montage as an experimental approach to reality geared toward its transformation. As Salazkina notes, "Chiarini and Barbaro were unlikely allies in the campaign to promote cinema's social and educational function as against its commercial use," despite their divergent investments in film as a mode of individual expression with the potential to edify the masses (Chiarini) or as a vehicle for generating class consciousness (Barbaro).[18] These ideals, developed in an educational space comparatively free of political scrutiny, later informed the postwar neorealist movement and its well-known appropriation in postrevolutionary Cuban cinema.[19] Efforts to give filmmakers practical training but also a cultural formation designed to have an edifying effect on audiences persisted in the school's later years. At a 1954 gathering of film schools (discussed in greater detail later), Giuseppe Sala, the CSC's director at the time, defined its aims as "the preparation of film professionals [and the fostering of] the country's film culture through scientific, filmographic and bibliographic research," insisting that "aesthetic problems are dominant in our school."[20] Framing CSC's activities in terms of "scientific" progress, Sala's description nevertheless privileges artistic questions over technical ones.

CSC focused on preparing Italian students for industry careers while also welcoming foreign students, and its policies created clear divisions between the two groups. The school offered tuition-free instruction, with scholarships available to help defray living expenses for Italian students, but their international classmates were not eligible until a policy change in 1972.[21] Until 1969, foreign students were technically allowed only to audit the school's programs, which by the late 1930s included acting, directing, screenwriting, editing, cinematography, sound, set design, and costume and make-up.[22] (Notably, during the 1930s only the programs in acting, set decoration, and costume and make-up were open to female students.)[23] Between 1937 and 1943, when Italy formed part of the Axis, most international students hailed from Germany, German-occupied territories, and Spain. Their presence was encouraged as a means of mitigating the "political and cultural isolation" stemming from Italy's foreign policy.[24]

International student enrollment at CSC reached its peak between 1950 and 1970.[25] In 1954 Sala described a ratio of two-thirds Italian students to one-third foreigners, with the latter concentrated in the acting school; three years later, an American student reported that non-Italians made up half of his cohort in the directing program.[26] By the end of the 1960s, foreigners actually outnumbered Italians in this program two to one.[27] However, until 1958 foreign auditors of CSC's courses were not provided resources to direct their own student films or allowed to be credited as directors, though both Birri and Gutiérrez Alea made films during their time at CSC in the early 1950s.[28] As a result, international students did not receive a diploma upon completing their studies, only a certificate of attendance.[29] Even after these policies changed, the school dedicated minimal resources to foreign students' film projects, which tended to be between a quarter and a third the length of those of their Italian classmates.[30] Nor were international students entitled to the paid year-long internship that Italian students had the option to pursue after their studies, though in practice some of them completed it.[31]

CSC proved a powerful draw for students from Latin America despite their unequal position in the school, likely due to the lure of neorealism and the historical ties between Italy and the region forged by massive Italian immigration, especially to Argentina and Brazil.[32] Between 1935 and 2020, Brazil and Colombia ranked second and third, after Greece, in the number of foreign students studying at CSC in the areas of directing, cinematography, and set design.[33] Beyond the school's best-known Latin American students—including Birri, Gutiérrez Alea, García Espinosa, and García Márquez, who roomed together during their studies—two dozen individuals from the region studied there during the 1950s and

1960s, including Cinema Novo filmmakers Paulo César Saraceni (who never completed his studies) and Gustavo Dahl as well as Rudá de Andrade, a future film educator and Cinemateca Brasileira staff member.³⁴ While certainly not all CSC graduates pursued neorealist strategies in their work, and the movement was already the subject of intense debate in Italy by the early 1950s, many were attracted by the movement's attention to pressing social problems and its challenge to Hollywood narrative and aesthetics. Neorealist practices like location shooting and casting non-professional actors allowed for more economical budgets, and thus were especially attractive for independent productions and in nations where industrial filmmaking was minimal or nonexistent.

Writing in 1954, Fernando Birri cited his impassioned response to neorealism as the root of his decision to study in Rome, suggesting how the movement's spirit suffused the CSC's activities: "We have gone into the street with our movie cameras to reflect the man in the street, with his problems regarding his daily bread and wine, the bicycle that carries him to work, his difficult years after the Second World War, his desire to believe again.... Propelled by an intimate ethical conviction, in this way I satisfied a profound aesthetic necessity."³⁵ In Birri's account, through the confrontations with everyday life embedded in the pedagogy of the CSC, the quotidian struggles of postwar Italy came to light, revealing to the spectator harsh conditions that were typically ignored or rendered invisible.³⁶ For Birri, neorealism's revelations resonated globally. He framed this insight in relation to dependency theory, which posits that a core of highly industrialized nations maintains the global periphery in a state of underdevelopment in order to extract value in the form of natural resources and cheap labor, a perspective that gained significant traction among Latin American intellectuals in the 1960s. In an interview conducted in the 1980s, Birri reflected, "Neo-realism is the cinema that discovers the Italy of underdevelopment, discovers in a country that apparently has the tinsel, and, what's more, the rhetoric of development, another reality, a hidden one, that of underdevelopment ... it was the cinema of the humble and offended. It was possible everywhere."³⁷

Beyond CSC's coursework—which students often found overly theoretical and insufficiently practical, a common complaint about European film school curricula—the school facilitated contact with industry professionals, who served as guest lecturers and even filmed in the school's studio spaces. The school's permanent facility, which opened in 1940, was adjacent to the Cinecittà studio complex. Gutiérrez Alea noted that Vittorio De Sica filmed in one of CSC's studios and attended

FIGURE 13. Fernando Birri with Alberto Cavalcanti in Rome in the 1950s. *Source:* Fernando Birri Archive of Multimedia Arts, John Hay Library, Brown University.

the opening ceremony for the 1951 academic year.[38] For his part, while in Italy Fernando Birri rubbed shoulders with Emilio Fernández, Mexico's most internationally renowned director in the period, and Alberto Cavalcanti, who played a pivotal role in the interwar French avant-gardes and British documentary of the 1930s before returning to his native Brazil in 1950 to head the Companhia Cinematográfica Vera Cruz.[39] Screenwriter Cesare Zavattini, the preeminent champion and theorist of neorealist aesthetics and a CSC instructor, became Birri's mentor. As David Brancaleone shows through reference to their abundant correspondence, Zavattini helped Birri secure a position working on Vittorio De Sica's 1956 film *Il tetto* (*The Roof*). In 1959 Birri took a preliminary edit of *Tire dié*—a portrait of impoverished residents of Santa Fe, Argentina, that Birri made collectively with his students at the Instituto de Cinematografía—to Rome to seek Zavattini's comments, which he incorporated "point by point" into the final version.[40]

Zavattini's mentorship of young Cuban filmmakers is perhaps the best-known instance of the cultural transfer of neorealist strategies brokered by the CSC. Zavattini visited Cuba in 1953 on a junket sponsored by Unitalia—the agency charged with promoting Italian film abroad—before traveling on to Mexico to work with independent producer Manuel Barbachano Ponce.[41] On the island, Zavattini met with members of the Sociedad Cultural Nuestro Tiempo, including Gutiérrez Alea and García Espinosa, whom he had met at the CSC four years earlier.[42] By letter, Zavattini advised the two Cuban filmmakers on the production of *El mégano* (Julio García Espinosa, 1955), a documentary short denouncing the inhumane working conditions of rural charcoal workers considered a key precursor of postrevolutionary Cuban cinema.[43] Zavattini returned to Cuba for an extended stay after the triumph of the Revolution in 1959 as an adviser to the newly created ICAIC. Yet Zavattini's relationships with ICAIC filmmakers quickly deteriorated in the process of bringing his screenplay for *El joven rebelde* (*The Young Rebel*, Julio García Espinosa, 1962) to the screen. According to Anastasia Valecce, García Espinosa and his Cuban collaborators were troubled by Zavattini's conception of the title character, a campesino who joins the guerrilla struggle against the dictatorship of Fulgencio Batista, as a youth with a "pure and savage nature."[44] Bereft of political consciousness, in Zavattini's version he undergoes an almost religious conversion to revolutionary ideology. More broadly, Valecce argues, the disagreement served as a pretext for a break with Zavattini that permitted the pursuit of a distinctly Cuban revolutionary aesthetic that nevertheless remained indebted to Italian neorealism. For his part, Joseph Francese suggests that Zavattini struggled to reconcile the ostensibly "universal" ethical truths that informed his neorealist scripts—rooted, despite his Communist affiliation, in a Christian morality that identified human evil rather than economic forces as the source of social ills—with the social and political particularities of revolutionary Cuba.[45]

Due to the discursive importance of Italian neorealism for practitioners and historians of NLAC, CSC's impact on filmmaking in the region has largely overshadowed that of IDHEC, which, as noted previously, trained a larger group of Latin American cineastes during the 1950s and 1960s. In the two decades following the school's opening in 1944, foreigners hailing from fifty-eight countries accounted for 44 percent of its enrollment. In this period, Brazilians were the second-largest contingent of international students at IDHEC after Americans.[46] Prominent Latin American directors and intellectuals who passed through IDHEC's doors include Simón Feldman, a major figure of the *generación del 60* (Argentina's new wave), and Humberto Ríos, a documentary filmmaker of Bolivian origin who mostly worked in Argentina; Paulo

Emílio Salles Gomes, longtime director of the Cinemateca Brasileira, and acclaimed documentary filmmaker Eduardo Coutinho, from Brazil; Francisco Norden, Jorge Pinto, and Abraham Zalzman, a group of Colombian filmmakers dubbed the "generación de los maestros" due to their training abroad; writer Salvador Elizondo and directors Felipe Cazals and Paul Leduc from Mexico; and Venezuelan filmmaker Margot Benacerraf. At least seventy-three Latin American students attended IDHEC prior to its restructuring as la Fémis (Fondation européenne pour les métiers de l'image et du son) in 1986, compared with the forty-nine Latin Americans who studied at CSC in the same period.[47] In the following section, I examine how French cultural diplomacy informed IDHEC's institutional project and shaped the careers of individual Latin American filmmakers. Attending to the influence of French pedagogy illuminates how the humanistic and often conservative bent of postwar film culture shaped the region's early film schools.

IDHEC: EXPORTING FRENCH CULTURAL
TRADITION AND TECHNIQUE

The founding of IDHEC in 1943 marked the implantation in France of a film pedagogy that fused theory and practice on the model of VGIK and the CSC, though it was preceded by the École technique de photographie et de cinématographie, opened in 1926, which focused exclusively on practical instruction.[48] Dudley Andrew notes, "Until 1968 IDHEC served not only as France's technical training school but as virtually the only recognized place for the sustained study of cinema in the entire country" with the exception of the Institut de filmologie at the Sorbonne, which pursued sociological and psychological approaches to the medium.[49] In fact, IDHEC initially had three divisions dedicated to technical training, research, and the expansion of film culture.[50]

The immediate impetus for IDHEC's creation—a long-standing ambition of its president, filmmaker Marcel L'Herbier, who had elaborated a plan for a "University of New Arts" between 1938 and 1942—stemmed from the profound disruption of World War II.[51] As the German army advanced, film industry workers fled to the south of the country, forming a cultural association that eventually solidified into IDHEC. Established as the Centre des jeunes du cinéma français near Cannes in 1940, the association was renamed the Centre artistique et technique des jeunes du cinéma and transferred to Nice in 1941.[52] In late 1943, the organization was reorganized as IDHEC under the auspices of the Direction générale de la cinématographie nationale (Office of National Cinema; DGCN) and transferred to Paris.⁵³ In 1946, the DGCN was replaced by the CNC, the agency dedicated to supporting and promoting French cinema, which heavily subsidized IDHEC. The school's activities were part of efforts to bolster French cinema in the face of renewed competition from foreign films—lowering barriers to the release of Hollywood films was a cornerstone of the Blum-Byrnes Accords that forgave France's war debt to the United States—and other challenges.

Despite state backing, the school's resources proved inadequate for purchasing camera equipment and film stock and for offering its personnel competitive salaries. Real estate proved to be one of IDHEC's thorniest problems. The school's eviction from its premises forced it to shut down during the 1950–1951 academic year for lack of a suitable space; thereafter, IDHEC's activities were dispersed across several locations, including a former studio in Saint-Cloud in the Paris suburbs.⁵⁴ In 1967, facing another forced move, IDHEC's longtime general administrator Rémy Tessonneau lamented the school's "chronically insufficient and precarious conditions," noting that it had "never received, since 1948 [when the school was informed it needed to relocate], the material means in space and financial support to fully implement its programs, notably in terms of practical work, the production of films and television programs."⁵⁵

While such problems placed practical limitations on the kind of hands-on training IDHEC could offer, from its inception the school's leadership had stressed the need to combine film practice with theory and to develop film culture, aims shared by VGIK and CSC. This pedagogical model was explicitly tied to nationalistic aspirations to global influence. In a speech delivered at IDHEC's opening ceremony, L'Herbier stressed that

> the essential goal of this Institute [is to] *create creators of films, in the right numbers, with an indisputable human quality*. Its second goal is to link itself with pure artistic or technical research, which does not concern only inventors, aestheticians or other dreamers: it concerns us all . . . The third goal of our official activities is to disseminate *film culture*. . . . What use is it to want to improve the quality of films if we do not, at the same time and with the same stubbornness, make an effort to improve the quality of the spectator? (emphasis in original)⁵⁶

The goal of transforming the audience—or, as L'Herbier put it on another occasion, to "raise the level of spectators; to refine their taste, to sharpen their critical faculties"—is yoked to patriotism in this speech.⁵⁷ L'Herbier declares, "A new clear-sightedness should demand, in our

FIGURE 14. Impressive-looking low-angle shot of IDHEC's studio facilities featured on the cover of a 1956 pamphlet, belying the school's struggles with resources and real estate. *Source:* © Fémis (Fondation européenne pour les métiers de l'image et du son). Scan courtesy of the Cinémathèque française.

opinion, *everything* from the man who, tomorrow, will express the nation through film—who by means of the film will be the spokesman of the nation to itself and to the world, who through the force, nuance, and poetry of film will influence the mass of workers, who are given over, usually defenseless, to the fearsome Lethe of the dark theater" (emphasis in original).[58] Acts of self-expression that simultaneously synthesized national sentiments are here cast as an antidote to cinema as an opiate for the masses, as suggested by the reference to the river Lethe, whose waters brought forgetfulness to the dead in the ancient Greek underworld.

Notably, L'Herbier's vision of film's educational impact is explicitly international in its scope. Further championing the school's future role in reproducing an idealized if vaguely defined Frenchness, L'Herbier continues: "From the Institut des hautes études cinematographiques, one must expect the formation of a phalanx of film artists and technicians who, when peace is restored, will be able to work not only in France, but also in the new centers of film production that are being established in great numbers overseas. . . . These men, in effect, will all be designated—as indirect ambassadors—to represent in distant lands, as at home, our culture, our taste, and above all, radiate through our cinematic knowledge, the purest French quality."[59] Like the Institut français d'Amérique latine discussed in chapter 1, IDHEC was attributed with the capacity to regenerate French prestige and influence, eroded by World War II, overseas.

If L'Herbier initially imagined IDHEC's French graduates as "indirect ambassadors" to the world, by the late 1940s this role partially shifted to the school's growing number of foreign students. These students were welcomed for the material and reputational benefits they might offer the school and, by extension, the French film industry. In the latter half of the 1940s, IDHEC reached out to French foreign embassies for help publicizing its summer courses to international students in an effort to "assure the coming of young foreigners to Paris, who, trained in French film technique, will become the best promoters of the art and industry of French cinema upon their return to their countries."[60] That these students would return home was both assumed and strongly encouraged by IDHEC officials; by design, significant barriers existed for graduates who sought to work in France. According to Tessonneau, French film professionals feared competition from foreigners—a concern intensified by the French film industry's precarious economic state—leading IDHEC to be leery of expanding its offerings of short-term training programs for foreign film professionals.[61]

Though their numbers were negligible in IDHEC's first three cohorts, with the fourth group of students admitted, foreigners came to account for over half of IDHEC's enrollees, a percentage that remained consistent through the 1960s.[62] In 1954 Tessonneau remarked, "We wanted the school to be international and it has become so to a great extent."[63] While French students attended tuition-free aside from their examination and registration fees (4,000 francs) in the early to mid-1950s, foreigners paid 48,000 francs (later raised to 75,000) annually, though roughly a quarter received scholarships from France's MAE.[64] Given IDHEC's relatively meager resources, foreign students' financial contribution doubtless made them valuable to the school (though tuition accounted for a tiny portion of the budget relative to subventions from the CNC).[65]

The separate admission process developed for non-French students suggests both IDHEC's commitment to recruiting them and their unequal status during and after their studies. Generally, French nationals could gain admission to IDHEC only after completing a university degree (with the exception of those pursuing programs in cinematography and set design) and undergoing a rigorous examination process.[66] By contrast, international students could be admitted either via examination or on the strength of their existing academic credentials (*sur titres*), with the latter being a far more common path.[67] Only foreigners who opted to take the entrance exams were eligible for the year-long internship required of French students and thus for the work card that had become indispensable for employment in the film industry.[68] Yet given that France's Ministry of Labor capped the number of foreign workers at 4 percent of each industry, their chances of employment were low.[69] In fact, in the mid-1950s foreign students who were admitted sur titres pledged in writing not to work in France after completing their studies at IDHEC, and the school encouraged the authorities responsible for issuing the cards to enforce this.[70]

Functioning as a major barrier to the future professionalization of foreign film students in France, IDHEC's entrance exams demanded deep knowledge of French literary and artistic history, signaling both the school's humanistic approach and its project of perpetuating a national cultural tradition through film. Students applying for admission in 1943 were instructed to prepare by reviewing Stendahl's *Le rouge et le noir* (*The Red and the Black*) and Flaubert's *L'Éducation sentimentale* (*Sentimental Education*) in order to comment on which author was more "adaptable to the screen."[71] A 1944 exam asked students to respond to the query: "Do you feel, based on your experience as a spectator, that French cinema from 1930 to today has accurately reflected society?"[72] Clearly, this question would have been challenging to answer for anyone who had been living outside France during the previous decade and a half. Not surprisingly, IDHEC officially enrolled only one foreign student in each of its first two cohorts.[73] By the mid-1950s, the subject matter covered on IDHEC's entrance exams had broadened significantly to include such topics as Cervantes's *Don Quixote*, the twentieth-century American novel, and African art, but still contained a significant component of French history and literature, and later exams were again dominated by European subject matter.[74] Given the rigor of the exams, many applicants enrolled in a preparatory class offered by Catholic film educator Henri Agel at the Lycée Voltaire. Some 40 percent of students who completed the course were accepted, whereas the school's overall acceptance rate was 8 to 12 percent, contributing to perceptions of IDHEC's elitism.[75] The relatively few foreign students who entered via examination were held up as evidence of the school's favorable international reputation. In 1951 a memo on the school's activities noted that four students from Belgium, Germany, Switzerland, and the United States had successfully gained admission via examination, "show[ing] that IDHEC's prestige abroad is greater than ever."[76]

Despite foreign students' disadvantageous position relative to their French classmates, internal and external communications emphasized their presence and accomplishments as a boon to the French film industry and to France's soft power more generally. A 1951 memo on the activities of IDHEC alumni highlighted the school's ambitions to "train foreign students using the methods and techniques of French cinema, so that these can later be applied to film production in their countries, propagating the prestige of ours.... IDHEC's *foreign* students are naturally the best agents of our cinematic propaganda in all the film-producing countries of the world" (emphasis in original).[77] The memo notes alumni's contributions to film production in Egypt and India and mentions Margot Benacerraf and three former students who worked with Alberto Cavalcanti at the Companhia Cinematográfica Vera Cruz—Martim Gonçalves (Brazil), Marcos Margulies (a Polish-born Brazilian), and John Waterhouse (United Kingdom)—as examples of successful graduates.[78] These last two individuals also participated in early efforts to establish film education in Brazil. In 1953 Waterhouse taught a course in "gramática do Cinema" (film language) and Margulies a class in "elementos da direção" (elements of direction) as part of a three-semester program combining aesthetic education and practical training offered through the Seminário de Cinema hosted by the Museu de Arte de São Paulo (MASP).[79]

In some cases, IDHEC administrators also worked to facilitate French alumni's participation in film production overseas. For instance, L'Herbier unsuccessfully petitioned the MAE's DGRC to help fund a return trip to Brazil for IDHEC graduate Roger Moride. Moride had crossed the Atlantic in a sailboat, filming the short documentary *Bahía la Sainte* (1951), on African-derived religious practices, upon his arrival in the city of Salvador. Moride's expeditions, L'Herbier argued, advanced France's international interests through their scientific and ethnographic character. This letter signals an investment in the anthropological uses of film shared with the Musée de l'Homme's Comité du Film Ethnographique, which also trained aspiring filmmakers.[80] In addition, IDHEC facilitated ethnographic filmmaking by sending students to North and Central Africa, Thailand, and Labrador, Canada.[81]

Like other French institutions of film culture, IDHEC actively forged connections between its counterparts around the world, beginning with a 1954 conference during the Cannes film festival. Representatives from the Soviet Union, Italy, France, Spain, the United States, and Poland (namely the Łódź national film school founded by Jerzy Toeplitz, who also served as FIAF's president for a quarter century) met to discuss best practices in film education.[82] CILECT—which counted MASP's Seminário de Cinema and Chile's Academia de Cine y Fotografía among its affiliates—was formally created the following year with the encouragement of Enrico Fulchignoni, a former CSC professor and director of UNESCO's Film Section.[83] Housed at IDHEC, CILECT operated with the support of the MAE.[84] At this inaugural meeting, the schools resolved to participate in exchanges of films and personnel to mutually support each other's development.[85] With the rapid growth of film schools in Eastern Europe, including in Hungary, Poland, and Czechoslovakia, CILECT, while remaining "balanced and apolitical," became an arena for Cold War tensions.[86] Its membership was evenly divided between schools in capitalist and communist countries; any time this parity was disrupted, the faction at a numerical disadvantage quickly recruited a new member to restore it.[87] Like FIAF (see chapter 2), CILECT's leadership attempted to mediate between these internal blocs by alternately holding meetings on each side of the Iron Curtain.[88]

IDHEC also prided itself on fostering the creation of film schools abroad, including in Egypt, Iran, and India and elsewhere in the Global South.[89] In 1965 Tessonneau visited the Pontificia Universidade Católica do Rio Grande do Sul in Porto Alegre, Brazil, to teach a seminar and help coordinate the creation of a film school, though the initiative never came to fruition.[90] Tessoneau also had a hand in the creation of the Film and Television Institute of Pune (FTIP) in western India; in a 1963 letter, he noted that FTIP had been operating "for two years according to my plans."[91] Yet by 1965 the links of cooperation between IDHEC and FTIP were strained when the Indian school signed a bilateral cooperation agreement with VGIK. Nevertheless, Tessonneau continued to insist that "the pedagogical influence of IDHEC should be the concrete and conceptual base of the cinematic training given at Poona."[92]

Despite its grand ambitions to boost the reputation of French cinema abroad and to facilitate international cooperation among film schools,

Film Pedagogy | 191

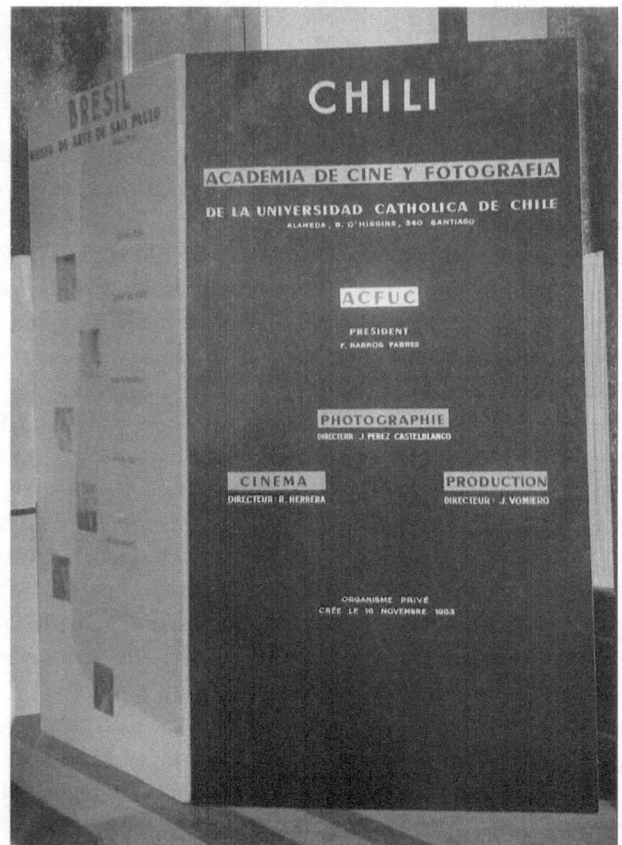

FIGURE 15. Displays dedicated to the Academia de Cine y Fotografía in Santiago de Chile and the Museu de Arte de São Paulo's Seminário de Cinema at a 1954 gathering of film schools in Cannes. *Source:* "Informe sobre las actividades efectuadas por la Academia de Cine y Fotografía de la Universidad Católica de Chile, 1954." 06IIF-0001—Instituto Fílmico—Rectorado de Alfredo Silva Santiago, Archivo de la Pontificia Universidad Católica de Chile.

IDHEC's finances, facilities, and administrative procedures were remarkably unstable through the late 1960s. In the early 1950s the school lacked a central building for instruction; classes were taught at multiple locations across Paris, leading the students to become "nomads who spent our time in the metro," in Benacerraf's words.[93] These challenges disproportionately affected Latin American students who arrived from abroad with limited guidance in navigating the school's bureaucracy. Germán

Puig, one of the founding members of the Cine Club de la Habana, arrived in Paris on a yearlong scholarship from Cuba's Ministry of Education, only to learn that IDHEC would not be accepting new students in the 1950–1951 academic year. Puig instead opted to study at the Sorbonne's Institut de filmologie.[94] Abraham Zalzman was more fortunate; after he belatedly received a scholarship from the Colombian government to study in France, he appealed to FIAF executive secretary Marion Michelle to intercede on his behalf so he could enroll in IDHEC.[95] Zalzman successfully capitalized on connections stemming from the film society and preservation movements—he was involved with the Cine Club de Colombia and the associated Cinemateca Colombiana, a FIAF member—to gain access to professional training in France, signaling the overlap between institutional networks of film preservation and film education. In other cases, such issues drove would-be students elsewhere. In 1951, Gutiérrez Alea, prevented from enrolling in IDHEC by its closure, complained that Puig had not told him CSC was still a viable alternative.[96] Fortunately, García Espinosa made inquiries on Gutiérrez Alea's behalf that allowed him to matriculate in time.[97] Communicating admissions requirements and timelines across the Atlantic proved a challenging task.

Beyond these logistical hiccups, aspiring Latin American filmmakers often complained (like their fellow classmates) about IDHEC's strong emphasis on the humanities and the lack of hands-on training, due in part to the school's limited resources.[98] When assigned projects, IDHEC students received roughly a third of the raw negative furnished to their counterparts at CSC relative to the running time of the finished film.[99] IDHEC failed to measure up to peer institutions on this metric well into the 1960s.[100] Rudá de Andrade, who attended IDHEC briefly in 1950, recalled that it had "extremely limited resources: lack of equipment, lack of film, lack of everything"; as a result, he switched to CSC.[101] For her part, Benacerraf "resented the IDHEC because it was very theoretical and I wanted to *make* films, to *touch* films, to learn the concrete techniques of *creating* cinema. The first year was all art history, history of literature, music history, film history. I felt above all that—I had already earned a university degree in humanities, and I wanted to study filmmaking! Even the production courses bored me because they were pure theory and numbers" (emphasis in original).[102] This emphasis on humanities courses reflected IDHEC's grounding in ideals of an erudite film culture informed by broader knowledge of arts and letters. This model proved influential across Latin America but also generated tension, especially when students perceived an urgent need for cinematic praxis that responded to a turbulent present.

Given the nature of IDHEC's curriculum, Benacerraf often skipped class and instead spent her time with other foreign students, building connections that helped lay the groundwork for pan-Latin American collaborations. For example, she connected Colombia-based cineclub organizer Luis Vicens with his counterparts in Venezuela during Vicens's trip to Paris.[103] One such encounter gave rise to a memorable anecdote highly suggestive of IDHEC's shortcomings in the eyes of Latin American students. Recalling a tour of the school Benacerraf gave him, Birri reminisced, "We saw some teams that were filming . . . ("not bad—again—roll camera—take one—take two"). . . . Later, as we left, I asked Margot, 'When will they see this material? When will they edit it?' She told me that never, because there was no film in the cameras, it was a simulation of filming."[104] Birri reflected on another occasion, "I chose the Centro Sperimentale essentially because it has theoretical and practical training (in IDHEC, it was predominantly theoretical), but above all because the Centro allowed me to be at the source of this cinematic movement that in just a few years influenced all of world cinema."[105]

Despite her reservations about IDHEC, Benacerraf went on to become one of its most prominent Latin American graduates, first with her films *Reverón* (1952) and *Araya* (1959), which won acclaim at European festivals, and later through her institution-building efforts in her home country, including the creation of the Cinemateca Nacional de Venezuela in 1966. Benacerraf made her directorial debut in an emerging genre pioneered in France: *films sur l'art*, or films on visual artists that often used their works as the basis for complex formal experiments, and became a staple of embassy film libraries and cineclub programming.[106] Benacerraf agreed to complete a portrait of the artist Armando Reverón at the urging of journalist and Franco-Bulgarian expatriate Amy Courvoisier and French cultural attaché Gaston Diehl, founders of the Cine-Club Venezuela. Diehl originally sought out Alain Resnais, who had also studied at IDHEC, as director, but Resnais declined as he was in the midst of filming *Guernica*, based on the works of Picasso.[107] *Reverón* took the top prize at a 1952 festival of films sur l'art organized by Diehl, and later screened at the Cinémathèque française at the invitation of Henri Langlois.[108] After working at a UNESCO field office in Pátzcuaro, Mexico, Benacerraf returned to Venezuela and shot her lyrical documentary *Araya*, which depicts traditional practices of extracting salt on a remote peninsula on the Caribbean on the cusp of their mechanization. Due partly to concerns about quality control in Venezuelan film laboratories, Benacerraf edited the footage in Paris on a compressed timeline, commissioning a voiceover by poet Pierre Seghers to meet the submission deadline for the Cannes film festival and fulfill the festival's requirement that all entries have French subtitles or dialogue.[109] At the festival, *Araya* won top honors from FIPRESCI and France's Commission Supérieure Technique (Superior Technical Commission).

Signaling how European institutions might mediate encounters between Latin American filmmakers, *Araya* served as an inspiration for Cinema Novo filmmaker Glauber Rocha. While attending Cannes as a journalist, Rocha interviewed Benacerraf; he later cited *Araya* as an inspiration for his feature film *Barravento* (*The Turning Wind*, 1962, Brazil).[110] Yet due in part to the lack of a Spanish-language version of the narration, *Araya* did not receive a theatrical release in Venezuela until 1977. As Julianne Burton-Carvajal observes, as a result *Araya* occupies an uneasy position within national and international film historiography. Hailed by many Euro-American critics as a masterpiece with universal qualities despite its "exotic" subject, the film is often dismissed by Venezuelan commentators for aestheticizing rather than politicizing exploitative forms of labor and thus failing to serve as a fitting precursor of NLAC.[111]

These critiques find ample purchase in the film's striking compositional precision and its approach to time. Dramatic contrasts of scale—particularly in shots where workers are dwarfed by the massive pyramids of salt amassed through their labor—continually draw attention to the artful arrangement of graphic elements within the frame. In alternation with striking high-angle shots, some taken from a construction crane encountered on site, *Araya*'s subjects are often filmed from low angles that exalt the rural worker in a manner reminiscent of Eduard Tissé's cinematography for Sergei Eisenstein's unfinished *Que Viva México* (1931, Mexico), a conscious point of reference for Benacerraf.[112] Their staging against dramatic cloud formations also recalls the "Golden Age" features of Mexican director Emilio Fernández and cinematographer Gabriel Figueroa, which were warmly received on the international festival circuit, though they are rarely recognized as examples of postwar art cinema today.[113] *Araya* thus evokes a visual repertoire of Latin American-ness that European audiences would have recognized from their limited exposure to films from the region, primarily on the festival circuit.

Araya's structure and voiceover also favor poetic exploration over social denunciation. We observe the daily tasks of salt miners and their families as they unfold over a twenty-four-hour period, with the implication they will be repeated without change the following day, creating a sense of time as cyclical. These repeated actions are dramatically interrupted by a dynamite explosion that announces the advent of industrial extraction on the peninsula, leaving the salt workers' fate uncertain. Yet for most of its running time, *Araya* sidesteps or even negates historical change. Its voiceover stresses that the gestures of the salt flat workers have remained unaltered since the colonial occupation of the peninsula by the Spanish over four hundred years earlier, suggesting that the workers are locked within a rigid set of labor relations rather than being agents of history. Marking a disconnect between the logic of postwar art cinema and the principles of socially conscious filmmaking later valorized by NLAC, *Araya*'s complex reception also reflects Benacerraf's transnational trajectory.

The career of Colombian documentarian Marta Rodríguez highlights an alternative path pursued by Latin American filmmakers trained in Europe. Rodríguez studied with Camilo Torres Restrepo, a priest who became a founding member of the School of Sociology at Colombia's Universidad Nacional and later died fighting with a leftist guerrilla group, the Ejército de Liberación Nacional. Beginning in 1961, Rodríguez trained as an ethnologist at Paris's Musée de l'Homme, where she studied with Jean Rouch. After her return to Colombia, Rodríguez collaborated with French institutions in Bogotá, running a film society at the AF and working in the French embassy's film collection.[114] The embassy supported the production of Rodríguez's documentary *Chircales* (*Brickmakers*, co-directed with her partner Jorge Silva, 1966/1971), which offers a striking counterpoint to Benacerraf's *Araya*. Both films, along with *El mégano*, are examples of what Salomé Aguilera Skvirsky calls the "process genre" in that they delve, step by step, into the stages of a product's production. This mode of filmmaking proved pivotal for NLAC due to its capacity to lay bare conditions of extreme labor exploitation.[115] In comparison with *Araya*, *Chircales*, which examines the manufacture of bricks on semi-rural estates on the margins of Bogotá, offers a far more trenchant and uncompromising look at relations of production.

Building on ethnographic work that Rodríguez had begun in 1958 under the guidance of Torres Restrepo, the film reflects the sweeping changes in documentary style that had occurred in the early 1960s, including Rouch and Edgar Morin's experiments with cinéma vérité. A

FIGURES 16A–16D. High-angle shots and contrasts of scale in *Araya* (1959) (A and B) and *Chircales* (1966/1971) (C and D). *Source: Araya*, directed by Margot Benacerraf (Harrington Park, NJ: Milestone Films, 2011), DVD; and *Chircales*, directed by Marta Rodríguez and Jorge Silva (Bogotá: Fundación Cine Documental, 2014), DVD.

mobile camera continually pans, tilts, and zooms to capture details like a bare foot immersed in mud and water. Despite this dynamism, careful composition is evident throughout. Like *Araya*, *Chircales* makes use of high-angle shots that allow a comprehensive view of sites of extraction; for instance, an image early in the film carefully frames two female workers guiding a wheelbarrow between the mud pit where clay

is extracted and a stack of drying bricks. Yet other shared strategies like contrasts of scale drive home miserable conditions in *Chircales*, diverging sharply from *Araya*'s move to highlight the monumentality of the laborers' achievements by using the salt pyramids as a striking compositional element. For instance, a medium close-up early in *Chircales* highlights the grotesque mismatch between the length of a pick designed for an adult and the height of the young girl who uses it to break up the soil in preparation for soaking and mixing the clay.

Similarly, the structure and soundtrack of *Chircales* explicitly politicize the situation of the brickworkers. Unlike *Araya*, which lacks direct testimony from the workers, *Chircales* makes extensive use of recorded interviews with the Castañeda family of brickmakers, interviews that interact dynamically with the image given the lack of synchronization. Omniscient narration offers an explicitly Marxist analysis of the brickmakers' position within a broader set of labor relations. Significantly, whereas the isolated peninsula of Araya appears in Benacerraf's film as a space outside politics, *Chircales* opens not at the brickmakers' worksite, but rather with election day in Bogotá's central Plaza Bolívar. Over images captured at the ballot box, we hear an interview with one of the Castañedas, who evokes La Violencia (1946–1966), the bloody clash between Liberals and Conservatives that drove internal migration, and comments on the ineffectiveness of electoral politics. Furthermore, *Chircales* ends by gesturing toward more radical possibilities, ending with a quotation from Torres Restrepo: "La lucha es larga, comencemos ya" ("the struggle is long, let us begin now").

The links between the Musée de l'Homme and Rodríguez's socially committed filmmaking practice suggest a genealogy that, along with the case of CSC, more neatly fits into the established trajectories of NLAC than Benacerraf's experience. Yet attending to alternate circuits of cultural exchange mediated by film pedagogy illuminates a more complex history that cannot be reduced to a prelude to radical filmmaking. This history comes into clearer focus if we examine the distinct institutional aims of early Latin American film schools and their shared politicization beginning in the mid-1960s.

FILM EDUCATION IN POSTWAR LATIN AMERICA

By contrast with the "national conservatory" model that dominated in Europe, in Latin America only one of the film schools founded in the two decades after World War II operated directly under the auspices of the state, Argentina's Escuela Nacional de Cinematografía. The rest were housed in universities, and their development is thus inseparable from broader shifts in higher education in the period. Transformations of Latin American universities in the decades following World War II were largely rooted in the rapid—if ultimately limited—expansion of access to higher education in the period, along with successive waves of university reform. First crystallized in 1918 at the Universidad Nacional de Córdoba in Argentina, the university reform movement lent Latin American institutions of higher education one of their most characteristic features: their claims to autonomy from direct state governance and police and military interference, although many were public institutions that received significant state support.

In postwar Latin America, film education and the production of educational film alike responded to the university reform movement's efforts to modernize education and improve its accessibility. Often, both the humanistic study of film and the professional training of filmmakers first entered higher education under the rubric of university extension, or intellectual activities targeted toward the broader community. College enrollments were also growing rapidly in the postwar period due to economic development and demographic expansion. In Venezuela, which saw the largest increase, the number of university students more than quintupled between 1955 and 1965; in Mexico and Brazil, this demographic more than doubled during the same timeframe.[116] Higher education shifted from an upper-class pursuit to a middle-class one as well, in turn driving the creation of private universities that offered greater exclusivity and academic prestige to elites.[117] Nevertheless, the overall percentage of young people pursuing higher education in Latin America remained low. In 1960 only 3 percent of college-age individuals in the region were enrolled in post-secondary education, with figures ranging from 11.8 percent in Argentina and 7.8 percent in Uruguay to 2.6 percent in Mexico and 1.6 percent in Brazil.[118] While the full realization of its egalitarian values often proved elusive, the university reform movement nevertheless helped drive film-related educational initiatives, mobilizing cinema as a pedagogical tool and working to render the technically complex, capital-intensive process of filmmaking more feasible in nations with nonexistent or troubled film industries.

Cinema's expanding presence in Latin America's postwar universities was rooted in diverse understandings of the medium's pedagogical role. Some of the earliest promoted film appreciation, a core goal of the film society and preservation movements, rather than technical training. As

Irene Rozsa notes, Cuban critic José Manuel Valdés-Rodríguez taught the earliest known college-level film studies course in Latin America, Cine, industria y arte de nuestro tiempo (Cinema, art and industry of our times), at the Universidad de la Habana's summer school. The school offered non-credit courses, including language and culture classes marketed to US residents.[119] Valdés-Rodríguez's course ran from 1943 to 1956, when the university was temporarily shuttered before its reorganization after the triumph of the revolution in 1959. As reconstructed from the instructor's memory in the 1960s, the course addressed film's historical, social, and technological dimensions as well as aesthetic questions ranging from "the specifically cinematic" to the medium's relationship to other arts.[120] In 1949 the university approved the creation of the Departmento de Cinematografía designed to help instructors incorporate film into their courses. The creation of a film archive supported these pedagogical activities and the year-round Cine Arte screening series that complemented Valdés-Rodríguez's course.[121] Although its institutional structure was looser and its resources more limited, the Instituto de Cine founded at the Universidad de Buenos Aires in 1955 constituted another early instance of film studies' emergence as an academic discipline in Latin America, even as the institute engaged in the production of short educational films and other activities.[122] By contrast with the Cuban case, where Valdés-Rodríguez's efforts predated the local emergence of cineclubs, in Brazil the film society and preservation movements help lay the groundwork for university film education. As Rafael Morato Zanatto notes, a 1958 course offered to cineclub organizers by the Cinemateca Brasileira left a strong imprint on film studies curricula that took shape at the Universidade de Brasília and Universidade de São Paulo in the 1960s.[123]

In countries where commercial film production was minimal, such as Uruguay and Chile, university film institutes like the Universidad de Chile's Instituto de Cinematografía Educativa (1929–1948) and Uruguay's ICUR (1950–1973) focused on the production of educational cinema rather than film appreciation or the training of fiction filmmakers.[124] Yet no firm distinction can be drawn between these various forms of film pedagogy; the output of most early Latin American film schools included not only student exercises, but also educational and sponsored films.[125] The region's film institutes proved to be flexible entities that adapted themselves to the varied and changing needs of the universities that housed them.

Founded by Rodolfo Tálice, a professor of parasitology in the Universidad de la República's medical school, ICUR reflected efforts to reorient the university toward research and knowledge production, as well as its pursuit of modern pedagogical methods that would help it manage rapid growth (the number of enrolled students more than tripled between the end of the 1930s and the late 1950s).[126] Utilizing specialized processes like microcinematography, ICUR's early output was dominated by medical and zoological topics, as suggested by early titles like *Cómo lucha Uruguay contra la tuberculosis* (How Uruguay fights tuberculosis, Rodolfo Tálice, José Martoy and Marcos Santa Rosa, 1950) and *Vida de termites del Uruguay* (The life of termites in Uruguay, Marcos Santa Rosa, M. J. Lastretti, and Jorge Radice, 1951).[127]

It was not until the mid-1960s that ICUR broadened the scope of its production activities to inventive ethnographic films like Mario Handler's *Carlos, cine-retrato de un "caminante"en Montevideo* (Carlos, cine-portrait of a Montevideo panhandler, 1965), which focused on the marginalized at a moment of deepening economic crisis.[128] In turning away from the hard sciences and a positivistic approach to social problems, Handler's work sparked debate within ICUR, particularly as he moved toward more openly politicized films like *El entierro de la universidad* (The burial of the university, 1965)—a freewheeling handheld record of a mock funeral students staged to protest the government's failure to release promised funds—and *Elecciones* (Mario Handler and Ugo Ulive, 1967), a record of the previous year's electoral campaigns.[129] Handler later helped found the Cinemateca del Tercer Mundo in 1969 (see chapter 2). The perceived politicization of ICUR no doubt contributed to its dissolution in 1973 following a right-wing coup. After a military intervention in the university, in which the ICUR's equipment was seized and staff fired, the institute was restructured as the Departamento de Medios Técnicos de Comunicación (Department of Technical Communications Media), which served the university's audiovisual needs and filmed promotional works commissioned by the military government.[130]

While ICUR's activities seem at first glance to be far removed from film appreciation, in fact they converged with the aesthetically oriented forms of film pedagogy cultivated by the film society movement, particularly in the second half of the 1960s. Eugenio Hintz and Walther Dassori Barthet, key figures of Uruguay's cineclub and film preservation movements, both worked at ICUR. Hintz was one of the organizers of the Cine Club del Uruguay, worked for the Cinemateca Uruguaya, and later became head of Uruguay's state film archive, Cine Arte del SODRE, while Dassori Barthet was a founder of Cine Universitario who also helped establish the Cinemateca Uruguaya. Signaling the overlap between his work for ICUR and his participation in the cineclub movement, Dassori Barthet organized screenings of scientific films for members of Cine Universitario and the general public in the mid- to late 1960s.[131] He also worked to incorporate filmology—a line of inquiry encompassing sociological, psychological, and artistic approaches to cinema rooted in the French academic tradition—into ICUR's activities, citing the precedent of a 1957 lecture series hosted by the institute that addressed cinema's educational, social, and aesthetic dimensions.[132]

In Chile, two university film institutes emerged in the 1950s, each striking a distinct balance between internal university needs for audiovisual content and the training of film professionals. Founded on the initiative of university students, in 1953 the Academia de Cine y Fotografía (Academy of Film and Photography) at the Pontificia Universidad Católica de Chile became the first academic program in filmmaking in Latin America. Initially, the academy enrolled approximately fifty aspiring photographers and filmmakers and operated a photo club and film society.[133] Yet the newly created program was soon roiled by administrative chaos—the school's status within the university was uncertain; its instructors held no contracts; no clear accounting was kept of its finances—and aesthetic and ideological tensions. According to the disgruntled ex-president of the academy, Fernando Barros Fabres, its new leader Giorgio Vomiero, "a connoisseur of the Neo-Realist School (which has experienced a boom in his homeland [Italy]) wants, by means of this school, . . . to fuse *truth* with *beauty*" (emphasis in original). By contrast, Barros Fabres affirmed that his Chilean colleagues "believed they were working to create a Film School that would elevate the basic standard of film crews and, at the same time, create an agitation in the [film] scene that could lead to the rise of a National Cinema."[134] Vomiero's aims, Barros Fabres implied, were overly lofty and cosmopolitan, while those of his Chilean colleagues were practical and patriotic. In turn, Vomiero alleged that Barros Fabres had not only failed in his duties as coordinator of the film society and as instructor of film technique but was viewed with disfavor by the OCIC and suspected of communist leanings.[135]

After these rocky beginnings, in 1955 the academy was restructured as the Instituto Fílmico under the leadership of Jesuit priest Rafael Sánchez. A planning document from August 1955 signals a departure from the humanistic tradition of the European film school, declaring, "Experience has demonstrated the need to channel the Academy's activities firmly towards the path of technical work, rather than pseudo-intellectual discussions," although aesthetic concerns did not disappear from the institute's curriculum altogether.[136] Over the next decade, the Instituto Fílmico produced a robust slate of thirty educational and sponsored films, becoming financially self-supporting by the early 1960s by shooting commissions and offering editing and laboratory services.[137] Its lab possessed the only 16mm film printer in Chile at the time, as one of its employees noted in a plea for new equipment from the Tools for Freedom program of the Alliance for Progress–backed Panamerican Development Foundation. This request itself indicates the university's strong anticommunist leanings and ties.[138] Despite the Instituto Fílmico's important functions within the local ecosystem of film production, limited demand for its graduates' skills led the school to close its courses to new enrollees in 1962. Instead, the academic unit took on a small number of student employees who honed their skills on the institute's internal and external commissions.[139] The institute's often conservative leanings notwithstanding, it counts among its alumni central figures of NLAC like Bolivian filmmaker Jorge Sanjinés and Chilean documentarian Patricio Guzmán.[140] In fact, Guzmán produced his film *El primer año* (The first year), a document of the early days of Salvador Allende's democratically elected socialist government, under the auspices of the Instituto Fílmico in 1972.[141] The institute had recently been brought under the umbrella of the Escuela de Artes de la Comunicación, a product of sweeping university reform sparked by massive student protests in 1967. In 1978, the school was dismantled and filmmaking activities ceased under the leadership of Jorge Swett Madge, an admiral installed by the regime of Augusto Pinochet after the 1973 coup that resulted in Allende's ouster and death.[142]

Film enthusiasts Sergio Bravo and René Kocher had also attended the Instituto Fílmico before founding the Centro de Cine Experimental at the Universidad de Chile, the country's leading public university.[143] Like the Instituto Fílmico of the early 1960s, Cine Experimental functioned more as a filmmaking laboratory than a formal program of study. In 1957 Bravo and Pedro Chaskel, who were members of the Cine Club Universitario, turned their energies to documentary filmmaking and created Cine Experimental with two other film enthusiasts. By Bravo's account, he was actually expelled from the film society for proposing the production of a documentary short.[144] Bravo convinced the school to serve as Cine Experimental's institutional home with the support of visiting British documentarian John Grierson. The university offered Cine Experimental space, the use of two 16mm cameras, and funds for film stock, but the center did not formally become part of its Departamento Audiovisual until 1961.[145] According to a 1959 article, Cine Experimental sought the advancement of educational filmmaking—the text cites "the university use of this form of knowledge" as one of its aims—alongside more pragmatic goals like the "rationalization of the production of films, that is to say, the creation of a stable material infrastructure and analysis of an adequate production policy" and "professionalization, that is, working with appropriate equipment that can be maintained in practical use so as to assure good technical results."[146] Focusing on nonfiction film, Cine Experimental's members shared a drive to investigate social realities, an impulse that took a turn toward openly politicized filmmaking in the mid-1960s.[147]

By contrast with the Chilean and Uruguayan cases, in Mexico and Argentina film schools arose in response to a perceived economic and aesthetic crisis in once-thriving national film industries.[148] The US government's decision to sharply reduce the export of raw film stock to Argentina during World War II due to the country's neutrality in the conflict had dealt a serious blow to its industry, contributing to a 50 percent decline in the number of Argentine films produced between 1942 and 1944.[149] During the presidency of Juan Domingo Perón (1946–1955), government subsidies and growing state control of media fed into an increasingly formulaic approach to film production, according to standard film histories of the period (though it should be noted that these accounts trace their roots to the vehemently anti-Peronist film society movement).[150] For many middle- and upper-class film enthusiasts, Perón's ouster in a 1955 military coup opened up new possibilities for artistic exploration through cinema; at the same time, it led to a rapid dismantling of state incentives for film production that triggered a profound crisis in the industry.[151] It is no coincidence that the following year, 1956, saw the creation of film schools in La Plata and Santa Fe.[152] (It should be noted that the earliest known university film institute in Argentina, the Universidad Nacional de Tucumán's Instituto Cinefotográfico, was founded a decade earlier. Yet due to limited resources, the Instituto struggled to maintain its core activity—the production of nonfiction shorts—and the project was largely abandoned by 1966 in favor of a university television channel.)[153]

The Argentine state moved to stimulate film production directly by creating a film school within INC, established on paper by the 1957 cinema law designed to revive the struggling industry. Yet the Escuela Nacional de Cinematografía (now known as the Escuela Nacional de Experimentación y Realización Cinematográfica) did not open its doors until 1965, when it began offering free courses designed to contribute to the "training of audiences" (*formación de público*) as well as future creators.¹⁵⁴ Classes in directing, producing, screenwriting, film criticism, film theory, and Argentine film history were taught by prominent critics like Roland (Andrés José Rolando Fustiñana) and young directors like Rodolfo Kuhn and Manuel Antín. In its first year, the school enrolled 736 students, 65 percent of whom were male, with an average age between twenty-five and thirty.¹⁵⁵ However, these free courses had a 55 percent drop-out rate, leading the school's organizers to propose more formal programs of study in directing, producing, screenwriting, and acting, with admission via entrance exam beginning in 1966.¹⁵⁶ Signaling an interest in international film school models, the institute invited representatives of IDHEC, CSC, the Svenska Filminstitutet (Swedish Film Institute), and Mexico's CUEC to commemorate the school's official opening in 1966, the event that opens this chapter.¹⁵⁷

Yet as previously noted, university film programs predated the Escuela Nacional by a decade. The Universidad Nacional de La Plata's Departamento de Cine emerged from a popular course in film appreciation offered by film and theater director Cándido Moneo Sanz that attracted over three hundred students.¹⁵⁸ The program imparted skills like screenwriting, editing, and cinematography and offered instruction in film and art history, though aesthetic questions were emphasized over technical ones.¹⁵⁹ Significantly, the school did not limit itself to training creatives who might revive the struggling film industry, but instead advocated for a broadened understanding of film production that incorporated "documentaries; scientific, technical, pedagogical shorts, [and] entertaining films for children."¹⁶⁰ One of the department's organizers observed, "It is obvious that the lack of trained directors with a strong foundation has contributed to the crisis. . . . But if the crisis has almost totally paralyzed industrial cinema, in other aspects, little has been accomplished for lack of initiative, of questing, of experimentation. The Department of Cinema understands that the total integration of Argentine cinema will be accomplished the day that the genres which now are lacking are practiced effectively."¹⁶¹ With IDHEC-trained documentarian Humberto Ríos as one of its instructors, the program implemented these ideals by making promotional and educational films for municipal and university partners, such as *Hacia el futuro* (Towards the future, 1957) for the Minors Division of the Province of Buenos Aires and *Pejerrey* (1960), shot for the campus's museum of natural history.¹⁶²

The Departamento de Cine had close ties to the film society and preservation movements—the Cinemateca Argentina furnished films for its history courses, and the archive's director, Roland, briefly headed the school in 1962—as well as the generación del 60.[163] Representatives of the movement like Kuhn, Simón Feldman, and José Martínez Suárez taught in the program.[164] Yet by the early 1970s few well-known figures remained on the faculty, leading to student complaints and the firing of instructors.[165] The Departamento de Cine ultimately closed its doors amid repression by the military junta that seized power in 1976 in the midst of political instability following the death of Juan Domingo Perón during his third presidency in 1974.[166] The regime was responsible for the deaths and disappearances of an estimated thirty thousand dissidents. The program reopened in 1990, seven years after the return to democracy.

The film school that embodied the most radical response to the crisis of Argentine cinema, along with the most direct influence of European film pedagogy in Latin America, was the aforementioned Instituto de Cinematografía, founded by filmmaker Fernando Birri at Santa Fe's Universidad Nacional del Litoral in December 1956. In part because the socially engaged filmmaking practices developed at the school are clear antecedents of the critical realism pursued by NLAC, the Instituto de Cinematografía is by far the best-known Latin American film school founded in the postwar period. The institute—informally known as the Escuela Documental de Santa Fe—emerged from a seminar that Birri was asked to offer through the university's Instituto Social, although the Cine Club Santa Fe had petitioned the institute to create it several months earlier.[167] The Instituto Social's director Angela Vera Romero described it as "a vehicle of the University's unity with the people," stressing that the mission of "[u]niversity extension was understood not as the simple education of inferior classes by 'elites,' but rather as an exchange."[168] For Romero, the Instituto de Cinematografía held out the promise of "a new form of communication with our people in their real dimensions" that would avoid both cliché and aesthetic radicalism: "Neither regionalism, nor the picturesque, nor avant-garde art."[169]

Aligned with the practice of university extension championed by Romero, Birri's pedagogical methods sought to make the people visible to themselves, a project inevitably fraught with contradictions. While inspired by CSC's model, Birri noted a clear disjuncture between the material conditions and pedagogical needs of Italy and Argentina. He reflected in a 1979 interview, "I returned from Italy thinking about a school that would have the Centro Sperimentale as a model, where directors, actors, cinematographers, costume designers, set designers, sound technicians were trained, in short: a school for the making of fiction films. When I arrived in Santa Fe and saw the actual conditions of the nation and the place, I realized it was somewhat premature to have a school like this." Rather than producing narrative features, Birri championed documentary works that would favor "the search for a national identity that was disconnected, lost, alienated by a type of cultural penetration, by a hegemony of an imperialist type in terms not only of political and economic infrastructure but also cultural superstructure. As a result, the Argentine did not recognize his own face, nor the face of his fellow man, nor the face of his nation."[170] Birri's wager is that documentary could generate self-recognition in the nation's citizens and by extension, collective recognition of Argentina's neo-colonial condition.

In hopes of generating this recognition, Birri's pedagogy drew heavily on Italian neorealism's interest in the everyday as a source of social consciousness. In his first four-day seminar—which used a Spanish translation of former CSC director Luigi Chiarini's *Il film nei problema dell'arte* (*The Film in the Problems of Art*) as a textbook—Birri publicly presented Italian photo-documentaries via magic lantern projection to spark discussion about the need to represent Argentine social realities.[171] After the projection of slides from "Un paese" ("A Country"), a photo essay with images by Paul Strand and text by Zavattini published in the Italian film magazine *Cinema Nuovo* in 1955, and "I bambini di Napoli" ("The Children of Naples"), with images by Chiara Sumgheo and text by Domenico Rea, the discussion lasted until nearly four in the morning.[172] Birri recalls:

> It was not a question ... of repeating, of simply copying a successful Italian experience, but instead of knowing, of proving to ourselves to what extent it was possible to assimilate all of this vital experience of neorealism (which, I do not tire of repeating, more than a cinematic style is a moral attitude) which has invigorated the cinematic art. In other words, it was not a question of making neorealist cinema in Argentina, but of making understood—and above all, felt—up to what point this realism, the realism of images, COULD NOT HELP BEING the reality of our region, of our nation (emphasis in original).[173]

For Birri, the denunciatory power of the image inevitably imbued it with social specificity; even if neorealist conventions were used, Argentine reality would necessarily emerge. In the second half of the course, Birri's students ventured out into the city to produce their own photodocumentaries with the support of the Foto Club de Santa Fe.[174] These were exhibited publicly in 1958 alongside a screening of an early version of *Tire dié* (1960) that attracted over four thousand spectators.[175] The documentary arose from the collaborative efforts of Birri and eighty-eight of his students, who recorded interviews and footage documenting the lives of Santa Fe's marginalized residents, including the children who run along the railroad tracks begging train passengers for coins. Their cries of "*tire dié*" (throw me a dime) give the film its title. Despite issues with over- and under-exposure and sound—recorded with cumbersome equipment so large and heavy it had to be carried by four people—the film received a warm reception locally and internationally and has been retrospectively hailed as a major forerunner of NLAC.[176]

In 1959, the Escuela Documental de Santa Fe gained new momentum. For the first time the institute was granted its own budget and was able to purchase cameras, raw stock, and laboratory and lighting equipment, as well as to hire thirty-one faculty and staff.[177] At this time, the school offered three-year programs (later extended to four years) in directing, producing, and cinematography. The curriculum included classes in photography, cinematography, screenwriting, and production alongside courses in film aesthetics, film criticism, sociology, and Argentine literature.[178] A memo outlining the curriculum noted that it drew on "the experiences of pedagogical organization and professional training of the Centro Sperimentale di Cinematografía de Cinecittà and IDHEC in Paris, analyzed critically to adjust them to our reality and circumstances, and additionally attempting to overcome their deficiencies."[179] Six months of each academic year were devoted to coursework and three to hands-on projects, referred to as the Taller Experimental (experimental workshop).[180] Instructors included the novelists Ernesto Sábato and Juan José Saer, Catholic film critic Jaime Potenze, Cine Club Núcleo founder Salvador Sammaritano, and generación del 60 directors Feldman and Martínez Suárez.[181] To make its program as accessible as possible, the Instituto de Cinematografía offered flexible hours suited to working students and waived the requirement of a high school diploma. It was even open to individuals who had not completed middle school, who were required to enroll in preparatory courses.[182] As a result, the institute's students were a remarkably heterogeneous group, according to Birri:

> students in chemistry and law, teachers, a carpenter, social workers, a lawyer, housewives, high school students, a musician in the police band, poets, painters, a non-commissioned army officer, film society members, a peasant [*campesino*] ... none of them feels like an artist in the romantic, minoritarian or exotic sense of the world.... Only with this spirit, free of any superiority, full of sure patience, of obstinate confidence, have they been able to work anonymously, with only their hands, borrowed cameras, sound

recorders provided by through other means, with partly donated film, to erect their Institute.[183]

As this account suggests, the Instituto de Cinematografía's approach sought to overturn class-based barriers to training in filmmaking and even to question the notion of professionalization itself. By contrast with the approach of IDHEC and many of its Latin American counterparts, this method of working de-emphasized individual self-expression and accordingly, the need for elevated film culture on the part of students. As Mariano Mestman and Christopher Moore observe, the Instituto de Cinematografía's mode of film practice deliberately eroded the distinction between professional and amateur filmmaking, engaging teachers and students alike in dialogue with the local community.[184] Birri sent students to conduct an extensive survey of *Tire dié*'s viewers after nineteen public screenings of the film in Santa Fe. Distributed to over eight hundred audience members, the questionnaires inquired whether or not respondents liked the film and why, and what subjects they would suggest for future projects.[185] Whereas the questionnaires used by cineclubs were designed to sharpen members' critical faculties in response to a pre-selected canon of films, this survey invited respondents to directly shape the institute's future work.

After a period of consolidation, the Instituto de Cinematografía faced new challenges in 1963, when the documentary-fiction hybrid *Los cuarenta cuartos* (The forty rooms, Juan Oliva), on the issue of overcrowding, was barred from release and its negative seized by the military government of José María Guido, which had ousted President Arturo Frondizi in a coup the previous year.[186] Birri left Argentina for Italy shortly thereafter, and the Instituto's programs in directing and screenwriting were cut for lack of funds.[187] Nevertheless, the school's institutional structure was further solidified under the leadership of the CSC-trained cinematographer Adelqui Camusso between 1962 and 1969.[188] In the second half of the decade, the institute cultivated a dense web of connections with Latin American and European institutions, including the Columbianum and Pesaro film festivals, respectively dedicated to Latin American film and new cinemas.[189] In the early 1970s, conflicts between the new administration and the student body over the censorship of film scripts led to a student strike and the temporary closure of the institute to new enrollees.[190] Like ICUR and the Universidad Nacional de La Plata's Departamento de Cine, the Instituto de Cinematografía was shuttered when right-wing military dictatorships rose to power across the Southern Cone.

Mexico—a regime often referred to as a *dictablanda* (soft dictatorship) due to the decades-long one-party rule of the Partido Revolucionario Institucional (Institutional Revolutionary Party; PRI)—did not experience the authoritarian coups that swept the Southern Cone in the 1960s and 1970s, although the brutal repression of student activism in the October 2, 1968, massacre in the Plaza de Tlatelolco made the state's authoritarianism devastatingly clear. The government's bid to host the 1968 Summer Olympics, which opened just ten days later, proved to be a precipitating factor, generating pressure to present an orderly face to the world. These political circumstances give unusual continuity to the trajectory of film education in Mexico; CUEC has operated largely without interruption since its founding in 1963.

Emerging from existing film-related activities on campus, including seminars, lecture series, and a thriving cineclub scene, CUEC's founding also responded to calls to reform Mexico's troubled film industry. In 1961 the Grupo Nuevo Cine, an association of young critics and would-be filmmakers, had called for the creation of a national film school. The school, it was hoped, would offer an alternative path into an industry they saw as closed to newcomers and in decline, both aesthetically and economically. They traced these woes to tight union control and a government subsidy scheme viewed as discouraging innovation while encouraging shoddy production values.[191] (Producers often applied for credits based on an inflated budget and then slashed it during production, pocketing the difference.) In light of these circumstances, the Grupo Nuevo Cine hailed auteurist ideals and European new waves, suggesting that bringing young directors' personal vision to the screen could help revitalize Mexico's flagging cinema. Although the direct institutional connections between Mexican and French film pedagogy are more tenuous than those that shaped cineclub and film preservation movements, CUEC built on the ideals of film culture articulated by IDHEC. Embodying aspects of European film schools' humanist tradition, CUEC's pedagogy suggested that the challenges facing Mexico's industry could be surmounted not by catering to the mass audience but by seeking to reform it.

CUEC: INSTITUTIONALIZING RUPTURE

The blossoming of university film culture in mid-century Mexico City was one aspect of a surge of cultural activity centered on UNAM. In the years following World War II, UNAM was increasingly seen as pivotal to the state's modernization projects and was granted unprecedented levels of government funding, some earmarked for the training of professionals and technocrats to support the programs of capitalist development pursued by the administrations of Manuel Ávila Camacho (1940–1946) and Miguel Alemán (1946–1952). This support took on highly visible form in the construction of UNAM's Ciudad Universitaria, a showpiece of state-sponsored development that fused modernist architecture with large-scale murals. Demographic trends further reshaped the university. The number of students living in Mexico City exploded as the nation's overall population doubled from the 1940s through the 1960s; UNAM's enrollment quadrupled during this period. Although the student body remained largely middle class, its composition had shifted somewhat by the mid-1960s, with nearly a quarter of students coming from working-class or *campesino* (peasant) backgrounds.[192] Tapping into the spirit of renewal fostered by the new campus, under the leadership of Jaime García Terres, UNAM's Dirección General de Difusión Cultural (Cultural Promotion Department; hereafter, Difusión Cultural) established the Casa del Lago, a cultural center frequented by writers like Octavio Paz, Carlos Fuentes, and Salvador Elizondo; organized the experimental theater series Poesía en voz alta (Poetry Out Loud); and bolstered the university's publishing activities, refashioning the *Revista de la Universidad* into an influential cultural magazine that devoted considerable space to film criticism.[193]

As Deborah Cohn observes, these university-affiliated entities proved pivotal in the efforts of cosmopolitan intellectuals like Paz, Fuentes, and Jaime García Ponce to forge alternatives to state-sponsored cultural nationalism in the 1950s.[194] This impulse was rooted in a broader cultural crisis. Utopian aspirations of social equality stemming from the Mexican Revolution (1910–1920) had largely evaporated, and the government's democratic legitimacy was eroded by the uninterrupted control of the PRI beginning in 1929.[195] Following the presidency of Lázaro Cárdenas (1934–1940), who championed land reform and mass education, the wartime and postwar administrations of Ávila Camacho and Alemán had favored business interests, the expansion of foreign investment, and a closer relationship with the United States. Prosperity fostered rapid industrialization and urbanization and the growth of Mexico's middle classes. Yet its benefits were distributed in a strikingly unequal manner: the wealthiest 30 percent of Mexicans saw their average income almost double between 1950 and 1963, while the poorest 30 percent actually saw a decline in real wages as the cost of living soared.[196] Class stratification, combined with widespread corruption and cronyism, contributed to a sense that Mexico's revolutionary project had reached a crisis point.

In the cultural sphere, the contradictions of an institutionalized revolution informed ongoing efforts to articulate Mexican national identity within a postwar global order, exemplified by Paz's renowned book *El laberinto de la soledad* (*The Labyrinth of Solitude*, 1950). Increasingly, intellectuals interrogated Mexico's place within a universal tradition and critiqued state-sponsored modes of cultural production. In particular, muralism and its epic visions of national history and politics were contested by visual artists who favored abstraction, referred to as "la generación de la ruptura" or "breakaway generation." In parallel with these efforts, the Grupo Nuevo Cine called both for a radical break with the current state of Mexican cinema and for institution-building efforts rooted in erudite notions of film culture.

The Grupo Nuevo Cine—an association of "filmmakers, aspiring filmmakers, critics, and film society organizers" that included young Mexican writers like Elizondo and Carlos Monsiváis as well as Spanish exiles Emilio García Riera, José Miguel "Jomí" García Ascot, and José de la Colina—publicly declared its existence in early 1961 with a polemical program of action to revitalize Mexican cinema.[197] According to González Casanova, the group originally coalesced around the Cine Club de México hosted by the Institut français d'Amérique latine (see chapter 1).[198] The "Manifiesto del Grupo Nuevo Cine" declared an urgent state of crisis, affirming the need to "overcome the depressing state of Mexican cinema."[199] Indeed, the domestic film industry's economic health and production values had declined sharply from its so-called Golden Age in the 1940s and early 1950s. This period had seen the consolidation of a nationalistic, visually polished cinema that drew broad audiences in Mexico, in the United States, and across the Spanish-speaking world with melodrama and popular song. Referring to the close relationship between major production companies and film industry unions that discouraged experimentation and blocked new players from entering the business, the manifesto's signatories frame the situation in terms of intergenerational conflict, insisting that "the doors should be opened to a new generation of filmmakers, which is more necessary every day."[200] Taking its cue from European new waves, the Grupo Nuevo Cine articulates an individualistic vision of the filmmaker as auteur, declaring "the filmmaker-creator has as much right as the writer, painter, or musician to express himself freely."[201] Rather than outlining a defined artistic or political program, the signatories champion "the free play of creation, with the diversity of aesthetic, moral, and political positions that this implies," imagining a mode of production free of ideological, censorship, and industry constraints.[202]

Surprisingly, alongside its call for artistic liberation, the "Manifiesto del Grupo Nuevo Cine" stresses an urgent need to create and support film-related cultural institutions—structures that by definition help give legitimacy and stability to cultural production. The signatories call for "the development of film culture in Mexico by means of the following points: the foundation of a serious institute of cinematic instruction specifically devoted to the training of new filmmakers; support and stimulus for the cineclub movement . . . the formation of a film archive that has the necessary resources and is in the hands of reliable and responsible persons; the existence of publications that orient the audience," beginning with the group's own magazine *Nuevo Cine*.[203] Invoking a need for seriousness, responsibility, and financial sustainability—terms that suggest concern about the fragility of cultural infrastructures—this portion of the manifesto abandons rhetoric championing individual freedom from film industry strictures. Instead, the text advocates for the founding of organizations that would foster the creation and preservation of filmic works and help "orient the audience," suggesting viewers needed structure and guidance.

How can one reconcile the Grupo Nuevo Cine's call for a cinema of individual expression freed from commercial and ideological limits with its emphasis on strengthening and creating film-related institutions? I contend that the Grupo Nuevo Cine's formative involvement with university film culture served to institutionalize its performative gestures of rupture and innovation. This move may appear contradictory due to the concerns about "'institutionalization,' 'academicization' or any 'ization' that would appear to dilute anti-establishment energies" that frequently crop up in discussions of experimental film, as Michael Zryd observes. He argues that "such complaints too often paint with far too broad a brush a portrait of 'The Institution' that ignores a historical understanding of how institutions have been necessary for the aesthetic, social, and political goals of the film and media community."[204] While the tension between innovation and institutionalization in the Grupo Nuevo Cine's manifesto may be a partly illusory one, the creation of CUEC nevertheless spoke to a paradoxical vision of postwar art cinema as an avant-garde for the masses. This paradox resonated with the contradictions of Mexico's "institutionalized revolution," which increasingly structured public discourse in the 1950s and 1960s. As the case of muralism indicates, the Mexican state had long legitimized and acted as a patron of modernist cultural forms. As noted previously, in the 1950s and 1960s, bourgeois, cosmopolitan intellectuals sought to dislodge state-sponsored cultural institutions—including the commercial film industry, which received the bulk of its financing from the Banco Nacional Cinematográfico, a joint venture between private capital and the state—and develop an alternative cultural infrastructure.[205] In Pierre Bourdieu's terms, this new intelligentsia sought to reshape the field of cultural production by endowing it with greater autonomy from the field of power, specifically from state patronage, rather than contesting the status of cultural production as an autonomous sphere separate from daily life, which Peter Bürger identifies as the key intervention of the early twentieth-century avant-gardes.[206] Instead, the cultural projects of the Grupo Nuevo Cine and university film culture sought to sidestep a contradiction inherent to the "new cinemas" that emerged on a global scale in the late 1950s and early 1960s: the imperative to embody an avant-garde while continuing to function as a mass medium.

Within Mexico City's shifting cultural scene, the forms of rupture and institution-building surrounding cinema were unusual in their emphasis on an approximation between popular audiences and cultural elites. At the conclusion of the "Manifiesto del Grupo Nuevo Cine," its signatories rhetorically enlist the support of an idealized film audience under construction, writing that "the Grupo Nuevo Cine hopes to rely on the support of a conscious film public, the ever-growing mass of spectators who see in cinema not only a form of entertainment, but one of the most formidable means of expression of our century."[207] Significantly, the "Manifiesto del Grupo Nuevo Cine" suggests that being attuned to cinema as a means of expression—an individualistic notion of art as the exteriorization of subjective interior states—could transmute a "mass of spectators" into a "conscious film public" or a critically inclined film audience. Similarly, in his 1962 film society manual ¿Qué es un cine-club?, Manuel González Casanova called for the creation of a "vanguard of spectators" (a term borrowed from French actor-director Louis Daquin) through the use of cineclubs to foster active critical engagement.[208]

The belief that fostering film culture could forge an avant-garde within the mass audience promised a fusion between the two categories, highlighting a tension inherent to the notion of an avant-garde. As Malte Hagener argues in the case of early twentieth-century European vanguards, by staking out a position "in advance" of the majority while agitating for transformations that would ultimately make its position mainstream, the avant-garde guarantees its own dissolution.[209] Continual breaks with the past are thus a necessity for the incessant production of the new—a dynamic Paz famously referred to in a 1974 essay as "the tradition of rupture."[210]

CUEC institutionalized critical reflection on Mexican cinema and its relationship with a mass public in a classroom setting, even as an approximation between the tastes of mass audiences and those of the intelligentsia remained a largely elusive goal. The institution-building efforts that led to the school's creation were rooted in the often top-down practices of UNAM's film societies and their efforts to reshape popular taste. Yet González Casanova also utilized the cineclub—which was incorporated into CUEC's curriculum—as a sort of laboratory, requiring students to survey viewers on their opinions of Mexican cinema and incorporating these observations into analysis of the national industry's challenges and opportunities.

The forms of informal film pedagogy, both university-sponsored and student-driven, that took shape at UNAM in the 1950s betray both optimism and concern regarding cinema's social impact and the future of the Mexican film industry.[211] In March 1954 García Terres presided over a seminar on cinema organized by Difusión Cultural, opening with the reflection: "Perhaps for the first time, the Universidad Nacional today opens its doors to the public, formal consideration of cinematic creation." García Terres went on to note cinema's "inexorable influence on all, or almost all, modes of contemporary thought" due to its functioning as a "peculiar means of expression capable of reaching millions of men," and further specified the seminar's "particular interest in the progress of Mexican cinema and the definitive elucidation of its problems."[212] The public lectures, which tackled the history, aesthetics, ethics, and sociology of film, were delivered by figures like Álvaro Custodio and García Ascot—two Spanish exiles and familiar faces on the cineclub circuit who had curated and introduced programs for IFAL's Cine Club de México— along with Paz and acclaimed modernist photographer Manuel Álvarez Bravo.[213]

By 1955 the cineclub movement, which had given rise to at least seven film societies in Mexico City, reached UNAM's campus.[214] That year, the *Gaceta de la Universidad* (university bulletin) applauded the efforts of the Cine Club de la Universidad run by Difusión Cultural and the independent Cine Club Progreso (which had a significant student contingent) to actively engage audiences and shape film tastes, "promoting in the public curiosity and discussions that will help orient them and lay the foundations for their preferences within this artistic genre."[215] The following year, private film societies began to disappear en masse due to tensions with distributors and the authorities surrounding questions of film censorship, further encouraging the rise of campus film societies.[216] According to event listings in the *Gaceta de la Universidad*, by the end of the decade cineclubs were operating in UNAM's schools of philosophy and letters, engineering, architecture, and sciences and one of the preparatory schools administered by UNAM, among other academic units. An on-campus Asociación de Cine Experimental also hosted screenings.

In 1959 González Casanova was appointed the head of the newly created Sección de Actividades Cinematográficas within Difusión Cultural.[217] The following year, the section launched the Cine Debate Popular, curated by Monsiváis, González Casanova and photographer Ricardo Vinós.[218] This screening series targeted a broader audience—totaling 13,443 spectators in 1965—and rigorously maintained film introductions and post-screening discussions.[219] Concretizing a cherished goal of Mexico's film society movement, the university founded a film archive in 1960, which loaned "classics" to university film societies.[220] Two informal courses in film appreciation offered in 1960 and 1962 featuring lectures by Grupo Nuevo Cine members Elizondo, García Riera, and de la Colina provided the most immediate impetus for the creation of CUEC under González Casanova's leadership.[221]

While the school's genesis was a collective effort, González Casanova's ideals of film pedagogy nevertheless shaped its broader institutional goals. In a speech delivered on the fifteenth anniversary of CUEC's founding, González Casanova declared, "Cinema is one of the great means of education at our disposal, given that its teachings extend to all social classes with particular influence on less educated groups. Not being a supporter of censorship, which I generally consider to be a negative solution, I saw no other path than to pursue an education, an elevated education for those responsible for film production. If their function is that of teachers who will educate the people, let us give them a teacher's training."[222] Rather than adopting the language of individual self-expression evident in the "Manifiesto del Grupo Nuevo Cine," González Casanova's speech echoes postwar discourses on the need for film appreciation as a bulwark against cinema's potential ills, arguing, in terms that echo L'Herbier's speech on the mission of IDHEC, that film schools had a major role to play in regulating the medium's social influence.

Like its European precursors, CUEC combined humanistic study with creative courses, and students often complained of an emphasis on

FIGURE 17. Program for a series on Mexican independent cinema presented by the Cine Club de la Universidad, illustrated by an image from Jomí García Ascot's *En el balcón vacío* (On the empty balcony, 1962), suggesting the close links between the Grupo Nuevo Cine and emerging institutions of university film culture. Source: *Sección de Actividades Cinematográficas—Anuario 1963* (Mexico City: Universidad Nacional Autónoma de México, 1963). Colección Filmoteca UNAM México.

theory over practice. During the first five years of the school's operation, its students completed only sixteen short films.[223] Enrollees lobbied for more filmmaking opportunities, achieving the addition of a fifth year to CUEC's curriculum to facilitate this in 1970.[224] Once again, limited resources and institutional structure seem to have played a role. CUEC was not consolidated as an official academic unit at UNAM until 1970, when it was brought under the umbrella of the university's extension school.[225] Like IDHEC in its early years, CUEC had no dedicated facility for its classes until 1965 and lacked a long-term home until a decade later, when the school set up shop in the Colonia del Valle roughly eight kilometers north of the Ciudad Universitaria.[226] The school possessed just three cameras, all 16mm, and two of them spring-wound, in the late 1960s.[227]

CUEC's first cohort of students took the following classes: Aesthetic Currents in Cinema, taught by Grupo Nuevo Cine member García Riera; Screenwriting, with instruction by the well-known novelist José

Revueltas;[228] Laboratory Technique; Editing; and Cinematography. A second set of courses planned for 1964 added additional classes in directing and a class in film analysis taught by Elizondo, who, as noted previously, belonged to the Grupo Nuevo Cine and had studied at IDHEC.[229] This first three-year curriculum also included classes on color, sound, and direction of actors, as well as a course in Mexican cinema taught by González Casanova himself, to which I return shortly.[230]

When the program was extended to four years with the entering class of 1966, additional theory and history courses were added alongside hands-on classes, including a screenwriting class taught by Gabriel García Márquez in 1967 as he was writing his acclaimed novel *Cien años de soledad (One Hundred Years of Solitude)*.[231] Paul Leduc, an IDHEC graduate, served as García Márquez's teaching assistant and took over the course when the writer gave up teaching to focus on his novel.[232] In year one, these humanities-style classes included Film History; Introduction to Aesthetics, Cinema and Literature; Film Theory (taught by Grupo Nuevo Cine member de la Colina); and Theory of Dramatic Art. Other examples include Cinema and Aesthetics (taught by critic Jorge Ayala Blanco) and Cinema and the Plastic Arts in year two; Mexican Cinema in year three; and Socioeconomic History of Cinema (taught by Monsiváis) and Cinema and Culture in year four.[233] While surviving documentation is fragmentary, student exams for Cinema and the Plastic Arts suggest how CUEC courses conveyed canons of Western art history and art cinema, even as the school attempted to respond to the unique challenges facing the Mexican film industry in the period. An exam submitted by one of CUEC's best-known graduates, director Jaime Humberto Hermosillo, features sketches of Egyptian bas relief and Corinthian columns alongside a discussion of framing in F. W. Murnau's *Nosferatu*. Another student commented on Gothic architecture while comparing composition in the work of Fritz Lang, Akira Kurosawa, and Mexican filmmaker Carlos Velo.[234]

Beyond the pedagogical principles that can be gleaned from course titles and exercises, archival records offer some sense of the material and social conditions of instruction at CUEC in the mid- to late 1960s. Keeping in mind UNAM's historical tendency to attract middle- and upper-class students, financial and logistical barriers to enrollment at CUEC seem to have been relatively low. While CUEC did not offer free classes to Mexican citizens as IDHEC and CSC did, tuition was fairly affordable. In the late 1960s, students paid 50 pesos to enroll after passing an entrance exam and 100 pesos per month in tuition, at a

FIGURE 18. Compositional strategies in *Nosferatu* (F. W. Murnau, 1922), drawn by future director Jaime Humberto Hermosillo for an exam in the course Cine y artes plásticas. Surviving exams indicate how established canons not only of cinema, but also art and architectural history, informed CUEC's curriculum. *Source:* IISUE/AHUNAM/Fondo Centro Universitario de Estudios Cinematográficos/Caja 6/Exp. 35.

time when the average daily minimum wage in Mexico was just under 28 pesos.[235] In this period, classes were generally held between the hours of 6:00 and 10:00 p.m., presumably to facilitate enrollment by working students as well as instruction by professors with other duties.[236] Surviving documents suggest that neither students nor instructors did an especially stellar job combining their obligations at CUEC with other activities. It was not uncommon for professors to miss half or even all of their classes in a month; similarly, the students who attended least often tended to miss roughly half of their classes, and many dropped out without completing the program.[237] If tuition was kept relatively low, so was compensation. García Márquez recalls that he "must have been paid around 150 pesos" for his course in 1967, though he did not recall the exact amount.[238] School records indicate that CUEC instructors typically received 400 pesos per course per month in 1969.[239] Women were a tiny minority of both faculty and students at CUEC in the mid-1960s; each entering class and slate of instructors typically had one to two women, if that.

If CUEC proved inclusive in some ways and less so in others, its pedagogy also shows traces of the simultaneously elitist and democratizing project of film education promoted by the cineclub. While it was not listed as an official part of the curriculum, CUEC students were apparently expected to participate in the Cine Club de la Universidad run by the Sección de Actividades Cinematográficas, as their attendance at its sessions was monitored.[240] This detail suggests that not only knowledge of cinema history, but engagement in the carefully regulated discussion of films as a means of building one's critical sensibilities, was considered a fundamental aspect of a future filmmaker's training.

A core ideal of the film society movement—the need to reshape audience tastes as a precondition for transforming film production—also left its mark on González Casanova's course in Mexican cinema. In 1967 students in the course completed a survey of moviegoers, with each conducting twenty-five interviews intended to gauge the public's attitudes toward Mexican cinema as well as other aspects of their film tastes.[241] Highlighting the class-based character of this audience analysis, spectators leaving the theater were asked for their occupation and level of education, as well as their opinion of Mexican cinema, the nationality of the films they most preferred, and their thoughts on the film they had just seen. Extant surveys record a range of mostly negative, often colorful, responses to queries about the state of Mexican cinema. For the most part, respondents described a decline in Mexican cinema over the previous fifteen years, marked by the pursuit of box office profits, unoriginal plots, a noticeable drop in production values, and a lack of investment and development. However, other moviegoers—often those with a lesser degree of formal education—expressed neutral or even highly positive attitudes toward Mexican cinema, complicating the dominant historical narrative of industry crisis inherited from the Grupo Nuevo Cine. This exercise transplanted the audience questionnaire—a staple of the cineclub circuit designed to determine audience preferences while also stimulating reflection in respondents—to a classroom setting. In so doing, the assignment also incorporated the rhetoric of industry crisis and need for innovation popularized by the Grupo Nuevo Cine members into CUEC's curriculum, framing the film school's activities as a possible means out of the impasse.

In the same course, students completed papers that analyzed the dire situation of Mexican cinema, offering possible solutions in terms that closely echoed González Casanova's call to reform the mass audience. Noting economic and structural factors like the loss of market share abroad and the barriers erected by industry unions to the entry of new directors, one student cited "the lack of cultural preparation of directors and producers and, in many cases, the eagerness to achieve high box-office profits by exploiting the bad taste of a large part of the public. Mexican directors become stagnant, due in large measure to their lack of familiarity with artistic movements in world cinema."[242] Another identified the "illiterate public" as the root of the problem, noting that "fortunately there are campaigns to improve it, although this process is still very slow."[243] A third called into question attempts to bridge the gap between mass audiences and the emerging generation of Mexican cineastes:

> There are new filmmakers and high hopes are placed on them; however, something strange is happening. The audience does not understand them, it does not identify with the cinema they make, save a few exceptions and this is due (personal opinion) to the fact that they are very pretentious. A great deal of genius and humility is needed to achieve the difficult simplicity necessary for the comprehension of all types of audiences. Now, if it's a matter of trying to make cinema a work of art, one should not worry about the mass audience's lack of understanding, since—say what you will—the work of art is never made for the masses but rather so that those who can understand it, do.[244]

As these comments indicate, students expressed a range of opinions regarding whether Mexican cinema could achieve the elusive reconciliation between high art and mass culture, but a strong thread of elitism runs through the essays. Another student suggested that Mexican cinema could prosper only if the influence of the intelligentsia were broadened. Contrasting the industrial power of Hollywood with the success of the French New Wave, he argued, "The relationship with the public that is bought in the United States [through large film budgets and advertising] is acquired somewhat more legitimately in France, and one could say it is acquired through the significant influence of the cultural elite on public opinion. . . . Mexico must create an elite with greater force within the world that can influence the cultural level of its cinema . . . in Mexico, it is essential that a contingent of intellectuals exert influence over a greater number of people with its ideas, and not only amongst themselves."[245] One can presume that these examples of student work blend their authors' opinions with their predictions of what the instructor wanted to hear in hopes of receiving a satisfactory grade. In this sense, they suggest the parameters and perspectives offered by González Casanova for making sense of Mexican cinema's condition in the period.

The paternalistic attitudes toward Mexican audiences that seem to have pervaded some aspects of CUEC instruction were thrown into sharp relief by the events that enveloped CUEC in 1968, the year after González Casanova's students submitted their evaluations of the state of Mexican cinema. Many CUEC students participated in the left-wing student movement, occupying the school's facilities and appropriating its equipment and facilities to document the movement. The resulting footage, which had to be smuggled out of the school under threat of a military occupation, was later edited by Leobardo López Arretche into the acclaimed documentary *El grito* (The cry, 1968).

How to reconcile these openly elitist positions on film culture with the radical energies of the 1968 student movement? First, one must recall that the push for political and cultural renewal in 1950s and 1960s Mexico was distinctly cosmopolitan and bourgeois, rather than radical and working class. The 1968 student movement itself had a highly significant middle-class contingent, although the mobilization was marked by a new solidarity between the students at UNAM and the largely working-class Instituto Politécnico Nacional (IPN). A July 1968 altercation involving students from two of IPN's preparatory schools, violently repressed by police, was the initial spark for the movement. Furthermore, UNAM's administration was initially supportive of the movement. The university's rector at the time, Javier Barros Sierra, led an orderly march in early August in protest of the military's violation of university autonomy following the violent takeover of UNAM preparatory schools, although he later called for students to return to classes as their activism escalated.

According to retrospective accounts, González Casanova and the rest of CUEC's staff backed the students' mobilization. Filmmaker Marcela Fernández Violante recalled that "it was amicably decided that the academic and administrative authorities should not represent the Center, it had to be us, the students, we weren't at war with them but nor were we inclined to accept them giving the movement marching orders."[246] Approximately twenty students ventured into the streets armed with CUEC's small battery of 16mm cameras and the film stock allotted for student exercises and the Sección de Actividades Cinematográficas's planned slate of documentaries.[247]

The students were forced to develop creative strategies for documenting the movement in the face of police and military violence. Fernández Violante tells a memorable story about removing the taillights of her car in order to allow López Arretche to film from the trunk undetected while Roberto Jaime Sánchez Martínez, her husband at the time,

FIGURE 19. Still from *El grito* (1968) showing CUEC students joining the student movement in front of and behind the cameras. Note the iconic "Mexico 68" logo of the Olympic Games partially visible on the façade of the Liverpool department store. *Source: El grito*, directed by Leobardo López Arretche (Mexico City: Filmoteca UNAM, 2018), DVD.

drove.²⁴⁸ Events that escaped documentation, including the Tlatelolco massacre itself, are reconstructed in the film via the dynamic treatment of still photographs in a manner that recalls the radical newsreels of Cuban filmmaker Santiago Álvarez. A layered soundtrack adds energy to decontextualized images of public protest, including recorded speeches (though the filmmakers were unable to capture direct sound and relied on recordings by the university's radio station to synchronize short portions of these discourses) and a voiceover containing translated commentary by Italian journalist Oriana Fallaci, herself a victim of military violence during the massacre.²⁴⁹ Yet *El grito* does not demand that the spectator synthesize complex political statements via montage in the manner of the most celebrated works of NLAC, such as the Grupo Cine Liberación's *La hora de los hornos* (*The Hour of the Furnaces*, 1967, Argentina).

CUEC played a decisive role in assuring *El grito*'s completion, but also in suppressing the film from public view. González Casanova helped safeguard the footage in advance of a military occupation of the university by dispersing the reels among CUEC students.[250] According to Fernández Violante, González Casanova also determined the authorship of the finished documentary after a conflict arose between López Arretche and Sánchez Martínez during the editing phase; González Casanova flipped a coin to determine who would take charge of the project, with López Arretche emerging the winner.[251] Other accounts—including González Casanova's statements in a 2007 interview—indicate that the coin toss never happened and that an assembly of CUEC students chose López Arretche to complete the film.[252] Regardless, the collective labor of image creation gave way to a more conventional mode of sole authorship. Furthermore, once *El grito* was completed, González Casanova opposed its screening as a political provocation that could damage CUEC and UNAM, and he convinced López Arretche not to premiere the film. The film's chances of public exhibition seemed even more remote after his brother Pablo González Casanova became university rector in 1970. *El grito* went largely unseen until 1971, when CUEC student Guillermo Díaz Palafox recovered a duplicate negative López Arretche had deposited with ICAIC and furnished prints to student organizations, resulting in his expulsion from the school.[253]

El grito emerged from an institution marked by deep contradictions. Committed to improving society through better films, CUEC nonetheless promoted an elitist notion of what these films would look like and placed limited faith in the aesthetic or political sensibilities of untrained spectators. Ultimately, so did the largely straightforward formal strategies of *El grito*, by contrast with the complex and intellectually demanding montage of a film like *La hora de los hornos*. CUEC's tuition and schedule had the potential to democratize access to professional film training, but it nevertheless operated in the context of a largely middle- and upper-class university whose class character shaped the student movement in ways that are not always fully acknowledged. As UNAM's students were radicalized by the movement, CUEC's leadership facilitated their filmmaking while maintaining arguably paternalistic control over the exhibition of the results.

CUEC's ideological project of reforming the mass audience, a project inherited in part from the cineclub movement, resonated with IDHEC's imperative to convey specialized cultural knowledge as a precondition for a thriving industry that would also enlighten viewers. Ultimately, the ideals of UNAM's film culture and the Grupo Nuevo Cine served less to reconcile cinematic modernism with mass taste than to institutionalize a cinema of celebrated auteurs—many of them, like Jaime Humberto

Hermosillo, trained at CUEC. This cinema gained renewed state support during the presidency of Luis Echeverría (1970–1976) without ever attracting the mass audiences that Mexican popular cinema had enjoyed from the late 1930s through the early 1950s.[254] The bid to gain autonomy for cinema by transforming cultural markets and overturning a failed mode of state-supported production proved unsuccessful; instead, film production was increasingly subsumed back into the cultural infrastructures of the state.

By the late 1970s, González Casanova's own position had shifted somewhat in light of the Marxist, anti-colonial critique that came to dominate Latin American intellectual spheres during the 1960s, as suggested by a text he delivered at the 1976 CILECT conference in Mexico City. Discussing the need to foster a national film industry as a means of combating cultural colonialism, he asserted: "The powerful interests which control film and television in a capitalistic society use them, as is natural, to their own advantage; they turn the spectacle into another means of securing political and economic control for themselves. By seeing to it that individuals and whole nations lose their identities, they degrade them and can thereby subjugate them more easily. Thus, the "American Way of Life" ceased to be just an American bourgeois ideal and became the symbol of the superiority of the capitalistic system, transforming even the most seemingly innocent cinematic production into a message destined to strengthen cultural colonization."[255] Even his evaluation of the Nuevo Cine Mexicano that CUEC's graduates helped forge was pessimistic: "The first attempts to leave this dependent-colonizing cinema behind resulted in very minor replicas of the successful European cinema."[256]

In spite of these uncompromising sentiments, elements of González Casanova's alternately cautionary and utopian rhetoric from the 1950s and early 1960s persist in this later public address. He observed, "It is no secret to any of you that human behavior at the present time is clearly affected, and I would add, determined by what is shown on the screen. Styles, habits and customs are becoming more uniform all over the world."[257] Despite media's role in what we now call globalization, González Casanova nevertheless held out hope for its use as a vehicle of international understanding: "The artificial barriers which have been erected throughout history will tumble when direct contact is established with the most intimate realities of life in the rest of the world.... Unfortunately, we have not yet reached that stage."[258] In the quest to construct what González Casanova called "the ideal society," film schools, he argued, had to "prepare future creators of cinema and television so that they are conscious of the social importance of the instrument that they are managing."[259]

Delivered more than a decade after CUEC's founding, these remarks at once echo the postwar rhetoric of cinema's threat and promise that animated González Casanova's institution-building efforts and highlight the transformation of these ideals within a more deeply polarized Cold War context. CUEC's development forms part of a largely unexplored history of film pedagogy in Latin America, which, far from simply paving the way for NLAC, was shaped by a range of institutional goals and geopolitical maneuvers, from the educational aims of individual universities to French efforts to regain lost cultural prestige through the training of foreign film technicians. Rather than consistently championing the notions of individual expression that animated much of the discourse on art cinema in the period, postwar film pedagogy often centered cinema's broader social effects but stopped short of instrumentalizing cinema as a tool for social justice, until the growing politicization of culture forced a dramatic confrontation with these older ideals. Film education thus became a key site where postwar film culture collided with emerging practices of socially engaged filmmaking and where understandings of the creator and the audience were alternately reinforced and reimagined.

Conclusion

The premise of Uruguay's 2011 submission to the Academy Awards, *La vida útil* (*A Useful Life*, Federico Veiroj), is a paean to cinephilia: after more than five decades, financial problems force an archive with an uncanny resemblance to the Cinemateca Uruguaya to shut its doors, setting longtime employee Jorge (Jorge Jellineck) existentially adrift. The film's self-conscious cinephilia is also evident in its form; its black-and-white cinematography evokes both "classics" and low-budget contemporary indies. *La vida útil*'s measured narrative, replete with dead times and minutely observed actions, partakes of the observational realism—some might say neorealism—characteristic of the Latin American cinema that has circulated widely on the festival and arthouse circuits since the turn of the twenty-first century, bolstered by new national film policies and transnational funding schemes.

This deliberate pace allows *La vida útil* to delve into the daily labor that sustains the institution in precarious circumstances, from the maintenance of heavily worn projectors to the live Spanish translation of intertitles in a Hollywood silent performed by the archive's director, who is played by its real-life director at the time, Manuel Martínez Carril. (It is no accident that the film in question is Erich von Stroheim's *Greed*, whose lost eight-hour version epitomizes the elusive object of cinephilic desire.) This on-the-spot translation, a common practice in postwar Latin American cineclubs, exemplifies the logistical frictions generated by cinema's circulation through the kind of alternative distribution infrastructure mapped in this book, often without the benefit of affordances like subtitles. This kind of cultural labor becomes all but impossible in the face of a neoliberal logic that instrumentalizes culture as an engine of economic growth, the film suggests in a scene where the protagonist and his boss Martínez appeal to a private foundation to increase its support to save the archive, only to have it yanked altogether on the grounds that the foundation can only fund self-sustaining ventures.[1] Encouragingly, in reality the opposite occurred; the Corporación Andina de Fomento, a Latin American development bank, set aside space for the archive in its new Montevideo headquarters. The building opened in 2018, attracting new audiences to the Cinemateca's upgraded screening rooms. *La vida útil* was the final film shown in the archive's old location.[2]

La vida útil offers a political economy of the prevailing perception, beginning at the turn of the twenty-first century, that cinephilia was in an inexorable decline, or at the least in the throes of a transformation that was rendering it unrecognizable. Susan Sontag's famous (or infamous) 1996 essay "The Decay of Cinema" blamed cinema's absorption into a swirl of ubiquitous screens.[3] For Sontag, rapid cutting and frenetic camera movement cheapened film aesthetics in a bid for viewer attention on small screens, while the easy accessibility of films on television and home video robbed the cinematic experience of its elusive, ephemeral, and transcendent qualities. As Sarah Keller notes, cinephilia has long been marked by anxieties surrounding technological change.[4] The year after Sontag's essay was published, the DVD was introduced in the United States, gaining widespread popularity and partially bridging the gap between theatrical viewing and the "degraded" experience offered by magnetic media like VHS, characterized by loss of resolution, poor color reproduction, and "panning and scanning" to reduce widescreen releases to Academy ratio proportions, thus threatening to erode the aura of the movie theater experience.[5]

Contra Sontag, critics like Thomas Elsaesser, Marijke de Valck, and Girish Shambu have hailed the emergence of a "new cinephilia" of the digital age marked by the seemingly infinite on-demand abundance of moving images.[6] Even as the sheer volume of available titles presents a profound challenge to the idea of a canon of historically and aesthetically significant films, this perception of abundance can conceal huge geographical and historical gaps in streamers' constantly changing catalogs. Nevertheless, the gulf between this experience and that of mid-century cinephiles obliged to forge connections across oceans and continents, developing a sprawling network of institutions simply to secure film "classics" could hardly be starker. Similarly, the explosion of online discourse about movies has democratized the role of cinematic tastemaker beyond the wildest dreams (or nightmares) of the mid-century cinephiles on both sides of the Atlantic who sought to elevate the film culture of the masses. At the same time, the free online availability of thoughtful amateur commentary on movies has rendered film criticism all but obsolete as a viable profession.[7]

Though the "new cinephilia" is hailed as refreshingly global, increasingly open to "non-Western" cinemas and defined by a geographically dispersed community of film lovers and trendsetters, its effects are not felt homogeneously, particularly in light of the "digital divide" in access to high-speed internet worldwide. In the Global South, non-networked digital technologies like (pirated) VCDs and Cuba's "paquete semanal" (weekly package) of media files circulated via hard drives passed from person to person can be much more significant and far-reaching than the online consumption of moving images. In recent years, Latin American film archives have been marked not only by intensified political repression in Brazil (see chapter 2) and Ecuador, where police occupied the Cinemateca Nacional during a state of emergency declared by the government to quell protests by indigenous groups—but also, as the case of the Cinemateca Uruguaya suggests, by massive investment in film archives as physical spaces for film exhibition. By 2018 Mexico's Cineteca Nacional and Colombia's Cinemateca Distrital (renamed the Cinemateca de Bogotá) had also moved into expansive, architecturally stunning new spaces equipped with ample screening rooms.[8] This development suggests that the physically isolated but digitally networked viewing experience that we envision as defining the "new cinephilia" is far from a universal one. These recent developments throw into question *La vida útil*'s pessimism about the future of film archives and non-commercial exhibition, suggesting they should be viewed not only in a light of nostalgia or loss, but also in terms of endurance. These new investments in non-commercial exhibition are a testament to the lasting impact of forms of film culture forged in postwar Latin America, despite their limitations and structural exclusions.

If *La vida útil* shows Jorge's devotion to film to be hopelessly quixotic, Jonathan Nossiter's 2020 film *Last Words* (France/Italy/United States) raises the question of cinephilia's relevance today to a fever pitch by setting it against irrevocable ecological devastation and humanity's total annihilation. The film's unnamed narrator (Kalipha Touray), who identifies himself at the start of the film as the last surviving person on earth, embarks on a pilgrimage to the Cineteca di Bologna after spotting its address on a film can discovered by chance. There, he meets the grizzled guardian of the archive's trove of films (Nick Nolte). Armed with raw negative and an improvised camera, plus a projector and films, the two set off in search of a colony of survivors, seeking "a last chance to leave a trace, a living trace, a testimony of us." In its joyous scenes of a picture show that threatens, each time, to be the last, *Last Words* makes the case that cinema can teach us to be human again in the grimmest of circumstances, celebrating the medium as a repository of world memory that may endure longer than humanity itself.

At a moment of climate emergency, rising authoritarianism worldwide, and Russian invasion in Ukraine—a development that, if one judges by the reaction of US commentators who perhaps had not been watching developments in the region closely, seemed unthinkable in a post–Cold War order—the efforts of French and Latin American film enthusiasts to train critically inclined viewers and encourage intercultural understanding feel at once quaint and poignant. Of course, as we have seen, these altruistic aims were inextricably intertwined with self-interested national agendas and desires for prestige. The protocols of sophisticated viewing that cinephiles sought to instill in order to help spectators to responsibly navigate threatening ideologies and rapidly shifting social and sexual mores seem woefully inadequate in the face of our algorithmically driven consumption of online media, which promotes the spread of misinformation and extreme views that encourage engagement and thus generate profit.

As temperature records are shattered and we continue to grapple with the uneven global toll of COVID-19, it is impossible to ignore how our lives depend on the fragile internationalism of accords like the necessary but insufficient Paris Agreement and the work of supranational bodies like the World Health Organization. Affirming that cinema can offer us a truly planetary consciousness, generating affective connections and solidarities that may help us to imagine other possible worlds, can feel hopelessly utopian in these times.[9] Girish Shambu writes, "'Life organized around films' is one widely accepted definition of traditional cinephilia. But at this moment, when the world is in turmoil and the planet on the edge of catastrophe, such a conception of cine-love seems irresponsible. What we need now is a cinephilia that is fully in contact with its present global moment—that accompanies it, that moves and travels with it."[10] It is worth recalling that mid-twentieth-century film enthusiasts and institution-builders aspired not only to advance patriotic aims and enhance their own prestige, but also to better the world by transforming the viewer, even if it is easy now to dismiss their utopian yet paternalistic hopes for the medium. With the very possibility of a human future now in doubt, whether cinephilia continues to matter remains an open question.

Notes

INTRODUCTION

1. For instance, France was the first nation to create an office solely dedicated to cultural diplomacy in its foreign ministry. Arndt, *First Resort of Kings*, xvii.

2. I use the term *Southern Cone* to refer to Argentina, Brazil, and Chile—sometimes called the "ABC countries" due to their historically high levels of wealth and industrialization relative to other Latin American nations—Paraguay, and Uruguay. Uruguay also industrialized early, while Paraguay's economic development was hindered by losses suffered in the War of the Triple Alliance (1864–1870) and Chaco War (1932–1935).

3. Bourdieu, "Forms of Capital."

4. For overviews of academic discourse on cinephilia, see Keathley, *Cinephilia and History*; and Keller, *Anxious Cinephilia*. On expanding our notion of cinephilia beyond erudite spectatorship, see Jullier and Leveratto, *Cinéphiles et cinéphilies*; for a rethinking of the historical emergence of cinephilia, see Cowan, *Film Societies in Austria and Germany*; and for discussion of contemporary cinephilia, see the conclusion of this study.

5. Nye, "Soft Power"; and Nye, *Soft Power*. Faye Bartram makes a similar argument regarding France's film-related cultural diplomacy vis-à-vis the USSR in "35mm Bridges."

6. Rolland, *La crise du modèle française*; and Matthieu, *Une ambition sud-américaine*.

7. Holloway, *Companion to Latin American History*, 32; and Leddy Phelan, "Genesis of the Idea of Latin America."

8. Bourdieu, *Distinction*.

9. López-Pedreros, *Makers of Democracy*, 1–7, 21–41; Parker and Walker, *Latin America's Middle Class*, 8–11; and Owensby, *Intimate Ironies*, 5.

10. The term was popularized by Fernando Solanas and Octavio Getino in their celebrated 1969 manifesto "Towards a Third Cinema" and has inspired enduring scholarly debate. Note that the categories of first, second, and third cinema do not map directly onto the First (capitalist), Second (communist), and Third (postcolonial/Global South) Worlds, but rather correspond with classical cinema, bourgeois art cinema, and radical political filmmaking.

11. Corrêa, *A Cinemateca Brasileira*; Souza, "A Cinemateca Brasileira"; Domínguez, *24 ilusiones por segundo*; Silveira, *Cultura y cinefilia*; Izquierdo, *Cine y preservación*; Broitman, "La cinefilia en la Argentina"; Rozsa, "On the Edge of the Screen"; Wschebor Pellegrino, "Ouvrir les boîtes"; and Amieva Collado, "La conformación del campo cinematográfico."

12. Bethell and Roxborough, "Introduction," 2–3.

13. Bethell and Roxborough, "Introduction," 22–23.

14. Crisp, *Classic French Cinema*, 51–53.

15. Cravenne, *Le tour du monde du cinéma français*, 70. All translations from French, Portuguese, and Spanish are the author's except where noted.

16. Hecht, *Radiance of France*, 208–209.

17. Mitchell, *International Cultural Relations*; and Arndt, *First Resort of Kings*, xvii–xix. The distinction between cultural diplomacy and cultural relations (and their overlap with related concepts like public diplomacy and soft power) is often murky; see Ang, Isar, and Mar, "Cultural Diplomacy," 365–369; and Gienow-Hecht and Donfried, "Model of Cultural Diplomacy."

18. This organization has variously been known as the Motion Picture Producers and Distributors of America (1922–1945); the Motion Picture Association of America (1945–2019), and the Motion Picture Association (2019–present).

19. Vasey, *World According to Hollywood*; Chung, *Hollywood Diplomacy*; and Shaw, *Hollywood's Cold War*.

20. Lee, *Cinema and the Cultural Cold War*; and Melnick, *Hollywood's Embassies*.

21. See Neale, "Art Cinema as Institution"; Staiger, "With the Compliments of the Auteur"; and Wilinsky, *Sure Seaters*.

22. For a recent study of the contradictions involved in efforts to construct alternative film cultures and ideal publics, see Trice, *City of Screens*.

23. Studies of cinema and the cultural Cold War, most focused on the United States and/or the USSR, include Shaw, *Hollywood's Cold War*; Shaw and Youngblood, *Cinematic Cold War*; Roth-Ey, *Moscow Prime Time*; and Gilburd, *To See Paris and Die*, 158–215. For a broader treatment (though mostly focused on Europe), see Lovejoy and Pajala, *Remapping Cold War Media*.

24. Littleton and Sykes, *Advancing American Art*.

25. Cockcroft, "Abstract Expressionism"; and Guilbaut, *How New York Stole the Idea of Modern Art*.

26. Galt and Schoonover, "Introduction," 5. On art cinema as a relational concept defined by films' "variable difference from the qualities usually associated with the commercial mainstream," see King, *Positioning Art Cinema*.

27. Bordwell, "Art Cinema as a Mode of Film Practice." On the history of art cinema as a concept in Latin America, see Couret, "Enduring Art Cinema."

28. Neale, "Art Cinema as Institution," 11.

29. Stonor Saunders, *Cultural Cold War*, 279–301; and Iber, *Neither Peace nor Freedom*.
30. Salazkina, *World Socialist Cinema*; Djagalov, *From Internationalism to Postcolonialism*; and Bystrom, Popescu, and Zien, *Cultural Cold War and the Global South*. See also Glaser and Lee, *Comintern Aesthetics*.
31. Westad, *Global Cold War*.
32. Garrard-Burnett, Lawrence, and Moreno, introduction to *Beyond the Eagle's Shadow*, 4–5; and Field, Krepp, and Pettinà, *Latin America and the Global Cold War*, 7.
33. Garrard-Burnett, Lawrence, and Moreno, *Beyond the Eagle's Shadow*; Joseph and Spenser, *In From the Cold*; and Griffith, "Cultural Turn in Cold War Studies."
34. Quoted in Cornick, "French Intellectuals," 40.
35. Jackson, *De Gaulle*, 379.
36. Judt, *Past Imperfect*, 1.
37. Costigliola, *France and the United States*, 46–47; and Cornick, "French Intellectuals."
38. Costigliola, *France and the United States*, 68, 83.
39. On tricontinentalism, see Garland Mahler, *From the Tricontinental to the Global South*; for an overview of NAM see Dinkel, *Non-Aligned Movement*.
40. Dinkel, *Non-Aligned Movement*, 118, 165.
41. Costigliola, *France and the United States*, xv.
42. Creswell, *Question of Balance*.
43. Quoted in Costigliola, *France and the United States*, 139–140.
44. Jackson, *De Gaulle*, 396.
45. Hellmann, *Communitarian Third Way*, 3–5.
46. Hellmann, *Communitarian Third Way*, 8.
47. Jackson, *De Gaulle*, 401–406, 420.
48. Jackson, *De Gaulle*, 427.
49. Zolov, *Last Good Neighbor*, 19.
50. Trouvé, "L'ambition et les contraintes," 106–110.
51. For an overview, see McLynn, "Ideology of Peronism."
52. Trouvé, "L'ambition et les contraintes," 110.
53. Vaïsse, introduction to *De Gaulle et l'Amérique latine*, 8–9. See also Jackson, *De Gaulle*, 605–606.
54. Lusnich, Aisemberg, and Cuarterolo, *Pantallas transnacionales*; Gunckel, *Mexico on Main Street*; Castro Ricalde and McKee Irwin, *Global Mexican Cinema*; Castro Ricalde and McKee Irwin, *El cine mexicano "se impone"*; and Gunckel, Horak, and Jarvinen, *Cinema between Latin America and Los Angeles*.
55. Paranaguá, "Of Periodizations and Paradigms."
56. Paranaguá, *Tradición y modernidad*; and Schroeder-Rodríguez, "Latin American Silent Cinema." See also Schroeder-Rodríguez, *Latin American Cinema*, 129–163.
57. Owensby, *Intimate Ironies*, 5–6.
58. López-Pedreros, *Makers of Democracy*, 5–10.
59. Parker, *Idea of the Middle Class*; Owensby, *Intimate Ironies*; Barr-Melej, *Reforming Chile*; Adamovsky, *Historia de la clase media argentina*; Parker and

Walker, *Latin America's Middle Class*; López Pedreros, *Makers of Democracy*; and Barbosa Cruz, López Pedreros, and Stern, *Middle Classes in Latin America*.

60. Owensby, *Intimate Ironies*, 27–35; and Parker, *Idea of the Middle Class*, 17–21.

61. Eineigel, "Revolutionary Promises Encounter Urban Realities."

62. Bulmer-Thomas, *Economic History of Latin America Since Independence*, 232, 235–236.

63. Bulmer-Thomas, *Economic History of Latin America Since Independence*, 268–272.

64. Roberts, *Cities of Peasants Revisited*, 146–149.

65. Roberts, *Cities of Peasants Revisited*, 146.

66. Bethell and Roxborough, "Introduction."

67. Pedreros-Lopez, *Makers of Democracy*, 34–36, 46–48; Owensby, *Intimate Ironies*, 4–6; and Parker, *Idea of the Middle Class*, ix, 3–5.

68. Mitchell, *International Cultural Relations*, 93.

69. Owensby, *Intimate Ironies*, 56; López-Pedreros, *Makers of Democracy*, 6–10; and Parker, *Idea of the Middle Class*, 4–5.

70. Owensby, *Intimate Ironies*, 8.

71. Wilinsky, *Sure Seaters*.

72. "Encuesta Sobre 'Manon,'" *Cine Club* (Montevideo), June 1950, 15; and "Actividad realizada," Cine Club Mendoza, 1953, F.I.C.C. Questionnaires, Rapports d'activités ciné-clubs, Cinémathèque française-Fonds Georges Sadoul (hereafter CF-SADOUL) 724-B51.

73. Amieva Collado, "La conformación del campo cinematográfico en Uruguay," 58.

74. Rodríguez Rodríguez, "Entrevista con Manuel González Casanova," 130, 137.

75. This paragraph draws extensively on Melo Souza, *Paulo Emílio no Paraíso*.

76. Wschebor Pellegrino, "Ouvrir les boîtes," 173.

77. Cortés, *Los amores contrariados*; and Rocco, *Gabriel García Márquez*.

78. "Rapport d'activité, 1958," quoted in Pendergast, "French Policy in UNESCO," 302.

79. Cravenne, *Le tour du monde du cinéma français*, 73.

80. The literature on this topic is ample, much of it generated by the French state itself. See, for instance, Balous, *L'action culturelle française dans la monde*; Salon, *L'action culturelle de la France dans le monde*; Ministère des Affaires Étrangères, *Le projet culturel exteriéur de la France*; Roche and Pigniau, *Histoires de diplomatie culturelle des origines*; Raymond, *L'action culturelle extérieure de la France*; and Lane, *French Scientific and Cultural Diplomacy*.

81. Matthieu, *Une ambition sud-américaine*, 15–25; and Rolland, *La crise du modèle français*, 75–84.

82. Bunker, *Creating Mexican Consumer Culture*, 99–133.

83. Rolland, *La crise du modèle française*.

84. Matthieu, "Un enjeu diplomatique"; and Matthieu, *Une ambition sud-américaine*, 131–149.

85. Rolland, *La crise du modèle français*, 266–314; and Jackson, *De Gaulle*, 605.

86. Matthieu, *Une ambition sud-américaine*, 198.
87. Horne, "'To Spread the French Language Is to Extend the *Patrie*.'"
88. Bruézière, *L'Alliance française*, 176.
89. Chaubet, *La politique culturelle française et la diplomatie de la langue*, 277.
90. "FICC—Activité administrative," CF-SADOUL724-B51; and Bedoya, "El Cine Club de Lima"; and Pierre Denis, French ambassador in Ecuador, to Georges Bidault, Minister of Foreign Affairs, February 2, 1953. Ministère des Affaires Étrangères, France (hereafter FRMAE)-241QO-215.
91. Paschalidis, "Exporting National Culture."
92. The Direction générale des relations culturelles was created in 1945. Between 1956 and 1966, it was known as the Direction générale des affaires culturelles et techniques (Office of Cultural and Technical Affairs).
93. See, for example, Report, French ambassador in Argentina to the Minister of Foreign Affairs [Georges Bidault], April 30, 1953, FRMAE-241QO-203.
94. Jean Binoche, French ambassador in Peru, to the Minister of Foreign Affairs Georges Bidault, July 15, 1953, FRMAE-241QO-216.
95. "Rapport sur l'activité du Service d'Information et de Presse de l'Ambassade de France au Brésil," January 25, 1950, FRMAE-241QO-207.
96. Jean-Paul Angles [French chargé d'affairs in Chile] to [Minister of Foreign Affairs] Georges Bidault, July 21, 1953, FRMAE-241QO-212.
97. Abel Verdier, French ambassador in Colombia, to the Minister of Foreign Affairs [Georges Bidault], July 8, 1953, FRMAE-241QO-214.
98. Report, French ambassador in Argentina to Minister of Foreign Affairs [Georges Bidault], May 26, 1952, FRMAE-241QO-203.
99. Francis Levasseur [French chargé d'affairs in Brazil] to [Minister of Foreign Affairs] Georges Bidault, November 28, 1953, FRMAE-241QO-207; and J. F. Charvet, "État des dépenses effectuées par le Service de Presse au cours du 2éme semestre 1951," January 3, 1952, FRMAE-241QO-212.
100. Database of Latin American cineclub screenings compiled by the author, available at transatlanticcinephilia.net.
101. On the history of COFRAM, see Cravenne, *Le tour du monde du cinéma français*, 48–61; Couret, "When New Waves Crash," 99–104; and Rodrigues Pereira, "La politique culturelle française du Brésil de 1945 à 1970." Documentation on COFRAM is held in the files of the CNC at France's national archives.
102. Matthieu, *Une ambition sud-américaine*, 193–199; and Cravenne, *Le tour du monde du cinéma français*, 49.
103. Cravenne, *Le tour du monde du cinéma français*, 55.
104. Cravenne, *Le tour du monde du cinéma français*, 72–73.
105. On the French film weeks, see Cravenne, *Le tour du monde du cinéma français*, 123–164; Bartram, "Reel Results after One Week"; and Bartram, "35mm Bridges."
106. French ambassador in Argentina to Minister of Foreign Affairs [Georges Bidault], June 26, 1953, FRMAE-241QO-203.
107. Cravenne, *Le tour du monde du cinéma français*, 77.
108. Cravenne, *Le tour du monde du cinéma français*, 87, 94.
109. Cravenne, *Le tour du monde du cinéma français*, 98.
110. Andrew, "Time Zones and Jet Lag," 70.

111. Moine, "La FIAPF," 256.

112. UNESCO Preparatory Commission, Draft Proposals for an Educational and Cultural Organisation of the United Nations, Conference for the Establishment of the United Nations Scientific, Educational, and Cultural Organization, 1945, https://unesdoc.unesco.org/ark:/48223/pf0000117626.locale=en.

113. Pendergast, "UNESCO and French Cultural Relations," 454.

114. Pendergast, "UNESCO and French Cultural Relations," 454–455.

115. Pendergast, "UNESCO and French Cultural Relations," 458.

116. UNESCO General Conference, First Session, 1946, Sub-Commission on Mass Communication, 159–160, https://unesdoc.unesco.org/ark:/48223/pf0000114580?posInSet=4&queryId=8d95e62c-e5fa-4dd1-86f0-9d20efe86762.

117. UNESCO General Conference, First Session, 1946, Sub-Commission on Mass Communication, 228.

118. See J. M. L. Peters's *Teaching about the Film*, published in Spanish (as *La educación cinematográfica*) and several other languages; and Lods, *Professional Training of Film Technicians*.

119. Langlois, "And Action!," 82; and Druick, 'UNESCO, Film and Education," 87.

120. Philippe Desjardins, "UNESCO Sums Up 1947–1948 Press, Radio, Film Needs," *UNESCO Courier*, October 1948, 4.

121. Desjardins, "UNESCO Sums Up 1947–1948 Press, Radio, Film Needs," 4.

122. Huttunen, *Politicised Cinema*.

123. Langlois, "And Action!" On these collaborations, see Longo, "Palimpsests of Power."

124. The Beirut Agreement was specific to film; the Florence Agreement was broader.

125. "UNESCO Helps Educational Films over Frontier Barriers," *UNESCO Courier*, March 1950, 2.

126. "Report by the Director-General on the Aid Furnished by UNESCO to the Latin American Educational Film Institute (ILCE)," Eighty-Third Meeting of the UNESCO Executive Board, Paris, September 19, 1969, 2, https://unesdoc.unesco.org/ark:/48223/pf0000193138_eng?posInSet=3&queryId=f71ac4dd-9e50-4a79-ac7a-114cd1d9df6b.

127. Cleppe, "Institutional Breeding Grounds of the Postwar Film on Art."

128. Corrêa, "O cinema como instituição," 90.

129. Brouillette, *UNESCO and the Fate of the Literary*.

130. Acland and Wasson, *Useful Cinema*.

131. For an overview of this literature, see the "Empire, Nation, and Travel" section of Chen and Gräfe, "Mapping the Nontheatrical"; see also Chan, "Under the Palms"; Blaylock, "The Persistent Instructor"; and Kwon, Odagiri, and Baek, *Theorizing Colonial Cinema*.

CHAPTER 1: THE CINECLUB MOVEMENT IN LATIN AMERICA

1. Cine Club de Colombia (hereafter CCC) program, September–October 1979, Fundación Patrimonio Fílmico Colombiano (hereafter FPFC). On this incident, see Concha Henao, *Historia social del cine en Colombia*, 347.

2. On disturbances in Colombian movie theaters, see Barón Leal, "Los cinemas bogotanos," 153–154; Ospina León, "Films on Paper," 45; and Lamaña, "Protohistoria de los públicos."

3. On Gaitán's political career and its aftermath, see Braun, *Assassination of Gaitán*.

4. Palacios, *Between Legitimacy and Violence*, trans. Richard Stoller, 142.

5. CCC program, September–October 1979, FPFC.

6. *Film society* is the term usually used in the Anglo-American context, while *ciné-club*, *cineclub*, and *cineclube* (or *clube de cinema*) are utilized in French, Spanish, and Portuguese, respectively. While one might argue each term corresponds to a distinct associative tradition and ethos, I use the two interchangeably here.

7. CCC, "Selección de la mejor película exhibida en Bogotá durante el año 1960," FPFC.

8. Reyes, *Politics of Taste*, 5.

9. Reyes, *Politics of Taste*, 8.

10. Acta de Constitución del Cine Club de Colombia, September 2, 1949, FPFC; and López-Pedreros, *Makers of Democracy*.

11. Rama, *The Lettered City*.

12. Souillés-Debats, *La culture cinématographique du mouvement ciné-club*; and Conway, "'New Wave of Spectators.'" There is some anecdotal evidence that French cineclubs achieved greater member participation than their counterparts elsewhere. After summarizing the results of a survey conducted by a cineclub in Annecy, a British film society magazine commented, "What most of our committees would like to know—how to get 500 members to answer a questionnaire—they don't say!" "Pour l'ambiance," *Film* (London), September–October 1955, 6.

13. CCC program, April 11, 1957, FPFC.

14. CCC program, January–February 1961, FPFC.

15. As Léo Souillés-Debats points out, no rigid distinction can be drawn between organizers and members, since individuals might occupy both roles at different times. Souillés-Debats, *La culture cinématographique du mouvement ciné-club*, 27.

16. See chapter 3 for more on this festival.

17. Andrade, "L'action des cine-clubs et des cinémathèques en Amérique Latine," 3.

18. Pick, *New Latin American Cinema*.

19. Ch[arles] de Vesme, "Ce que doivent être le Ciné-Club et son Journal," *Le journal du ciné-club*, January 1920, n.p.

20. Filmmaker Walter Lima Júnior noted in an interview that many Rio de Janeiro cineclubs of the 1960s were communist fronts. Freire, "Cópias de filmes e salas de exibição, cineclubes e cinematecas," 132.

21. Bethell and Roxborough, "Introduction," 2; and Broitman, "La cinefilia en la Argentina," 212–213.

22. The two organizations later merged, becoming the Club français du cinéma. Gauthier, *La passion du cinéma*, 17–65. See also Abel, *French Film Theory and Criticism*, 198–199, 324–325, 425–426.

23. Gauthier, *La passion du cinéma*, 170; and Smoodin, *Paris in the Dark*, 42.

24. Crisp, *Classic French Cinema*, 228; and Gauthier, *La passion du cinéma*, 171–179.
25. Hankins, "Iris Barry, Writer and Cineaste." On Barry's life and career, see Sitton, *Lady in the Dark*.
26. Hagener, *Moving Forward, Looking Back*, 96–97.
27. Hagener, *Moving Forward, Looking Back*, 89; and Cowan, *Film Societies in Austria and Germany*, 181–245.
28. Two short-lived cineclubs existed in Uruguay in 1930 and 1936 according to Hintz, *Algo para recordar*, 7–8.
29. Artundo, "Institución, arte y sociedad, 13; Peña, "Amigos del cine," 59–63; Couselo, *Cine argentino en capítulos sueltos*, 95–99; and Cuarterolo, "Gaze Turned towards Europe."
30. Rozsa, "On the Edge of the Screen," 93–95.
31. De los Reyes, "La idea del cine club en México en la etapa muda"; and de los Reyes, *Sucedió en Jalisco*, 263–264.
32. Rodríguez Álvarez, "La sociedad de los cinéfilos," 74–78; and Rodríguez Álvarez, "*Contemporáneos* y Cineclub Mexicano."
33. Clariana Rodagut, "Mujeres iberoamericanas mediadoras."
34. On the Chaplin Club see, among others, Xavier, *Sétima arte*, 199–263; Santos, "A apoteose da imagem"; and Heise and Tudor, "Constructing (Film) Art."
35. "Sessão especial do Chaplin-Club: Apresentação de 'A Caixa de Pandora,'" *O Fan*, January 1930, 4.
36. The club seems to have operated sporadically through 1936, sometimes under the name Cineclub Bolívar. Pérez, "El cineclubismo en Venezuela," 133–134.
37. See, for instance, "Desarrollo hispanoamericano de los cineclubs," *La Gaceta Literaria*, August 15, 1931, 10.
38. Agustín Aragón Leiva, "Fundación del Cineclub," *Contemporáneos*, April/May/June 1931, 187–189, trans. Abel Plenn.
39. Rodríguez Álvarez, "*Contemporáneos* y el Cineclub Mexicano," 280–281; Agustín Aragón Leiva, "Bulletin No. 1 of the Mexican Cine Club," trans. Abel Plenn, *Experimental Cinema*, no. 4 (1932): 34.
40. "Fundación del Cineclub," *Contemporáneos*, April/May/June 1931, 187–189.
41. "Estatutos do Chaplin-Club," *O Fan*, January 29, 1929, 4.
42. "Sessões do Chaplin-Club," *O Fan*, June 1930, 89–90; and Pérez, "El cineclubismo en Venezuela," 133.
43. See Peña, "Amigos del cine," 59.
44. Rozsa, "On the Edge of the Screen," 93; Aragón Leiva, "Bulletin No. 1 of the Mexican Cine Club"; and Ortiz de Montellano, *Epistolario*, 127–130.
45. Clariana Rodagut, "Mujeres iberoamericanas mediadoras."
46. Borge, "Lettered Clown."
47. Wells, "Parallel Modernities?"
48. Wells, "Parallel Modernities?," 156; and Rozsa, "On the Edge of the Screen," 93.
49. Such titles included *Frauennot—Frauenglück* (Women's misery, women's happiness, 1930, Switzerland), a hybrid documentary-fiction film on abortion

directed by cinematographer Eduard Tissé, a frequent collaborator of Eisenstein, and *Troika* (Vladimir Strizhevsky, Germany, 1930). See Ortiz de Montellano, *Epistolario*, 127–130; and Rodríguez Álvarez, "*Contemporáneos* y Cineclub Mexicano," 296.

50. Rodríguez Álvarez, "*Contemporáneos* y Cineclub Mexicano," 303–304.

51. Peña, "Amigos del cine," 61; and Guillermo de Torre, "El 'cineclub' de Buenos Aires," *La Gaceta Literaria*, April 1, 1930, 5, published in English translation in Navitski and Poppe, *Cosmopolitan Film Cultures in Latin America*, 176–179.

52. Crisp, *Classic French Cinema*, 229. Fans could mingle with celebrities at two cineclubs sanctioned by the occupiers, each run by a German film magazine with a French-language edition, but viewing and discussing films seems not to have been part of their activities. See Smoodin, *Paris in the Dark*, 57–59.

53. Broitman, "La cinefilia en la Argentina," 142; and "Programas presentadas en Cine-Arte," in Villegas López, *El film documental*, 38–48.

54. "Rapport des activités pour l'année 1948," 1, Compte-rendus des séances de la F.I.C.C, CF-SADOUL 734-B52; "Rapport annuel d'activité—Fédération tunisienne" (July 1953), FICC—Activité administrative, CF-SADOUL724-B51. On the Indian case, see Ghosh, "Memories of Action"; Cherian, *India's Film Society Movement*; and Majumdar, *Art Cinema and India's Forgotten Futures*, 92–123.

55. Crisp, *Classic French Cinema*, 229.

56. Souillés-Debats, "Les pratiques cinéphiles," 53.

57. Souillés-Debats, *La culture cinématographique du mouvement ciné-club*, 40–42.

58. Souillés-Debats, *La culture cinématographique du mouvement ciné-club*, 47.

59. Souillés-Debats, *La culture cinématographique du mouvement ciné-club*, 553.

60. The phrase recurs in the title of Héctor García Mesa and José del Campo, "¿Qué es un cine-club? Algunas ideas sobre la organización de cine-clubs," *Cine Cubano* 1, no. 2 (1960): 64–66.

61. González Casanova, *¿Qué es un cine-club?*, 23.

62. The quotation appears in Louis Daquin, "Les ciné-clubs et la défense du cinéma," in Jacques Chevallier, ed., *Regards neufs sur le cinéma* (Paris: Seuil, 1953), 143. González Casanova mentions Daquin's text in a letter to Georges Sadoul dated December 29, 1954, FICC—Activité administrative, CF-SADOUL724-B51.

63. Cine Club Núcleo, "Comunicado no. 6," July 1959, 1, Cine Club Núcleo folder, Museo del Cine Pablo C. Ducrós Hicken (hereafter MCPDH). The original text is by Orencio Ortega Frisón.

64. Amieva Collado, "La conformación del campo cinematográfico en Uruguay," 237–238.

65. Cine Club Núcleo, "Comunicado no. 6," 1. The original text dates from February-March 1956.

66. Navitski, "Latin American Film Society Magazines."

67. Mignolo, "Many Faces of Cosmo-polis," 721.

68. González Casanova, *¿Qué es un cine-club?*, 23.

69. Sánchez, *El cine*, 30.

70. Manuel González Casanova, "Despertar la conciencia del creador; formarlo cultural y técnicamente," *Revista de Cine*, March 1966, 54.

71. For Catholic calls for the development of film culture, see, for instance, Monsignor Angelo Dell'Acqua, "É necessário fomentar a cultura cinematográfica," *Revista de Cultura Cinematográfica*, July–August 1957, 35–37; Ildo Aveta, "Possibilidades e limites da verdadeira cultura cinematográfica," *Revista de Cultura Cinematográfica*, December 1958–January 1959, 6–9, reprinted from *Latinoamérica*.

72. [José] Agustín Mahieu, "A treinta años de los comienzos de una entidad de legendaria influencia," *La Opinón*, June 27, 1972.

73. "Salvador Sammaritano, un hombre de cine," *La Nación*, September 24, 2000. For an in-depth study of Gente de Cine and Núcleo, see Broitman, "La cinefilia en la Argentina," 180–375.

74. Amy B. Courvoisier to Luis Vicens, June 27, 1952, FPFC.

75. Vincenot, "Germán Puig, Ricardo Vigón et Henri Langlois."

76. Navitski, "Cine Club de Colombia."

77. On amateur filmmaking and non-commercial film culture see Rozsa, "On the Edge of the Screen," 158–219; and Amieva Collado, "La conformación del campo cinematográfico en Uruguay," 292–403.

78. "Primer Concurso Nacional de Cine-Aficionados," 1952, FPFC.

79. Carlos Barrios Barón, "Vigésimo aniversario del Cine Club Argentino," *16mm*, June 1952, 1–2. On the Cine Club Argentino, see Broitman, "La cinefilia en la Argentina," 142–143.

80. Foster, "Cinema Section of Foto Cine Clube Bandeirante"; and Hermanson Meister, *Fotoclubismo*, 165.

81. Program, Cine Universitario, December 15, 1950, Cinémathèque française (hereafter CF)-HL3497; "Cine Club Gente de Cine 1942–1954," Biblioteca de la Escuela Nacional de Experimentación y Realización Cinematográfica (hereafter B-ENERC); and Foster, "Cinema Section of Foto Cine Clube Bandeirante," 100.

82. Zúñiga, "Sección Cine-Clubs," in *Anuario del cine argentino*, 432; "El cineclub en el sube y baja," *Panorama*, March 4, 1956, 52; and questionnaire, "Cine Club de Tucumán," F.I.C.C. Activité administrative, CF-SADOUL724-B51. On film societies outside the city of Buenos Aires, see Broitman, "La cinefilia en la Argentina," 147–163.

83. Francia, *Nuevo Cine Latinoamericano en Viña del Mar*, 53–54; Luisa Ferrari, "Tercer Festival: Un festival que despierta interés," *Cine Foro*, November 1965, n.p.; and "Mística para un festival," *Cine Foro*, April 1966, 5–6.

84. Hintz, *Algo para recordar*, 9–14. See also Amieva Collado, "La conformación del campo cinematográfico en Uruguay," 292–403; and Amieva Collado, "El 'amateur avanzado' como cine nacional."

85. Costa and Scavino, *Por amor al cine*, 9–18.

86. "Cartelera abril," *Film*, April 1952, 23; and "Cartelera octubre," *Film*, October 1952, 31. For an overview, see Amieva Collado, "La conformación del campo cinematográfico en Uruguay," 305–308.

87. Melo Souza, *Paulo Emílio no Paraíso*, 300–304; and Corrêa, *A Cinemateca Brasileira*, 102–114.

88. Manuel Gallardo Olmos, "El Cine Club Universitario: Su trayectoria y sus actividades," *Anales de la Universidad de Chile* 107–108 (1957): 461–471; and Andrade, "L'action des cine-clubs et des cinémathèques en Amérique Latine," 21.

89. Ian Newton, "Film Society Newsreel," *Film* (London), November/December 1959, 38; Abraham Zalzman, "En cine, Colombia se agita," *Cine Cubano*, December 1963, 60–63; "Cine clubes y clubes de cine," *Guiones*, May 1963, 46; "Cine-Club Universitario 63 de Manziales," *Guiones*, June 1963, 3; and Andrade, "L'action des ciné-clubs et des cinémathèques en Amérique Latine," 31.

90. González Casanova, *¿Qué es un cine-club?*, 16–20. See also Pensado, *Rebel Mexico*, 174–179; and Rodríguez Álvarez, *Manuel González Casanova*, 20, 31–32.

91. "Funciones del 'Cine Club de la Universidad,'" *Gaceta de la Universidad*, November 7, 1955, 8.

92. Amieva Collado, "La conformación del campo cinematográfico en Uruguay," 39–149; and Amieva Collado, "Cine Arte del SODRE."

93. Amieva Collado, "La conformación del campo cinematográfico en Uruguay," 51.

94. Rozsa, "Institutionalization of Film Exhibition in Cuba."

95. Watson, *Elementos para un cine-debate*, 17.

96. Ruszkowski, *Cine, sus grandezas y miserias*.

97. "'Decadent' Films Hurt West in Cold War, Catholic Cinema Official Says," *Motion Picture Daily*, November 28, 1960, 1, 4.

98. On the OCIC's history, see Bonneville, *Soixante-dix ans au service du cinéma*; Convents, "Resisting the Lure of the Modern World"; Ortiz, "Catholic Church and Its Attitude to Film"; Trumpbour, "Belgium and the Making of an International Catholic Film Movement"; Boes, Engelen, and Vande Winkel, "Roman Catholic Engagements with Audio-Visual Media"; and Boes, Engelen, and Vande Winkel, "Clerics, Laymen, and Cinema."

99. Ramírez Llorens, "So Close to God"; Butruce, "Cineclubismo no Brasil," 118; Cáceres Mateus, "El cine moral y la censura," 208–211; and Ramos, "Cine e iglesia Católica en Cuba," 111–113.

100. Ramírez Llorens, "So Close to God," 327; and Cáceres Mateus, "El cine moral y la censura," 212–213.

101. Bonneville, *Soixante-dix ans au service du cinéma*, 36–37; and Boes, Engelen, and Vande Winkel, "Clerics, Laymen, and Cinema," 379.

102. Bonneville, *Soixante-dix ans au service du cinéma*, 37–38.

103. Boes, Engelen, and Vande Winkel, "Roman Catholic Engagements with Audio-Visual Media," 12.

104. Office catholique international du cinéma, *IV Congreso Internacional de Cine*, 101–102.

105. Bonneville, *Soixante-dix ans au service du cinéma*, 55.

106. Ramos, "Cine, medios, comunicación"; and Bonneville, *Soixante-dix ans au service du cinéma*, 262–263; on Penichet, see Silveira Gusmão, Costa Santos, and Duarte, "Mulheres em projetos de educação pelo/para o cinema."

107. Bonneville, *Soixante-dix ans au service du cinéma*, 87; Andrade, *Cronologia da cultura cinematográfica no Brasil*, 15; "Curso de Formación

Cinematográfica," undated pamphlet from the Centro de Educación Cinematográfica (Santiago de Chile), Cinemateca Uruguaya-Archivo Walther Dassori Barthet (hereafter CU-AWDB); Rozsa, "Institutionalization of Film Exhibition in Cuba," 161; Bedoya, "El Cine Club de Lima," 177; and "Cinemateca Colombiana/OCIC: Cursos de Cine," FPFC.

108. Butruce, "Cineclubismo no Brasil," 118; and Rozsa, "Institutionalization of Film Exhibition in Cuba," 159. On Catholic cineclubs in Brazil, see Silveira Gusmão and Costa Santos, "Cinema e católicos no Brasil"; Costa Santos, "Um trajeto católico de educação pelo/para o cinema no Brasil"; Moreira Chaves, "Sob o desígnio moral"; Nunes Guimarães Paes, "Olhar ativo"; Malusá, "Católicos e cinema na capital paulista"; Andrade, *Cronologia da cultura cinematográfica no Brasil*; and Américo Ribeiro, *O cinema em Belo Horizonte*, 47–50, 94–103, 157–162.

109. This attitude is also manifest in the controversial festival prizes awarded by OCIC.

110. Bedoya, "El Cine Club de Lima," 179; and Jorge Pucinellli, "Cinémathèque du Pérou—Rapport des activités dans le période d'organisation iniciale," October 10, 1953, Correspondance entre la FIAF et ses membres, Fédération internationale des archives du film (hereafter FIAF)-COR/028.

111. Jean Binoche to Georges Bidault, January 8, 1954, FRMAE-241QO-216.

112. Ramírez Llorens, "So Close to God," 332.

113. "Conversa da redação," *Revista de Cultura Cinematográfica*, September–October 1957, 2–3.

114. Bonneville, *Soixante-dix ans au service du cinéma*, 138–143.

115. For a case study of Czechoslovakia's diplomatic use of film, see Česálková, "Film as Diplomat."

116. Federación Argentina de Cineclubes, Boletín de Informaciones no. 2, 4, Correspondance entre la FIAF et ses membres Argentine–Allemande, FIAF-COR/018.

117. Cine Club Mendoza, "Actividad realizada," 1953, F.I.C.C. Questionnaires—Rapports d'activités ciné-clubs, CF-SADOUL724-B51; and Broitman, "La cinefilia en la Argentina," 199.

118. Luis Vicens to Servicios Franceses de Información, French Embassy, November 5, 1949, FPFC; and Luis Vicens to Jean-Georges Auriol (editor of *Le Revue du Cinéma*), November 14, 1949, FPFC.

119. Chonchol and Martinière, *L'Amérique latine et la latino-américainisme en France*, 75–76. On the attempt to move the IICI, see Dumont-Quessard, "La défaite de 1940," 21–24.

120. R. Fiasson, "L'Institut Français d'Amérique latine," *Bulletin de l'I.F.A.L.*, January–February 1945, 1.

121. Horne, "Global Cultural Fronts."

122. Rolland, *Vichy et la France libre au Mexique*; and Rolland, "L'exil structure l'émigration."

123. Jean-François Ricard [Revel] to Henri Langlois, April 1, 1950, uncatalogued internal archives, CF; quoted in Boulanger, "L'aventure du Ciné Club de Mexico," 1015.

124. French ambassador in Mexico to Minister of Foreign Affairs, August 6, 1951, 3, FRMAE-100QO/21-16.
125. French ambassador in Mexico to Minister of Foreign Affairs, August 6, 1951, 2, and November 8, 1951, 2, FRMAE-100QO/21-16.
126. French ambassador in Mexico to Minister of Foreign Affairs, August 6, 1951, 2, FRMAE-100QO/21-16.
127. Rodríguez Álvarez, *Manuel González Casanova*, 17.
128. "Note sur le ciné-club de l'Institut français de México," undated (c. late 1951), FRMAE-100QO/21-16.
129. Rodríguez Álvarez, *Manuel González Casanova*, 17–19; "Cine – El CCM," *Hispano*, July 13, 1951, 42; de la Vega Alfaro, *Nuevo Cine*, 12; and "Note sur le ciné-club de l'Institut français de México," FRMAE-100QO/21-16.
130. Henri Langlois to J[ean]-F[rançois] Ricard [Revel], October 25, 1950, uncatalogued internal archives, CF.
131. Henri Langlois to J[ean]-F[rançois] Ricard [Revel], April 12, 1950, uncatalogued internal archives, CF. See also "Note sur le ciné-club de l'Institut français de México," FRMAE-100QO/21-16.
132. Henri Langlois to Raymond Borel, February 20, 1951, uncatalogued internal archives, CF.
133. Luis Vicens to Gaston Diehl, October 29, 1951, FPFC; and J[ean]-F[rançois] Ricard [Revel] to Henri Langlois, July 6, 1950, uncatalogued internal archives, CF.
134. Amy B. Courvoisier to Luis Vicens, June 27, 1952, and program, September 1954, FPFC.
135. Henri Langlois to J[ean]-F[rançois] Ricard [Revel], April 16, 1952; and J[ean]-F[rançois] Ricard [Revel] to Henri Langlois, April 21, 1952, uncatalogued internal archives, CF. The exchange is also quoted in Boulanger, "L'aventure du Ciné Club de Mexico," 1018.
136. Henri Langlois to Raymond Borel, May 24, 1951, uncatalogued internal archives, CF.
137. J[ean]-F[rançois] Ricard [Revel] to Henri Langlois, October 25, 1950, uncatalogued internal archives, CF.
138. [Illegible] to Yvonne Dornes, December 31, 1952, uncatalogued internal archives, CF.
139. "Note sur le ciné-club de l'Institut français de México," undated (c. late 1951), FRMAE-100QO-16.
140. Navitski, "Latin American Film Society Magazines."
141. The clubs included are the Cine Club de Colombia in Bogotá; Gente de Cine in Buenos Aires; Cine Club Núcleo in Buenos Aires (1948–1954, incomplete); Cine Club del Uruguay in Montevideo (1948–1954, incomplete); Cine Universitario in Montevideo (1950–1953, incomplete); and Cine Club Progreso, Mexico City (May, July–December 1954). A limited number of screenings from the Cine Club Santa Fe, Cine Club Tucumán, and Cine Club Eva Perón in Argentina and the Cine Club de Barranquilla and Cine Club de Medellín in Colombia are also included. The dataset can be accessed at transatlantic cinephilia.net.

142. Some screenings were reconstructed from year-end programming summaries, which lack print sources. For comparison, Columbia Pictures supplied forty-five prints during the same period and United Artists twenty-nine.

143. Navitski, "Latin American Film Society Magazines."

144. Fein, "From Collaboration to Containment," 139.

145. See chapter 3 of this study.

146. I owe this insight to Mariana Amieva Collado.

147. Rodríguez Álvarez, *Manuel González Casanova*, 20; and programs, Cine-Club Progreso, FICC, Activité administrative, CF-SADOUL724-B51.

148. Ramírez Llorens, *Noches de sano esparcimiento*, 210.

149. Ramírez Llorens, *Noches de sano esparcimiento*, 210; and "Actividades de la Cinemateca Colombiana en el mes de Noviembre 1965," FPFC.

150. "Cine Club Gente de Cine 1942–1954," B-ENERC.

151. Questionnaire, Cine Club Eva Perón, Questionnaires—Rapports d'activités ciné-clubs, CF-SADOUL724-B51; "Circulación de películas de la Cinemateca Argentina en 1953," Correspondance diverse membres FIAF années 1950, FIAF-COR/005.

152. CCC program, September 25, 1958, FPFC.

153. CCC program, September 3, 1960, FPFC.

154. CCC programs, September–October 1962, September–October 1963, FPPC.

155. Acland and Wasson, *Useful Cinema*.

156. Cine Club Núcleo, "Comunicado del mes de mayo," 1957, Cine Club Núcleo folder, MCPDH.

157. Cine Club Mendoza, "Actividad realizada," 1953, F.I.C.C. Questionnaires, Rapports d'activités ciné-clubs, CF-SADOUL724-B51.

158. Gente de Cine, "Comunicado no. 29—Análisis de los cuestionarios," March 1955, Gente de Cine folder, MCPDH.

159. The estimate is from Andrés José Rolando Fustiñana, "Informe del Club Gente de Cine para la Fédération Internationale des Ciné-Clubs," 1953, 2. F.I.C.C. Questionnaires, Rapports d'activités ciné-clubs, CF-SADOUL724-B51.

160. Gente de Cine thanks a long list of commercial distributors in a commemorative program from the late 1940s; see figure 3.

161. Informe del Tesorero [del Cine Club de Colombia] a la Asamblea General, October 18, 1955, and Relación de los gastos del Cine Club de Colombia, January 15, 1964, FPFC.

162. Cine Club de Colombia (unsigned) to Francisco Jaramillo, 2 October 1951, FPFC.

163. Valck, *Film Festivals*, 125–30.

164. "Gran Labor ha Desarrollado en Nueve Años el 'Cine Club': Entrevista con el Secretario General," unidentified press clipping, September 1958, FPFC.

165. Concha Henao, *Historia social del cine colombiano*, vol. II, *1930–1959*, 477–478. I thank Ramiro Arbeláez for bringing this to my attention.

166. Hintz, *Algo para recordar*, 47–48.

167. CCC program, March 23, 1954, FPFC. See also CCC program, September 1, 1953, FPFC.

168. CCC program, February 16, 1954, FPFC.

169. Acta de la Junta Directiva del Cine Club de Colombia, March 31, 1965, June 10, 1966, March 3, 1967, and June 19, 1969, FPFC.
170. CCC program, August 2, 1960, FPFC.
171. For instance, just over 4 percent of films with a known print source screened at the CCC screenings between 1949 and 1965 were from the Cinemateca Colombiana's collection or gifts or loans from other archives. On Argentine and Uruguayan cineclubs' screenings of archival prints, see Amieva Collado, "La conformación del campo cinematográfico en Uruguay," 256–258; and Tadeo Fuica, "Tracing Past Exchanges."
172. Vignaux, "Georges Sadoul et la Fédération française des ciné-clubs." See also "La Fédération Internationale des Ciné-Clubs est née," *Ciné-Club*, November 1947, 1.
173. "F.I.C.C.—Accord de Rome," November 26, 1949, Comptes-rendu F.I.C.C., CF-SADOUL721-B50. See also FIAF, "Compte-Rendu - Congrès de Rome 1949," 56–62; and Corrêa, "O cinema como instituição," 38–41.
174. Baecque, *La cinéphilie*, 63–96.
175. Vignaux, "Georges Sadoul et la Fédération française des ciné-clubs," 187.
176. Manuel González Casanova to Georges Sadoul, December 29, 1954, FICC—Activité administrative, CF-SADOUL724-B51.
177. Ne[lly] Ka[plan], "Jornadas en Marly-le-Roi," *Gente de Cine*, November 1953, 2; and Ronald Shields, "Marly," *Film* (London), September–October 1955, 27. On the seminars, see Conway, "New Wave of Spectators."
178. Melo Souza, *Paulo Emílio no Paraíso*, 128–130.
179. Décio de Almeida Prado to Paulo Emílio Salles Gomes, July 3, 1939, Cinemateca Brasileira-Arquivo Paulo Emílio Salles Gomes (hereafter CB-APESG), PE/CP.0253.
180. Décio de Almeida Prado to Paulo Emílio Salles Gomes, July 3, 1939, CB-APESG, PE/CP.0253.
181. Melo Souza, *Paulo Emílio no Paraíso*, 291.
182. Georges Sadoul to Paulo Emílio Salles Gomes, November 4, 1947, CB-APESG, PE/CP.0482.
183. "Compte-rendu de la IIème Assemblée Générale de la Fédération Internationale des Ciné-Clubs," 2 CF-SADOUL734-B52.
184. Quoted in Corrêa, *Cinemateca Brasileira*, 106.
185. Andrew, "Time Zones and Jet Lag," 69–75.
186. FICC meeting notes, June 27, 1946, 2, Comptes-rendus des séances de la F.I.C.C., CF-SADOUL734-B52.
187. FICC meeting notes, June 27, 1946, 2, CF-SADOUL734-B52. These notes predate the founding of known postwar cineclubs in Chile and Uruguay, so it is unclear which organizations are being referred to.
188. Broitman, "La cinefilia en la Argentina," 207–209; Sección Latinoamericana de la FIAF—Congreso de Punta del Este, January 25–30, 1955, 3, Cinemateca Brasileira-Archivo Histórico (hereafter CB-AH); "Accord entre la Federación Argentina de Cine-Clubes et la Cinemateca Argentina," Correspondance entre la FIAF et ses members, FIAF-COR/018; and José María Podestá and Raúl Benavides to President of FIAF [Jerzy Toeplitz], January 1954, Correspondance entre la FIAF et ses membres, FIAF-COR/028.

189. Regional federations were also founded in the Northeast and in Rio. Andrade, *Cronologia da cultura cinematográfica no Brasil*, 12, 16, 19–21, 25.

190. González Casanova, *¿Qué es un cine-club?*, 18.

191. Brancaleone, *Cesare Zavattini's Neo-Realism*; 228 (no source is cited for this claim, however); and "Declaración de principios de la Federación Mexicana de Cine-Clubs," September 1955, reprinted in Rodríguez Álvarez, *Atlas del cineclub*, 215.

192. *Cine Club* (Barranquilla), August 1957, CF-SADOUL816-B63; Luis Vicens to Maritza de Urdinola, March 15, 1959, FPFC; program, Cine Club de Medellín, May 1966, FPFC; Hernando Salcedo Silva to Álvaro Cepeda [Samudio], September 15, 1959, FPFC; Caicedo González, "Los cineclubes bogotanos," 249; and "Cine-Clubs Federados," *Guiones*, June 1963, 30.

193. Caicedo González, "Los cineclubes bogotanos," 249.

194. "Boletín de Informaciones no. 2," Federación Argentina de Cineclubes, 4, Correspondance entre la FIAF et ses membres, FIAF-COR/018.

195. Questionnaire, Cine Club de Tucumán, Questionnaires—Rapports d'activités ciné-clubs, CF-SADOUL724-B51; overleaf, *Film*, November–December 1953, 1; and Hintz, *Algo para recordar*, 75.

196. Owensby, *Intimate Ironies*, 63–64, 96–97; Parker, *Idea of the Middle Class*, 41–42; and Garguin, "'Los Argentinos Descendemos de los Barcos.'"

197. "Encuesta Sobre 'Manon,'" *Cine Club* (Montevideo), June 1950, 15.

198. "Actividad realizada," Cine Club Mendoza, 1953, F.I.C.C. Questionnaires—Rapports d'activités ciné-clubs, CF-SADOUL724-B51.

199. Souillés-Debats, *La culture cinematographique du mouvement ciné-club*, 151.

200. Watson, *Elementos para un cine-debate*, 20.

201. Tavares de Sá, *Cinema e educação*, 157.

202. "Encuesta Sobre 'Manon,'" *Cine Club* (Montevideo), June 1950, 15.

203. Walther Dassori Barthet to Marta Ottino de Sambarino, May 6, 1969, CU-AWDB.

204. Arias Osorio, "Movie Audiences, Modernity, and Urban Identities," 238–246.

205. Isabel Larguía de Pastor to Andrés José Rolando Fustiñana, July 27, 1953, 1. F.I.C.C. Questionnaires—Rapports d'activités ciné-clubs, CF-SADOUL724-B51.

206. "Tribuna de los socios," *Gente de Cine*, September 1952, 11.

207. Watson, *Elementos para un cine-debate*, 104–105.

208. Watson, *Elementos para un cine-debate*, 18–19, 24. See also Sánchez, *El cine*, 30.

209. Bronx [pseud. Serna], *El cine foro y elementos de cinematografía*, 48.

210. Undated questionnaire, Cine Club Enfoques folder, MCPDH.

211. On the short, see Podalsky, *Specular City*, 92–94.

212. Feldman, *La generación del 60*, 15–18; and Broitman, "La cinefilia en la Argentina," 298, 367.

213. Undated questionnaire (c. 1958), Cine Club Núcleo folder, MCPDH.

214. Questionnaire, Cine Club Santa Fe. Questionnaires—Rapports d'activités ciné-clubs, CF-SADOUL724-B51.

215. [José] Sanz to Paulo Emílio Salles Gomes, April 23, 1952, CB-APESG, PE/CP.0847.
216. Cine Club de Medellín, bulletin, undated, FPFC.
217. Barón Leal, "Los cinemas bogotanos," 136.
218. "Cine Club: Criticar es aprender," *Semana*, March 22, 1954.
219. Acta de Constitución del Cine Club de Colombia, September 2, 1949, FPFC.
220. Acta de la Asamblea General de Socios del Cine Club de Colombia, September 6, 1949, FPFC.
221. Estatutos del Cine Club de Colombia, FPFC. The CCC organized a contest for amateur photographers in 1950.
222. Luis Guerrero, "Cineclub," *El Liberal* (Bogotá), September 8, 1949, unpaginated press clipping, FPFC.
223. Guerrero, "Cineclub," *El Liberal*, September 8, 1949, FPFC. Some accounts suggest Zalamea's objections were rooted in Carné's choice to make films under the Vichy regime during World War II. Caicedo González, "Langostas, libros, y cine," 67.
224. Bourdieu, *Distinction*, 80–92. Bourdieu notes that cultural forms like cinema that have not yet fully been legitimated by the educational system offer a particularly compelling investment for those with limited social capital.
225. Conway, "New Wave of Spectators," 40–41; and Acland, "Classrooms, Clubs, and Community Circuits."
226. Fernán Torres León, "La Cinemateca Colombiana será centro distribuidor para el Norte de América," *El Tiempo*, undated/unpaginated press clipping [1959], FPFC.
227. Alberto León, "Entrevista a Hernando Salcedo Silva," *Cine* 9 (1982): 70. Roland similarly described Gente de Cine as an obligatory rendezvous point for local intellectuals. Feldman, *La generación del 60*, 15.
228. CCC programs, June 27, 1950, August 11, 1953, and November 6, 1956, FPFC.
229. Luis Vicens to Amy B. Courvoisier, July 18, 1952, FPFC.
230. I am indebted to Juan Sebastián Ospina León for his insights on this point.
231. CCC program, January 18, 1955, FPFC.
232. "Cineclubes y clubes de cine," *Guiones*, May 1963, 46.
233. CCC meeting notes, October 7, 1966, FPFC.
234. See, for example, CCC programs, May 24, 1955 and March 16, 1954, FPFC.
235. CCC program, March 16, 1954, FPFC. CCC members offered a handful of comments on Luis Buñuel's *Robinson Crusoe* and Russell Rouse's *The Thief*. CCC programs, August 9, 1955 and March 21, 1957, FPFC.
236. CCC program, July 5, 1955, FPFC.
237. Acta de la Junta Directiva del Cine Club de Colombia, June 19, 1969, FPFC.
238. "Cine Club," *Cinemés* 7 [1969?], n.p.
239. Zalzman is likely referring to the CCC (Bogotá), Cine Club de Medellín, Cine Club de Barranquilla, Cine Club La Tertulia (Cali), and Cine Club

de Cartagena, although other film societies also existed in Colombia in this period.

240. Abraham Zalzman, "En cine, Colombia se agita," *Cine Cubano*, December 1963, 61. Zalzman himself founded a film society at Bogotá's Universidad Nacional, a hotbed of student activism, in 1960. Becerra Venegas, "Colombia," 222.

241. Reportaje del Director Ejecutivo del Cine Club de Colombia a la Asamblea General, February 12, 1970, FPFC. In 1977, the CCC reportedly had 150 stable members and another fifty who participated intermittently. Valverde, *Reportaje crítico al cine colombiano*, 266–267.

242. Hagener, *Moving Forward, Looking Back*, 105–107. On the rivalry between cineclubs and the expanding arthouse circuit in 1960s Buenos Aires, see Broitman, "La cinefilia en la Argentina," 300–302.

243. "El cine club en el sube y baja," *Panorama*, March 4, 1969, 53.

244. See also Solanas and Getino, "Towards a Third Cinema."

CHAPTER 2: TOWARD A GLOBAL FILM PRESERVATION PRACTICE?

1. The archive's holdings were seized by the Soviet army, and some were deposited at Moscow's Gosfilmofond. Le Roy, "La Rapatriement des films spoilés pour les nazis," 50.

2. Minutes, FIAF executive committee meeting, April 16, 1948, www.fiafnet.org /images/tinyUpload/History/FIAF-Archives/Digitized%20docs/EC%20meetings /1948-04-Paris_Red.pdf; and minutes, 1948 FIAF conference in Copenhagen, 1, www.fiafnet.org/images/tinyUpload/History/FIAF-Archives/Digitized%20docs /Congresses/1948%2009%2013-15%20FIAF%20Congress%20Copenhague %20Review.pdf.

3. See FIAF's digital Affiliation History Map for a sense of the organization's geographic reach in different periods, at www.fiafnet.org/pages/History/Map -FIAF-Institutions-History-Full-Screen.html.

4. Minutes, 1976 FIAF congress in Mexico, 29, https://www.fiafnet.org /images/tinyUpload/E-Resources/Official-Documents/Protected%20Files /Congress-Reports/1976-Mexico%20GA%20MinutesRED.pdf; and minutes, 1964 FIAF congress in Moscow, 5, https://www.fiafnet.org/images/tinyUpload /History/FIAF-Archives/Digitized%20docs/Congresses/1964%20Moscow _Congress%20minutes%20EN_Red.pdf.

5. Trujillo and del Amo, "Escuela sobre ruedas 2004–2005"; and Giuliani, "African Heritage and the School on Wheels Experience."

6. FIAF members are institutions whose primary purpose is film preservation and that hold significant audiovisual collections. Associate members preserve films as one among many activities and/or currently lack significant collections. For FIAF's membership lists, see www.fiafnet.org/pages/Community/Affiliates.html.

7. On APEX, see Suárez and Vizner, "Education through International Collaboration."

8. Danilo Trelles of Cine Arte del SODRE proposed a competing project for regional cooperation between Latin American film archives in this period.

Amieva Collado, "La conformación del campo cinematográfico en Uruguay," 143; and minutes, 1955 Latin American Pool conference in Punta del Este, 1, Cinemateca Brasileira-Archivo Histórico (hereafter CB-AH). Documents from this source are uncatalogued.

9. Frick, *Saving Cinema*, 158; and Ceja Alcalá, "Imperfect Archives," 75–76.

10. Dimitriu, "La Cinemateca Argentina," 15; and Corrêa, *A Cinemateca Brasileira*, 102–114; Navitski, "Cine Club de Colombia," 818; and Vincenot, "Germán Puig, Ricardo Vigón et Henri Langlois," 21–26.

11. "F.I.C.C.—Accord de Rome," November 26, 1949, CF-SADOUL-721-B50.

12. For instance, the Cinemateca Uruguaya organized screenings sporadically from its inception but began to offer memberships that allowed individuals to attend all its programs only in 1975. Silveira, *Cultura y cinefilia*, 19.

13. Domínguez, *24 ilusiones por segundo*, 39; and minutes, 1955 Latin American Pool conference in Punta del Este, 3, CB-AH.

14. Frick, *Saving Cinema*. On the preservation of Brazilian and Colombian film in the 1950s, see Corrêa, *A Cinemateca Brasileira*, 124, 159; and "Rapport de Monsieur Louis Vicens," 1–2, XIIIe Congres de la FIAF-Antibes, Octobre 1957, Tome I, Annexe A, FIAF-CON/11B. In Uruguay, collecting domestically produced films was first discussed as a priority in the mid-1960s. Amieva Collado, "La conformación del campo cinematográfico en Uruguay," 81.

15. Minutes, 1948 FIAF conference in Copenhagen, 1, 33–34, www.fiafnet.org /images/tinyUpload/History/FIAF-Archives/Digitized%20docs/Congresses/1948 %2009%2013-15%20FIAF%20Congress%20Copenhague%20Review.pdf.

16. Cormon, "FIAF Member Service/FIAF Pool"; Resolutions, 1952 FIAF Congress in Amsterdam, 3–4, www.fiafnet.org/images/tinyUpload/History/FIAF -Archives/Digitized%20docs/Congresses/1952%2010-11%2025-01%20FIAF %20Congress%20Amsterdam%20R%C3%A9sum%C3%A9%20LR.pdf.

17. Corrêa, "O cinema como instituição."

18. Borde, *Les cinémathèques*, 122–124; and Houston, *Keepers of the Frame*, 37–38.

19. Lenk and Stufkens, "'Then Began the Battle Royal.'" In addition to her administrative role at FIAF beginning in 1956, Michelle is a fascinating figure in her own right, who had a romantic and creative partnership with Dutch leftist filmmaker Joris Ivens. See Waugh, *Conscience of Cinema*, 333–393.

20. Borde, *Les cinémathèques*, 107–112.

21. Corrêa, *A Cinemateca Brasileira*, 108; and Langlois to José María Podestá, March 4, 1954, 3, CU, uncatalogued.

22. Rudá de Andrade, quoted in Melo Souza, *Paulo Emílio no Paraíso*, 588n3.

23. Rudá de Andrade, quoted in Melo Souza, *Paulo Emílio no Paraíso*, 588n3.

24. Tadeo Fuica, "Tracing Past Exchanges," 32–34.

25. Resolutions, 1946 FIAF Congress in Paris, 4, www.fiafnet.org/pages /History/Archival-Documents-about-FIAF-Congresses.html; and minutes, FIAF executive committee, May 19 and 20, 1957, 2, www.fiafnet.org/images/tiny Upload/History/FIAF-Archives/Digitized%20docs/EC%20meetings/1957-05 -Paris-RED.pdf.

26. Tadeo Fuica, "Tracing Past Exchanges," 32–34.

27. Tadeo Fuica, "Tracing Past Exchanges," 37.

28. Henri Langlois to [Louis] Joxe, undated letter [received January 2, 1947], FRMAE-241Q0-3.

29. The MAE recommended that Langlois's request be granted. J[ean] Marx to Director of the Centre national de la cinématographie [Michel Fourré-Cormeray], February 3, 1947, FRMAE-241Q0-3.

30. Borde, *Les cinémathèques*; Slide, *Nitrate Won't Wait*; and Houston, *Keepers of the Frame*. On Langlois, see Myrent and Langlois, *Henri Langlois*; and Roud, *Passion for Films*. Bliss Cua Lim's forthcoming book *The Archival Afterlives of Philippine Cinema* and Juana Suárez's *Moving Images Archives, Cultural History, and the Digital Turn in Latin America* (in preparation) promise to partially address this gap.

31. Corrêa, *A Cinemateca Brasileira*; Domínguez, *24 ilusiones por segundo*; Silveira, *Cultura y cinefilia*; and Izquierdo, *Cine y preservación*. Doctoral and master's theses on the topic include Souza, "A Cinemateca Brasileira"; and Araújo Quental, "A preservação cinematográfica."

32. Ceja Alcalá, "Imperfect Archives," 74.

33. Frick, *Saving Cinema*, 158, 165–168.

34. "Rapport des Membres effectifs et provisoires de l'Amérique Latine," 1956, Congrès 1956—Dubrovnik, FIAF-CON/010A.

35. Wood, "Archivos, discursos y memoria."

36. Bluff [pseud.], "Peço a palavra! . . .," *Fon-Fon*, December 7, 1912, n.p.

37. *Cinearte*, February 6, 1929, n.p.

38. Torres Bodet, "Películas del pasado," 157–158.

39. De los Reyes, "La idea del cine club en México en la etapa muda."

40. Dimitriu, "La Cinemateca Uruguaya," 41.

41. MacLean Switz, "Educational Film Elsewhere Abroad," 468.

42. Mario Zavala T., "La Filmoteca Nacional: Nueva aportación de Elena Sánchez Valenzuela," *Cinema Repórter*, February 26, 1944, 12–13; and Torres San Martín, *Elena Sánchez Valenzuela*, 174.

43. Torres San Martín, *Elena Sánchez Valenzuela*, 180–191.

44. Wood, "Archivos, discursos y memoria."

45. Izquierdo, *Cine y preservación*, 1–20, 37–38.

46. Jorge F. Oubiña to FIAF, September 5, 1963, Correspondence 1963, Archives membres FIAF par pays, FIAF-AFF/003.

47. The archive's statutes closely resemble those of the short-lived Primer Museo Cinematográfico Argentino founded in 1941 by collector Manuel Peña Rodríguez, according to Amieva Collado, "La conformación del campo cinematográfico en Uruguay," 46. For more on the archive, see Izquierdo, *Cine y preservación*, 23–26.

48. "SODRE—Cine Arte," unsigned manuscript document, ca. 1948, Montevideo–SODRE, Archives membres FIAF par pays, FIAF-AFF/004.

49. SODRE, *Su organización y cometidos*, 195–196; and Amieva Collado, "Cine Arte del SODRE en la conformación de un campo audiovisual en Uruguay."

50. Torres, "El surgimiento de la radiodifusión pública en Hispanoamérica." For histories of SODRE, see Casanova Delfino and Campodónico, *Historias del SODRE*; and SODRE, *SODRE: Cincuenta años de aplausos*.

51. SODRE, *Su organización y cometidos*, 198.
52. SODRE, *Su organización y cometidos*, 198–199; and Danilo Trelles, "Rapport de la Cinémathèque d'Uruguay—SODRE," 1948, Montevideo–SODRE, Archives membres FIAF par pays, FIAF-AFF/004.
53. Amieva Collado, "La conformación del campo cinematográfico en Uruguay," 51.
54. Amieva Collado, "Cine Arte del SODRE en la conformación de un campo audiovisual en Uruguay"; and Amieva Collado, "¿Cómo el Uruguay no hay?"
55. Danilo Trelles to FIAF President, March 15, 1948, and "SODRE—Cine Arte," unsigned manuscript document, c. 1948, Montevideo–SODRE, Archives membres FIAF par pays, FIAF-AFF/004.
56. "SODRE—Cine Arte," unsigned manuscript document, c. 1948, and "Liste des films se trouvant dans la Cinémathèque d'Uruguay," c. 1948, Montevideo–SODRE, Archives membres FIAF par pays, FIAF-AFF/004.
57. Henri Langlois to José María Podestá, March 4, 1954, 1, uncatalogued document, CU.
58. Henri Langlois to José María Podestá, March 4, 1954, 1, CU.
59. Henri Langlois to José María Podestá, March 4, 1954, 3, CU.
60. Tadeo Fuica, "¿Qué mostrar? ¿Cómo cuidar?," 61.
61. Melo Souza, *Paulo Emílio no Paraíso*; Corrêa, *A Cinemateca Brasileira*; and Souza, "A Cinemateca Brasileira."
62. 1948 FIAF conference in Copenhagen, 62, www.fiafnet.org/images/tiny Upload/History/FIAF-Archives/Digitized%20docs/Congresses/1948%2009 %2013-15%20FIAF%20Congress%20Copenhague%20Review.pdf.
63. Galvão, *Burguesia e cinema*; and Garcia Durand, *Arte, privilégio e distinção*, 117–145.
64. *Estado de São Paulo*, Suplemento Literario, November 8, 1958.
65. Francisco Matarazzo Sobrinho to Paulo Emílio Salles Gomes, February 4, 1949, CB-APESG, PE/CP.0553. See also Corrêa, *A Cinemateca Brasileira*, 102–114; and Melo Souza, *Paulo Emílio no Paraíso*, 305–306.
66. Paulo Emílio Salles Gomes to Francisco Matarazzo Sobrinho, February 25, 1949, CB-APESG, PE/CA.0221.
67. Lourival [Gomes Machado] to Paulo Emílio Salles Gomes, October 25, 1950, CB-APESG, PE/CP.0770.
68. Paulo Emílio Salles Gomes to Henri Langlois, January 9, 1951, CB-APESG, PE/CA.0248.
69. On film-related cultural diplomacy during World War II, see Busko Valim, *Brazil, the United States, and Good Neighbor Policy*.
70. Paulo Emílio Salles Gomes to Francisco Matarazzo Sobrinho, September 30, 1949, CB-APESG, PE/CA.0231.
71. On Barry and MoMA's Film Library, see Wasson, *Museum Movies*; and Sitton, *Lady in the Dark*.
72. Iris Barry to Paulo Emílio Salles Gomes, November 1, 1948, CB-APESG, PC/CP.0544.
73. Notes, FIAF executive committee meeting, February 24–25, 1955, 6, www.fiafnet.org/images/tinyUpload/History/FIAF-Archives/Digitized%20docs /EC%20meetings/1955-02-Paris-RED.pdf.

74. Henri Langlois to Paulo Emílio Salles Gomes, July 31, 1957, CB-APESG, PE/CP 0994.

75. Novais Teixeira to Paulo Emílio Salles Gomes, July 8, 1962, CB-APESG, PE/CP.1560.

76. "A Filmoteca movimenta-se para adquirir filmes velhos," *Cine-Reporter*, August 27, 1955, 5; and Corrêa, *A Cinemateca Brasileira*, 124, 159.

77. Souza, "A Cinemateca Brasileira," 68.

78. A major conflict irrupted between the two archives in 1956 when Salles Gomes organized a film retrospective in Rio and reneged on a promise to provide films to the Cinemateca do MAM-Rio. See Araújo Quental, "A preservação cinematográfica," 97–100.

79. Araújo Quental, "A preservação cinematográfica," 85–90.

80. Araújo Quental, "A preservação cinematográfica," 109–114; and Ruy Pereira da Silva, "Jornal de viagem," *Boletim mensal do Departamento de Cinema do Museu de Arte Moderna do Rio de Janeiro*, November 1957, December 1957, and January 1958, n.p., Museu de Arte Moderna do Rio de Janeiro (hereafter MAM-Rio).

81. Araújo Quental, "A preservação cinematográfica," 126.

82. "Liste des films appartenant à l'archive de la Cinémathèque du Musée de l'Art Moderne de Rio de Janeiro," Correspondance diverse membres FIAF années 1950 (Borde 1), FIAF-COR/005; and Araújo Quental, "A preservação cinematográfica," 132.

83. Vincenot, "Germán Puig, Ricardo Vigón et Henri Langlois," 25–26; and Rozsa, "On the Edge of the Screen," 100.

84. Henri Langlois to Raymond Borel, February 7, 1951, uncatalogued internal archives, CF.

85. Vincenot, "Germán Puig, Ricardo Vigón et Henri Langlois," 18–25. See also resolutions, 1951 FIAF Congress in Cambridge, 59–60, www.fiafnet.org/images/tinyUpload/History/FIAF-Archives/Digitized%20docs/Congresses/1951%20FIAF%20Congress%20Cambridge%20Rapport%20LR.pdf.

86. Germán Puig, "Rapport de Cuba," 1957, XIIIe Congres de la FIAF, Antibes, Octobre 1957, Tome 1, Annèxe B, 10, FIAF-CON/011C; see also Vincenot, "Germán Puig, Ricardo Vigón et Henri Langlois," 31; and Rozsa, "On the Edge of the Screen," 100–102.

87. Puig, "Rapport de Cuba," 9, FIAF-CON/011C; Vincenot, "Germán Puig, Ricardo Vigón et Henri Langlois," 33–34; and Rozsa, "On the Edge of the Screen," 101–102.

88. Rozsa, "On the Edge of the Screen," 102.

89. Minutes, Cine Club de Colombia executive committee, April 29, 1966, FPFC. Documents from this source uncatalogued.

90. Program, Cine Club de Colombia, September 6, 1955, FPFC.

91. Minutes, 1955 FIAF Congress in Warsaw, 11, www.fiafnet.org/images/tinyUpload/History/FIAF-Archives/Digitized%20docs/Congresses/1955_Warsaw_Congress_Decisions_Red.pdf; and Gabriel García Márquez, untitled report, Congrès Warsawa—Cinemateca Colombiana, FIAF-CON/009A. See also Rito Torres Alberto, "García Márquez: Cinéfilo, cineclubista, crítico de cine y representante del primer archivo fílmico de nuestro país," http://patrimonio

filmico.org.co/documentos-y-publicaciones/documentos/192-garcia-marquez
-cinefilo-cineclubista-critico-de-cine-y-representante-del-primer-archivo-filmico
-del-pais.

92. "Rapport de Monsieur Louis Vicens," XIIIe Congres de la FIAF, Tome 1: Antibes, Octobre 1957, Annexe A, FIAF-CON/11B, 1–2.

93. "Rapport de Monsieur Louis Vicens," FIAF-CON/11B, 2–3.

94. A 1961 report to FIAF mentions three additional Colombian feature films held in the Cinemateca Colombiana's collection; the source of this discrepancy is unclear. "Informe de actividades de la Cinemateca Colombiana, mayo de 1960 a septiembre de 1961," Courrier reçu pour le secrétariat 1960–1963, FIAF-COR/003.

95. Inventario de Películas de Cinemateca Colombiana, May 26, 1966, FPFC.

96. Margot Benacerraf to Jerzy Toeplitz, October 29, 1953, Correspondance entre la FIAF et ses membres, FIAF-COR/028.

97. Luis Álvarez Marcano to Jerzy Toeplitz, August 28, 1958, Correspondance entre la FIAF et ses membres, FIAF-COR/028.

98. Jorge Pucinelli, "Rapport d'activities dans la période d'organisation iniciale," October 10, 1953, and Claudio Capasso to Henri Langlois, October 4, 1954, Correspondance entre la FIAF et ses membres, FIAF-COR/28.

99. Minutes, 1959 Latin American Pool conference in Mar del Plata, 5, CB-AH.

100. The universities involved were the Universidad Nacional Mayor de San Marcos, Pontificia Universidad Católica del Perú, Universidad Nacional de Ingeniería, and Universidad Nacional Agraria La Molina. Wiener Fresco, *Estudio y propuesta*, 57–58.

101. "Informe de la Cinemateca Universitaria del Perú (CUP)," *Cine Cubano* 73–75 (November 1972): 139.

102. Wiener Fresco, *Estudio y propuesta*, 100–106.

103. Dimitriu, "La Cinemateca Argentina," 15; "Vida de los Cine Clubes," *Cine Club* (Montevideo), December 1949, n.p.; minutes, 1951 FIAF Congress in Cambridge, 64, www.fiafnet.org/images/tinyUpload/History/FIAF-Archives/Digitized%20docs/Congresses/1951%20FIAF%20Congress%20Cambridge%20Rapport%20LR.pdf; and minutes, 1949 FIAF Congress in Rome, 17, www.fiafnet.org/images/tinyUpload/History/FIAF-Archives/Digitized%20docs/Congresses/1949%2011%2023-26%20FIAF%20Congr%C3%A8s%20Rome%20Compte%20Rendu%20LR.pdf.

104. Minutes, 1955 Latin American Pool conference in Punta del Este, 3, CB-AH; and "Accord entre la Federación Argentina de Cine-Clubes et la Cinemateca Argentina," Correspondance entre la FIAF et ses membres, FIAF-COR/018.

105. "Rapport de l'Argentine," XIIIe Congres de la FIAF, Tome 1: Antibes, Octobre 1957, 50, FIAF-CON/011A.

106. Salvador Sammaritano to Fédération Internationale des Archives du Film, October 16, 1957, "Resolución," Federación Argentina de Cineclubes, June 1958, and "Comunicado de la Cinemateca Argentina," July 1, 1958, in Correspondence diverse membres FIAF anneés 1950 (Borde), FIAF-COR/005; and memo signed by FIAF President Jerzy Toeplitz and André José Rolando Fustiñana, Buenos Aires, January 23, 1961, CB-AH.

107. Domínguez, *24 ilusiones por segundo*, 33.

108. Domínguez, *24 ilusiones por segundo*, 38–39; resolutions, 1952 FIAF Congress in Amsterdam, 6, www.fiafnet.org/images/tinyUpload/History/FIAF-Archives/Digitized%20docs/Congresses/1952%2010-11%2025-01%20FIAF%20Congress%20Amsterdam%20R%C3%A9sum%C3%A9%20LR.pdf.; and "Cartas," *Cine Club*, July 1953, 33–42.

109. Domínguez, *24 ilusiones por segundo*, 39.

110. José María Podestá and Raúl Benavides to President of FIAF [Jerzy Toeplitz], January 1954, Correspondance entre la FIAF et ses membres, FIAF-COR/028.

111. Minutes, 1955 Latin American Pool conference in Punta del Este, 3, CB-AH.

112. Minutes, 1956 Latin American Pool conference in São Paulo, 3, CB-AH.

113. Pedro Noa Romero, "La primera savia nutricia: La Filmoteca Universitaria," *Cine Cubano*, July–December 2011, 113. See also Rozsa, "On the Edge of the Screen," 50; and Eduardo Manet, "Cine y cultura en la Universidad de la Habana," *Cine Cubano* 1, no. 2 (1961): 54–55.

114. The Filmoteca UNAM was initially known as the Filmoteca Universitaria and later the Cinemateca de la Universidad.

115. Universidad Nacional Autónoma de México, *25 años Filmoteca UNAM*, 13.

116. "Filmoteca de la Universidad," *Gaceta de la Universidad*, July 18, 1960, 1.

117. On this point, see García Blizzard, *White Indians of Mexican Cinema*, 170–175.

118. "La Cinemateca de la UNAM," *Cine Cubano* 73–75 (November 1972): 136.

119. Universidad Nacional Autónoma de México, *25 años Filmoteca UNAM*, 13; and "Filmoteca Universitaria," *Gaceta de la Universidad*, June 27, 1960, 3.

120. Daniel Adolfo Urria, "Una cinemateca: Un vacío que debe ser llenado," *Séptimo Arte* 3 (1956): 4; and advertisement, *Séptimo Arte* 3 (1956): 19.

121. Mouesca, *El documental chileno*, 66–67.

122. Cineteca Universitaria, annual report, 1961 FIAF congress in Budapest, FIAF-CON/015.

123. "Problemas y planes de la Cineteca Universitaria y Cine Experimental: Habla su director," *Boletín de la Universidad de Chile* 27 (1966): 50–53.

124. Pedro Chaskel, "Informe Cineteca de la Universidad de Chile," *Cine Cubano* 73–75 (November 1972): 137.

125. Rozsa, "On the Edge of the Screen."

126. Rozsa, "Institutionalization of Film Exhibition in Cuba," 162; see also Rozsa, "On the Edge of the Screen," 137–142.

127. Cinemateca de Cuba, annual report, 1963 FIAF conference in Belgrade, FIAF-AFF/041.

128. Héctor García Mesa, "Cinemateca de Cuba," *Cine Cubano* 1, no. 5 (1961): 44–45.

129. García Mesa, "Cinemateca de Cuba," 47.

130. Rozsa, "On the Edge of the Screen," 140.

131. Héctor García Mesa, annual report, 1962 FIAF Conference in Rome, FIAF-AFF/041.

132. Héctor García Mesa, "Los programas de la Cinemateca," *Cine Cubano* 5, no. 30 (1965): 27–35.

133. Octavio Cortázar's documentary short *Por primera vez* (For the first time, 1967, Cuba) played a major role in publicizing this practice.

134. García Mesa, "Cinemateca de Cuba," 49; "Cinemateca de Cuba—Report to the XXVIII FIAF Congress—Annex 2—ICAIC Mobile Film Units" [1972], 2, FIAF-AFF/041.

135. Héctor García Mesa, Cinemateca de Cuba, annual report, 1961 FIAF Congress in Budapest, FIAF-CON/015; and "Entrevista con Héctor García Mesa, Director de la Cinemateca de Cuba," *Cine Cubano* 1, no. 5 (1961): 62–63.

136. Cineteca Universitaria, annual report at 1961 FIAF Congress in Budapest, 2, FIAF-CON/015; Pedro Chaskel to Marion Michelle, August 6, 1962, Courrier reçu pour le secrétariat 1960–1963, FIAF-COR/003; and Informe sobre la XIV Asamblea Ordinaria del Cine Club de Colombia, October 28, 1965, FPFC.

137. Cinemateca de Cuba, annual report, 1963 FIAF Conference in Belgrade, 2, FIAF-AFF/041.

138. Grioni, *Margot Benacerraf*, 44–47. See also Schwartzman et al., "Interview with Margot Benacerraf," 72–73.

139. Fernando Pérez, "Cuatro entrevistas en Venezuela: Margot Benacerraf," *Cine Cubano* 89–90, 89.

140. Corrêa, "O cinema como instituição."

141. Resolutions, 1952 FIAF Congress in Amsterdam, 4, www.fiafnet.org/images/tinyUpload/History/FIAF-Archives/Digitized%20docs/Congresses/1952%2010-11%2025-01%20FIAF%20Congress%20Amsterdam%20R%C3%A9sum%C3%A9%20LR.pdf.

142. Minutes, FIAF Executive Committee notes, Knokke-sur-Mer, June 28–July 1, 1949, 8, www.fiafnet.org/images/tinyUpload/History/FIAF-Archives/Digitized%20docs/EC%20meetings/1949-06-Knocke_Red.pdf.

143. Iran's national film institute, which joined FIAF in 1949, was the only member operating outside these regions at the time. Resolutions, 1952 FIAF Congress in Amsterdam, 3–4.

144. Minutes, 1952 FIAF Congress in Amsterdam, 98–99, www.fiafnet.org/images/tinyUpload/2022/02/10-1952_Congress_Report_CORRECT_VERSION_Amsterdam_CON-006B_RED.pdf.

145. Henri Langlois, "Le pool de circulation," 25, XIIIe Congres de la FIAF-Antibes, Octobre 1957, Annèxe B, 25–26, FIAF-CON/011C.

146. "Congrès Lausanne, Resultats des Trauvaux et Resolutions," 8, FIAF-CON/008.

147. FICC, minutes, June 27, 1946, Ciné-clubs—Compte-rendus des séances de la F.I.C.C. (1946–1950), CF-SADOUL734-B52; and Vignaux, "Georges Sadoul et la Fédération française des ciné-clubs," 189.

148. Henri Langlois to Paulo Emílio Salles Gomes, July 11, 1949, CB-APESG, PE/CP.0576. See also Paulo Emílio Salles Gomes to Henri Langlois, undated

[1949], CB-APESG, PE/CA.0235; "F.I.C.C.–Accord de Rome," November 26, 1949, CF-SADOUL721-B50; and minutes, 1949 FIAF Congress in Rome, 56–62.

149. Quoted in Vignaux, "Georges Sadoul et la Fédération française des ciné-clubs," 189. See also Corrêa, "O cinema como instituição," 38–41.

150. Jacques Ledoux, "Exposé sur la Fédération Internationale des Ciné-Clubs," 74–76, XIIIe Congres de la FIAF, Tome 1: Antibes, Octobre 1957, Annèxe B, FIAF-CON/011C.

151. Henri Langlois to José María Podestá, March 4, 1954, 3, uncatalogued, CU.

152. Minutes, 1955 Latin American Pool conference in Punta del Este, 2–4. CB-AH.

153. Eugenio Hintz to Marion Michelle, November 14, 1962, Courrier reçu pour le secrétariat 1960–1963, FIAF-COR/003.

154. Minutes, 1956 Latin American Pool conference in São Paulo, 9–11, CB-AH.

155. On sending prints via the diplomatic pouch see Hoek, "Films in the Diplomatic Bag." Minutes, 1956 Latin American Pool conference in São Paulo, 9–10, CB-AH.

156. Paulo Emílio Salles Gomes to Marion Michelle, March 17, 1963, Courrier reçu pour le secrétariat 1960–1963, FIAF-COR/003.

157. Minutes, 1955 Latin American Pool conference in Punta del Este, 2, CB-AH.

158. Marion Michelle to Hernando Salcedo Silva, December 12, 1963. Courrier reçu pour le secrétariat 1960–1963, FIAF-COR/003.

159. FIAF's *Journal of Film Preservation* became a trilingual English/Spanish/French publication with its October/November 1999 issue; FIAF's statutes were updated to reflect the organization's widespread use of Spanish a decade and a half later. See meeting notes, 2014 FIAF Congress in Skopje, 7. My thanks to Christophe Dupin for clarifying this point.

160. "Section Latino-Américaine de FIAF," 2, CB-AH.

161. Eugenio Hintz to Marion Michelle, November 14, 1962, Courrier reçu pour le secrétariat 1960–1963, FIAF-COR/003.

162. Minutes, 1956 Latin American Pool conference in São Paulo, 5–6, CB-AH. Lasala mentions pulling strings (including diplomatic ones) to obtain a seat but being discouraged from attending at the last minute by Langlois.

163. For example, Salles Gomes asked Francisco Luiz de Almeida Salles, who was working at the Brazilian embassy in Paris, to pay the Cinemateca Brasileira's FIAF dues on his behalf. Paulo Emílio Salles Gomes to Francisco Almeida Salles, October 5, 1962, CB-APESG, PE/CA.0418. IDHEC student Abraham Zalzman also paid part of the Cinemateca Colombiana's outstanding balance. Hernando Salcedo Silva to Marion Michelle, January 2, 1962, Courrier reçu pour le secrétariat 1960–1963, FIAF-COR/003.

164. Paulo Emílio Salles Gomes to Eugenio Hintz, January 16, 1963, CB-APESG, PE/CA.0423.

165. Pedro Chaskel to Marion Michelle, January 26, 1963, Courrier reçu pour le secrétariat 1960–1963, FIAF-COR/003; and Eugenio Hintz to Marion Michelle, November 22, 1965, Members Montevideo SODRE–Moscow Gosfilmofond, FIAF-AFF/048.

166. Notes, FIAF executive committee meeting, June 16–17, 1956, 17–18, www.fiafnet.org/images/tinyUpload/History/FIAF-Archives/Digitized%20docs/EC%20meetings/1956-09-Paris-RED.pdf.
167. Juan Pivel Devoto to André Thirifays, December 14, 1959, Courrier reçu pour le secrétariat 1960–1963, FIAF-COR/003.
168. Minutes, 1960 Latin American Pool conference, 4, CB-AH.
169. Lenk and Stufkens, "'Then Began the Battle Royal,'" 211–212.
170. Olmeta, *La Cinémathèque française*, 108.
171. Eugenio Hintz to Rudá de Andrade, February 15, 1960, CB-AH.
172. Minutes, 1960 Latin American Pool conference, 14–20, CB-AH.
173. Lenk and Stufkens, "'Then Began the Battle Royal,'" 204; Paulo Emílio Salles Gomes to Jerzy Toeplitz, February 26, 1960, CB-APESG, PE/CA.0357; and Paulo Emílio Salles Gomes to Henri Langlois, June 30, 1961, CB-APESG, PE/CP.0384.
174. Paulo Emílio Salles Gomes to Antonio Moniz Vianna and José Sanz, February 14, 1960, CB-APESG, PE/CA.0355.
175. Andrés José Rolando Fustiñana to Jerzy Toeplitz, March 25, 1965, Dossiers affiliés 5, Fundación Cinemateca Argentina, FIAF-AFF/016.
176. Núñez, "Notas para um estudo," 66; and Corrêa, "O cinema como instituição," 151.
177. Domínguez, *24 ilusiones por segundo*, 68–69.
178. Danilo Trelles to Jerzy Toeplitz, March 22, 1960, 2, Congrès Budapest 1961—SODRE. FIAF-CON/015.
179. Eugenio Hintz to Marion Michelle, November 14, 1962, Courrier reçu pour le secrétariat 1960–1963, FIAF-COR/003.
180. Henri Langlois to Maria Adriana Prolo, quoted in Lenk and Stufkens, "'Thus Began the Battle Royal,'" 217n84.
181. Minutes, 1965 FIAF Congress in Oslo, 9, Congrès Oslo 1965 à Congrès Sofia, FIAF-CON/19.
182. Minutes, 1967 FIAF Congress in East Berlin, 5–7, www.fiafnet.org/images/tinyUpload/2021/09/Minutes_Congress_Berlin_1967_RED.pdf.
183. Amieva Collado, "La conformación del campo cinematográfico en Uruguay," 12, 81.
184. Ernest Lindgren to Eugenio Hintz, June 10, 1966, Members Montevideo SODRE–Moscow Gosfilmofond, FIAF-AFF/048.
185. Eugenio Hintz to Ernest Lindgren, January 30, 1968, Members Montevideo SODRE–Moscow Gosfilmofond, FIAF-AFF/048.
186. Domínguez, *24 ilusiones por segundo*, 83.
187. "Declaración de Cinematecas/UCAL," February 23, 1965, RR1 Carpeta 2 D/RR—Correspondencia enviada/recibida Cinemateca Uruguaya, CU-AWDB.
188. "Fundación de UCAL," Dossiers affiliés 5, Fundación Cinemateca Argentina, FIAF-AFF/016. See also Núñez, "Notas para um estudo," 71; and Domínguez, *24 ilusiones por segundo*, 83.
189. "Fundación de UCAL," Dossiers affiliés 5, Fundación Cinemateca Argentina, FIAF-AFF/016.
190. Pick, *New Latin American Cinema*.

191. Domínguez, *24 ilusiones por segundo*, 84; UCAL members to Foreign Minister Vasco Leitão de Cunha, September 25, 1965, RR5, Carpeta 2 D/RR—Correspondencia enviada/recibida Cinemateca Uruguaya, CU-AWDB.

192. Walther Dassori Barthet to Miguel Reynel Santillana, January 25, 1966, C2RR14, Carpeta 2 D/RR—Correspondencia enviada/recibida Cinemateca Uruguaya, CU-AWDB.

193. Eugenio Hintz to Ernest Lindgren, January 30, 1968, Members Montevideo SODRE–Moscow Gosfilmofond, FIAF-AFF/048.

194. Ely Azeredo, "Cinema," *Tribuna da Imprensa*, May 22, 1967, sec. 2, 3.

195. See, for example, Eugenio Hintz to Jacques Ledoux, March 17, 1970, Members Montevideo SODRE–Moscow Gosfilmofond, FIAF-AFF/048.

196. Walther Dassori Barthet to Kerry Oñate, April 17, 1969, R2, Carpeta 2 D/RR—Correspondencia enviada/recibida Cinemateca Uruguaya, CU-AWDB.

197. Manuel González Casanova to Walther Dassori Barthet, November 4, 1965, RR7, Carpeta 2 D/RR—Correspondencia enviada/recibida Cinemateca Uruguaya, CU-AWDB; and Eugenio Hintz to Jacques Ledoux, October 14, 1969, Members Montevideo SODRE–Moscow Gosfilmofond, FIAF-AFF/048.

198. Walther Dassori Barthet to Manuel González Casanova, May 18, 1966, RR17a, Carpeta 2 D/RR—Correspondencia enviada/recibida Cinemateca Uruguaya, CU-AWDB. Portions of the letter are reproduced in Domínguez, *24 ilusiones por segundo*, 84–86.

199. Eugenio Hintz to Jacques Ledoux, February 25, 1969, 1, Members Montevideo SODRE–Moscow Gosfilmofond, FIAF-AFF/048.

200. Hintz to Ledoux, February 25, 1969, 1–2, FIAF-AFF/048.

201. Hintz to Ledoux, February 25, 1969, 2, FIAF-AFF/048.

202. Hintz to Ledoux, February 25, 1969, 2, FIAF-AFF/048.

203. Wschebor Pellegrino, "Ouvrir les boîtes," 172–175.

204. "Proposition cubaine," https://www.fiafnet.org/images/tinyUpload/2020/12/proposition_cubaine_RED.pdf.

205. On Latin American film archives under dictatorship see Silveira, *Cultura y cinefilia*; and Núñez, "La acción de las cinematecas latinoamericanas."

206. See Schwarz, "Culture and Politics in Brazil, 1964–1969."

207. "Declaración del VI Congreso de la Unión de Cinematecas de América Latina," *Cine Cubano* 73/75 (November 1972): 116.

208. "Declaración del VI Congreso de la Unión de Cinematecas de América Latina," 116.

209. See "Una Cinemateca ausente: La Cinemateca del Tercer Mundo," *Cine Cubano* 73/75 (November 1972): 138. There is a growing body of work on the Cinemateca del Tercer Mundo; for the most sustained study to date, see Wschebor Pellegrino, "Ouvrir les boîtes," 304–387.

210. Ceja Alcalá, "Imperfect Archives," 81–82; and Domínguez, *24 ilusiones por segundo*, 138.

211. Minutes, 1972 FIAF Congress in Bucharest, 14, 31–32, www.fiafnet.org/images/tinyUpload/E-Resources/Official-Documents/Protected%20Files/Congress-Reports/1972-%20Bucharest%20GA%20minutesRED.pdf.

212. Emilio Massobrio and Gustavo Ferrand to FIAF, November 21, 1974, Members Montevideo SODRE–Moscow Gosfilmofond, FIAF-AFF/048. See also Núñez, "Notas para um estudo," 76; and Silveira, *Cultura y cinefilia*, 169.
213. Domínguez, *24 ilusiones por segundo*, 142.
214. Minutes, 1976 FIAF Congress in Mexico, 28, www.fiafnet.org/images/tinyUpload/E-Resources/Official-Documents/Protected%20Files/Congress-Reports/1976-Mexico%20GA%20MinutesRED.pdf; and Domínguez, *24 ilusiones por segundo*, 148–149. The archives stipulated that although some RCCS members had left UCAL, the two entities were not in conflict.
215. Dimitriu, "Cinemateca Uruguaya," 51.
216. Mario Handler, one of the Cinemateca del Tercer Mundo's founders, had also clashed with Martínez Carril in a series of bitter professional disputes, suggesting how personal and political antipathies often overlapped. Domínguez, *24 ilusiones por segundo*, 107–113, 117–118.
217. Núñez, "La acción de cinematecas latinoamericanas en tiempos de dictadura," 48; Silveira, *Cultura y cinefilia*, 203–219, 261–268; and Wschebor Pellegrino, "Ouvrir les boîtes," 197–210.

CHAPTER 3: BROKERING ART CINEMA

1. André Bazin, "Le voyage à Punta del Este," *Cahiers du Cinéma*, April 1956, 26.
2. The town of Yorkton in the Canadian province of Saskatchewan hosted an international documentary film festival in October 1950; however, the event seems to have received little to no industry press coverage at the time. Thanks to Jonathan Petrychyn for sharing this information. Homero Alsina Thevenet, "Una muestra del cine francés," *Film*, March–April 1953, 18–19.
3. Bazin, "Le voyage à Punta del Este," 26.
4. Bazin, "Le voyage à Punta del Este," 26.
5. On film festival prizes, see English, *Economy of Prestige*, 288–289.
6. Latil, *Le festival de Cannes*, 51–52, 130–149.
7. Bartram, "35mm Bridges," 47.
8. This was a stipulation of FIAPF regulations. Pisu, "Transnational Love-Hate Relationship," 116–118.
9. Fein, "From Collaboration to Containment," 129–137, 142–157.
10. The first Reseña Mundial de los Festivales Cinematográficos took place in Mexico City; it was held regularly in Acapulco until 1968.
11. These distances were often stressed in French press accounts of the festivals. See Henry Magnan, "Punta del Este: Km 12,000," *Cahiers du Cinéma*, April 1951, 58–60; and Pierre Billard, "Le festival du bout du monde," *Cinéma 60*, May 1960, 4–8, 139–140.
12. José Manuel Valdés-Rodríguez, "Sin el avión jamás podría América requisar su gran riqueza y relacionar sus pueblos," *El Mundo*, April 17, 1948, 15.
13. Some sources cite 1933 as the date of FIAPF's founding and others 1939. Moine, "La FIAPF," 256.

14. Category A festivals were competitive international events and Category B festivals noncompetitive international events. Category C was used for special events such as UNESCO's film festival, while Category D events were national in scope. Moine, "La Fédération internationale des associations de producteurs de films," 98–99; and Pisu, "Transnational Love-Hate Relationship."

15. "Uruguay Festival, after Fight for Right to Give Prizes, Doesn't," *Variety*, February 9, 1955, 2.

16. "Bars Reds from Council Federation," *Motion Picture Herald*, November 12, 1955, 34. See also Moine, "La Fédération internationale des associations de producteurs de films," 99.

17. Wong, *Film Festivals*, 42; and Valck, *Film Festivals*, 51.

18. Gideon Bachmann, "Two Kinds of Film Festivals," *Variety*, May 8, 1963, 109.

19. "Reds in Orbit at Festivals," *Variety*, May 2, 1962, 226.

20. Salazkina, *World Socialist Cinema*, 1, 36, 103.

21. Hugo R. Alfaro, Jorge A. Arteaga and Calvero [pseud. Emir Rodríguez Monegal], "¿Un festival de gusto southamericano?," *Marcha*, January 14, 1955, 13.

22. "Uruguay Fest Needs and Gets H'wood Backing," *Variety*, December 1, 1954, 10.

23. Alfaro, Arteaga, and Calvero, "¿Un festival de gusto southamericano?," 13; and Hugo R. Alfaro, Jorge A. Arteaga, and Calvero [pseud. Emir Rodríguez Monegal], "Los remiendos del caos," *Marcha*, January 21, 1955, 12.

24. Alfaro, Arteaga, and Calvero, "¿Un festival de gusto southamericano?," 13.

25. "El 'gran festival': 55 páginas a mimeógrafo," *Marcha*, February 8, 1952, 10.

26. The word *criollo* originally referred to a person of Spanish parentage born in the colonial territories. It is frequently used in Argentina and Uruguay to describe a local, hybrid cultural identity. Alfaro, Arteaga, and Calvero, "Los remiendos del caos," 12.

27. Quoted in Edward C. Burks, "In the Chips: Argentine Resort Comes to Life Again with the Reopening of its Casino," *New York Times*, June 16, 1963, 330.

28. On Mar del Plata, see Kriger, "'Inolvidables jornadas vivió Mar del Plata'"; Triana Toribio, "El festival de los cinéfilos transnacionales"; and Neveleff, Monforte, and Ponce de León, *Historia del Festival Internacional*. On other Latin American festivals of the period, see Amieva Collado, "¿Cómo el Uruguay no hay?"; and Morato Zanatto, "O I Festival Internacional de Cinema do Brasil (1954)."

29. The Film Festival Research Network's website lists hundreds of articles and books on the topic. For surveys of the subfield, see Iordanova, *Film Festival Reader*; and Valck, Kredell, and Loist, *Film Festivals*.

30. Ross, "Film Festival as Producer."

31. Harbord, "Film Festivals—Time—Event."

32. Andrew, "Time Zones and Jet Lag," 69–75.

33. The consortium of film schools met at Cannes in 1955, 1956, 1957, and 1961.

34. Schwartz, *It's So French!*, 65.

35. Latil, *Le festival de Cannes*; and Gallinari, "L'URSS au festival de Cannes."
36. Abraham [Z]alzman, "Sobre el festival de Cartagena," *Cine Cubano*, April 1963, 53.
37. The popular and scholarly literature on Cannes is vast. See, for instance, Beauchamp and Béhar, *Hollywood on the Riviera*; Le Clézio and Chazal, *Les années Cannes*; and Schwartz, *It's So French!*, 57–99.
38. Latil, *Le festival de Cannes*, 11–56; Schwartz, *It's So French!*, 59–61; Wong, *Film Festivals*, 38–39; and Valck, *Film Festivals*, 48.
39. Schwartz, *It's So French!*, 57–58.
40. "Elements de réponse à la Cour des Comptes," unsigned, undated manuscript (likely 1948), Ministère des Affaires Étrangères, France—Association française d'action artistique—Services des échanges artistiques (hereafter FRMAE-554 INVA)-922.
41. Schwartz, *It's So French!*, 62, 67.
42. "Pays invités en 1939 qui avaient accepté et solicités à nouveau/Pays nouveaux invités en 1946," Festival de Cannes 1946—Participations, Cinémathèque française—Festival Internacional du Film de Cannes—Service Administration (hereafter CF-FIFA)49-B8.
43. Between 1947 and 1953, jury members were all French. Latil, *Le festival de Cannes*, 145–146; and "Membres du jury au Festival International de Cannes, Septembre–Octobre 1946," Festival de Cannes 1946, Participations, CF-FIFA49-B8.
44. Robert Favre Le Bret to Pierre Blanchar, July 17, 1946, Festival de Cannes 1946, Récompenses, CF-FIFA37-B6; and Wong, *Film Festivals*, 39.
45. Latil, *Le festival de Cannes*, 275–278.
46. Schwartz, *It's So French!*, 72.
47. See Rueda, "Films latino-américains, festivals français"; and Schroeder-Rodríguez, *Latin American Cinema*, 129–163.
48. Podalsky, *Specular City*.
49. Nicolas Mouneu to Robert Favre Le Bret, April 6, 1953, Festival de Cannes 1953, Participations A à D, CF-FIFA279-B43.
50. Latil, *Le festival de Cannes*, 129, 213–215; Bartram, "35mm Bridges," 52–53.
51. Gallinari, "L'URSS au festival de Cannes," 29; and Bartram, "35mm Bridges," 45–70.
52. Pisu, "Transnational Love-Hate Relationship," 122.
53. Cannes organizing committee meeting notes, October 30, 1963, 2, FRMAE-554 INVA-933.
54. Cannes organizing committee meeting notes, July 1, 1959, 8, FRMAE-554 INVA-930.
55. Cannes organizing committee meeting notes, October 25, 1962, FRMAE-554 INVA-930.
56. "Note pour le cabinet de Monsieur le Sécretaire d'État," undated (likely 1964), FRMAE-554 INVA-933.
57. Rueda, "Films latino-américains, festivals français," 88; and Bartram, "35mm Bridges," 68.
58. On the characteristics of festival films, see Wong, *Film Festivals*, 65–99.

59. Favre Le Bret to Nicholas Mouneu, February 28, 1957, Festival de Cannes 1957, Participations A à F, CF-FIFA473-B82.

60. Telegram, Favre Le Bret to APDPM, March 24, 1953, and APDPM to Festival International du Film de Cannes, March 27, 1953, Festival 1953, Participations I à S, CF-FIFA281-B45.

61. Nicolas Mouneu to Robert Favre Le Bret, March 6, 1961, Festival 1961, Participations A à I, CF-FIFA689-B116.

62. Telegram, Jean Basvedant to French embassy in Cuba, March 23, 1963, and Campredon, draft telegram to French embassy in Cuba, March 18, 1963, COFRAM, Correspondence pays, Archives nationales, France—Pierrefitte-sur-Seine (hereafter ANF)-CNC-20050584/57. See also folder labeled Cannes 63—Cuba, FRMAE-554 INVA-930.

63. Ramírez Llorens, *Noches de sano esparcimiento*, 127.

64. Amy Courvoisier to Robert Favre Le Bret, March 29, 1962, Festival de Cannes 1962, Participations A à B, CF-FIFA743-B123.

65. Latil, *Le festival de Cannes*, 174.

66. Undated telegram, Robert Favre Le Bret to Oswaldo Massaini, Festival de Cannes 1962, Participations A à B, CF-FIFA743-B123. Cannes files do not specify the requested cuts; the concerns may have been due to its overall length.

67. M[ay] Delanney to [Francisco Luiz de Almeida] Salles, April 7, 1964, Festival de Cannes 1964, Participations B à S, CF-FIFA847-B138.

68. Luís Edgar de Andrade, "Cannes quis salvar Baleia para alegrar *Vidas Secas*, mas produtor não permitiu," *Jornal do Brasil*, April 30, 1964, 8. Danilo Trelles, the head of Cine Arte del SODRE (see chapter 2), was also a co-producer of the film.

69. Avancini and Penna, "Antologia da Crítica Cinematográfica em *Vidas Secas*," 86.

70. Martin-Márquez, "Coloniality and the Trappings of Modernity," 96–97.

71. Martin-Márquez, "Coloniality and the Trappings of Modernity," 96–97.

72. General Manager of Argentina Sono Film to Jean Touzet, November 3, 1950, Festival de Cannes 1951, Participations A à E, CF-FIFA200-B26.

73. Jaime Prades to Robert Favre Le Bret, January 29, 1951, Robert Favre Le Bret to Jaime Prades, February 5, 1951, and Nicolas Mouneu to Robert Favre Le Bret, February 21, 1951, Festival de Cannes 1951, Participations A à E, CF-FIFA200-B26.

74. Phu, "Bigger at the Movies," 49–50.

75. Nicolas Mouneu to Robert Favre Le Bret, February 21, 1962, Festival de Cannes 1962, Participations A à B, CF-FIFA743-B123.

76. Robert Favre Le Bret to Nicolas Mouneu, February 26, 1962, Festival de Cannes 1962, Participations A à B, CF-FIFA743-B123.

77. Acevedo-Muñoz, *Buñuel and Mexico*, 75—77; Keating, "Volcano and the Barren Hill," 201; and Martin-Márquez, "Coloniality and the Trappings of Modernity," 99.

78. Bazin, *Cinema of Cruelty*, 59–60, trans. Sabine d'Estrée and Tiffany Fliss.

79. Martin-Márquez, "Coloniality and the Trappings of Modernity," 98.

80. Paz, "Buñuel the Poet," 188–190, trans. Michael Schmidt.

81. APDPM to Festival Internacional de Cinéma de Cannes, February 23, 1951, Festival de Cannes 1951, Programmation Japon-Pologne, CF-FIFR47-B13.
82. Polizzotti, *Los olvidados*, 73–74.
83. Telegram, Robert Favre Le Bret to Jean Sirol, February 23, 1953, Festival 1953, Participation I à S, CF-FIFA281-B45.
84. Jean Sirol to Robert Favre Le Bret, March 6, 1953, Festival 1953, Participation I à S, CF-FIFA281-B45.
85. Robert Favre Le Bret to the Ambassador of Brazil in France, February 7, 1951, Festival de Cannes 1951, Participations A à E, CF-FIFA200-B26.
86. Martin-Márquez, "Coloniality and the Trappings of Modernity," 98.
87. A number of observers compared the film to Astruc's *Le rideau cramoisi* (*The Crimson Curtain*, 1953). Nicolas Mouneu to Favre Le Bret, April 12, 1957, Festival de Cannes 1957, Participations A à F, CF-FIFA473-B82.
88. Telegram, Nicholas Mouneu to Robert Favre Le Bret, March 13, 1961, Festival de Cannes 1961, Participations A à I, CF-FIFA689-B116.
89. Leopoldo Torre Nilsson to Robert Favre Le Bret, March 9, 1965, Festival 1965, Participations A à H, CF-FIFA898-B144.
90. Gloria Alcorta, "Note confidentielle à propos du film de Torre Nilsson 'LE TROU DE SERRURE,'" Festival de Cannes 1965, Participations A à H, CF-FIFA898-B144.
91. Gloria Alcorta, "Recherche des films—Argentine," Festival de Cannes 1965, Participations A à H, CF-FIFA898-B144. For other contacts between Alcorta and the festival, including an unsuccessful request for the event to subsidize her trip, see FRMAE-554 INVA-933.
92. Cannes organizing committee meeting notes, April 23, 1965, 3, FRMAE-554 INVA-933.
93. Sala, "Casarse con una viuda," 64.
94. Feldman, *La generación del 60*, 71–72.
95. Robert Favre Le Bret to José Enrique Lozano, April 23, 1965, Festival de Cannes 1965, Participations A à H, CF-FIFA898-B144.
96. Robert Favre Le Bret to Philippe Erlanger, April 29, 1965, FRMAE-554 INVA-933.
97. Telegram, INC to Robert Favre Le Bret, undated, Festival de Cannes 1965, Participations A à H, CF-FIFA898-B144.
98. Telegram, INC to Robert Favre Le Bret, April 29, 1965, Festival de Cannes 1965, Participations A à H, CF-FIFA898-B144, Cannes organizing committee meeting notes, April 23, 1965, 3, FRMAE-554 INVA-933; and telegram, [Christian de] Margerie to Ministère des Affaires Étrangères, April 29, 1965, 1, FRMAE-554 INVA-933.
99. Telegram, INC to Robert Favre Le Bret, April 29, 1965, and telegram, René Mujica to May Delanney, May 10, 1965, Festival de Cannes 1965, Participations A à H, CF-FIFA898-B144.
100. Robert Favre Le Bret to Alberto Ugalde Portela, March 4, 1958, Festival 1958, Festival Divers, CF-FIFA520-B89.
101. Nicolas Mouneu to Robert Favre Le Bret, February 21, 1962, Festival de Cannes 1962, Participations A à B, CF-FIFA743-B123.

102. "Argentine Festival Asides," *Variety*, April 4, 1962, 5.
103. Bartram, "35mm Bridges," 67–68.
104. Ernesto Salcedo [Salazar] to Robert Favre Le Bret, March 28, 1963, Films à Inviter. CF-FIFA793-B131.
105. Robert Favre Le Bret to Ernesto Salcedo [Salazar], April 1, 1963, Films à Inviter. CF-FIFA793-B131.
106. "Arnold Picker says UA's Latin American Gross to 'Nearly Double' in 1955," *Motion Picture Daily*, January 28, 1955, 3.
107. H[omero] A[lsina] T[hevenet], "El Festival de Mar del Plata: Truenos en varios formatos," *El País*, undated press clipping, MCPDH.
108. See Lee, *Cinema and the Cultural Cold War*, 18–20, 68–91.
109. "Punta del Este, Uruguay Seen as Coming So. American Tourist Spot," *Variety*, December 5, 1951, 15.
110. Advertisement in Fernández, *Travelling en el festival*, 56. On the history of the Cantegril Country Club and the festival, see Polo Risso, *Historia de Punta del Este*, 239–245, 263–273, 278; and Trochon Ghislieri, *Punta del Este*, 151–155, 161–175.
111. Milton Bracker, "Uruguay Festival," *New York Times*, March 11, 1951, 101. See also Fernández, *Travelling en el festival*, 11; and Potenze, *El Festival Internacional de Cine*, 12.
112. "Revisión del festival: Las nueces, solamente," *Marcha*, March 16, 1951, 12.
113. Milton Bracker, "Uruguay Festival," *New York Times*, March 11, 1951, 101.
114. Fernández, *Travelling en el festival*, 9–10.
115. "Diario de Punta del Este: El ruido con sus nueces," *Marcha*, March 9, 1951, 14. Electrical problems recurred in later years; see, for instance, Alfaro, Arteaga, and Calvero, "Los remiendos del caos," 12.
116. Gallinari, "L'URSS au festival de Cannes," 28.
117. Potenze, *El Festival Internacional de Cine*, 16; and Fernández, *Travelling en el festival*, 5–6. See also Hugo R. Alfaro and H[omero] Alsina Thevenet, "El Segundo festival," *Marcha*, September 7, 1951, 10.
118. "No Participará el Cine Nacional del Certamen de Punta del Este," *La Época*, February 13, 1951, 10.
119. "Uruguay Fest Picks Italian Film; Names Swanson, Hull Top Actress," *Variety*, March 7, 1951, 20.
120. H[omero] A[lsina] T[hevenet], "Finanzas del festival cinematográfico," *Marcha*, June 22, 1951, 16; "Nobody Really to Blame, Why Point?" *Variety*, April 10, 1963, 3; and executive committee meeting notes, I Festival Internacional de Cinema de São Paulo, December 8, 1953, Livro de Atas, CB. Cannes did cover celebrity guests' travel in 1946; see "Elements de réponse à la Cour des Comptes," unsigned, undated manuscript (likely 1948), FRMAE-554 INVA-922.
121. "Diario de Punta del Este: El ruido con sus nueces," *Marcha*, March 9, 1951, 15; and Milton Bracker, "Uruguay Festival," *New York Times*, March 11, 1951, 101.
122. "If There's a Uruguayan Pic Festival Next Year, Better Start Training Now," *Variety*, March 14, 1951, 14.

123. "Diario de Punta del Este: El ruido con sus nueces," *Marcha*, February 23, 1951, 13; "Diario de Punta del Este: El ruido con sus nueces," *Marcha*, March 2, 1951, 12; and Potenze, *El Festival Internacional de Cine*, 13.

124. "Diario de Punta del Este: El ruido con sus nueces," *Marcha*, February 23, 1951, 13.

125. Freda Bruce Lockhart, "At the Film Festival in Uruguay," *Focus*, May 1951, 133; and Potenze, *Festival Internacional de Cine*, 28–29.

126. Potenze, *Festival Internacional de Cine*, 34–35.

127. "Diario del Festival: El ruido con sus nueces," *Marcha*, March 2, 1951, 12; Potenze, *El Festival Internacional de Cine*, 19–20.

128. "Diario de Punta del Este: El ruido con sus nueces," February 23, 1951, 13; and Potenze, *El Festival Internacional de Cine*, 10.

129. "Only RKO, UA from U.S. Enter Films At Uruguay Fete," *Variety*, January 16, 1952, 7. See also Milton Bracker, "Italian Film Wins Uruguayan Prize," *New York Times*, March 6, 1951, 25. Sixty-six non-US delegates attended the festival. H[omero] A[lsina] T[hevenet], "Finanzas del festival cinematográfico," *Marcha*, June 22, 1951, 11.

130. T[hevenet], "Finanzas del festival cinematográfico," 16.

131. Amieva Collado, "La conformación del campo cinematográfico en Uruguay," 8.

132. "Revisión del festival," *Marcha*, March 16, 1951, 12.

133. Arias, "Gobiernos reformistas en Uruguay 1947–1958."

134. Bulmer-Thomas, *Economic History of Latin America*, 264.

135. "El gran festival," *Marcha*, January 18, 1952, 7.

136. Bolaña, "El fenómeno de los 'cantegriles' montevideanos," 102.

137. "¿Podemos perder tiempo en Cantegril?," *Marcha*, February 1, 1952, 4.

138. "Uruguay Fete, with Relaxed P.A. Sked, Better Run Than in '51," *Variety*, January 30, 1952, 4.

139. "Diario de Punta del Este: El ruido con sus nueces," *Marcha*, January 25, 1952, 13.

140. H[omero] A[lsina] T[hevenet], "El segundo festival de Punta del Este," *Film*, March 1952, 2; Hugo R. Alfaro and H[omero] Alsina Thevenet, "El segundo festival," *Marcha*, January 11, 1952, 12; and "Diario de Punta del Este: El ruido con sus nueces," *Marcha*, January 18, 1952, 13.

141. Uruguayan press outlets fielded a critic's jury, a feature of many festivals. "Uruguay Accedes to IFP," *Motion Picture Daily*, December 6, 1951, 2.

142. Alfaro and Thevenet, "El segundo festival," 2; and "El gran festival," *Marcha*, January 18, 1952, 7.

143. "Only RKO, UA from U.S. Enter Films At Uruguay Fete," *Variety*, January 16, 1952, 7.

144. Antonio J. Grompone, "Punta del Este 1952," *Cine Club*, June 1952, 9.

145. "El 'gran festival': 55 páginas a mimeógrafo," *Marcha*, February 8, 1952, 10; and "Diario de Punta del Este: El ruido con sus nueces," *Marcha*, January 18, 1952, 13.

146. Édouard-Félix Guyon to Georges Bidault, March 23, 1953, 1, FRMAE-241QO-218. See also Homero Alsina Thevenet, "Una muestra del cine francés," *Film*, March–April 1953, 18–19.

147. Édouard-Félix Guyon to Georges Bidault, March 23, 1953, 3, FRMAE-241QO-218.

148. "Set Film Festivals in South America, Europe for 1954," *Motion Picture Daily*, January 13, 1954, 10.

149. J[ulio] L. M[oreno], "Cine italiano e inglés: Algo viejo y algo nuevo," *Film*, June 1954, 20–23.

150. Homero Alsina Thevenet, "Punta del Este 1955," *Film*, March 1955, 2.

151. "Uruguay Fest Needs and Gets H'wood Backing," *Variety*, December 1, 1954, 10.

152. H[omero] A[lsina] T[hevenet], "Punta del Este 1955," *Film*, March 1955, 2; and Alfaro, Arteaga, and Calvero, "¿Un festival de gusto southamericano?," 13.

153. T[hevenet], "Punta del Este 1955," 4–5; and Hugo R. Alfaro, Jorge A. Arteaga, and Calvero [pseud. Emir Rodríguez Monegal], "Festival vs. Cine," *Marcha*, January 28, 1955, 12.

154. "Fallo del Jurado," *Film*, March 1955, 6; "Festival de Punta del Este: Fallo del jurado," *Séptimo Arte*, August 1955, 12; and "Tercer Festival Cinematográfico Internacional de Punta del Este: Fallo del Jurado Oficial," *Gente de Cine*, January–March 1955, 16.

155. Hugo R. Alfaro and Calvero [pseud. Emir Rodríguez Monegal], "Liquidación de un Festival Cinematográfico," *Marcha*, February 4, 1955, 12.

156. Alfaro and Calvero, "Liquidación de un Festival Cinematográfico," 12.

157. T[hevenet], "Punta del Este 1955," 3.

158. Punta del Este festival regulations, 1958; Festival de Cannes 1958—Festivals divers, CF-FIFA520-B89; and Salvador Sammaritano, "Festival de Punta del Este," *Tiempo de Cine*, February/March 1961, 23–26.

159. Prizes were awarded in each of these categories at the 1956 festival. Catalog, II Festival Internacional de Cine Documental y Experimental, n.p.

160. Catalog, II Festival Internacional de Cine Documental y Experimental, n.p.

161. Catalog, II Festival Internacional de Cine Documental y Experimental, n.p.

162. Amieva Collado, "¿Cómo el Uruguay no hay?," 18–21; and Amieva Collado, "La conformación del campo cinematográfico en Uruguay," 58, 84–106.

163. López, "Naming and Defining."

164. Feldman et al., "Primer Congreso Latino Americano de Cineístas Independientes," 539.

165. Feldman et al., "Primer Congreso Latino Americano de Cineístas Independientes," 539.

166. Feldman et al., "Primer Congreso Latino Americano de Cineístas Independientes," 541–542.

167. "O problema do dia: O festival," *Boletim do Festival*, February 11, 1954, 3.

168. Executive committee meeting notes, I Festival Internacional de Cinema do Brasil, November 8, 1953, Livro de Atas, CB.

169. "O problema do dia: O festival," *Boletim do Festival*, February 11, 1954, 3.

170. Galvão, *Burguesia e cinema*; and Durand, *Arte, privilégio e distinção*, 117–145.

171. Francisco Luiz de Almeida Sal[l]es, "Como nasceu o festival do Brasil," *Boletim do Festival*, February 11, 1954, 3.
172. H[omero] A[lsina] T[hevenet], "São Paulo 1954," *Film*, June 1954, 2.
173. Morato Zanatto, "O I Festival Internacional de Cinema do Brasil (1954)," 116.
174. Melo Souza, *Paulo Emílio no Paraíso*, 349–350.
175. Corrêa, *A Cinemateca Brasileira*, 144.
176. Morato Zanatto, "O I Festival Internacional de Cinema do Brasil (1954)," 116.
177. Morato Zanatto, "O I Festival Internacional de Cinema do Brasil (1954)," 116–118.
178. Kriger, "'Inolvidables jornadas vivió Mar del Plata'," 118–131.
179. "Plush Casinos, Auto Races, Pix, Cafés to Spruce Up 1st Arg. Film Festival," *Variety*, February 18, 1948, 19.
180. Pastoriza and Torre, *Mar del Plata*, 31, ch. 5.
181. "Argentine Pixers Set Two Film Festivals," *Variety*, November 26, 1947, 15.
182. José Manuel Valdés-Rodríguez, "Estuvieron representadas Europa y América en el primer festival del cine argentino," *El Mundo*, April 21, 1948, unpaginated press clipping, MCPDH. See also "Destacados periodistas asistieron al gran festival cinematográfico," *Set*, April 1948, 10.
183. Colonel Domingo Mercante, speech delivered at the Primer Festival de Cine Argentino, published in *Set*, April 1948, 3–4.
184. Mercante, speech delivered at the Primer Festival de Cine Argentino, 4.
185. Mercante, speech delivered at the Primer Festival de Cine Argentino, 4.
186. "Historia del Peronismo: El Festival de Mar del Plata," *Primera Plana*, June 25, 1968, 49.
187. Kriger, "'Inolvidables jornadas vivió Mar del Plata.'"
188. "Robinson's Art Visits, Pidgeon's Bearing, Flynn Win Gauchos at Pix Fest," *Variety*, March 17, 1954, 2.
189. "Historia del Peronismo: El Festival de Mar del Plata," *Primera Plana*, June 25, 1968, 48.
190. Kriger, "'Inolvidables jornadas vivió Mar del Plata,'" 120.
191. By law, only half of box office proceeds could be remitted abroad; due to economic challenges, Argentina's central bank released only small quantities of dollars at a time, creating a backlog. "Despite Only $500,000 Unfrozen in Arg., Yank Distribs Hopeful of Future," *Variety*, December 23, 1953, 12.
192. "Perón will Release Funds of U.S. Films," *New York Times*, March 12, 1954, 15; "Pakistan Tighter, Denmark Easier on Remittances," *Variety*, March 17, 1954, 3; and "French, Italo Pix Weeks Okayed but Arg. Board Stalls Metro Anni Fete," *Variety*, November 10, 1954, 12.
193. Andrew Sarris, "Breaks Jaw: Best Actress; But Yanks Snub Mar del Plata," *Variety*, April 7, 1965, 5.
194. "C'Scope Okayed for Arg. Film Fete; WB Wants to Exhib 'Wax' Via 3-D," *Variety*, March 3, 1954, 7.
195. "El Festival de Mar del Plata," unidentified, undated press clipping, MCPDH.

196. Morato Zanatto, "O I Festival Internacional de Cinema do Brasil (1954)," 110.
197. Dupont, "Searching for Nelly Kaplan," 22–23.
198. Nid Ember, "ARC-120: Poor Man's Cinerama," *Variety*, January 18, 1961, 5; and "More Strong Yank Films Than Ever Competing in Mar del Plata Fest," *Variety*, January 11, 1961, 4.
199. Neveleff, Monforte, and Ponce de León, *Historia del Festival Internacional*, 49–50.
200. "Prep Mar del Plata Fest Hope for Adequate Power," *Variety*, January 24, 1962, 13.
201. "Argentine's Fest Tone Very 'Local,'" *Variety*, February 1, 1961, 15.
202. "Peculiar Is the Word for Argentine Films," *Variety*, January 5, 1955, 202.
203. "IV Festival Internacional de Mar del Plata," *Lyra*, January 1962, n.p.
204. "Mar del Plata: Un festival que ya no está en el fin del mundo," *Primera Plana*, March 12, 1963, 37.
205. "Mar del Plata," 37.
206. Billard, "Le festival du bout du monde," 4.
207. Salazkina, *World Socialist Cinema*, 36.
208. "Buenos Aires Crix Okay Plan to Organize 1959 Arg. Int'l Film Fest," *Variety*, November 5, 1958, 25. See also Broitman, "La cinefilia en la Argentina," 191–194.
209. "Mar del Plata's Fest in March," *Variety*, August 22, 1962, 21.
210. "Despite Inner Rows, Mar Del Plata Fest Promises to Be Annual Affair," *Variety*, May 6, 1959, 11. SICA's opposition can be traced to a conflict that erupted at a national film festival held in Río Hondo in 1958. When the jury declined to award the prize for best Argentine film, actor/director Hugo del Carril attacked critic Raimundo "Calki" Calcagno, leading to a feud between critics and the industry. González Centeno, "Raimundo Calcagno."
211. "Buenos Aires Crix Okay Plan to Organize 1959 Arg. Int'l Film Fest," *Variety*, November 5, 1958, 25; and "Despite Inner Rows, Mar Del Plata Fest Promises to Be Annual Affair," *Variety*, May 6, 1959, 11.
212. Neveleff, Monforte, and Ponce de León, *Historia del Festival Internacional*, 145–146.
213. Neveleff, Monforte, and Ponce de León, *Historia del Festival Internacional*, 100; and Jorge Montes, "Un festival de puertas adentro," *Atlántida*, April 1959, 23.
214. "Despite Inner Rows, Mar Del Plata Fest Promises to Be Annual Affair," *Variety*, May 6, 1959, 11.
215. Carlos García-Rivas, "Estrategias de vigilancia policia en el Festival Internacional de Cine de Mar del Plata"; and Ramírez Llorens, *Noches de sano esparcimiento*, 210. This practice was by no means unique to Mar del Plata; see Wäfler, "Surveillance of Film Festivals in Switzerland."
216. H[omero] A[lsina] T[hevenet], "Contratiempos, fallos y realizaciones," *El País*, undated press clipping, MCPDH.
217. El V Festival de Cine de Mar del Plata," *Cine Cubano*, July 1963, 16.
218. "B.A. Madly Mauls U.S. Stars," *Variety*, April 15, 1964.
219. Enzo Ardigó, "Welcome," *Gaceta del Festival*, March 9, 1960, n.p.

220. "Encuentro de teóricos," *Gaceta del Festival*, March 27, 1965, n.p.
221. Billard, "Le festival du bout du monde," 6.
222. Hans Ehrmann, "Film Art Eggheads—Rear View," *Variety*, April 11, 1962, 21.
223. Ehrmann, "Film Art Eggheads," 21.
224. "V Festival: Un caos donde el que más valía fue obligado a valer menos," *Primera Plana*, April 2, 1963, 36.
225. Vincent Canby, "US Stars (Sí), Frondizi (No)," *Variety*, April 4, 1962, 5.
226. "Llegaron ayer las delegaciones de España, Alemania e Italia," unidentified, undated press clipping, MCPDH.
227. Domingo di Núbila, "Decision to Skip 1967 Mar del Plata for 'Austerity' Reasons Is Contested," *Variety*, December 28, 1966, 4.
228. Ramírez Llorens, "Cine, autoritarismo y política de medios en Argentina."
229. Ramírez Llorens, "Cine, autoritarismo y política de medios en Argentina," 150–151; Domingo di Núbila, "Procrastinated Law Divides Unions, but Mar del Plata Goes On," *Variety*, March 6, 1968, 22.
230. "Ramírez Llorens, "Cine, autoritarismo y política de medios en Argentina," 153; and "'Don't Think Your Arty Fest Excuses You from Us'—Censors to Ridruejo," *Variety*, March 27, 1968, 24.
231. "10th for Mar del Plata; Journalists Warn of News Blackout If Film Choices Censored; Hopes on Rise," *Variety*, January 14, 1970, 28; and Domingo di Núbila, "Hey, Amigos, Nothing's Cut: Latins Rocked by 'Free' Fest," *Variety*, March 18, 1970, 7.
232. Simon Lantieri, "Premières rencontres avec le cinéma du Amérique Latine," *Cinéma 60*, August–September 1960, 111; for a similar sentiment, see Olivier de Tourmel, "Festivals," *Cahiers du Cinéma*, August 1960, 51.
233. Guy Gauthier, "Le cinéma d'Amérique Latine a Sestri Levante," *Image et Son*, July 1963, 24.
234. Pick, *New Latin American Cinema*.
235. Oscar Yoffe, "Nada sin fe en Sestri Levante," *Tiempo de Cine*, October–November 1963, 24.
236. The festival was held in Santa Margherita Ligure in 1960 and 1961, in Sestri Levante in 1962 and 1963, and in Genoa in 1965.
237. Alfredo Guevara, "Sestri Levante: IV Reseña del Cine Latinoamericano," *Cine Cubano*, July 1963, 54–61.
238. Yoffe, "Nada sin fe en Sestri Levante," 24.
239. Rocha, "Esthetic of Hunger."
240. López, "Naming and Defining."
241. Luisa Ferrari, "Tercer Festival: Un festival que despierta interés," *Cine Foro*, November 1965, n.p.; and "Mística para un festival," *Cine Foro*, April 1966, 5–6.

CHAPTER 4: FILM PEDAGOGY BETWEEN
LATIN AMERICA AND FRANCE

1. "Manuel González Casanova, "Despertar la conciencia del creador; formarlo cultural y técnicamente," *Revista de Cine*, March 1966, 54.

2. González Casanova, "Despertar la conciencia del creador," 54.

3. On ethical questions and professional film training, see Hjort, introduction to *Education of the Filmmaker in Africa, the Middle East, and the Americas*, 2–6.

4. On the professional training of filmmakers, see Baldi, *La scuola italiana del cinema*; Hjort, *Education of the Filmmaker in Europe, Australia, and Asia*; Hjort, *Education of the Filmmaker in Africa, the Middle East, and the Americas*; Petrie and Stoneman, *Educating Film-makers*; and Petrie, "New Art for a New Society?" On film schools as nodes of transnational exchange, see Salazkina, "Moscow-Rome-Havana"; Salazkina, "Soviet-Italian Cinematic Exchanges"; and Chomentowski, "Filmmakers from Africa and the Middle East at VGIK during the Cold War." On the academic study of film, see Polan, *Scenes of Instruction*; Grieveson and Wasson, *Inventing Film Studies*; Decherney, *Hollywood and the Culture Elite*; Bolas, *Screen Education*; and Askari, *Making Movies into Art*.

5. Petrie and Stoneman, *Educating Film-makers*, 17–18.

6. See, for instance, Hess, "Neo-realism and New Latin American Cinema"; Paranaguá, *Tradición y modernidad*, 170–199; Ruberto and Wilson, *Italian Neorealism and Global Cinema*; Mestman, "From Italian Neorealism to New Latin American Cinema"; and Valecce, *Neorealismo y cine en Cuba*.

7. The school was renamed the Scuola Nazionale di Cinema in 2004.

8. Petrie and Stoneman, *Educating Film-makers*, 17.

9. At first the school coexisted with a competing institution in Petrograd, which was dissolved in 1927. Kepley, "Building a National Cinema," 7–13.

10. Kepley, "Building a National Cinema," 10–18; and Miller, "Educating the Filmmakers," 480–482. See also Kepley, "Eisenstein as Pedagogue"; and Salazkina, "(V)GIK and the History of Film Education in the Soviet Union."

11. Miller, "Educating the Filmmakers," 464–467; and Kepley, "Building a National Cinema," 16–18.

12. Kepley, "Building a National Cinema," 17–18.

13. Petrie and Stoneman, *Educating Film-makers*, 41.

14. Chomentowski, "Filmmakers from Africa and the Middle East," 1–2. According to a preliminary tally compiled from VGIK's internal statistics by Gabrielle Chomentowski, 116 Latin American students studied there from the 1960s through the 1990s, with the largest number hailing from Cuba, Chile, and Colombia. Gabrielle Chomentowski, email communication, March 3, 2020. See also Woll, "Russian Connection."

15. Miller, "Educating the Filmmakers," 479–480.

16. Petrie and Stoneman, *Educating Film-makers*, 23.

17. Salazkina, "Soviet-Italian Cinematic Exchanges," 188.

18. Salazkina, "Soviet-Italian Cinematic Exchanges," 189.

19. Salazkina, "Moscow-Rome-Havana"; Valecce, *Neorealismo y cine en Cuba*.

20. IDHEC, *Première Rencontre*, 28–29.

21. Aldo Philipson, "Italian Experiment," *Sight and Sound* 8, no. 31 (1939): 118–119; and Laviosa, "Six Continents," 267–268.

22. Laviosa, "Six Continents," 267.

23. Philipson, "Italian Experiment," 119.

24. Laviosa "Six Continents," 263.

25. Laviosa et al., "International Students," 197.
26. IDHEC, *Première Rencontre*, 28–29; Robert J. Rauch, "An American in a European Film School," *Hollywood Quarterly* 10, no. 1 (1957): 9–11.
27. Maben and Jacobson, "Centro Sperimentale di Cinematografia," 33.
28. Philipson, "Italian Experiment"; Maben and Jacobson, "Centro Sperimentale di Cinematografia," 8–9; and IDHEC, *Première Rencontre*, 29.
29. Laviosa, "Six Continents," 267.
30. Laviosa, "Six Continents," 267–268.
31. IDHEC, *Première Rencontre*, 32.
32. Laviosa, "Six Continents," 265.
33. Laviosa et al., "International Students," 177.
34. Francese, "Influence of Cesare Zavattini on Latin American Cinema," 431; and Paranaguá, "Cinéastes latino-americains formés en Europe," 67.
35. Fernando Birri, "Autoretrato de Fernando Birri," *El Hogar*, April 1954, unpaginated press clipping, box 38, folder 36, John Hay Library, Brown University-Fernando Birri Archive of Multimedia Arts (hereafter JH-FBAMA).
36. See also García Espinosa, "Recuerdos de Zavattini."
37. Chanan, *New Cinema of Latin America Part I*, quoted in Hess, "Neorealism and New Latin American Cinema," 110.
38. Tomás Gutiérrez Alea to Germán Puig, November 22, 1952, reprinted in Ibarra, *Titón*, 24.
39. "Fotos con Maestros," "Fernando Birri con Cavalcanti," box fotos 4, folder 4, JH-FBAMA.
40. Brancaleone, *Cesare Zavattini's Neo-Realism*, 240, 245–246.
41. On Zavattini's links with Mexico, see the correspondence collected in Rodríguez Álvarez, *Cartas a México*.
42. Valecce, *Neorealismo y cine en Cuba*, 54–56; and Brancaleone, *Cesare Zavattini's Neo-Realism*, 213–215.
43. Valecce, *Neorealismo y cine en Cuba*, 102–117.
44. The phrase appears in a letter to Zavattini from ICAIC head Alfredo Guevara. Valecce, *Neorealismo y cine en Cuba*, 137.
45. Francese, "Influence of Cesare Zavattini," 434–435.
46. IDHEC, *Annuaire des anciens éleves de l'IDHEC*, vi. Although they seem not to have been included in official enrollment counts, US soldiers also took film appreciation courses at IDHEC. IDHEC, "Rapport sur l'organisation et fonctionnement des service de l'Institut des hautes études cinématographiques," 1945, 5, IDHEC—Organisation des services—Presentation et fonctionnement, ANF-IDHEC 20100344/29; and "Paris Education," *Motion Picture Herald*, December 15, 1945.
47. Paranaguá, "Cinéastes latino-americains formés en Europe," 66–67; and Laviosa et al., "International Students," 188–190.
48. The school trained camera operators, sound recordists, and laboratory technicians. Crisp, *Classic French Cinema*, 203.
49. Andrew, "IDHEC," 51.
50. IDHEC, "Rapport sur le fonctionnement de l'Institut des hautes études cinématographiques," 1944, 4–8, Organisation des services—Presentation et fonctionnement, ANF-IDHEC-20100344/29.
51. Rémy Tessonneau, "L'IDHEC et ses activités," 6.

52. IDHEC opened its doors in January 1944. Crisp, *Classic French Cinema*, 204–205; Andrew, "IDHEC," 50–51; Tessonneau, "L'IDHEC et ses activités," 6–7; and Lods, *Professional Training of Film Technicians*, 30.

53. Crisp, *Classic French Cinema*, 206; and IDHEC, "Rapport sur le fonctionnement de l'Institut des hautes études cinématographiques."

54. IDHEC-CNC, communiqué, July 1950, Correspondances adressées à Marcel L'Herbier, président du conseil d'administration (1947–1967), ANF-IDHEC-20100344/30; and Lucien Aguettand, "Pour un centre de recherches et d'études cinématographiques," February 10, 1952, 3, Dossiers, rapports et essais relatifs aux arts et opérateurs du spectacle, ANF-IDHEC-20100344/32.

55. Rémy Tessonneau to Marcel L'Herbier, April 4, 1967, Correspondances adressées à Marcel L'Herbier, président du conseil d'administration (1947–1967), ANF-IDHEC-20100344/30.

56. Marcel L'Herbier, "Allocution de M. Marcel L'Herbier le 10 janvier à la séance inaugurale de l'Institut des Hautes Études Cinematographiques," reprinted in L'Herbier, *La tête qui tourne*, 322–323.

57. Marcel L'Herbier, undated form letter, Organisation des services—Presentation et fonctionnement, ANF-IDHEC-20100344/29.

58. L'Herbier, *La tête qui tourne*, 321.

59. L'Herbier, *La tête qui tourne*, 321.

60. Form letter, Ministère des Affaires Étrangères to the Mexican cultural attaché, undated (c. 1945–1947), FRMAE 241QO-4.

61. IDHEC, *Première Rencontre*, 110.

62. Percentages were calculated from a list of IDHEC graduates compiled by Rémy Tessonneau. CF-AGP258-B36. See also IDHEC, *Annuaire des anciens éleves de l'IDHEC*.

63. IDHEC, *Première Rencontre*, 91.

64. Lods, *Professional Training of Film Technicians*, 50; IDHEC, *Première Rencontre*, 108; and IDHEC administrative council meeting notes, January 22, 1952, 4, Conseil d'administration 1943–1967, ANF-IDHEC-20100344/24. In 1951, the minimum wage in Paris was 100 francs per hour; forty hours of labor at this rate would have been needed to pay the entrance exam fees. Salles Gomes received one such grant in 1946 but never completed his studies at IDHEC. Melo Souza, *Paulo Emílio no Paraíso*, 266.

65. In 1959, IDHEC received 66,462,000 francs from the CNC, 600,000 francs from exam and registration fees, and 4,400,000 from tuition (that is, 6 percent of the budget). IDHEC administrative council meeting notes, November 8, 1959, 4, Conseil d'administration 1943–1967, ANF-IDHEC-20100344/24.

66. IDHEC, *Première Rencontre*, 93.

67. See IDHEC, *Les carrières du cinéma*, 1954, 24–26; and IDHEC, *Première Rencontre*, 95.

68. IDHEC, *Les carrières du cinéma*, 1954, 54–56; and Crisp, *Classic French Cinema*, 206.

69. IDHEC, *Première Rencontre*, 95.

70. [Alfred] Rosier, Directeur de la Main d'œuvre to Rémy Tessonneau, December 30, 1955, IDHEC—Commission d'étude de l'organisation et de la formation professionnelle de la cinématographie, ANF-IDHEC-20100344/49.

71. Untitled manuscript document listing 1943 entry criteria, "Concours d'entrée—1943–1948," Bibliothèque nationale, France-Arts du spectacle—Fonds Marcel L'Herbier (hereafter BNF-AS-FMH), FOL-LOL-198 (111); and IDHEC, "Programme de concours d'entrée pour la section Réalisateurs, Directeurs de production, Monteurs," 1943, Organisation des services—Presentation et fonctionnement, ANF-IDHEC-20100344/29.

72. "Concours d'entrée—1943–1948," BNF-AS-FMH, FOL-LOL-198 (111).

73. IDHEC, *Annuaire des anciens éleves de l'IDHEC.*

74. IDHEC, *Les carrières du cinéma et de la television*, 1954, 39, 47; "Programs de concours d'entrée," 1960, included in Ghislain Cloquet, "La formation professionelle des opérateurs de prise de vues," report to Congrès international des écoles de cinéma et télévision, Dossiers, rapports et essais relatifs aux arts et opérateurs du spectacle, ANF-IDHEC-20100344/32.

75. Crisp, *Classic French Cinema*, 206.

76. "Note sur l'activité de L'I.D.H.E.C," unsigned manuscript document, November 10, 1951, BNF-AS-FMH, 4-COL-198 (1743).

77. "Note sur l'activité de L'I.D.H.E.C," BNF-AS-FMH, 4-COL-198 (1743).

78. "Note concernant l'activité des anciens élèves de l'IDHEC," November 12, 1951, BNF-AS-FMH, 4-COL-198 (1743).

79. Armando Pinheiro de Mello, "O Brasil tem escolas de cinema," *A Cena Muda*, May 27, 1953, 24–25. On the Seminário, see Uchôa, "O Seminário de Cinema do MASP."

80. Marcel L'Herbier to Louis Joxe, February 25, 1952; and Louis Joxe to Marcel L'Herbier, March 12, 1952, BNF-AS-FMH, 4-COL-198 (1741).

81. Ruth Karpf, "School of the Cinema," *New York Times*, October 19, 1947, SM33.

82. IDHEC, *Première Rencontre*, 10.

83. IDHEC, *Deuxième Rencontre*, 3, 15–16, IDHEC—Programmes des cours—Congrès International des Ecoles de Cinéma et de Télévision, CF-SADOUL755-B55; and IDHEC administrative council meeting notes, July 23, 1953, 1–2, Conseil d'administration 1943–1967, ANF-IDHEC-20100344/24.

84. Rémy Tessonneau to [Jean-Pierre] Campredon, December 14, 1961, Relations avec le Ministère des affaires étrangères, ANF-IDHEC-20100344/51.

85. IDHEC, *Deuxième Rencontre*, 15.

86. Rémy Tessonneau to Jean-Pierre Campredon, June 9, 1964, Relations avec le Ministère des affaires étrangères, ANF-IDHEC-20100344/51.

87. Williams, "CILECT," 100–102.

88. Petrie and Stoneman, *Educating Film-makers*, 5.

89. Resolution, Association de l'IDHEC meeting, April 22, 1963, Statuts et listes des membres actifs de l'Association de 1951 a 1963, ANF-20100344/23; and IDHEC administrative council meeting notes, May 31, 1961, 1, 5, Conseil d'administration 1943–1967, ANF-IDHEC-20100344/24.

90. "Pequenas notas," *Jornal do Dia*, March 12, 1965, 7.

91. Rémy Tessonneau to M. Campredon, June 4, 1963, Relations avec le Ministère des affaires étrangères, ANF-IDHEC-20100344/51.

92. Rémy Tessonneau to Jean Basdevant, September 14, 1965, Ministère des affaires étrangères—Correspondance (1955–1968), ANF-IDHEC-20100344/51.

93. Schwartzman et al., "Interview with Margot Benacerraf," 55.
94. Vincenot, "Germán Puig, Ricardo Vigón et Henri Langlois," 21, 24.
95. Abraham Zalzman to Marion Michelle, August 30, 1960, Courrier reçu pour le secrétariat 1960–1963, FIAF-COR/003.
96. Vincenot, "Germán Puig, Ricardo Vigón et Henri Langlois," 25.
97. Tomás Gutiérrez Alea to Germán Puig, November 22, 1952, reprinted in Ibarra, *Titón*, 23.
98. On foreign students' dissatisfaction with this aspect of IDHEC, see, for instance, IDHEC, *Première Rencontre*, 34, 108; and "Notes on the Institut des Hautes Études Cinématographiques," *Documentary Film News*, July 1948, 83.
99. IDHEC, *Première Rencontre*, 34, 108.
100. IDHEC administrative council meeting notes, April 15, 1966, 2, Conseil d'administration 1943–1967, ANF-IDHEC-20100344/24.
101. Melo Souza, *Paulo Emílio no Paraíso*, 292.
102. Schwartzman et al., "Interview with Margot Benacerraf," 55.
103. Luis Vicens to Amy B. Courvoisier, July 18, 1952, uncatalogued document, FPFC; Schwartzman et al., "Interview with Margot Benacerraf," 55.
104. Fernando Birri, "Seminario Memoria y Futuro: La Escuela Documental de Santa Fe y el Nuevo Cine Latinoamericano," 11, box 28, folder 55, JH-FBAMA.
105. Interview with Fernando Birri, "Las raíces del realismo documental" in Burton-Carvajal, *Cine y cambio social en América Latina*, 28. Interviews were conducted in Spanish, but the volume first appeared in English as Burton-Carvajal, *Cinema and Social Change in Latin America*. I use my translation rather than the published English-language version, which omits some details.
106. On this genre, see Jacobs, Cleppe, and Latsis, *Art in the Cinema*.
107. Schwartzman et al., "Interview with Margot Benacerraf," 55; and Fernando Pérez, "Cuatro entrevistas en Venezuela: Margot Benacerraf," *Cine Cubano* 89/90 (1973): 85.
108. Schwartzman et al., "Interview with Margot Benacerraf," 60–61.
109. Schwartzman et al., "Interview with Margot Benacerraf," 68–69; and Grioni, *Margot Benacerraf*, 31.
110. Burton-Carvajal, "*Araya* across Time and Space," 62–63; see also Grioni, *Margot Benacerraf*, 69.
111. Burton-Carvajal, "*Araya* across Time and Space."
112. Schwartzman et al., "Interview with Margot Benacerraf," 66–67; and Howie Movshovitz, "Restored 'Araya' Revisits Venezuela's Salt Mines," *National Public Radio*, October 7, 2009, www.npr.org/templates/story/story.php?storyId=113570680.
113. Keating, "Volcano and the Barren Hill," 201, 215.
114. West and West, "Conversation with Marta Rodríguez"; and Pineda Moncada, "Entre la verdad y la ilusión," 71.
115. Aguilera Skvirsky, *Process Genre*, 149–151.
116. Wickham-Crowley, "Winners, Losers, and Also-Rans," 142.
117. Levy, *Higher Education and the State in Latin America*, 38–47.
118. Levy, *Higher Education and the State in Latin America*, 40–41.

119. Rozsa, "On the Edge of the Screen," 54, 59; and Pedro R. Noa Romero, "La primera savia nutricia: la Filmoteca Universitaria," *Cine Cubano*, July–December 2011, 110–115.

120. Valdés-Rodríguez, *El cine, industria y arte de nuestro tiempo*.

121. Rozsa, "Film Culture and Education in Republican Cuba"; Rozsa, "Filmoteca Universitaria and Mid-Century Cinephilia at the University of Havana," forthcoming. See also Eduardo Manet, "Cine y cultura en la Universidad de la Habana," *Cine Cubano*, 1, no. 2 (1960): 54–55.

122. Robles and Bilbao, "Vanguardia, Universidad y Cinematografía." The institute was shuttered in 1966 after student protests against military intervention in public universities following the coup that overthrew Arturo Illia, foreshadowing the closures of university film schools across the region in the 1970s.

123. Morato Zanatto, "O Curso para Dirigentes de Cineclubes."

124. On the Instituto de Cinematografía Educativa, see Álvarez, Colleoni, and Horta, "El cine en el aula."

125. On sponsored films at the "Escuela Documental de Santa Fe," see Neil and Peralta, "1956–1976,"46–49.

126. Wschebor Pellegrino, "Del documento al documental uruguayo," n.p.

127. Wschebor Pellegrino, "Los orígenes del cine científico en Uruguay," 46–47.

128. Wschebor Pellegrino, "Ouvrir les boîtes," 219– 228.

129. Wschebor Pellegrino, "Ouvrir les boîtes," 228–257.

130. Wschebor Pellegrino, "Cine, universidad y política audiovisual."

131. Walther Dassori Barthet to Manuel González Casanova, May 18, 1966, folder 2, RR17a–Correspondencia enviada/recibida Cinemateca Uruguaya, CU-AWDB; and Walther Dassori Barthet, "Una experiencia de cine científico y público general," September 1969, folder 2, P5-ICUR/Cine documental y científico, CU-AWDB.

132. Lowry, *Filmology Movement*. A faculty member in filmology was hired by the ICUR in 1969. "Promoción de la Filmología en el Uruguay," undated manuscript document [1968], folder 3-X3, CU-AWDB; Walther Dassori Barthet, "Informe de la comisión especial nombrada por el consejo administrativo de Cine Universitario del Uruguay para estudiar la organización de iniciativas relacionadas con la filmología," April 29, 1968, folder 3-X10, CU-AWDB; and "Ciclo sobre Cine–Programa de conferencias organizadas por el Instituto de Cinematografía de la Universidad de la República," 1957, CU-AWDB.

133. "Informe sobre las actividades efectuadas por la Academia de Cine y Fotografía de la Universidad Católica de Chile," "Relación de los trabajos y estudios efectuados por la AFUC, en el período abril–diciembre de 1954," Archivo Histórico de la Pontificia Universidad Católica de Chile-Rectorado de Alfredo Silva Santiago (hereafter AHPUCC-RASS), 06IIF-0001.

134. Fernando Barres Fabres to Rector [Alfredo Silva Santiago], July 20, 1954, AHPUCC-RASS, 06IIF-0001.

135. "Informe sobre las actividades efectuadas por la Academia de Cine y Fotografía de la Universidad Católica de Chile," 1–2, AHPUCC-RASS, 06IIF-0001.

136. "Programa a desarrollar en los años 1955 y 1956," AHPUCC-RASS, 06IIF-0001.

137. As of this writing, the output of the Instituto Fílmico and its successors can be viewed online through the website of the university's film archive, at http://archivofilmico.uc.cl/. "Memoria General del Instituto Fílmico de la Universidad Católica de Chile, agosto 1955–1967," part III, 1–2, AHPUCC-RASS, 06IIF-0501.

138. Andrés Grau to Basilio Liacuris, November 10, 1967, AHPUCC-RASS, 07IIF-0101.

139. "Memoria General del Instituto Fílmico de la Universidad Católica de Chile, agosto 1955–1967," part I, 4, AHPUCC-RASS, 06IIF-0501.

140. On Sanjinés's time at the Instituto Fílmico, see Wood, *El espectador pensante*, 27–28.

141. For documents relating to the film's production, see Archivo Histórico de la Pontificia Universidad Católica de Chile, Rectorado de Fernando Castillo Velasco, 07IIF-0201.

142. Hurtado, "50 años de teatro en la Universidad Católica," 45–46.

143. Mouesca, *El documental chileno*, 64; and Salinas Muñoz and Stange Marcus, *Historia del Cine Experimental*, 48–49.

144. The other founding members were Enrique Rodríguez and Pedro Chaskel. Salinas Muñoz and Stange Marcus, *Historia del Cine Experimental*, 33–35.

145. Salinas Muñoz and Stange Marcus, *Historia del Cine Experimental*, 35–40.

146. "Se organiza Centro de Cine: 4 cortometrajes da en junio," *Boletín de la Universidad de Chile* 2 (1959): 67.

147. Horta Canales, "La subversión de las imágenes."

148. A brief account of the creation of film schools in Argentina, including lists of prominent graduates, can be found in Feldman, *La generación del 60*, 38–39.

149. Falicov, "Hollywood's Rogue Neighbor," 257.

150. Núbila, *Historia del cine argentino*; see also España, *Cine argentino*.

151. Castagna, "La generación del 60."

152. A third university film program was founded at the Universidad Nacional de Córdoba in 1964. See Moreschi, "Construir la memoria."

153. Cossalter, "Del centro a la periferia," 11–12.

154. Jorge Eneas Cromberg, "Hacer cine pero también entenderlo," *Revista de Cine*, March 1966, 86.

155. "El INC: Mucho más que un banco de préstamos," *Revista de Cine*, July–August 1965, 60.

156. Eneas Cromberg, "Hacer cine pero también entenderlo," *Revista de Cine*, March 1966, 87.

157. "Escuelas de cine: Para un nuevo creador responsable," *Revista de Cine*, March 1966, 51.

158. Massari, Peña, and Vallina, *Escuela de Cine*, 12–13.

159. Massari, Peña, and Vallina, *Escuela de Cine*, 16–17, 22; and Truglio, "El cine de las escuelas de cine," 316–317.

160. Ulises Craig, "Mentes nuevas para un cine nuevo," *El Mundo*, May 6, 1959, unpaginated press clipping, MCPDH.

161. Craig, "Mentes nuevas para un cine nuevo," MCPDH.

162. Truglio, "El cine de las escuelas de cine," 318; and Massari, Peña, and Vallina, *Escuela de Cine*, 21.
163. "Rapport de l'Argentine," XIIIe Congres de la FIAF, 1957, 49, FIAF-CON/011A.
164. Massari, Peña, and Vallina, *Escuela de Cine*, 24–25.
165. Truglio, "El cine de las escuelas de cine," 320–321.
166. The university moved to eliminate the program in 1976, and it ceased operations in 1978. Massari, Peña, and Vallina, *Escuela de Cine*, 33–34.
167. Neil and Peralta, "1956–1976," 17–18.
168. Angela Romero Vera, "Prólogo," *Exposición de Fotodocumentales*, Series E2.5A, Escritos con Fernando Birri—Didácticos—Escuela Documental de Santa Fe, box 15, folder 40, JH-FBAMA.
169. Romero Vera, "Prólogo," n.p.
170. Interview with Fernando Birri, "Las raíces del realismo documental," 30. My translation.
171. Birri, *La escuela documental de Santa Fe*, 18. On the Italian photodocumentary's impact in Argentina, see Mestman and Moore, "On the Origins of Birri's Documentary School of Santa Fe," 154–157.
172. Birri, *La escuela documental de Santa Fe*, 18–19.
173. Birri, *La escuela documental de Santa Fe*, 19.
174. Truglio, "El cine de las escuelas de cine," 309.
175. Birri, *La escuela documental de Santa Fe*, 30, 53.
176. Truglio, "El cine de las escuelas de cine," 309.
177. Gutiérrez and Benito, *El Instituto de Cinematografía*, 15; and Neil and Peralta, "1956–1976," 33–34,
178. Birri, *La escuela documental de Santa Fe*, 131–132; undated organizational chart, box 4, folder 43, JH-FBAMA; and Sendrós, *Fernando Birri*, 14–17. For a full list of courses, see Neil and Peralta, "1956–1976," 29.
179. Eduardo Pallero to university rector Josué Gollán, quoted in Neil and Peralta, "1956–1976," 28.
180. Birri, *La escuela documental de Santa Fe*, 130–131.
181. "Instituto de Cinematografía: Organograma 1960" and undated organizational chart, box 4, folder 43, FBAMA; and Gutiérrez and Benito, *El Instituto de Cinematografía*, 14–15.
182. Sendrós, *Fernando Birri*, 14. The requirement of middle school completion was reinstituted in 1969. Neil and Peralta, "1956–1976," 29.
183. Birri, *La escuela documental de Santa Fe*, 56–57.
184. Mestman and Moore, "On the Origins of Birri's Documentary School of Santa Fe," 151.
185. Mestman and Moore, "On the Origins of Birri's Documentary School of Santa Fe," 160–161.
186. Documents relating to the incident are reprinted in Birri, *La escuela documental de Santa Fe*, 167–172.
187. Gutiérrez and Benito, *El Instituto de Cinematografía*, 18–20.
188. For instance, protocols for hiring instructors were formalized. Neil and Peralta, "1956–1976," 36–38.
189. Neil and Peralta, "1956–1976," 43–44.

190. Truglio, "El cine de las escuelas de cine," 314; and Neil and Peralta, "1956–1976," 56–72.
191. On this perceived decline of Mexican cinema, see Salvador Elizondo, "El cine mexicano y la crisis," *Nuevo Cine*, August 1962, 4–8, reprinted in Fundación Mexicana de Cineastas, *Hojas de cine* 2:37–46; Ramírez Berg, *Cinema of Solitude*, 37–46; and Baugh, "Developing History/Historicizing Development."
192. Pensado, *Rebel Mexico*, 21–23.
193. Eder Rozencwaig, *Desafío a la estabilidad*.
194. Cohn, "Mexican Intelligentsia."
195. The party was previously known as the Partido Nacional Revolucionario (1929–1938) and the Partido de la Revolución Mexicana (1938–1946).
196. Pensado, *Rebel Mexico*, 19.
197. "Manifiesto del Grupo Nuevo Cine," *Nuevo Cine*, April 1961, 3, reprinted in Fundación Mexicana de Cineastas, *Hojas de cine* 2:33–35.
198. Rodríguez Rodríguez, "Entrevista a Manuel González Casanova," 129.
199. "Manifiesto del Grupo Nuevo Cine," 33.
200. "Manifiesto del Grupo Nuevo Cine," 33.
201. "Manifiesto del Grupo Nuevo Cine," 33.
202. "Manifiesto del Grupo Nuevo Cine," 33.
203. "Manifiesto del Grupo Nuevo Cine," 34.
204. Zryd, "In Defense of Institutions in Experimental Film and Media." Zryd stresses the grassroots and often ephemeral nature of experimental film institutions.
205. Ramírez Berg, *Cinema of Solitude*, 44–47.
206. Bourdieu, "Field of Cultural Production"; and Bürger, *Theory of the Avant-Garde*.
207. "Manifiesto del Grupo Nuevo Cine," 34–35.
208. González Casanova, *¿Qué es un cine-club?*, 23.
209. Hagener, *Moving Forward, Looking Back*, 11–14.
210. Paz, "La tradición de la ruptura."
211. For an overview, see Medina Ávila, "Cultura y espíritu."
212. Jaime García Terres, "El cine en la Universidad," *Revista de la Universidad de México*, March 1954, 22–23.
213. Rodríguez Álvarez, *Manuel González Casanova*, 27; and García Terres, "El cine en la Universidad," 23.
214. For an in-depth account, see Rodríguez Álvarez, "Raíces y metamórfosis del cineclubismo universitario."
215. "Funciones del 'Cine Club de la Universidad,'" *Gaceta de la Universidad*, November 7, 1955, 8.
216. Rodríguez Álvarez, *Manuel González Casanova*, 28.
217. Rodríguez Álvarez, *Manuel González Casanova*, 29.
218. On Monsiváis's curating practice and program notes, see Rodríguez Álvarez, "Monsiváis y la cinefilia."
219. Dirección General de Difusión Cultural, *Anuario 1963 and Anuario 1965*, n.p.
220. Universidad Nacional Autónoma de México, *25 años "Filmoteca UNAM*, 11–12.
221. González Casanova, "El CUEC, un sueño imposible," 31–32.

222. González Casanova, "El CUEC, un sueño imposible," 31–32.
223. Rodríguez Rodríguez, "*El grito*," 35.
224. Joskowicz Bobrownicki, "Algunas reflexiones sobre el área de realización," 42.
225. González Casanova, "El CUEC, un sueño imposible," 32–33.
226. González Casanova, "Despertar la conciencia del creador," 54; "Inauguran el edicio del Centro Universitario de Estudios Cinematográficos," *Gaceta UNAM*, April 7, 1975, 20.
227. Rodríguez Cruz, *El 68 en el cine mexicano*, 18; and Rodríguez Rodríguez, "*El grito*," 39.
228. For more on Revueltas's approach to screenwriting see Revueltas, *El conocimiento cinematográfico*.
229. Dirección General de Difusión Cultural, *Anuario 1963*, n.p.
230. Dirección General de Difusión Cultural, *Anuario 1965*, n.p.
231. This was not García Márquez's first foray into film education; in 1960, he had outlined plans for a film school in Barranquilla, Colombia. See Gilard, "García Márquez."
232. Fernández Violante, "Gabriel García Márquez," 16, 2.
233. Dirección General de Difusión Cultural, *Anuario 1965*, n.p.
234. Trabajos presentados por alumnos de la materia Cine y Artes Plásticas, Caja 6, Expediente 35 and Caja 6, Expediente 37, Sección Escolar, Archivo Histórico de la Universidad Nacional Autónoma de México-Fondo Centro Universitario de Estudios Cinematográficos (hereafter AHUNAM-CUEC).
235. Registro de Colegiaturas 1966–1969, Caja 6, Expediente 30, Sección Escolar, AHUNAM-CUEC; and Joskowicz Bobrownicki, "Algunas reflexiones sobre el área de realización," 42.
236. Relaciones de asistencia de profesores, 1966, Caja 1, Expediente 1 and Expediente 2, Sección Escolar, AHUNAM-CUEC.
237. Relaciones de asistencia de profesores, 1966; and Relaciones de asistencia de alumnos 1966, Caja 3, Expediente 14, AHUNAM-CUEC; and Rodríguez Rodríguez, "*El grito*," 35.
238. Fernández Violante, "Gabriel García Márquez," 19.
239. Facturas 1967–1969, Caja 11, Expediente 68, Sección Administrativa, AHUNAM-CUEC.
240. Relaciones de asistencia de alumnos 1966, Caja 3, Expediente 15, Sección Escolar, AHUNAM-CUEC.
241. Trabajos de alumnos, 1967, Caja 7, Expediente 39 and Expediente 40, Sección Documentos del CUEC, AHUNAM-CUEC.
242. Jaime Ponce Barandika, "Situación actual del cine mexicano," 1, Trabajos de alumnos, 1967, Caja 7, Expediente 40, Sección Documentos del CUEC, AHUNAM-CUEC.
243. Miguel Ángel Sanromán, "Trabajo sobre cine mexicano: Su situación y posible solución," 2. Trabajos de alumnos, 1967, Caja 7, Expediente 40, Sección Documentos del CUEC, AHUNAM-CUEC.
244. José Luis Lira, "La situación actual del cine mexicano," 2, Trabajos de alumnos, 1967, Caja 7, Expediente 40, Sección Documentos del CUEC, AHUNAM-CUEC.

245. Luc-Toni Kuhn, "La situación crítica del cine mexicano y su solución," Trabajos de alumnos, 1967, Caja 7, Expediente 40, Sección Documentos del CUEC, AHUNAM-CUEC.
246. Rodríguez Cruz, *El 68 en el cine mexicano*, 18.
247. Muñiz García, "*El grito, México 1968*," 414.
248. Rodríguez Cruz, *El 68 en el cine mexicano*, 18.
249. Rodríguez Rodríguez, "*El grito*," 43, 50–52.
250. Rodríguez Cruz, *El 68 en el cine mexicano*, 20; and Rodríguez Rodríguez, "*El grito*," 45.
251. Rodríguez Cruz, *El 68 en el cine mexicano*, 20.
252. Rodríguez Rodríguez, "Entrevista con Manuel González Casanova," 139; and Rodríguez Rodríguez, "*El grito*," 47–48.
253. Rodríguez Rodríguez, "*El grito*," 53–56.
254. Ramírez Berg, *Cinema of Solitude*, 44–50.
255. González Casanova, "Participation of Our Schools," 3.
256. González Casanova, "Participation of Our Schools," 4.
257. González Casanova, "Participation of Our Schools," 3.
258. González Casanova, "Participation of Our Schools," 3.
259. González Casanova, "Participation of Our Schools," 7.

CONCLUSION

1. On this turn in UNESCO policy, see Brouillette, *UNESCO and the Fate of the Literary*.
2. Santacreu and Trelles, "La Cinemateca Uruguaya," 106–109.
3. Susan Sontag, "The Decay of Cinema," *New York Times*, February 25, 1996, sec. 6, 60.
4. Keller, *Anxious Cinephilia*.
5. See Tashiro, "Videophilia"; and Kendrick, "Aspect Ratios and Joe Six-Packs."
6. Shambu, *New Cinephilia*. Elsaesser uses the phrases "cinephilia take one" and "cinephilia take two" in "Cinephilia, or the Uses of Disenchantment." See also Lucia and Hamid, *Cinéaste on Film Criticism, Programming, and Preservation in the New Millennium*; and Tryon, *On-Demand Culture*.
7. See Frey and Sayad, *Film Criticism in the Digital Age*.
8. Suárez, "New Buildings, New Pathways."
9. See, for instance, White, *Women's Cinema/World Cinema*; and Schoonover and Galt, *Queer Cinema in the World*.
10. Shambu, "For a New Cinephilia," 34.

Bibliography

ARCHIVES

ANF	Archives nationales, Pierrefitte-sur-Seine, France	
	CNC	Centre national de la cinématographie
	IDHEC	Fonds du Centre artistique et technique des jeunes du cinéma (CATJC) (1941–1948) et de l'Institut des hautes études cinématographiques (IDHEC) (1943–1948)
AHPUCC	Archivo Histórico de la Pontificia Universidad Católica de Chile, Santiago de Chile	
	RASS	Rectorado de Alfredo Silva Santiago
	RFCV	Rectorado de Fernando Castillo Velasco
AHUNAM	Archivo Histórico de la Universidad Nacional Autónoma de México, Mexico City	
	CUEC	Fondo Centro Universitario de Estudios Cinematográficos
B-ENERC	Biblioteca de la Escuela Nacional de Experimentación y Realización Cinematográfica, Buenos Aires	
BNF	Bibliothèque nationale, France—Site Richelieu, Paris	
	AS-FMH	Arts du spectacle—Fonds Marcel L'Herbier
CB	Cinemateca Brasileira, São Paulo	
	AH	Archivo Histórico
	APESG	Arquivo Paulo Emílio Salles Gomes
CF	Cinémathèque française, Paris	
	AGP	Fonds Anne et Gérard Philipe

	FIFA	Festival Internacional du Film de Cannes—Service Administration
	FIFR	Festival Internacional du Film de Cannes—Service Régie
	SADOUL	Fonds Georges Sadoul
CU		Cinemateca Uruguaya, Montevideo
	AWDB	Archivo Walther Dassori Barthet
FIAF		Fédération internationale des archives du film, Brussels, Belgium
FPFC		Fundación Patrimonio Fílmico Colombiano, Bogotá
		Documents are uncatalogued.
FRMAE		Ministère des Affaires Étrangères, La Courneuve, France
	554 INVA	Association française d'action artistique—Service des échanges artistiques
	241QO	Direction générale des relations culturelles
	100QO/21	Amérique/Mexique 1944–1952
JH		John Hay Library, Brown University, Providence, United States
	FBAMA	Fernando Birri Archive of Multimedia Arts
MCPDH		Museo del Cine Pablo C. Ducrós Hicken, Buenos Aires, Argentina
MAM-Rio		Museu de Arte Moderna do Rio de Janeiro, Brazil

SECONDARY SOURCES

Abel, Richard. *French Film Theory and Criticism: A History/Anthology*. Volume I, *1907–1939*. Princeton, N.J.: Princeton University Press, 1993.

Acevedo-Muñoz, Ernesto. *Buñuel and Mexico: The Crisis of National Cinema*. Berkeley: University of California Press, 2003.

Acland, Charles R. "Classrooms, Clubs, and Community Circuits: Cultural Authority and the Film Council Movement, 1946–1957." In *Inventing Film Studies*, edited by Lee Grieveson and Haidee Wasson, 149–181. Durham, NC: Duke University Press, 2008.

Acland, Charles R., and Haidee Wasson, eds. *Useful Cinema*. Durham, NC: Duke University Press, 2011.

Adamovksy, Ezequiel. *Historia de la clase media argentina: Apogeo y decadencia de una ilusión*. Buenos Aires: Planeta, 2009.

Aguilera Skvirsky, Salomé. *The Process Genre: Cinema and the Aesthetic of Labor*. Durham, NC: Duke University Press, 2020.

Álvarez, Analía, Daniela Colleoni, and Luis Horta. "El cine en el aula: El Instituto de Cinematografía Educativa de la Universidad de Chile (1929–1948)." *Cuadernos Chilenos de Historia de la Educación* 2 (2014): 20–46.

Américo Ribeiro, José. *O cinema em Belo Horizonte: Do cineclubismo à produção cinematográfica na década de 60*. Belo Horizonte: Editora Universidade Federal de Minas Gerais.

Amieva Collado, Mariana. "Cine Arte del SODRE en la conformación de un campo audiovisual en Uruguay: Políticas públicas y acciones individuales." *Cine Documental* 6 (2012). http://revista.cinedocumental.com.ar/6/articulos_01.html.

———. "¿Cómo el Uruguay no hay? La participación del Festival de Cine Documental y Experimental del SODRE en las redes de festivales y sus particularidades." *Cine Documental* 18 (2018): 8–36.

———. "El 'amateur avanzado' como cine nacional: El caso del cine uruguayo en la década de 1950." *Imagofagia* 16 (2017): 142–166.

———. "La conformación del campo cinematográfico en Uruguay 1944–1963: Políticas públicas, cineclubismo y la emergencia del movimiento de realizadores," PhD diss., Universidad Nacional de La Plata, 2021.

Andrade, Rudá de. *Cronologia da cultura cinematográfica no Brasil*. São Paulo: Cinemateca Brasileira, 1962.

———. "L'action des cine-clubs et des cinémathèques en Amérique Latine pour le développement de la culture cinématographique." Roundtable presentation, "Le cinéma en Amérique Latine," at the II Rassegna del Cinema Latinoamericano, Santa Margherita Ligure, May 16, 1961.

Andrew, Dudley. "IDHEC." *Journal of the University Film Association* 35, no. 1 (1983): 50–54.

———. "Time Zones and Jet Lag: The Flows and Phases of World Cinema." In *World Cinemas, Transnational Perspectives*, edited by Nataša Ďurovičová and Kathleen Newman, 59–89. New York: Routledge, 2010.

Ang, Ien, Yudhishthir Raj Isar, and Philip Mar. "Cultural Diplomacy: Beyond the National Interest?" *International Journal of Cultural Policy* 21, no. 4 (2015): 365–381.

Araújo Quental, José Luiz de. "A preservação cinematográfica no Brasil e a construção de uma cinemateca na Belacap: A Cinemateca do Museu de Arte Moderna do Rio de Janeiro." Master's thesis, Universidade Federal Fluminense, 2010.

Arias, Cecilia. "Gobiernos reformistas en Uruguay 1947–1958: ¿profundización de la democracia en los inicios de la Guerra Fría?" *Nuevo Mundo Mundos Nuevos* (2018), n.p.

Arias Osorio, María Fernanda. "Movie Audiences, Modernity, and Urban Identities in Cali, Colombia, 1945–1980." PhD diss., Indiana University, 2014.

Arndt, Richard T. *The First Resort of Kings: American Cultural Diplomacy in the Twentieth Century*. Dulles, VA: Potomac Books, 2005.

Artundo, Patricia M. "Institución, arte y sociedad: la Asociación Amigos del Arte." In *Amigos del Arte, 1924–1942*, edited by Patricia M. Artundo and Marcelo E. Pacheco, 13–30. Buenos Aires: Museo de Arte Latinoamericano de Buenos Aires, 2008.

Askari, Kaveh. *Making Movies into Art: Picture Craft from the Magic Lantern to Early Hollywood*. London: British Film Institute, 2014.

Avancini, Atílio, and Julianna Penna. "Antologia da Crítica Cinematográfica em *Vidas Secas*." *Revista Brasileira de História da Mídia* 3, no. 2 (2014): 81–90.

Baecque, Antoine de. *La cinéphilie: Invention d'un regard, histoire d'une culture 1944–1968*. Paris: Librarie Arthème Fayard, 2003.

Baldi, Alfredo. *La scuola italiana del cinema, Il Centro Sperimentale di Cinematografia dalla storia alla cronaca (1930–2017)*. Soveria Mannelli: Rubbettino, 2018.

Balous, Suzanne. *L'action culturelle française dans la monde*. Paris: Presses universitaires de France, 1970.
Barbosa Cruz, Mario, A. Ricardo López Pedreros, and Claudia Stern, *The Middle Classes in Latin America: Subjectivities, Practices, and Genealogies*. New York: Routledge, 2022.
Barón Leal, Luis Alfredo. "Los cinemas bogotanos: Los edificios de la hechicera criatura." In *Bogota fílmica: Ensayos sobre cine y patrimonio*, edited by Sergio Becerra Venegas, 122–172. Bogotá: Instituto Distrital de las Artes, 2012.
Barr-Melej, Patrick. *Reforming Chile: Cultural Politics, Nationalism, and the Rise of the Middle Class*. Chapel Hill: University of North Carolina Press, 2002.
Bartram, Faye. "Reel Results after One Week: The Cinema and French Cold War Diplomacy with the USSR." *Journal of the Western Society for French History* 44 (2016): 30–41.
———. "35mm Bridges: Cultural Relations and Film Exchange between France and the Soviet Union, 1945 to 1972." PhD diss., University of Iowa, 2017.
Baugh, Scott L. "Developing History/Historicizing Development in Mexican Nuevo Cine Manifestoes around 'la Crisis.'" *Film & History* 34, no. 2 (2004): 25–37.
Bazin, André. *The Cinema of Cruelty: From Buñuel to Hitchcock*. Translated by Sabine d'Estrée. New York: Seaver Books, 1982.
Beauchamp, Cary, and Henri Béhar, *Hollywood on the Riviera: The Inside Story of the Cannes Film Festival*. New York: William Morrow, 1992.
Becerra Venegas, Sergio. "Colombia: En torno a Camilo Torres y el Movimiento Estudiantil." In *Las rupturas del 68 en el cine latinoamericano*, edited by Mariano Mestman, 217–248. Buenos Aires: Ediciones AKAL, 2016.
Bedoya, Ricardo. "El Cine Club de Lima." *Contratexto* 17 (2009): 175–182
Bethell, Leslie, and Ian Roxborough. "Introduction: The Postwar Conjuncture in Latin America—Democracy, Labor, and the Left." In *Latin America between the Second World War and the Cold War, 1944–1948*, edited by Leslie Bethell and Ian Roxborough, 1–32. Cambridge: Cambridge University Press, 1992.
Birri, Fernando. *La escuela documental de Santa Fe: Una experiencia-piloto contra el subdesarrollo cinematográfico en Latinoamérica*. Santa Fe: Universidad Nacional del Litoral, 1964.
Blaylock, Jennifer. "The Persistent Instructor: 45 Years of *Kofi the Good Farmer* in Ghana." *Journal of African Cinemas* 12, no. 1 (2020): 71–86.
Boes, Lieven, Leen Engelen, and Roel Vande Winkel. "Clerics, Laymen, and Cinema: The Troubled Relations between the Vatican and the Office Catholique International du Cinéma." *Journal of Italian Cinema & Media Studies* 5, no. 3 (2017): 375–392.
———. "Roman Catholic Engagements with Audio-Visual Media around the World (1928–2001): Exploring and Utilizing the OCIC and UNDA Archives." Leuven, Belgium: KADOC KU Leuven, 2018.
Bolaña, María José. "El fenómeno de los 'cantegriles' montevideanos, 1946–1973." *Contemporánea* 7, no. 7 (2016): 87–104.
Bolas, Terry. *Screen Education: From Film Appreciation to Media Studies*. Bristol: Intellect, 2009.

Bonneville, Léo. *Soixante-dix ans au service du cinéma et de l'audiovisuel: Organisation catholique internationale du cinéma*. Anjou, Québec: Editions Fides, 1998.
Borde, Raymond. *Les cinémathèques*. Paris: L'Áge d'Homme, 1983.
Bordwell, David. "The Art Cinema as a Mode of Film Practice." *Film Criticism* 4, no. 1 (1979): 56–64.
Borge, Jason. "The Lettered Clown: Chaplin and the Latin American Avant-Garde." *Revista de Estudios Hispánicos* 42, no. 2 (2008): 261–278.
Boulanger, Philippe. "L'aventure du Ciné Club de Mexico." *Commentaire* 29, nos. 113–116 (2006): 1014–1018.
Bourdieu, Pierre. *Distinction: A Social Critique of the Judgement of Taste*. Translated by Richard Nice. Cambridge, MA: Harvard University Press, 1984.
———. "The Field of Cultural Production, or: The Economic World Reversed." In *The Field of Cultural Production: Essays on Art and Literature*, 29–73. New York: Columbia University Press, 1993.
———. "The Forms of Capital." In *Handbook of Theory and Research for the Sociology of Education*, edited by John Richardson, 241–258. New York: Greenwood Press, 1986.
Brancaleone, David. *Cesare Zavattini's Neo-Realism and the Afterlife of an Idea*. New York: Bloomsbury Academic, 2021.
Braun, Herbert. *The Assassination of Gaitán*. Madison: University of Wisconsin Press, 1986.
Broitman, Ana. "La cinefilia en la Argentina: Cineclubes, crítica y revistas de cine en las décadas de 1950 y 1960." PhD diss., Universidad de Buenos Aires, 2021.
Bronx, Humberto [pseud. Jaime Serna]. *El cine foro y elementos de cinematografía*. Medellín: Secretariado Arquidiocesano de Cine, 1959.
Brouillette, Sarah. *UNESCO and the Fate of the Literary*. Stanford, CA: Stanford University Press, 2019.
Bruézière, Maurice. *L'Alliance française: Histoire d'une institution*. Paris: Hachette, 1983.
Bulmer-Thomas, Victor. *The Economic History of Latin America Since Independence*. 2nd ed. Cambridge: Cambridge University Press, 2003.
Bunker, Steven B. *Creating Mexican Consumer Culture in the Age of Porfirio Díaz*. Albuquerque: University of New Mexico Press, 2012.
Bürger, Peter. *Theory of the Avant-Garde*. Translated by Michael Shaw. Manchester: Manchester University Press, 1984.
Burton-Carvajal, Julianne. "*Araya* across Time and Space: Competing Canons of National (Venezuelan) and International Film Histories." In *Visible Nations: Latin American Film and Video*, edited by Chon Noriega, 51–81. Minneapolis: University of Minnesota Press, 2000.
———, ed. *Cine y cambio social en América Latina: Imágenes de un continente*. Mexico City: Diana, 1991.
———, ed. *Cinema and Social Change in Latin America: Conversations with Filmmakers*. Austin: University of Texas Press, 1986.
Busko Valim, Alexandre. *Brazil, the United States, and the Good Neighbor Policy: The Triumph of Persuasion during World War II*. Lanham, MD: Lexington Books, 2019.

Butruce, Débora. "Cineclubismo no Brasil: Esboço de uma história." *Acervo* 16, no. 1 (2003): 117–124.

Bystrom, Kerry, Monica Popescu, and Katherine Zien, eds. *The Cultural Cold War and the Global South: Sites of Contestation and Communitas*. New York: Routledge, 2021.

Cáceres Mateus, Sergio Armando. "El cine moral y la censura, un medio empleado por la Acción Católica Colombiana 1934–1942." *Anuario de Historia Regional y de Fronteras* 16 (2011): 208–218.

Caicedo González, Juan Diego. "Langostas, libros y cine." *Ensayos: Historia y teoría del arte* 18, no. 26 (2014): 64–84.

———. "Los cineclubes bogotanos: Siguen actuando las manos del padre Hernando Salcedo Silva." In *Bogota fílmica: Ensayos sobre cine y patrimonio*, edited by Sergio Becerra Venegas, 224–269. Bogotá: Instituto Distrital de las Artes, 2012.

Casanova Delfino, Eduardo, and Miguel Ángel Campodónico. *Historias del SODRE*. Montevideo: SODRE, 2011.

Castagna, Gustavo J. "La generación del 60: Paradojas de un mito." In *Cine argentino: La otra historia*, edited by Sergio Wolf, 243–264. Buenos Aires: Ediciones Letra Buena, 1993.

Castro Ricalde, Maricruz, and Robert McKee Irwin, eds. *El cine mexicano "se impone": Mercados internacionales y penetración cultural en la época dorada*. Mexico City: Universidad Nacional Autónoma de México, 2011.

———. *Global Mexican Cinema: Its Golden Age*. London: BFI Publishing, 2013.

Ceja Alcalá, Janet. "Imperfect Archives and the Principle of Social Praxis in the History of Film Preservation in Latin America." *Moving Image* 13, no. 1 (2013) 66–97.

Česálková, Lucie. "Film as Diplomat: The Politics of Postwar Screenings at Czechoslovak Foreign Embassies." *Film History* 27, no. 1 (2015): 85–110.

Chan, Nadine. "Under the Palms: The Unruly Lives of Colonial Educational Films in British Malaya." PhD diss., University of Southern California, 2015.

Chanan, Michael. *The New Cinema of Latin America Part I: Cinema of the Humble*. Joseph Plateau Productions, 1983.

Chaubet, François. *La politique culturelle française et la diplomatie de la langue: L'Alliance Française (1883–1940)*. Paris: L'Harmattan, 2006.

Chen, Hongwei Thorn, and Sophia Gräfe. "Mapping the Nontheatrical Field: A Useful Teaching Bibliography." *Journal of Cinema and Media Studies* 6, no. 1 (2021). https://quod.lib.umich.edu/cgi/t/text/idx/j/jcms/18261332.0060.607/--mapping-the-nontheatrical-field-a-useful-teaching?rgn=main;view=fulltext.

Cherian, V. K. *India's Film Society Movement: The Journey and Its Impact*. Los Angeles: Sage, 2016.

Chomentowski, Gabrielle. "Filmmakers from Africa and the Middle East at VGIK during the Cold War." *Studies in Russian and Soviet Cinema* 13, no. 2 (2019): 189–198.

Chonchol, Jacques, and Guy Martinière. *L'Amérique latine et la latino-américainisme en France*. Paris: Éditions de l'IHEAL/L'Harmattan, 1985.

Chung, Hye Seung. *Hollywood Diplomacy: Film Regulation, Foreign Relations, and East Asian Representations.* New Brunswick, NJ: Rutgers University Press, 2020.

Clariana Rodagut, Ainamar. "Mujeres iberoamericanas mediadoras y sus redes en los cineclubes de finales de los años 20 y 30: Lola Álvarez Bravo, Victoria Ocampo y María Luz Morales." Conference presentation, 1st Seminario de Cineclubismos Latinoamericanos (virtual), 2021.

Cleppe, Birgit. "The Institutional Breeding Grounds of the Postwar Film on Art: Key Figures and Networks behind the First International Conference on Art Films." In *Art in Cinema: The Mid-Century Art Documentary*, edited by Steven Jacobs, Birgit Cleppe, and Dimitrios Latsis, 39–65. London: Bloomsbury, 2021.

Cockcroft, Eva. "Abstract Expressionism, Weapon of the Cold War." *Artforum* 12, no. 10 (1974): 39–41.

Cohn, Deborah. "The Mexican Intelligentsia, 1950–1968: Cosmopolitanism, National Identity, and the State." *Mexican Studies/Estudios Mexicanos* 21, no. 2 (2005): 141–182.

Concha Henao, Álvaro. *Historia social del cine en Colombia.* Volume II, 1930–1959. Bogotá: BlackMaria Publicaciones, 2021.

Convents, Guido. "Resisting the Lure of the Modern World: Catholics, International Politics, and the Establishment of the International Catholic Office for Cinema (1918–1928)." In *Moralizing Cinema: Film, Catholicism, and Power*, edited by Daniel Biltereyst and Daniela Treveri Gennari, 19–34. New York: Routledge, 2015.

Conway, Kelley. "'A New Wave of Spectators': Contemporary Responses to *Cléo from 5 to 7*." *Film Quarterly* 61, no. 1 (2007): 38–47.

Cormon, Catherine. "FIAF Member Service/FIAF Pool: Sharing Film Prints in the 1960s." Conference presentation, 2019 FIAF Symposium in Lausanne, April 9, 2019.

Cornick, Martyn. "French Intellectuals, Neutralism, and the Search for Peace." In *France: From the Cold War to the New World Order*, edited by Tony Chafer and Brian Jenkins, 39–52. Houndmills: Macmillan, 1998.

Corrêa, Fausto Douglas, Jr. *A Cinemateca Brasileira: Das luzes aos anos de chumbo.* São Paulo: Editora Universidade Estadual Paulista, 2010.

———. "O Cinema como instituição: A Federação Internacional dos Arquivos de Filmes, 1948–1960." PhD diss., Universidade Estadual de São Paulo, 2012.

Cortés, María Lourdes. *Los amores contrariados: Gabriel García Márquez y el cine.* Caracas: Fundación del Nuevo Cine Latinoamericano, 2014.

Cossalter, Javier. "Del centro a la periferia: Las escuelas de cine nacionales, las rupturas del cortometraje y las nuevas formas de representación de las clases populares en la transición del cine clásico al moderno." *Folia Histórica del Nordeste* 32 (2018): 7–33.

Costa, Jaime E., and Carlos Scavino, *Por amor al cine: Historia de Cine Universitario del Uruguay.* Montevideo: Taller Gráfico Impresos Flograf, 2009.

Costa Santos, Raquel. "Um trajeto católico de educação pelo/para o cinema no Brasil: Redes, práticas, memórias." PhD diss., Universidade Estadual do Sudoeste da Bahia, 2016.

Costigliola, Frank. *France and the United States: The Cold Alliance since World War II*. New York: Twayne, 1992.
Couret, Nilo. "Enduring Art Cinema." In *The Routledge Companion to Latin American Cinema*, edited by Marvin D'Lugo, Ana M. López, and Laura Podalsky, 235–248. New York: Routledge, 2017.
———. "When New Waves Crash: The Friction of Transnational Film Distribution in Brazil, 1931–1959." *Film History* 31, no. 2 (2019): 89–115.
Couselo, Jorge Miguel. *Cine argentino en capítulos sueltos*. Mar del Plata: Festival Internacional de Cine de Mar del Plata, 2008.
Cowan, Michael. *Film Societies in Austria and Germany, 1910–1933: Tracing the Social Life of Cinema*. Amsterdam: Amsterdam University Press, 2023.
Cravenne, Robert. *Le tour du monde du cinéma français*. Paris: Editions Dixit, 1995.
Creswell, Michael. *A Question of Balance: How France and the United States Created Cold War Europe*. Cambridge, MA: Harvard University Press, 2006.
Crisp, Colin. *The Classic French Cinema, 1930–1960*. Bloomington: Indiana University Press, 1993.
Cuarterolo, Andrea. "A Gaze Turned towards Europe: Modernity and Tradition in the Work of Horacio Coppola." In *Cosmopolitan Film Cultures in Latin America, 1896–1960*, edited by Rielle Navitski and Nicolas Poppe, 180–201. Bloomington: Indiana University Press, 2017.
Daquin, Louis. "Les ciné-clubs et la défense du cinéma." In *Regards neufs sur le cinéma*, edited by Jacques Chevallier, 143–147. Paris: Editions du Seuil, 1953.
De la Vega Alfaro, Eduardo. *Nuevo Cine: Edición facsimilar*. Mexico City: DGE Equibrilista, 2015.
De los Reyes, Aurelio. "La idea del cine club en México en la etapa muda." In *Atlas del cineclub: Metodologías, estrategias y herramientas*, edited by Gabriel Rodríguez Álvarez, 135–158. Mexico City: PROCINECDMX/Filmoteca UNAM, 2020.
———. *Sucedió en Jalisco o los Cristeros: De cine, cultura y aspectos del México de 1924 a 1929*. Mexico City: Universidad Nacional Autónoma de México, 2013.
Decherney, Peter. *Hollywood and the Culture Elite: How the Movies Became American*. New York: Columbia University Press, 2005.
Dimitriu, Christian. "La Cinemateca Argentina: Entrevista con Guillermo Fernández Jurado." *Journal of Film Preservation*, nos. 74–75 (2007): 15–34.
———. "La Cinemateca Uruguaya: Entrevista con Manuel Martínez Carril." *Journal of Film Preservation*, nos. 78/80 (2009): 37–58.
Dinkel, Jürgen. *The Non-Aligned Movement: Genesis, Organization, and Politics, 1927–1992*. Leiden: Brill, 2019.
Dirección General de Difusión Cultural. *Departamento de Actividades Cinematográficas: Anuario 1965*. Mexico City: Universidad Nacional Autónoma de México, 1965.
———. *Sección de Actividades Cinematográficas: Anuario 1963*. Mexico City: Universidad Nacional Autónoma de México, 1963.

Djagalov, Rossen. *From Internationalism to Postcolonialism: Literature and Cinema between the Second and Third Worlds.* Montreal: McGill-Queen's University Press, 2020.

Domínguez, Carlos María. *24 ilusiones por segundo: La historia de Cinemateca Uruguaya.* Montevideo: Cinemateca Uruguaya, 2013.

Druick, Zoë. "UNESCO, Film and Education: Mediating Postwar Paradigms of Communication." In *Useful Cinema*, edited by Charles Acland and Haidee Wasson, 81–102. Durham, NC: Duke University Press, 2011.

Dumont-Quessard, Juliette. "La défaite de 1940: Une étape dans la redéfinition des relations culturelles entre la France et les intellectuels latino-américains." In *De Gaulle et l'Amérique latine*, edited by Maurice Vaïsse, 17–36. Rennes: Presses universitaires de Rennes, 2014.

Dupont, Joan. "Searching for Nelly Kaplan." *Film Quarterly* 71, no. 4 (2018): 22–32.

Durand, José Carlos. *Arte, privilégio e distinção: Artes plásticas, arquitetura e class dirigente no Brasil, 1855–1985.* São Paulo: Editora Perspectiva, 1989.

Eder Rozencwaig, Rita, ed. *Desafío a la estabilidad: Procesos artísticos en México 1952–1967.* Mexico City: Universidad Nacional Autónoma de México, 2014.

Eineigel, Susanne. "Revolutionary Promises Encounter Urban Realities for Mexico's Middle Class, 1915–1928." In *The Making of the Middle Class: Toward a Transnational History*, edited by A. Ricardo López-Pedreros and Barbara Weinstein, 253–266. Durham, NC: Duke University Press, 2012.

Elsaesser, Thomas. "Cinephilia, or the Uses of Disenchantment." In *Cinephilia: Movies, Love, and Memory*, edited by Marijke de Valck and Malte Hagener, 27–43. Amsterdam: Amsterdam University Press, 2005.

English, James F. *The Economy of Prestige: Prizes, Awards, and the Circulation of Cultural Value.* Cambridge, MA: Harvard University Press, 2005.

España, Claudio, ed. *Cine argentino: Modernidad y vanguardias, 1957–1983.* Buenos Aires: Fondo Nacional de las Artes, 2005.

Falicov, Tamara L. "Hollywood's Rogue Neighbor: The Argentine Film Industry during the Good Neighbor Policy, 1939–1945." *The Americas* 63, no. 2 (2006): 245–260.

Fein, Seth. "From Collaboration to Containment: Hollywood and the International Political Economy of Mexican cinema after the Second World War." In *México's Cinema: A Century of Film and Filmmakers*, edited by Joanne Hershfield and David R. Maciel, 123–164. Wilmington, DE: Scholarly Resources Books, 1999.

Feldman, Simón. *La generación del 60.* Buenos Aires: Ediciones Legasa, 1990.

———, et al. "Primer Congreso Latinoamericano de Cineístas Independientes promovido por el SODRE a través de su departamento de cine-arte." In *Hojas de cine: Testimonios y documentos del Nuevo Cine Latinoamericano*, vol. 1, *Centro y Sudamérica*, edited by the Fundación Mexicana de Cineastas, 537–543. Mexico City: Fundación Mexicana de Cineastas, 1988.

Fernández, Gualberto. *Travelling en el festival de cine de Punta del Este.* Montevideo: Talleres Gráficos Prometeo, 1951.

Fernández Violante, Marcela. "Gabriel García Márquez: México, el cine y el CUEC." In *La docencia y el fenómeno fílmico: Memoria de los XXV años del CUEC, 1963–1988*, edited by Marcela Fernández Violante, 13–30. Mexico City: Universidad Nacional Autónoma de México, 1988.

Field, Thomas C., Jr., Stella Krepp, and Vanni Pettinà, eds. *Latin America and the Global Cold War*. Chapel Hill: University of North Carolina Press, 2020.

Film Daily. *The Film Daily Yearbook 1960*. New York: Wid's Film and Film Folk, 1960.

———. *The 1950 Film Daily Year Book of Motion Pictures*. New York: Wid's Film and Film Folk, 1950.

Foster, Lila. "The Cinema Section of Foto Cine Clube Bandeirante: Ideals and Reality of Amateur Film Production in São Paulo, Brazil." *Film History* 30, no. 1 (2018): 86–113.

Francese, Joseph. "The Influence of Cesare Zavattini on Latin American Cinema: Thoughts on *El joven Rebelde* and *Juan Quin Quin*." *Quarterly Review of Film and Video* 24, no. 5 (2007): 431–444.

Francia, Aldo. *Nuevo Cine Latinoamericano en Viña del Mar*. Santiago de Chile: Centro de Estudios Sociales, 1990.

Freire, Rafael de Luna. "Cópias de filmes e salas de exibição, cineclubes e cinematecas: O caso do Centro de Cultura Cinematográfica." *Faces da História* 9, no. 1 (2022): 127–148.

Frey, Mattias, and Cecilia Sayad, eds. *Film Criticism in the Digital Age*. New Brunswick, NJ: Rutgers University Press, 2015.

Frick, Caroline. *Saving Cinema: The Politics of Preservation*. Oxford: Oxford University Press, 2011.

Fundación Mexicana de Cineastas, ed. *Hojas de cine: Testimonios y documentos del Nuevo Cine Latinoamericano*. 2 vols. Mexico City: Secretaría de Educación Pública, 1988.

Gallinari, Pauline. "L'URSS au festival de Cannes 1946–1958: Un enjeu des relations franco-soviétiques à l'heure de la 'guerre froide.'" *189:5 Revue d'histoire du cinéma* 51 (2007): 22–43.

Galt, Rosalind, and Karl Schoonover. "Introduction: The Impurity of Art Cinema." In *Global Art Cinema: New Theories and Histories*, edited by Rosalind Galt and Karl Schoonover, 3–30. Oxford: Oxford University Press, 2010.

Galvão, Maria Rita. *Burguesia e cinema: O caso Veracruz*. Rio de Janeiro: Civilização Brasileira, 1981.

García Blizzard, Mónica. *The White Indians of Mexican Cinema: Racial Masquerade throughout the Golden Age*. Albany: SUNY Press, 2021.

Garcia Durand, José Carlos. *Arte, privilégio e distinção*. São Paulo: Editora Perspectiva, 1989.

García Espinosa, Julio. "Recuerdos de Zavattini." *Cinemais* 34 (2003): 83–89.

García-Rivas, Carlos. "Estrategias de vigilancia policia en el Festival Internacional de Cine de Mar del Plata entre 1959 y 1960." *Comunicación y Medios* 42 (2020): 85–93.

Garguin, Enrique. "'Los Argentinos Descendemos de los Barcos': The Racial Articulation of Middle-Class Identity in Argentina, 1920–1960." In *The

Making of the Middle Classes: Toward a Transnational History, edited by A. Ricardo López-Pedreros and Barbara Weinstein, 355–376. Durham, NC: Duke University Press, 2012.

Garland Mahler, Anne. *From the Tricontinental to the Global South: Race, Radicalism and Transnational Solidarity*. Durham, NC: Duke University Press, 2018.

Garrard-Burnett, Virginia, Mark Atwood Lawrence, and Julio E. Moreno, eds. *Beyond the Eagle's Shadow: New Histories of Latin America's Cold War*. Albuquerque: University of New Mexico Press, 2012.

Gauthier, Christophe. *La passion du cinéma: Cinéphiles, ciné-clubs et salles specialisées à Paris de 1920 a 1920*. Paris: Association Française de Recherche sur l'Histoire du Cinéma, 1999.

Ghosh, Abhija. "Memories of Action: Tracing Film Society Cinephilia in India." *BioScope* 9, no. 2 (2018): 137–164.

Gienow-Hecht, Jessica C. E., and Mark C. Donfried. "The Model of Cultural Diplomacy: Power, Distance, and the Promise of Civil Society." In *Searching for a Cultural Diplomacy*, edited by Jessica C. E. Gienow-Hecht and Mark C. Donfried, 13–29. New York: Berghahn Books, 2010.

Gilard, Jacques. "García Márquez: Un projet d'école de cinéma." *Cinémas d'Amérique Latine* 3 (1995): 24–32.

Gilburd, Eleonory. *To See Paris and Die: The Soviet Lives of Western Culture*. Cambridge, MA: Harvard University Press, 2018.

Giuliani, Luca. "African Heritage and the School on Wheels Experience." *Journal of Film Preservation* 89 (2003): 31–34.

Glaser, Amelia, and Steven S. Lee, eds. *Comintern Aesthetics*. Toronto: University of Toronto Press, 2020.

González Casanova, Manuel. 'El CUEC, un sueño imposible.'" Reprinted in *La docencia y el fenómeno fílmico: Memoria de los XXV años del CUEC, 1963–1988*, edited by Marcela Fernández Violante, 31–34. Mexico City: Universidad Nacional Autónoma de México, 1988.

———. "The Participation of Our Schools in the Defense and Diffusion of National Culture." *Journal of the University Film Association* 29, no. 2 (1977): 3–7.

———. *¿Qué es un cine-club?* Mexico City: Universidad Nacional Autónoma de México, 1962.

González Centeno, Carolina. "Raimundo Calcagno: El periodismo como vocación." *Imagofagia* 5 (2012). www.asaeca.org/imagofagia/index.php/imagofagia/article/view/700/679.

Grieveson, Lee, and Colin MacCabe, eds. *Empire and Film*. London: British Film Institute, 2011.

———. *Film and the End of Empire*. London: British Film Institute, 2011.

Grieveson, Lee, and Haidee Wasson, eds. *Inventing Film Studies*. Durham, NC: Duke University Press, 2008.

Griffith, "The Cultural Turn in Cold War Studies." *Reviews in American History* 29, no. 1 (2001): 150–157.

Grioni, Luciana. *Margot Benacerraf*. Caracas: Cinemateca Nacional de Venezuela, 2009.

Grupo Nuevo Cine. "Manifiesto del Grupo Nuevo Cine." In *Hojas de cine: Testimonios y documentos del Nuevo Cine Latinoamericano*, vol. 2, *México*, edited by Fundación Mexicana de Cineastas, 33–37. Mexico City: Secretaría de Educación Pública, 1988.

Guilbaut, Serge. *How New York Stole the Idea of Modern Art: Abstract Expressionism, Freedom, and the Cold War*. Chicago: University of Chicago Press, 1983.

Gunckel, Colin. *Mexico on Main Street: Transnational Film Culture in Los Angeles before World War II*. New Brunswick, NJ: Rutgers University Press, 2015.

Gutiérrez, Iberia Ester, and Luis Alberto Benito. *El Instituto de Cinematografía de la Universidad Nacional del Litoral*. Santa Fe: Ediciones Asociación del Magisterio de Santa Fe, 1996.

Hagener, Malte. *Moving Forward, Looking Back: The European Avant-garde and the Invention of Film Culture, 1919–1939*. Amsterdam: Amsterdam University Press, 2007.

Hankins, Leslie K. "Iris Barry, Writer and Cineaste, Forming Film Culture in London, 1924–1926: *The Adelphi*, *The Spectator*, the Film Society, and the British *Vogue*." *Modernism/Modernity* 11, no. 3 (2004): 433–515.

Harbord, Janet. "Film Festivals—Time—Event." In *The Film Festival Reader*, edited by Dina Iordanova, 127–133. St Andrews: St. Andrews University Press, 2013.

Hecht, Gabrielle. *The Radiance of France: Nuclear Power and National Identity after World War II*. Cambridge, MA: MIT Press, 1998.

Heise, Tatiana, and Andrew Tudor. "Constructing (Film) Art: Bourdieu's Field Model in a Comparative Context." *Cultural Sociology* 1, no. 2 (2007): 165–187.

Hellmann, John. *The Communitarian Third Way: Alexandre Marc and Ordre Nouveau, 1930–2000*. Montréal-Kingston: McGill-Queens University Press, 2002.

Hermanson Meister, Sarah, ed. *Fotoclubismo: Brazilian Modernist Photography, 1946–1964*. New York: Museum of Modern Art, 2021.

Hess, John. "Neo-realism and New Latin American Cinema: *Bicycle Thieves* and *Blood of the Condor*." In *Mediating Two Worlds: Cinematic Encounters in the Americas*, edited by John King, Ana M. López, and Manuel Alvarado, 104–118. London: British Film Institute, 1993.

Hintz, Eugenio. *Algo para recordar: La verdadera historia de Cine Club del Uruguay*. Montevideo: Ediciones de la Plaza, 1998.

Hjort, Mette, ed. *The Education of the Filmmaker in Africa, the Middle East, and the Americas*. London: Palgrave Macmillan, 2013.

———. *The Education of the Filmmaker in Europe, Australia, and Asia*. London: Palgrave Macmillan, 2013.

Hoek, Lotte. "Films in the Diplomatic Bag: Sovereignty, Censorship, and the Foreign Mission Film in East Pakistan and Bangladesh." In *Media and the Constitution of the Political: South Asia and Beyond*, edited by Ravi Vasudevan, 23–50. New Delhi: Sage, 2021.

Holloway, Thomas. *A Companion to Latin American History*. London: Wiley, 2008.
Horne, Janet. "Global Cultural Fronts: The Alliance Française and the Cultural Propaganda of the Free French." *European Review of History* 25, no. 2 (2018): 222–241.
———. "'To Spread the French Language Is to Extend the *Patrie*': The Colonial Mission of the Alliance Française." *French Historical Studies* 40, no. 1 (2017): 95–127.
Horta Canales, Luis. "La subversión de las imágenes: La producción de cortos documentales en la Universidad de Chile y su rol en la renovación del cine nacional 1960–1965." *Imagofagia* 12 (2015): 1–22.
Houston, Penelope. *Keepers of the Frame: The Film Archives*. London: British Film Institute, 1994.
Hurtado, María de la Luz. "50 años de teatro en la Universidad Católica: Crear es andar detrás de la verdad." *Latin American Theatre Review* 29, no. 1 (1995): 39–53.
Huttenen, Miia. *Politicised Cinema: Post-War Film, Cultural Diplomacy and UNESCO*. New York: Routledge, 2022.
Ibarra, Mirta, ed. *Titón: Volver sobre mis pasos*. Havana: Ediciones Unión, 2008.
Iber, Patrick. *Neither Peace nor Freedom: The Cultural Cold War in Latin America*. Cambridge, MA: Harvard University Press, 2015.
Institut des hautes études cinématographiques (IDHEC). *Annuaire des anciens éleves de l'IDHEC, 1944–1964*. Paris: Institut des hautes études cinématographiques, 1964.
———. *Deuxième Rencontre Internationale des Écoles de Cinéma et de Télévision: Comptes Rendus sténographiés des séances du congrès relatives*. Paris: IDHEC, 1955.
———. *Les carrières du cinéma et de la télévision: Programmes et matières des concours et conditions d'admissions sur titres*. Paris: Librarie Vuibert, 1954.
———. *Première Rencontre Internationale des Écoles du Cinéma: Comptes Rendus de l'Exposition Documentaire et des Séances du Congrès*. Paris: IDHEC, 1954.
Instituto Social/Instituto de Cinematografía de la Universidad del Litoral, *Exposición de fotodocumentales*. Santa Fe: Instituto Social/Instituto de Cinematografía de la Universidad Nacional del Litoral, 1958.
Iordanova, Dina, ed. *The Film Festival Reader*. St Andrews: St Andrews Film Studies, 2013.
Izquierdo, Eugenia. *Cine y preservación: Los archivos cinematográficos en la Argentina (1940–2001)*. Buenos Aires: Imago Mundi, 2020.
Jackson, Julian. *De Gaulle*. Cambridge, MA: Harvard University Press, 2018.
Jacobs, Steven, Birgit Cleppe, and Dimitrios Latsis, eds. *Art in the Cinema: The Mid-Century Art Documentary*. London: Bloomsbury, 2020.
Joseph, Gilbert M., and Daniela Spenser, eds. *In from the Cold: Latin America's New Encounter with the Cold War*. Durham, NC: Duke University Press, 2008.

Joskowicz Bobrownicki, Alfredo. "Algunas reflexiones sobre el área de realización." In *La docencia y el fenómeno fílmico: Memoria de los XXV años del CUEC, 1963–1988*, edited by Marcela Fernández Violante, 41–49. Mexico City: Universidad Nacional Autónoma de México, 1988.

Judt, Tony. *Past Imperfect: French Intellectuals, 1944–1956*. Berkeley: University of California Press, 1992.

Jullier, Laurent, and Jean-Marc Leveratto. *Cinéphiles et cinéphilies: Une histoire de la qualité cinématographique*. Paris: Armand Colin, 2010.

Keathley, Christian. *Cinephilia and History, or the Wind in the Trees*. Bloomington: Indiana University Press, 2006.

Keating, Patrick. "The Volcano and the Barren Hill: Gabriel Figueroa and the Space of Art Cinema." In *Global Art Cinema: New Theories and Histories*, edited by Rosalind Galt and Karl Schoonover, 201–17. Oxford: Oxford University Press, 2010.

Keller, Sarah. *Anxious Cinephilia: Pleasure and Peril at the Movies*. New York: Columbia University Press, 2020.

Kendrick, James. "Aspect Ratios and Joe Six-Packs: Home Theater Enthusiasts Battle to Legitimize the DVD Experience." *Velvet Light Trap* 56 (2005): 58–70.

Kepley, Vance, Jr. "Building a National Cinema: Soviet Film Education, 1918–1934." *Wide Angle* 9, no. 3 (1987): 6–13.

———. "Eisenstein as Pedagogue." *Quarterly Review of Film & Video* 14, no. 4 (1993): 1–16.

King, Geoff. *Positioning Art Cinema: Film and Cultural Value*. London: Bloomsbury Academic, 2019.

Kriger, Clara. "'Inolvidables jornadas vivió Mar del Plata': Perón junto a las estrellas." *Archivos de la Filmoteca* 46 (2004): 118–132.

Kwon, Nayoung Aimee, Takushi Odagiri, and Moonim Baek, eds. *Theorizing Colonial Cinema: Reframing Production, Circulation, and Consumption of Film in Asia*. Bloomington: Indiana University Press, 2022.

Lamaña, Julio. "Protohistoria de los públicos: Asonadas, disturbios y otras manifestaciones del público de cine en Colombia." Paper presented at the Primer Seminario de Cineclubismos Latinoamericanos, July 22, 2021.

Lane, Philippe. *French Scientific and Cultural Diplomacy*. Liverpool: Liverpool University Press, 2013.

Langlois, Suzanne. "And Action! UN and UNESCO Coordinating Information Films, 1945–1951." In *A History of UNESCO: Global Actions and Impacts*, edited by Poul Duedahl, 73–94. London: Palgrave Macmillan, 2016.

Latil, Loredana. *Le festival de Cannes sur la scène international*. Paris: Nouveau Monde, 2005.

Laviosa, Flavia. "Six Continents at the Centro Sperimentale di Cinematografia in Rome: Flavia Laviosa in Conversation with Alfredo Baldi." *Journal of Italian Cinema and Media Studies* 9, no. 2 (2020): 261–270.

Laviosa, Flavia, et al. "International Students at the Centro Sperimentale di Cinematografia in Rome: A History to Be Written, 1935–2020." *Journal of Italian Cinema and Media Studies* 9, no. 2 (2021): 175–209.

Le Clézio, J.M.G. and Robert Chazal. *Les années Cannes: 40 ans de festival*. Renens: 5 Continents, 1987.
Le Roy, Eric. "La Rapatriement des films spoilés pour les nazis." *Journal of Film Preservation* 68 (2004): 46–51.
Leddy Phelan, John. "Pan-Latinism, French Intervention in Mexico (1861–1867), and the Genesis of the Idea of Latin America." In *Conciencia y autenticidad históricas: Escritos en homenaje a Edmundo O' Gorman*, edited by Juan Antonio Ortega y Medina, 279–298. Mexico City: Universidad Nacional Autónoma de México, 1986.
Lee, Sangjoon. *Cinema and the Cultural Cold War: US Diplomacy and the Origins of the Asian Cinema Network*. Ithaca, NY: Cornell University Press, 2020.
Lenk, Sabine, and André Stufkens, "'Then Began the Battle Royal': Marion Michelle and the FIAF Crisis." *Moving Image* 13, no. 1 (2013): 199–217.
Levy, Daniel C. *Higher Education and the State in Latin America: Private Challenges to Public Dominance*. Chicago: University of Chicago Press, 1986.
L'Herbier, Marcel. *La tête qui tourne*. Paris: Pierre Belfond, 1979.
Lim, Bliss Cua. *The Archival Afterlives of Philippine Cinema*. Durham, NC: Duke University Press, 2024.
Littleton, Taylor D., and Maltby Sykes. *Advancing American Art: Painting, Politics, and Cultural Confrontation at Mid-Century*. Tuscaloosa: University of Alabama Press, 2005.
Lods, Jean. *Professional Training of Film Technicians*. Paris: UNESCO, 1951.
Longo, Regina. "Palimpsests of Power: UNESCO-'Sponsored' Film Production and the Construction of a 'Global Village, 1948–1953.'" *Velvet Light Trap* 75 (2015): 88–106.
López, Ana M. "Naming and Defining: From 'New' National Cinemas to the New Latin American Cinema." Unpublished manuscript, n.d.
López-Pedreros, A. Marcos. *Makers of Democracy: A Transnational History of the Middle Classes in Colombia*. Durham, NC: Duke University Press, 2019.
Lovejoy, Alice. *Army Film and the Avant-Garde: Cinema and Experiment in the Czechoslovak Military*. Bloomington: Indiana University Press, 2015.
Lovejoy, Alice, and Mari Pajala. *Remapping Cold War Media: Institutions, Infrastructures, Translations*. Bloomington: Indiana University Press, 2022.
Lowry, Edward. *The Filmology Movement and Film Study in France*. Ann Arbor: UMI Research Press, 1982.
Lucia, Cynthia, and Rahul Hamid, eds. *Cinéaste on Film Criticism, Programming, and Preservation in the New Millennium*. Austin: University of Texas Press, 2017.
Lusnich, Ana Laura, Alicia Aisemberg, and Andrea Cuarterolo, eds. *Pantallas transnacionales: El cine argentino del período clásico*. Buenos Aires: Imago Mundi, 2017.
Maben, Adrian, and Gerald Jacobson. "The Centro Sperimentale di Cinematografia." *Cinéaste* 3, no. 1 (1969): 8–10.
MacLean Switz, Theodore. "The Educational Film Elsewhere Abroad." In *Film and Education*, edited by Godfrey M. Elliott, 468–470. New York: Philosophical Library, 1948.

Majumdar, Rochona. *Art Cinema and India's Forgotten Futures: Film and History in the Postcolony.* New York: Columbia University Press, 2021.

Malusá, Vivian. "Católicos e cinema na capital paulista: O cine-clube do Centro Dom Vital e a Escola Superior de Cinema São Luís, 1958–1972." Master's thesis, Universidade de Campinas, 2007.

Mannoni, Laurent. *Histoire de la Cinémathèque française.* Paris: Gallimard, 2006.

Martin-Márquez, Susan. "Coloniality and the Trappings of Modernity in *Viridiana* and *The Hand in the Trap.*" *Cinema Journal* 51, no. 1 (2011): 96–114.

Massari, Romina, Fernando Martín Peña, and Carlos Alberto Vallina. *Escuela de Cine—Universidad Nacional de La Plata: Creación, rescate y memoria.* La Plata: Universidad Nacional de La Plata, 2006.

Matthieu, Gilles. "Un enjeu diplomatique: La politique culturelle de la France en Amérique du Sud dans l'entre deux guerres." *Cahiers des Amériques Latines* 9 (1990): 131–138.

———. *Une ambition sud-américaine: Politique culturelle de la France (1914–1940).* Paris: L'Harmattan, 1991.

McLynn, F. J. "The Ideology of Peronism: The Third Way and the Logic of the Excluded Middle." *Government and Opposition* 19, no. 2 (1984): 193–206.

Medina Ávila, Virginia. "Cultura y espíritu: La UNAM en la formación de la cultura cinematográfica en los años cincuenta, sesenta y setenta del siglo XX." *Multidisciplina* 15 (2013): 107–128.

Melnick, Ross. *Hollywood's Embassies: How Movie Theaters Projected American Power Around the World.* New York: Columbia University Press, 2022.

Melo Souza, José Inácio de. *Paulo Emílio no Paraíso.* Rio de Janeiro: Editora Record, 2002.

Mestman, Mariano. "From Italian Neorealism to New Latin American Cinema: Ruptures and Continuities in the 1960s." In *Global Neorealism: The Transnational History of a Film Style,* edited by Saverio Giovacchini and Robert Sklar, 138–149. Jackson: University Press of Mississippi, 2011.

Mestman, Mariano, and Christopher Moore. "On the Amateur Origins of Fernando Birri's Documentary School of Santa Fe." In *Global Perspectives on Amateur Film Histories and Cultures,* edited by Masha Salazkina and Enrique Fibla-Gutiérrez, 149–168. Bloomington: Indiana University Press, 2020.

Mignolo, Walter D. "The Many Faces of Cosmo-polis: Border Thinking and Critical Cosmopolitanism," *Public Culture* 12, no. 3 (2000): 721–748.

Miller, Jamie. "Educating the Filmmakers: The State Institute of Cinematography in the 1930s." *Slavonic and East European Review* 85, no. 3 (2007): 462–490.

Ministère des Affaires Étrangères. *Le projet culturel extérièur de la France.* Paris: Ministère des Affaires Étrangères, 1984.

Mitchell, J. M. *International Cultural Relations.* London: Allen & Unwin, 1986.

Moine, Caroline. "La Fédération internationale des associations de producteurs de films: Un acteur controversé de la promotion du cinéma après 1945." *Le mouvement social* 2 (2013): 91–103.

———. "La FIAPF, une fédération de producteurs au coeur des relations internationales après 1945." In *Les producteurs: Enjeux créatifs, enjeux financiers,* edited by Laurent Creton et al., 246–266. Paris: Nouveau Monde, 2011.

Moore, Christopher. "Cine Local: Argentine Documentary Film and the Politics of Presence, 1948–1978." PhD diss., Indiana University, 2017.
Morato Zanatto, Rafael. "O Curso para Dirigentes de Cineclubes (1958): Momento decisivo para a formação dos cursos universitários de cinema no Brasil." *C-Legenda* 1, no. 40 (2022): 71–90.
———. "O I Festival Internacional de Cinema do Brasil (1954)." *Aniki* 8, no. 1 (2021): 101–130.
Moreira Chaves, Geovano. "Sob o desígnio moral: o cinema além do filme (1900–1964)." PhD diss., Universidade Federal de Minas Gerais, 2018.
Moreschi, Oscar. "Construir la memoria: El Departamento de Cine de la Escuela de Artes de la Universidad Nacional de Córdoba." *Toma Uno* 1 (2012): 207–222.
Mouesca, Jacqueline. *El documental chileno*. Santiago de Chile: LOM Ediciones, 2005.
Muñiz García, Elsa Ernestina. "*El grito, México 1968* o los sonidos del silencio: Una narración en imágenes del Movimiento Estudiantil de 1968." *Alegatos* 22, no. 70 (2008): 411–428.
Myrent, Glenn, and Georges P. Langlois. *Henri Langlois, First Citizen of Cinema*. Translated by Lisa Nesselson. New York: Twayne, 1995.
Navitski, Rielle. "The Cine Club de Colombia and Postwar Cinephilia in Latin America: Forging Transatlantic Networks, Schooling Local Audiences." *Historical Journal of Film, Radio and Television* 38, no. 4 (2018): 808–827.
———. "Latin American Film Society Magazines: Nodes in Mid-Century Networks of Film Culture." In *Global Movie Magazine Networks*, edited by Eric Hoyt and Kelley Conway. Under contract with University of California Press, expected 2024.
Navitski, Rielle, and Nicolas Poppe, eds. *Cosmopolitan Film Cultures in Latin America, 1896–1960*. Bloomington: Indiana University Press, 2017.
Neale, Steve. "Art Cinema as Institution." *Screen* 22, no. 1 (1981): 11–40.
Neil, Claudia, and Sergio Peralta. "1956–1976: Instituto de Cinematografía de la Universidad Nacional del Litoral." In *Fotogramas santafesinos: Instituto de Cinematografía de la UNL, 1956–1976*, edited by Claudia Neil et al., 10–81. Santa Fe: Universidad Nacional del Litoral, 2007.
Neveleff, Julio, Miguel Monforte, and Alejandra Ponce de León. *Historia del Festival Internacional de Cine de Mar del Plata—Primera época: 1954–1970—De la epopeya a la resignación*. Buenos Aires: Corregidor, 2013.
Núbila, Domingo di. *Historia del cine argentino*. Olivos, Argentina: Ediciones Cruz de Malta, 1959.
Nunes Guimarães Paes, Daniel. "Olhar ativo: A Central Católica de Cinema do Rio de Janeiro (1954–1971)." Master's thesis, Pontifícia Universidade Católica do Rio de Janeiro, 2010.
Núñez, Fabián. "La acción de cinematecas latinoamericanas en tiempos de dictadura: El caso de la Cinemateca do Museu de Arte Moderna do Rio de Janeiro." *Archivos de la Filmoteca* 73 (2017): 43–56.
———. "Notas para um estudo sobre a Unión de Cinematecas de América Latina." *Significação* 42, no. 44 (2015): 63–81.
Nye, Joseph S., Jr. "Soft Power." *Foreign Policy*, August 1990, 153–171.

———. *Soft Power: The Means to Success in World Politics*. New York: Public Affairs, 2005.
Office catholique international du cinéma. *IV Congreso Internacional de Cine: Orientaciones Internacionales del Cine*. Madrid: Talleres Gráficas Jesús Álvarez, 1950.
Olmeta, Patrick. *La Cinémathèque française: De 1936 à nos jours*. Paris: CNRS Éditions, 2013.
Ortiz, Gaye. "The Catholic Church and Its Attitude to Film as an Arbiter of Cultural Meaning." In *Mediating Religion: Conversations in Media, Religion, and Culture*, edited by Jolyon P. Mitchell and Sophia Marriage, 179–188. London: T&T Clark Ltd., 2003.
Ortiz de Montellano, Bernardo. *Epistolario*. Edited by María Lourdes Franco Bagnouls. Mexico City: Universidad Nacional Autónoma de México, 1999.
Ospina León, Juan Sebastián. "Films on Paper: Early Colombian Cinema Periodicals, 1916–1920." In *Cosmopolitan Film Cultures in Latin America, 1896–1960*, edited by Rielle Navitski and Nicolas Poppe, 39–65. Bloomington: Indiana University Press, 2017.
Owensby, Brian P. *Intimate Ironies: Modernity and the Making of Middle-Class Lives in Brazil*. Stanford, CA: Stanford University Press, 1999.
Palacios, Marcos. *Between Legitimacy and Violence: A History of Colombia, 1875–2002*. Translated by Richard Stoller. Durham, NC: Duke University Press, 2006.
Paranaguá, Paulo Antonio. "Cinéastes latino-americains formés en Europe." *Cinémas d'Amérique Latine* 2 (1994): 66–67.
———. "Of Periodizations and Paradigms: The Fifties in Comparative Perspective." *Nuevo Texto Crítico* 11, nos. 21/22 (1998): 31–44.
———. *Tradición y modernidad en el cine de América Latina*. Madrid: Fondo de Cultura Económica de España, 2003.
Parker, David S. *The Idea of the Middle Class: White-Collar Workers and Peruvian Society, 1900–1950*. University Park: Pennsylvania State University Press, 1998.
Parker, David S., and Louise E. Walker, eds. *Latin America's Middle Class: Unsettled Debates and New Histories*. Lanham, MD: Lexington Books, 2012.
Paschalidis, Gregory. "Exporting National Culture: Histories of Cultural Institutes Abroad." *International Journal of Cultural Policy* 15, no. 3 (2009): 275–289.
Pastoriza, Elisa, and Juan Carlos Torre. *Mar del Plata: Un sueño de los argentinos*. Buenos Aires: EDHASA, 2021.
Paz, Octavio. "Buñuel the Poet," translated by Michael Schmidt. In *Manifestos and Global Cinema Cultures: A Critical Anthology*, edited by Scott MacKenzie, 188–190. Berkeley: University of California Press, 2014.
———. "La tradición de la ruptura." In *Los hijos del limo: Del romanticismo a la vanguardia*, 13–136. Barcelona: Seix Barral, 1974.
Peña, Fernando Martín. "Amigos del cine," in *Amigos del Arte, 1924–1942*, edited by Patricia M. Artundo and Marcelo E. Pacheco, 59–64. Buenos Aires: Museo de Arte Latinoamericano de Buenos Aires, 2008.

Pendergast, William Richard. "French Policy in UNESCO." PhD diss., Columbia University, 1971.
———. "UNESCO and French Cultural Relations, 1945–1970." *International Organization* 30, no. 3 (1976): 453–483.
Pensado, Jaime M. *Rebel Mexico: Student Unrest and Authoritarian Political Culture during the Long Sixties.* Stanford, CA: Stanford University Press, 2013.
Pérez, Nelson. "El cineclubismo en Venezuela (1907–1966)." *Revista UCSAR* 3, no. 6 (2012): 128–136.
Peters, J. M. L. *Teaching about the Film.* Paris: UNESCO, 1961.
Petrie, Duncan. "A New Art for a New Society? The Emergence and Development of Film Schools in Europe." In *The Emergence of Film Culture: Knowledge Production, Institution Building and the Fate of the Avant-Garde in Europe, 1919–1945*, edited by Malte Hagener, 268–282. New York: Berghahn Books, 2014.
Petrie, Duncan, and Rod Stoneman, *Educating Film-makers: Past, Present, and Future.* New York: Intellect Books, 2014.
Phu, Thy. "Bigger at the Movies: *Sangre Negra* and the Cinematic Projection of *Native Son*." *Black Camera* 2, no. 1 (2010): 36–57.
Pick, Zuzana M. *The New Latin American Cinema: A Continental Project.* Austin: University of Texas Press, 1993.
Pineda Moncada, Gloria. "Entre la verdad y la ilusión: El paradigma de la objetividad en el cine político marginal de los años sesenta y setenta en Colombia." *Calle 14* 11, no. 18 (2015): 62–74.
Pisu, Stefano. "A Transnational Love-Hate Relationship: The FIAPF and the Venice and Cannes Film Festivals (1950–1970)." In *International Film Festivals: Contemporary Cultures and History Beyond Venice and Cannes*, edited by Tricia Jenkins, 109–131. London: I. B. Tauris, 2020.
Podalsky, Laura. *Specular City: Transforming Culture, Consumption, and Space in Buenos Aires, 1955–1973.* Philadelphia: Temple University Press, 2004.
Polan, Dana. *Scenes of Instruction: The Beginnings of the U.S. Study of Film.* Berkeley: University of California Press, 2007.
Polizzotti, Mark. *Los olvidados.* London: British Film Institute, 2006.
Polo Risso, Juan Ignacio. *Historia de Punta del Este: Desde el descubrimiento de América hasta el siglo XXI.* Montevideo: Editorial Sudamericana, 2007.
Potenze, Jaime. *El Festival Internacional de Cine de Punta del Este: Diario de un Jurado.* Buenos Aires: Editorial Criterio, 1951.
Rama, Ángel. *The Lettered City.* Translated by John Charles Chasteen. Durham, NC: Duke University Press, 1996.
Ramírez Berg, Charles. *A Cinema of Solitude: A Critical Study of Mexican Film.* Austin: University of Texas Press, 1992.
Ramírez Llorens, Fernando. "Cine, autoritarismo y política de medios en Argentina: El Festival de Mar del Plata de 1968." *Historia Crítica* 72 (2019): 139–159.
———. *Noches de sano esparcimiento: Estado, católicos y empresarios en la censura del cine en la Argentina.* Buenos Aires: Libraria Ediciones, 2016.

———. "So Close to God, So Close to Hollywood: Catholics and the Cinema in Argentina." *Journal of Latin American Cultural Studies* 23, no. 4 (2014): 325–344.
Ramos, Alberto. "Cine e iglesia Católica en Cuba (1934–1950)." In *Huellas olvidadas del cine cubano: Memorias del XV Taller Nacional de Crítica Cinematográfica*, edited by Armando Pérez Padrón, 106–124. Santiago de Cuba: Editorial Oriente, 2010.
———. "Cine, medios, comunicación: El apostolado de la imagen," *Espacio Laical* 2, no. 7 (2006). www.espaciolaical.org/contens/07/0761.pdf.
Raymond, Jean-François de. *L'action culturelle extérieure de la France*. Paris: La documentation française, 2000.
Revueltas, José. *El conocimiento cinematográfico y sus problemas*. Mexico City: Centro Universitario de Estudios Cinematográficos, 1965.
Reyes, Ana María. *The Politics of Taste: Beatriz González and Cold War Aesthetics*. Durham, NC: Duke University Press, 2019.
Rivas Polo, Carlos. *Revista Mito: Vigencia de un legado cultural*. Medellín: Editorial Universidad de Antioquia, 2010.
Roberts, Bryan R. *The Making of Citizens: Cities of Peasants Revisited*. London: Halstead Press, 1995.
Robles, Nadia y Sofía Bilbao. "Vanguardia, Universidad y Cinematografía: La experiencia del Instituto de Cine de la Universidad de Buenos Aires." Presented at IX Jornadas de Sociología, Universidad de Buenos Aires, 2011.
Rocco, Alessandro. *Gabriel García Márquez and the Cinema: Life and Works*. Woodbridge: Tamesis, 2014.
Rocha, Glauber. "An Esthetic of Hunger," translated by Randal Johnson and Burnes Hollyman. In *New Latin American Cinema*, vol. 1, *Theory, Practices and Transcontinental Articulations*, edited by Michael T. Martin, 59–61. Detroit: Wayne State University Press, 1997.
Roche, François, and Bernard Pigniau. *Histoires de diplomatie culturelle des origines à 1995*. Paris: La documentation française, 1995.
Rodrigues Pereira, Marcio. "La politique culturelle française du Brésil de 1945 à 1970: Institutions, acteurs, moyens et enjeux." PhD diss., University of Strasbourg, 2014.
Rodríguez Álvarez, Gabriel, ed. *Atlas del cineclub: Metodologías, estrategias y herramientas*. Mexico City: PROCINECDMX, 2020.
———, ed. *Cartas a México: Correspondencia de Cesare Zavattini, 1954–1988*. Mexico City: Universidad Nacional Autónoma de México, 2007.
———. "*Contemporáneos* y Cineclub Mexicano: Revistas y cineclubes, la experiencia mexicana." Undergraduate thesis, Universidad Nacional Autónoma de México, 2002.
———. "La sociedad de los cinéfilos." *Luna Córnea* 24 (2002): 74–79.
———. *Manuel González Casanova: Pionero del cine universitario*. Guadalajara: Universidad de Guadalajara, 2009.
———. "Monsiváis y la cinefilia." *Memoria* 275, no. 3 (2020). https://revistamemoria.mx/?p=3071.
———. "Raíces y metamórfosis del cineclubismo universitario." *Toma* 32 (2014): 67.

Rodríguez Cruz, Olga, ed. *El 68 en el cine mexicano*. San Andrés Cholula: Universidad Iberoamericana Plantel Golfo-Centro, 2000.
Rodríguez Rodríguez, Israel. "*El grito*: Una historia hecha de fragmentos." In *El grito: Memoria en movimiento*, edited by Filmoteca UNAM, 33–57. Mexico City: Filmoteca UNAM, 2018.

———. "Entrevista a Manuel González Casanova." In "Entre la preocupación existencial y el cine social: La obra de Leobardo López Arretche." Undergraduate thesis, Universidad Nacional Autónoma de México, 2008.

Rolland, Denis. *La crise du modèle française: Marianne et l'Amérique Latine*. Paris: L'Harmattan, 2011. First published 2000.

———. "L'exil structure l'émigration (Mexique, Second Guerre Mondiale)." *Matériaux pour l'histoire de notre temps* 67 (2002): 66–77.

———. *Vichy et la France libre au Mexique: Guerre, culture et propagandes pendant la Deuxième Guerre mondiale*. Paris: Editions de l'Institut des hautes études de l'Amérique Latine/L'Harmattan, 1990.

Ross, Miriam. "The Film Festival as Producer: Latin American Films and Rotterdam's Hubert Bals Fund." *Screen* 52, no. 2 (2011): 261–267.

Roth-Ey, Kristin. *Moscow Prime Time: How the Soviet Union Built the Media Empire That Lost the Cultural Cold War*. Ithaca, NY: Cornell University Press, 2014.

Roud, Richard. *A Passion for Films: Henri Langlois and the Cinémathèque Française*. New York: Viking, 1983.

Rozsa, Irene. "Film Culture and Education in Republican Cuba: The Legacy of José Manuel Valdés-Rodríguez." In *Cosmopolitan Film Cultures in Latin America, 1896–1960*, edited by Rielle Navitski and Nicolas Poppe, 298–323. Bloomington: Indiana University Press, 2017.

———. "The Institutionalization of Film Exhibition in Cuba, 1959–64." *Studies in Spanish and Latin American Cinemas* 14, no. 2 (2017): 153–170.

———. "On the Edge of the Screen: Film Culture and Practices of Noncommercial Cinema in Cuba (1948–1966)." PhD diss., Concordia University, 2019.

Ruberto, Laura E., and Kristi M. Wilson, eds. *Italian Neorealism and Global Cinema*. Detroit: Wayne State University Press, 2007.

Rueda, Amanda. "Films latino-américains, festivals français." *Caravelle* 83 (2004): 87–104.

Ruszkowski, Andrés. *Cine, sus grandezas y miserias*. Translated by Clara Estrada. Buenos Aires: Dirección Central de Cine y Teatro de la Acción Católica Argentina, 1956.

Sala, Jorge. "Casarse con una viuda: *El reñidero* y la reescritura fílmica de éxitos teatrales en el nuevo cine argentino." *Anclajes* 21, no. 2 (2017): 59–75.

Salazkina, Masha. "Moscow-Rome-Havana: A Film Theory Map." *October* 139 (2012): 97–116.

———. "Soviet-Italian Cinematic Exchanges: Transnational Film Education in the 1930s." In *The Emergence of Film Culture: Knowledge Production, Institution Building and the Fate of the Avant-Garde in Europe, 1919–1945*, edited by Malte Hagener, 180–198. New York: Berghahn Books, 2014.

———. "(V)GIK and the History of Film Education in the Soviet Union, 1920s–1930s." In *A Companion to Russian Cinema*, edited by Birgit Beumers, 68–86. Chichester: Wiley-Blackwell, 2016.

———. *World Socialist Cinema: Alliances, Affinities, and Solidarities in the Global Cold War*. Oakland: University of California Press, 2023.

Salinas Muñoz, Claudio, and Hans Stange Marcus. *Historia del cine experimental en la Universidad de Chile, 1957–1973*. Santiago de Chile: Uqbar Editores, 2008.

Salon, Albert. *L'action culturelle de la France dans le monde*. Paris: Fernand Nathan, 1983.

Sánchez, Rafael. *El cine: Estética—Técnica—Moral—Cine-forum*. Santiago de Chile: Ediciones Paulinas, 1955.

Santacreu, María José, and Alejandra Trelles. "La Cinemateca Uruguaya: Desde la inviabilidad crónica hacia un nuevo futuro." *Journal of Film Preservation*, April 2020, 102–110.

Santos, Fabricio Felice Alves dos. "A apoteose da imagem: Cineclubismo e crítica cinematográfica no Chaplin Club." Master's thesis, Universidade Federal de São Carlos, 2012.

Schoonover, Karl, and Rosalind Galt. *Queer Cinema in the World*. Durham, NC: Duke University Press, 2016.

Schroeder-Rodríguez, Paul A. *Latin American Cinema: A Comparative History*. Oakland: University of California Press, 2016.

———. "Latin American Silent Cinema: Triangulation and the Politics of Criollo Aesthetics." *Latin American Research Review* 43, no. 3 (2008): 33–57.

Schwartz, Vanessa. *It's So French! Hollywood, Paris, and the Making of Cosmopolitan Film Culture*. Chicago: University of Chicago Press, 2007.

Schwartzman, Karen, et al. "An Interview with Margot Benacerraf: *Reverón, Araya*, and the Institutionalization of Cinema in Venezuela." *Journal of Film and Video* 44, nos. 3–4 (1993): 51–75.

Schwarz, Roberto. "Culture and Politics in Brazil, 1964–1969." In *Misplaced Ideas*, edited by John Gledson, 126–159. New York: Verso, 1992.

Sendrós, Paraná. *Fernando Birri*. Buenos Aires: Centro Editor de América Latina, 1994.

Servicio Oficial de Difusión Radio Eléctrica (SODRE). *SODRE: Cincuenta años de aplausos*. Montevideo: SODRE, 1979.

———. *Su organización y cometidos: Memoria del labor realizado entre 1930–1962*. Montevideo: Servicio Oficial de Difusión Radio Eléctrica, 1963.

Shambu, Girish. "For a New Cinephilia." *Film Quarterly* 72, no. 3 (2019): 32–34.

———. *The New Cinephilia*. 2nd ed. Montreal: Caboose Books, 2020.

Shaw, Tony. *Hollywood's Cold War*. Amherst: University of Massachusetts Press, 2007.

Shaw, Tony, and Denise J. Youngblood. *Cinematic Cold War: The American and Soviet Struggle for Hearts and Minds*. Lawrence: University Press of Kansas, 2010.

Silveira, Germán. *Cultura y cinefilia: Historia del público de la Cinemateca Uruguaya*. Montevideo: Cinemateca Uruguaya, 2019.

Silveira Gusmão, Milene de Cássia, and Raquel Costa Santos. "Cinema e católicos no Brasil: Entre a ação pastoral-religiosa e a ação cultural-educacional." *Alceu* 15, no. 30 (2015): 146–167.

Silveira Gusmão, Milene de Cássia, Raquel Costa Santos, and Rosalia Maria Duarte. "Mulheres em projetos de educação pelo/para o cinema." *Educação Temática Digital* 19, no. 2 (2017): 456–481.
Sitton, Robert. *Lady in the Dark: Iris Barry and the Art of Film*. New York: Columbia University Press, 2014.
Slide, Anthony. *Nitrate Won't Wait: A History of Film Preservation in the United States*. Jefferson, NC: McFarland, 1992.
Smoodin, Eric. *Paris in the Dark: Going to the Movies in the City of Light, 1930–1950*. Durham, NC: Duke University Press, 2020.
Solanas, Fernando, and Octavio Getino, "Towards a Third Cinema: Notes and Experiences for the Development of a Cinema of Liberation in the Third World." In *New Latin American Cinema*, vol. 1, *Theory, Practices and Transcontinental Articulations*, edited by Michael T. Martin, 33–58. Detroit: Wayne State University Press, 1997.
Souillés-Debats, Léo. *La culture cinématographique du mouvement ciné-club: Une histoire de cinéphilies (1944–1999)*. Paris: Association Française de recherche sur l'histoire du cinéma, 2017.
———. "Les pratiques cinéphiles au prisme de la programmation des ciné-clubs: Du choix des animateurs aux goûts des adhérents." *1895: Revue d'histoire du cinéma* 81 (2017): 53–70.
Souza, Carlos Roberto de. "A Cinemateca Brasileira e a preservação de filmes no Brasil." PhD diss., Universidade de São Paulo, 2009.
Staiger, Janet. "With the Compliments of the Auteur: Art Cinema and the Complexities of its Reading Strategies." In *Interpreting Films: Studies in the Historical Reception of American Cinema*, 178–195. Princeton, NJ: Princeton University Press, 1992.
Stonor Saunders, Frances. *The Cultural Cold War: The CIA and the World of Arts and Letters*. New York: The New Press, 1999.
Suárez, Juana. "New Buildings, New Pathways: Toward Dynamic Archives in Latin America and the Caribbean." *Moving Image* 21, nos. 1–2 (2021): 26–54.
Suárez, Juana, and Pamela Vizner. "Education through International Collaboration: The APEX Program." *Synoptique* 6, no. 1 (2018): 102–112.
Tadeo Fuica, Beatriz. "¿Qué mostrar? ¿Cómo cuidar? Análisis de colaboraciones entre incipientes cinematecas para enfrentar dilemas comunes durante los años cincuenta." *Revista Encuentros Latinoamericanos* 4, no. 2 (2020): 52–68.
———. "Tracing Past Exchanges between European and South American Cinematheques: A Key to Understanding the Impact of Sharing." *Iluminace* 31, no. 1 (2019): 27–42.
Tashiro, Charles Shiro. "Videophilia: What Happens When You Wait for It on Video." *Film Quarterly* 45, no. 1 (1991): 7–17.
Tavares de Sá, Irene. *Cinema e educação*. São Paulo: Agir Editora, 1965.
Tessonneau, Rémy. "L'IDHEC et ses activités." In *IDHEC: Pâques 1953*. Paris: Institut des hautes études cinématographiques, 1953.
Torres Bodet, Jaime. "Películas del pasado." In *La cinta de plata*, edited by Luis Mario Schneider, 157–158. Mexico City: Universidad Nacional Autónoma de México, 1986.

Torres, María Inés de. "El surgimiento de la radiodifusión pública en Hispanoamérica: Contexto, modelos y el estudio de un caso singular; el SODRE, la radio pública estatal de Uruguay (1929)." *Revista internacional de Historia de la Comunicación* 5 (2015): 122–142.

Torres San Martín, Patricia. *Elena Sánchez Valenzuela*. Guadalajara: Universidad de Guadalajara, 2018.

Triana Toribio, Núria. "El festival de los cinéfilos transnacionales: Festival Cinematográfico Internacional de la República Argentina en Mar del Plata, 1959–1970." *Secuencias: revista de historia del cine* 25 (2007): 25–45.

Trice, Jasmine Nadua. *City of Screens: Imagining Audiences in Manila's Alternative Film Culture*. Durham, NC: Duke University Press, 2021.

Trochon Ghislieri, Yvette. *Punta del Este: El edén oriental, 1907–1997*. Montevideo: Editorial Fin de Siglo, 2017.

Trouvé, Matthieu. "L'ambition et les contraintes: Les discours et messages du général de Gaulle en Amérique latine et leur réception; la voix et les voies de la politique latino-américaine de la France (1964)." In *De Gaulle et l'Amérique latine*, edited by Maurice Vaïsse, 115–128. Rennes: Presses universitaires de Rennes, 2014.

Truglio, Marcela. "El cine de las escuelas de cine." In *Generaciones 60/90: Cine argentino independiente*, edited by Fernando Martín Peña, 308–325. Buenos Aires: Museo de Arte Latinoamericano de Buenos Aires, 2003.

Trujillo, Iván, and Alfonso del Amo, "Escuela sobre ruedas 2004–2005." *Journal of Film Preservation* 69 (2005): 40–44.

Trumpbour, John. "Belgium and the Making of an International Catholic Film Movement." In *Selling Hollywood to the World: U.S. and European Struggles for the Mastery of the Global Film Industry, 1920–1950*, 211–25. Cambridge: Cambridge University Press, 2001.

Tryon, Chuck. *On-Demand Culture: Digital Delivery and the Future of Movies*. New Brunswick, NJ: Rutgers University Press, 2013.

Uchôa, Fábio Raddi. "O Seminário de Cinema do MASP e a produção documental de Ozualdo Candeias (1955–1966)." *Famecos* 24, no. 2 (2017): n.p.

United Nations. *United Nations Demographic Yearbook 1951*. New York: United Nations, 1951.

———. *United Nations Demographic Yearbook 1961*. New York: United Nations, 1961.

Universidad Nacional Autónoma de México. *25 años Filmoteca UNAM*. Mexico City: Universidad Nacional Autónoma de México, 1986.

Vaïsse, Maurice. Introduction to *De Gaulle et l'Amérique latine*, edited by Maurice Vaïsse. Rennes: Presses universitaires de Rennes, 2014.

Valck, Marijke de. *Film Festivals: From European Politics to Global Cinephilia*. Amsterdam: Amsterdam University Press, 2007.

Valck, Marijke de, Brendan Kredell, and Skadi Loist, eds. *Film Festivals: History, Theory, Method, Practice*. London: Routledge, 2016.

Valdés Rodríguez, José Manuel. *El cine, industria y arte de nuestro tiempo*. Havana: Letras Cubanas, 1966.

Valecce, Anastasia. *Neorealismo y cine en Cuba: Historia y discurso en torno a la primera polémica de la Revolución*. West Lafayette, IN: Purdue University Press, 2021.
Valverde, Umberto. *Reportaje crítico al cine colombiano*. Bogotá: Editorial Toronueva, 1978.
Vasey, Ruth. *The World According to Hollywood, 1918–1939*. Madison: University of Wisconsin Press, 1997.
Vignaux, Valérie. "Georges Sadoul et la Fédération française des ciné-clubs ou Contribution à une histoire des usages non commerciaux du cinéma." *Cinémas: Revue d'études cinématographiques/Cinémas: Journal of Film Studies* 27, nos. 2–3 (2017): 179–194.
Villegas López, Manuel. *El film documental: Introducción a la teoría y práctica del cinema*. Buenos Aires: Ediciones Cine Arte, 1942.
Vincenot, Emmanuel. "Germán Puig, Ricardo Vigón et Henri Langlois, pionniers de la Cinemateca de Cuba." *Caravelle* 83 (2004): 11–42.
Wäfler, John. "The Surveillance of Film Festivals in Switzerland: The Case of the Locarno International Film Festival." In *Cultural Transfer and Political Conflicts: Film Festivals in the Cold War*, edited by Andreas Kötzig and Caroline Moine, 141–152. Göttingen: V&R Unipress, 2017.
Wasson, Haidee. *Museum Movies: The Museum of Modern Art and the Birth of Art Cinema*. Berkeley: University of California Press, 2005.
Watson, Nora. *Elementos para un cine-debate*. Buenos Aires: Dirección Central de Cine y Teatro de la Acción Católica Argentina, 1957.
Waugh, Thomas. *The Conscience of Cinema: The Works of Joris Ivens, 1926–1989*. Amsterdam: Amsterdam University Press, 2016.
Wells, Sarah Ann. "Parallel Modernities? The First Reception of Soviet Cinema in Latin America." In *Cosmopolitan Film Cultures in Latin America, 1896–1960*, edited by Rielle Navitski and Nicolas Poppe, 151–175. Bloomington: Indiana University Press, 2017.
West, Dennis, and Joan M. West. "Conversation with Marta Rodríguez." *Jump Cut*, no. 38 (1993): 39–44.
Westad, Odd Arne. *The Global Cold War: Third World Interventions and the Making of Our Times*. Cambridge: Cambridge University Press, 2007.
White, Patricia. *Women's Cinema/World Cinema: Projecting Contemporary Feminisms*. Durham, NC: Duke University Press, 2015.
Wickham-Crowley, Timothy P. "Winners, Losers, and Also-Rans: Toward a Comparative Sociology of Latin American Guerilla Movements." In *Power and Popular Protest: Latin American Social Movements*, rev. ed., edited by Susan Eckstein, 132–181. Berkeley: University of California Press, 2001.
Wiener Fresco, Christian H. *Estudio y propuesta sobre conservación y difusión del material cinematográfico y audiovisual peruano*. Lima: Ministerio de Cultura, 2015.
Wilinsky, Barbara. *Sure Seaters: The Emergence of Art House Cinema*. Minneapolis: University of Minnesota Press, 2001.
Williams, Don G. "CILECT: The Early Years." *Journal of the University Film Association* 22, no. 4 (1970): 100–102.

Woll, Josephine. "The Russian Connection: Soviet Cinema and the Cinema of Francophone Africa." In *Focus on African Films*, edited by Françoise Pfaff, 223–240. Bloomington: Indiana University Press, 2004.

Wong, Cindy Hing-Yuk. *Film Festivals: Culture, People, and Power on the Global Screen*. Rutgers, NJ: Rutgers University Press, 2011.

Wood, David M. J. "Archivos, discursos y memoria de la imagen en movimiento: Límites y estrategias." In *Archivo, memoria y presente en el cine latinoamericano*, edited by Mauricio Durán Castro and Claudia Salamanca, 59–74. Bogotá: Editorial Pontificia Universidad Javieriana, 2012.

———. *El espectador pensante: El cine de Jorge Sanjinés y el Grupo Ukamau*. Mexico City: Universidad Nacional Autónoma de México, 2017.

Wschebor Pellegrino, Isabel. "Cine, universidad y política audiovisual: El Departamento de Medios Técnicos de Comunicación de la Universidad de la República (1973–1980)." *Contemporánea: Historia y problemas del siglo XX* 5, no. 5 (2014): 125–146.

———. "Del documento al documental uruguayo: El Instituto de Cinematografía de la Universidad de La República (1950–1973)." *Revista F@ro* 2, no. 14 (2011): n.p.

———. "Los orígenes del cine científico en Uruguay y la conformación del Instituto de Cinematografía de la Universidad de la República." In *Uruguay se filma: Prácticas documentales (1920-1990)*, edited by Georgina Torello, 43–63. Montevideo: Irrupciones Grupo Editor, 2018,

———. "Ouvrir les boîtes d'archives: Présence, absence et parcours du cinéma politique et militant produit en Uruguay entre 1965 et 1975." PhD diss., Université Paris Sciences et Lettres/Universidad de la República, 2022.

Xavier, Ismail. *Sétima arte, um culto moderno: O idealismo estético e o cinema*. São Paulo: Editora Perspectiva, 1978.

Zolov, Eric. *The Last Good Neighbor: Mexico in the Global Sixties*. Durham, NC: Duke University Press, 2020.

Zryd, Michael. "In Defense of Institutions in Experimental Film and Media." Conference presentation, Think:Film International Experimental Cinema Conference, Berlin, October 13, 2012. www.thinkfilm.de/panel/experiment-institution-michael-zryd.

Zúñiga, Guillermo, ed. *Anuario del cine argentino, 1949–1950*. Buenos Aires: Editorial Cinematográfica Americana, 1950.

Index

abstraction in art, 10, 99–100, 212. *See also* avant-garde; experimental film
Academia de Cine y Fotografía, 190–91, 191*fig.*, 202–3
Africa: cineclubs, 47; film education, 179; film festivals, 129; film preservation, 85–86, 112; Non-Aligned Movement, 12–13. *See also individual countries*
Allende, Salvador, 107, 123, 203
Alliance for Progress, 15, 18, 203
Alliance française, 23–26, 28, 40, 59–60
Almeida Salles, Francisco Luiz de, 71, 106*fig.*, 131*fig.*, 133, 159, 258n163
Alsina Thevenet, Homero, 148, 152, 156
amateur film, 32, 88, 209; and cineclub activities, 7, 42, 51, 53–54, 79, 203, 172
amateur photography, 53, 79, 207, 249n221
Andrade, Rudá de, 39–40, 90, 116, 168, 192
animation, 47, 64, 66, 157
Antonioni, Michelangelo, 83, 109, 151, 162
Araya, 193–98, 196*fig.*, 197*fig.*
Argentina: Catholic film culture, 55–57; cineclubs, 25, 43–53, 48*map*, 49*map*, 59, 65–67, 73–77, 83, 97, 105, 201–2, 208, 245n141; cinema, 7–8, 15, 20, 28, 64, 77, 83, 104, 127, 135–41, 143–47, 171–72, 204, 223; film education, 174, 176, 180–83, 199, 204–9; film exhibition, 2–3, 26–27; film festivals, 34, 127–28, 133, 135–41, 143–50, 154–55, 160–72; film preservation, 22, 59, 65, 88, 90, 95–97, 102, 105–6, 112–14, 117–21, 123, 155, 205–6; history and politics, 15, 18, 42, 95–96, 121, 160–65, 169–70, 204
art cinema: concept, 9–10, 15, 29–30, 99, 173, 194–95, 213; film festivals as arbiter, 34, 127–28, 133–48, 150, 159; reception in Latin America, 16, 19–20, 38–39, 63–64, 74, 83, 92, 107–10, 124, 218
Asia: cineclubs; 47; cinema, 9, 30, 44, 68, 189; film education, 190; film festivals, 129, 135, 148, 153–54; film preservation, 85–86, 112, 257n143; Non-Aligned Movement, 12–13. *See also individual countries*
audiences: composition, 26, 61, 65, 74–75, 96, 107, 122; efforts to train, 6, 10, 20, 39, 50–52, 54–58, 68, 75–77, 83–84, 99, 108–9, 123, 176–77, 179, 185–86, 205, 210, 213–16, 220–22, 224; film festival, 126, 138–41, 144, 146, 148, 152–53, 165, 173; impact of film on, 23, 42, 108–9, 225; resistance to cineclub ideals,

309

audiences (continued)
33, 77–82; tastes, 7–8, 20, 35, 68, 79–83, 127–28, 130, 212, 220–21, 225; unruly behavior, 37–39, 80
avant-garde: concept, 206, 213–15; films, 1, 44–46, 66–67, 99, 142–44, 157

Barbachano Ponce, Manuel, 107, 183
Barravento, 172, 194
Barry, Iris, 43, 88, 100, 111
Batlle Berres, Luis, 151, 153
Battleship Potemkin, 65, 109
Bazin, André, 125–26, 128, 130, 142, 156
Benacerraf, Margot, 110, 184, 189, 191–96, 198
Bergman, Ingmar, 68, 83, 109, 154
Berlin film festival, 129, 132
Birri, Fernando, 16, 139, 157–58, 176, 180–82, 182*fig.*, 193, 206–9
Brazil: Catholic film culture, 56–58; cineclubs, 41–44, 47, 71, 73; cinema, 7, 15, 47, 64, 110, 136, 139–40, 143, 172, 194; film education, 180–84, 189–90, 200; film exhibition, 2–3, 20, 26–28; film festivals, 139–40, 143, 150, 152, 156–60, 168–69; film preservation, 85–88, 90, 93–94, 97–101, 113, 115–21; history and politics, 13, 15, 17–18, 21, 24, 41, 121, 169, 199
Brickmakers, 195–98, 197*fig.*
British Film Institute, 30, 65, 89, 97, 159
Bronenosets Potiomkin, 65, 109
Buñuel, Luis: at Cannes, 136, 140, 142–43, 171; films, 46, 58, 109, 155, 162

Caiçara, 136, 143, 152
cangaceiro, O, 64, 136, 171
Cannes film festival, 22, 34–35, 134–48, 151, 171, 194; as meeting place, 71, 133, 190, 262n33; prizewinning films, 58, 64, 135, 139–40, 154, 194
Cantegril Country Club, 149–50, 153
Cartagena film festival, 127, 134, 147
casa del ángel, La, 143–45, 171
Catholic film culture, 47–49, 52, 55–58, 75–77, 104
Cavalcanti, Alberto, 109, 143–44, 152, 159, 171, 182*fig.*, 189
Centre international de liaison des écoles de cinéma et télévision, 133, 190, 225, 262n33
Centre national de la cinématographie, 23, 47, 185, 187
Centro de Cine Experimental, 107, 203–4

Centro Sperimentale di Cinematografia, 16, 176, 178–84, 192, 205–7, 209
Centro Universitario de Estudios Cinematográficos, 22, 35, 176–78, 210–26
Cercle du cinéma, 21, 71, 97
chapeau de paille d'Italie, Un, 65, 99
Chaplin Club, 43–44, 46–47
Chaskel, Pedro, 107, 122, 168, 203
Chiarini, Luigi, 179, 207
Chile: Catholic film culture, 52, 202–3; cineclubs, 48*map*, 49*map*, 52–54, 73, 107; cinema, 88, 200; film education, 190–91, 191*fig.*, 202–4; film exhibition, 2–3, 26; film festivals, 54, 119, 132, 135, 172–73; film preservation, 94, 107, 110, 116, 119, 122–23; history and politics, 18, 107, 121, 123
Chircales, 195–98, 197*fig.*
Cine Arte del Servicio Oficial de Difusión Radio Eléctrica: archive, 97–98, 116–18, 120, 122–23, 201, 250n8; film series, 55, 96–97; film festival, 157–58
Cine Arte movie theater (Argentina), 47, 105
Cine Arte screening series (Cuba), 102, 106
Cine Club de Buenos Aires, 43, 45–46, 52–53
Cine Club de Colombia, 33, 37–39, 53, 73, 79, 192; audiences, 78–83; programming, 59, 62–68
Cine Club de la Habana (1927), 43, 53
Cine Club de la Habana (1948), 102–3
Cine Club de la Universidad, 54, 215–16, 217*fig.*, 220
Cine Club de Lima, 25, 58, 104
Cine Club del Uruguay, 22, 67–68, 74–75, 105, 151, 245n141
Cine Club de Medellín, 73, 78
Cine Club de México (1931), 43–46, 45*fig.*
Cine Club de México (1950), 41, 59–62, 68, 70, 212, 215
Cine Club de Rosario, 53, 75
Cine Club Eva Perón, 53, 65, 245n141
Cine Club Mendoza, 25, 53, 59, 66–67, 74
Cineclub Mexicano, 43–46, 45*fig.*
Cine Club Núcleo, 50–51, 53, 66, 77, 208
Cine Club Progreso, 42, 54, 64–65, 70, 215
Cine Club Santa Fe, 53, 65, 77, 206, 245n141
Cine Club Tucumán, 53, 74, 245n141
Cine-Club Venezuela, 31, 43, 53, 62, 104, 119
Cine Club Viña del Mar, 53–54, 172
cineclubs: during World War II, 47; federations, 7, 21–22, 28, 40, 64, 59, 69–76, 82–83, 88, 105, 112; ideals, 33,

39–40, 50–52, 63, 67, 77–78, 80–84; in interwar period, 41–47; in postwar period, 47–49; relations with arthouse theaters, 52–53, 83. *See also individual clubs*
Cine Experimental, 107, 203–4
Cinemateca Argentina, 22, 155, 205–6; relations with cineclubs, 59, 65, 96, 102, 105; relations with FIAF, 118, 120; relations with Langlois and the Cinémathèque française, 90, 106; relations with Latin American archives, 113–14, 119–20, 123
Cinemateca Brasileira: emergence in art world, 97–101; fires suffered by, 86–87, 101, 113; relations with cineclubs, 98, 113, 200; relations with Cinémathèque française and Henri Langlois, 90, 97, 100, 116; relations with FIAF, 85, 98, 115, 118; relations with Latin American archives, 113, 115, 119–20, 254n78; role in film education, 181, 184, 200; in the twenty-first century, 86–87
Cinemateca Colombiana, 65, 102–4, 110, 113, 192, 247n171, 255n94, 258n163
Cinemateca de Cuba: prerevolutionary, 102–3; postrevolutionary, 96, 108–10, 118, 123–24
Cinemateca del Tercer Mundo, 122–23, 201, 261n216
Cinemateca do Museu de Arte Moderna do Rio de Janeiro, 101, 117, 123, 254n78
Cinemateca Nacional (Argentina), 96, 119
Cinemateca Nacional de Venezuela, 104, 110, 119, 193
Cinemateca Universitaria del Perú, 104, 119
Cinemateca Uruguaya, 155, 251n12; links with cineclubs, 22, 97, 102, 105; relations with Latin American archives, 113, 115–16, 119, 122–23; in the twenty-first century, 227–29
Cinemateca Venezolana, 104, 117–18
Cinémathèque française: relations with FIAF, 85, 89–91, 116–17; relations with Latin American archives, 87–91, 97–101, 103–4; relations with Latin American cineclubs, 7, 21, 60–62, 83; source of festival programming, 155, 159, 100. *See also* Langlois, Henri
cinephilia: concept of, 1–2, 133, 227–31. *See also* film culture
Cineteca Universitaria (Chile), 107, 119, 122
Cine Universitario, 50–51, 54, 74–75, 97, 105, 201–2

Clair, René, 65–66, 99, 152
Clube de Cinema de São Paulo, 21, 47, 54, 98–99. *See also* Cinemateca Brasileira
Cold War: culture, 4, 8–11, 15, 30, 38, 40, 51, 100; film festivals, 126, 129, 133, 164; film preservation, 65–66, 90; in France, 11–15; impact on international organizations, 28–30, 90, 114, 190; in Latin America, 4–6, 121, 226; revisionist histories of, 11. *See also* communism; Eastern bloc; socialism; Soviet Union
Colina, José de la, 61, 212, 216, 218
Colombia: Catholic film culture, 56–57, 77; cineclubs, 25, 33, 37–41, 48–49, 54, 70, 73, 75, 78–83, 193; cinema, 68, 103, 127, 147, 255n95; film education, 180, 184, 192, 195–98; film exhibition, 2–3, 27, 36, 56, 79–83; film preservation, 65, 88, 101–4, 110, 112–13, 119; history and politics, 18, 37–38
communism: followers among cineclub organizers, 20–22, 42–43, 47, 65, 69–70, 102, 158, 239n20; followers among film educators, 202; followers among filmmakers, 6, 183; opposition to, 9, 56, 161, 166, 203; in world politics, 5–6, 11–15, 18, 161. *See also* Cold War; Eastern bloc; socialism; Soviet Union
Companhia Cinematográfica Vera Cruz, 136, 143, 152, 159, 182
Congo: Belgian, 47; Republic of, 85
Consortium franco-américain, 26–27, 59, 64, 101, 138
co-production, 9, 104, 147; agreements, 27, 164–65, 168–69; festival selections, 140–41, 144
Courvoisier, Amy Bakaloff, 53, 62, 80, 104, 117, 139, 193
Cuba: Catholic film culture, 56–57; cineclubs, 43, 48*map*, 49*map*, 55; cinema, 30, 172, 179, 182–83, 223; Cuban Revolution, 5, 17, 19, 38, 168; film education, 176, 179, 192, 200, 272n14; film exhibition, 1–3, 27, 229; film festivals, 138, 155, 172; film preservation, 88, 96, 102–3, 108–10, 118, 121, 123–24; history and politics, 13, 24, 38, 103, 168
cultura cinematográfica, 1, 52
cultural capital, 4–6; of individuals, 1, 33–34, 40, 52, 69–70, 74, 81–82, 199; of nations, 24, 29, 59–60, 125, 176, 187, 226; of organizations, 34–35, 40,

cultural capital (*continued*)
71, 67, 69, 88, 92, 98, 128, 138, 144, 147–49, 154, 156, 173, 189
cultural Cold War. *See* Cold War, culture
cultural diplomacy, 1–4, 9, 26, 58–59, 64, 234n17. *See also* France, cultural diplomacy
currency exchange rates, 31, 87, 115–16, 118, 149
Custodio, Álvaro, 70, 215
Cravenne, Robert, 8, 27, 147
Czechoslovakia: cineclubs, 26, 64–65; cinema, 64–65; film education, 190; film festivals, 129, 135, 165; film preservation, 65, 103, 109–10; history and politics, 12

Dassori Barthet, Walther, 22, 119–20, 168, 201–2
de Gaulle, Charles, 12–15, 60
De Sica, Vittorio, 64, 67, 76*fig.*, 154, 181–82
de-Stalinization, 29, 90, 114, 136
Diary of a Country Priest, 151–52
Diehl, Gaston, 31, 53, 62, 104, 193
Direction générale des relations culturelles, 25–26, 91, 189
distribution of films, 2–3; commercial, 2, 7, 9, 20, 23–24, 26–27, 55, 63, 67–68, 126, 132, 162; non-commercial, 23, 25–26, 30–31, 55, 59–62, 69, 88, 112–13, 119; remittances of box office profits, 138, 162; screen quotas, 27, 126, 138, 145, 162, 185; trade agreements, 27, 31, 165, 168

Eastern bloc: cinema, 10, 64–65, 109; distribution, 27; film education, 178–79, 190; film festivals, 129, 136, 150, 155, 157–58, 169; film preservation, 250n1, 90, 103, 109–10. *See also individual countries*
Ecuador: film culture, 2–3, 25, 49*map*, 229; history and politics, 13
educational film, 30–32, 66, 93–94, 174, 179, 199–205
Egypt, 135, 189–90
Eisenstein, Sergei, 42–44, 46, 65, 109, 178, 194, 240n49
Elizondo, Salvador, 61, 184, 211–12, 216, 218
Encuentros de Teóricos, 164–65, 168–69, 170*fig.*
En el balcón vacío, 172, 217*fig.*

Escuela Documental de Santa Fe, 158, 176, 182, 206–9
Escuela Nacional de Cinematografía (Argentina), 22, 199, 204–5
ethnographic film, 93–94, 157, 189–90, 195–98, 201
experimental film, 1, 44–46, 66–67, 99, 142–44, 157

Favre Le Bret, Robert, 136–41, 143–44, 146–47
Fédération française des ciné-clubs, 47–48, 69–70
Fédération internationale des archives du film, 21–22, 33–34, 69–71, 82–93, 96–124, 133
Fédération internationale des associations de producteurs de films, 128–30, 137, 154–56, 159, 162, 164, 166
Fédération internationale des ciné-clubs: and global circulation of films, 69–70, 73, 82–83, 112; impact in Latin America, 21, 70–71, 69*fig.*, 105; role in French cultural diplomacy, 7, 28, 40, 64
Fédération internationale du film d'art, 31. *See also films sur l'art*
Feldman, Simón, 145, 183, 206, 208
Fernández, Emilio, 61, 107, 182; films at festivals, 64, 135, 141–42, 152, 171, 194
Fernández Violante, Marcela, 222, 224
Festival del Cine Nuevo Latinoamericano, 54, 119, 132, 172
Figueroa, Gabriel, 61, 135, 141–42, 194
film criticism, 43–44, 52–53, 75–76, 103, 139–42, 158–61, 229; and canon formation, 4, 39, 63–64; at film festivals, 22, 35, 164–66, 168–69; high standards in Latin America, 126, 148, 153, 156
film culture, 1, 52
film education, 175. *See also individual schools*
film exhibition. *See individual countries*
film festivals, 125–34. *See also individual festivals*
filmology, 184, 192, 202
Filmoteca do Museu de Arte Moderna de São Paulo. *See* Cinemateca Brasileira
Filmoteca Nacional (Mexico), 94–96, 95*fig.*
film preservation, 85–86. *See also* Fédération internationale des archives du film; *and individual archives*
film schools, 175. *See also individual schools*
film societies. *See* cineclubs
films sur l'art, 25, 31, 66, 101, 193

Index | 313

France, 1–4, 6–8; cineclubs, 21, 39, 41–42, 47–51, 69–71, 97; cinema, 58, 63–66, 79, 99, 103, 109, 115, 135, 151–52, 163; cultural diplomacy, 23–29, 33–35, 40, 58–64, 83, 90–91, 125, 154–55, 161; film education, 7, 35, 176–78, 183–93, 208–10, 216–18; film exhibition, 2–3, 7; film festivals, 134–47, 150; history and politics, 11–15
Frondizi, Arturo, 15, 165–66, 169, 209
Fröken Julie, 57–58, 68, 72*fig.*, 109, 154, 162

Gance, Abel, 57, 162–63
García Ascot, José Miguel, 61, 172, 212, 215
García Espinosa, Julio, 16, 172, 176, 180, 183, 192
García Márquez, Gabriel, 22, 79, 103, 176, 180, 218–19, 281n231
García Mesa, Héctor, 108–10
García Riera, Emilio, 61, 212, 216–17
García Terres, Jaime, 211, 215
Gavaldón, Roberto, 64, 152
generación del 60, 77, 127, 136, 145, 172, 183, 206, 208
Gente de Cine: film society, 22, 25, 47, 53, 59, 63–65, 67, 69*fig.*, 249n227; magazine, 64, 75–76
Germany: cineclubs, 42–43, 64–65, 99; cinema, 7, 46, 64–65, 109–10; cultural diplomacy, 25, 59, 241n52; film education, 180, 189; film exhibition, 27–28; film festivals, 135, 153, 168; film preservation, 85, 90, 97, 110; history and politics, 7, 13–14, 21, 24–26
Getino, Octavio, 83, 172, 234n10
Given Word, The, 139, 171
Global South. *See* Third World
González Casanova, Manuel, 22, 50–52, 61, 70, 120, 174–76, 214–26
Gosfilmofond, 65, 90, 103, 109–10, 250n1
grito, El, 222–24, 223*fig.*
Grupo Nuevo Cine, 61, 172, 210, 212–14, 216–18, 220, 224
Gutiérrez Alea, Tomás, 102, 176, 180–83, 192

Hand in the Trap, The, 138, 140, 143–44
Handler, Mario, 201, 261n216
Hermosillo, Jaime Humberto, 218–19, 219*fig.*, 224–25
higher education. *See* universities
Hintz, Eugenio, 22, 106*fig.*, 113, 115–18, 120–21, 133, 201

Hollywood. *See* United States, cinema
House of the Angel, The, 143–45, 171
humanism, 6, 10, 15, 28, 57–58, 70, 175
Hungary: cinema, 65, 166; film education, 190

import-substitution industrialization, 6, 18–19, 153, 160, 165
India: cineclubs, 47; cinema, 189; film education, 190; film festivals, 135, 148
inflation, 19, 27, 34, 90, 115–16
informal communities, 65, 107, 153
Institut de filmologie, 184, 192
Institut des hautes études cinématographiques, 7, 35, 176–78, 183–93, 186*fig.*, 208–10, 216–18
Institut français d'Amérique latine, 33, 59–62, 60*fig.*, 187, 212
Institut international de coopération intellectuelle, 29–30, 59
Instituto Cubano de Arte e Industria Cinematográficos, 55, 102, 108–10, 138, 172, 183, 224
Instituto de Cinematografía de la Universidad de la República, 22, 200–2
Instituto de Cinematografía de la Universidad Nacional del Litoral, 158, 176, 182, 206–9
Instituto de Cinematografía Educativa (Chile), 94, 200
Instituto Fílmico, 190–91, 191*fig.*, 202–3
Instituto Nacional de Cinematografía (Argentina), 139, 144–47, 165–66, 169, 204–5
internationalism, 6–7, 38, 44, 52, 70, 73, 129, 133–35, 157, 225
inundados, Los, 139, 157
Iran, 85, 190, 257n143
Italian Straw Hat, The, 65, 99
Italy: cinema, 5–6, 58, 64–65, 67; cultural diplomacy, 25–26, 28, 59, 101, 183; film education, 16, 35, 175–83, 190, 202, 206–7; film festivals, 40, 76*fig.*, 101, 135, 150–52, 154–55, 161–62, 164; history and politics, 7

Japan: cinema, 68, 109; film exhibition, 27; film festivals, 135, 153–55; film preservation, 85
Journal d'un curé de campagne, 151–52

Karlovy Vary film festival, 129, 165
Klimovsky, León, 43, 47, 53, 105, 136
Kohon, David José, 77, 145, 172

Kuhn, Rodolfo, 144–45, 172, 205–6
Kukuli, 53, 104
Kurosawa, Akira, 68, 154, 218

Langlois, Henri, 21, 33, 60–62, 88–92, 97–105, 110–20, 168
Latin American Pool, 33–34, 87, 89, 93, 110–16, 123–24, 133
Ledoux, Jacques, 89, 120, 122
Leduc, Paul, 184, 218
L'Herbier, Marcel, 184–87, 189
Lindgren, Ernest, 89, 117–18, 120, 159
López Arretche, Leobardo, 222–24

mano en la trampa, La, 138, 140, 143–44
Marcha, 130, 132, 149, 152–54, 156
Mar del Plata film festival, 8, 34–35, 127–28, 130, 132–34, 147–49, 151, 155, 157, 160–70, 167*fig.*, 170*fig.*; archivists, critics, and educators at, 22, 115, 117–18, 120, 127, 133, 168–70
María Candelaria, 107, 135, 141–42
Matarazzo Sobrinho, Francisco, 98–99, 159
mégano, El, 183, 195
Mexico: cineclubs, 33, 41–46, 48*map*, 49*map*, 50, 54–55, 59–65, 70, 73; cinema, 7, 15–16, 20, 30, 55, 58, 64, 127, 155, 162, 177, 194; film education, 174, 176–77, 184, 210–25; film exhibition, 1–3, 27–28; film festivals, 127–28, 133, 135–36, 138, 140–43, 147, 150, 152, 167*fig.*, 171–72; film preservation, 93–95, 106–7, 114, 121–23; history and politics, 4, 17–18, 24, 199, 210–13, 222
Michelle, Marion, 89, 113–14, 117, 192, 251n19
middle classes, 1, 16–21, 149; cineclub members, 38–39, 42, 51–52, 58, 74, 80, 96; university students, 199, 211, 222
Middle East, 85–86, 129, 135, 179, 189–90. *See also individual countries*
military dictatorships, 18; Argentina, 123, 165, 169–70, 204, 277n122; Brazil, 15, 21, 54, 121; Chile, 121, 123, 203; Cuba, 103, 183; Mexico, 17, 210; Southern Cone, 90, 121, 123, 169, 209; Uruguay, 123, 201
Ministère des affaires étrangères (France) 23, 28, 62, 134, 187, 190, 233n1; cultural affairs division, 25–26, 91, 189
Miss Julie, 57–58, 68, 72*fig.*, 109, 154, 162
Monsiváis, Carlos, 61, 212, 216, 218
Morin, Edgar, 168, 174, 195

Motion Picture Association of America, 9, 127, 154, 162
Mouneu, Nicholas, 136–38, 141, 144
moviegoers. *See* audiences
Musée de l'Homme, 189, 195, 198
Museu de Arte de São Paulo, 189–90
Museu de Arte Moderna do Rio de Janeiro, 101, 117, 123, 254n78
Museu de Arte Moderna de São Paulo, 21, 54, 85, 97–101, 155
Museum of Modern Art (New York), 10, 62, 85, 97–98, 100, 102

Národní filmový archiv, 65, 103, 109–10
National Film Library (United Kingdom), 30, 65, 89, 97, 159
Native Son, 141, 150
neorealism, 5–6, 64–65, 143, 157, 175–77, 179–83, 207
New Latin American Cinema, 5, 16, 41, 83, 175, 194–98, 203, 223, 226; film festivals, 132, 148, 158, 171–73; film preservation, 91–93, 119–24; influence of neorealism, 64, 175–77, 180–84, 206–9

Office catholique international du cinéma, 33, 55–58, 202
olvidados, Los, 58, 109, 136, 142–43
On the empty balcony, 172, 217*fig.*

Pabst, Georg Wilhelm, 44, 99
pagador de promessas, O, 139, 171
Paz, Octavio, 142–43, 211–12, 215
Pereira dos Santos, Nelson, 136, 139–40, 157–58
Perón, Juan Domingo: death, 206; ideology, 15, 42, 161, 165–66; film policy, 95–96, 127, 150, 157, 160–65, 204; international relations, 153–55, 161; ouster, 96, 164–65, 204
Peru: Catholic film culture, 57–58; cineclubs, 25, 49*map*, 53, 58; cinema, 30, 104; film exhibition, 2–3, 25–26; film festivals, 168; film preservation, 95, 97, 104, 119; history and politics, 17–18
photography: amateur, 53, 79, 207; 249n221; courses, 202, 208; photo-essays, 207; professionals, 43, 46, 74, 79
Poland: film education, 133, 190; film festivals, 135; history and politics, 114–15, 134
prestige. *See* cultural capital
Pudovkin, Vsevolod, 42, 47, 65, 178–79

Puig, Germán, 53, 88, 102–3, 191–92
Punta del Este film festival, 8, 34, 125–34, 147–57, 150*fig.*, 162, 164; as meeting place, 113–15

Raíces, 107, 171
Rashomon, 68, 154
Rassegna del Cinema Latino-americano, 40, 171–72
Reichsfilmarchiv, 85, 90
reñidero, El, 144–47
Resnais, Alain, 83, 109, 193
Reynel, Miguel, 104, 119, 168
Ríos, Humberto, 183, 205
Robinson Crusoe (film), 143, 155, 249n235
Rocha, Glauber, 136, 139, 172, 194
Rockefeller, Nelson, 98, 100–101. See also Museum of Modern Art (New York)
Rodríguez, Marta, 195–98
Roland (Andrés José Rolando Fustiñana), 22, 131*fig.*, 168; as archivist, 88, 104–6, 106*fig.*, 112, 114; as cineclub organizer, 53, 71, 83, 112; as critic, 53, 76, 133; as educator, 205–6
Romero, Angela Vera, 206
Roots, 107, 171
Ruszkowski, Andrzej, 56–58, 104

Sadoul, Georges, 47, 69–70, 112, 168
Salcedo Salazar, Ernesto, 147–48
Salcedo Silva, Hernando, 67, 80–81, 114
Salles Gomes, Paulo Emílio, 20–22; archivist, 88, 92, 97–101, 106*fig.*, 112–13, 115, 117, 254n78; cineclub organizer, 54, 71; festival curator and jury member, 100, 131*fig.*, 133, 159; film student, 183–84, 274n64; UNESCO delegate, 29–30
Sammaritano, Salvador, 53, 168, 208
Sánchez, Rafael, 52, 202
Sánchez Martínez, Roberto Jaime, 222–24
Sánchez Valenzuela, Elena, 94–95, 95*fig.*, 160–61
Sangre negra, 141, 150
São Paulo film festival, 21, 97, 99–100, 113, 134, 158–60
Saraceni, Paulo César, 172, 181
scientific films, 109, 157, 176–77, 189, 200–202
screen quotas, 27, 126, 138, 145, 162, 185
Sección/Seção Latino(-)americana, 33–34, 87, 89, 93, 110–16, 123–24, 133
Séfert, Jean, 26, 59. See also Consortium franco-américain

Semaine du cinéma français, 27, 125, 154–55
Seminário de Cinema, 189–90, 191*fig.*
Service des œuvres françaises à l'étranger, 24, 91
Servicio Oficial de Difusión Radio Eléctrica. See Cine Arte del Servicio Oficial de Difusión Radio Eléctrica
Sindicato de la Industria Cinematográfica Argentina, 166, 270n210
16mm: cameras, 217, 222; printers, 203; prints, 40, 62, 107; projectors, 25, 98, 109; stock, 31
socialism, 5–6, 11–15, 21, 102, 107–10, 203. See also communism
socialist realism, 10, 70, 100
Sociedad Cultural Nuestro Tiempo, 53, 102, 183
soft power. See cultural diplomacy
Solanas, Fernando, 83, 172, 234n10
South Africa, 47, 135
Soviet Union: cinema, 42, 46–47, 56, 64–66, 70, 90, 97, 99, 103–4, 109–10; film education, 176, 178–79; film festivals, 129, 136, 149, 161, 167*fig.*, 168; film preservation, 65, 90, 103, 109–10, 250n1; history and politics, 11–15, 21; participation in international organizations, 29, 90. See also Cold War; communism; Eastern bloc; socialism
Spain: cineclubs, 44, 50; cinema, 140; exiles, 70, 212, 215; film education, 180, 190; film festivals, 135, 140, 155, 161; history and politics, 24, 195
spectators. See audiences
Stalin, Joseph, 12–13, 29, 90, 136
Stalinism, 14, 21, 114; and culture, 10, 70, 100; de-Stalinization, 29, 90, 114, 136
Stroheim, Erich von, 158, 227

Tessonneau, Rémy, 185, 187, 190
Third Way, 12, 14–15, 161
Third World: economic development, 29–32; film culture, 112, 129, 133, 190, 229, 234n10; liberation of, 11–14, 18, 38, 171
Tire dié, 182, 207–9
Toeplitz, Jerzy, 89, 105, 115, 117–18, 190
Torre Nilsson, Leopoldo, 34, 136, 138, 140, 143–44, 171–72
Torres Bodet, Jaime, 46, 94
trade agreements, 27, 31, 165, 168
translation, 44, 169, 207, 238n118; subtitles, 26, 61, 66, 146, 153, 194, 227–28

Trelles, Danilo, 20, 96–98, 117–18, 158, 250n8, 264n68
Turning Wind, The, 172, 194

Ugalde Portela, Alberto, 131*fig.*, 147, 150
Umberto D., 64, 154
Unifrance, 8, 23, 27–28, 53, 64, 147; agents' work with Cannes film festival, 136–39, 141, 144; French Cinema Week, 27, 125, 154–55; relations with cineclubs and archives, 59, 101
Unión de Cinematecas de América Latina, 34, 90–93, 107, 110, 117–24, 133, 168
Union of Soviet Socialist Republics. *See* Soviet Union
Unitalia, 59, 101, 183
United Kingdom: cineclubs, 42–43; cinema, 64, 151, 162, 168; film festivals, 135, 150–51, 161–62, 164; film preservation, 30, 65, 89, 97, 159; history and politics, 19
United Nations Educational, Scientific and Cultural Organization, 28–32, 39, 66, 94, 190, 193
United States: cinema, 5, 10, 47, 109, 120, 151, 155, 162–63, 221; film education, 189–90; film exhibition, 2–3; film festivals, 129, 134–36, 150, 152, 154–55, 162–63, 165; global circulation of films from, 2–3, 7, 9, 20, 23, 41, 55, 58–59, 63–64, 109, 162, 185; history and politics, 4–5, 11, 13–19, 24–25, 29, 31–32; influence in Latin America, 5, 15, 17, 38, 40, 88, 129, 169, 211
Universidad de Buenos Aires, 65, 200
Universidad de Chile, 54, 94, 107, 200, 203–4
Universidad de la Habana, 102, 106, 200
Universidad de la República, 22, 200–202
Universidad Nacional Autónoma de México: cultural activities, 22, 54–55, 174, 210–11, 215–17; expansion, 54, 210–11; film education, 215–25; film preservation, 95, 106–7, 119–20
Universidad Nacional de Córdoba, 199, 278n152
Universidad Nacional de La Plata: film school, 22, 204–6
universities: cineclubs, 54–55, 65, 74–75, 81–82, 96, 102, 215–16; expansion, 49, 176, 199, 210–11; extension programs, 65, 102, 200, 206, 217; film education, 22, 102, 176, 190, 199–210, 215–26; filmmaking, 22, 201, 203–5, 207–9, 222–24; film preservation, 91, 94–95, 104, 106–7, 119, 124; student activism and reform movement, 199, 201, 210, 222–24, 223*fig.*
Uruguay: cineclubs, 43, 48*map*, 49*map*, 50, 53–55, 67–68, 73–75; cinema, 88, 200, 227–28; film education, 200–202; film exhibition, 2–3, 90; film festivals, 8, 34, 125–34, 148–58; film preservation, 22, 85, 88, 90, 96–97, 105, 113, 115–23; history and politics, 18, 121, 153

Valdés-Rodríguez, José Manuel, 43, 46, 102–3, 106, 128, 160, 200
Variety, 128–29, 151–52, 155, 160–64, 166, 169
Velo, Carlos, 107, 210
Venezuela: cineclubs, 20, 31, 43–45, 48*map*, 49*map*, 53–54, 62, 65; cinema, 30, 184, 193–98; exiles 20, 65; film education, 184, 192–98; film exhibition, 2–3, 27; film festivals, 132, 193–94; film preservation, 96, 104, 110, 117–19
Venice film festival, 129–30, 134–35, 154, 156, 167*fig.*
Vera Cruz film studio, 136, 143, 152, 159, 182
Vicens, Luis, 53, 62, 79–80, 88, 103, 112
Vichy regime, 7, 14, 24, 59–60
Vidas secas, 136, 139–40, 140*fig.*
vida útil, La, 227–29
viewers. *See* audiences
Vsesoiuznyi Gosudarstvenny Institut Kinematografii, 176, 178–79, 184–85, 190

Watson, Nora, 55–56, 75–77
women: in archives, 94–95, 110; in cineclubs, 46, 75, 81; in film education, 180, 189, 191–98, 219–20
working-class viewers, 65, 74–75, 107, 220

Zalamea, Jorge, 79–80, 249n223
Zalzman, Abraham, 81, 184, 192, 250n240, 258n163
Zavattini, Cesare, 6, 73, 182–83, 207

Founded in 1893,
UNIVERSITY OF CALIFORNIA PRESS
publishes bold, progressive books and journals
on topics in the arts, humanities, social sciences,
and natural sciences—with a focus on social
justice issues—that inspire thought and action
among readers worldwide.

The UC PRESS FOUNDATION
raises funds to uphold the press's vital role
as an independent, nonprofit publisher, and
receives philanthropic support from a wide
range of individuals and institutions—and from
committed readers like you. To learn more, visit
ucpress.edu/supportus.

www.ingramcontent.com/pod-product-compliance
Lightning Source LLC
Chambersburg PA
CBHW021336230426
43666CB00006B/317